D1234018

Preserving the Family Farm

Revisiting Rural America
Pete Daniel and Deborah K. Fitzgerald, Series Editors

Mary Neth ▪ *Preserving the Family Farm: Women, Community, and the Foundations of Agribusiness in the Midwest, 1900–1940*

Sally McMurry ▪ *Transforming Rural Life: Dairying Families and Agricultural Change, 1820–1885*

VILLA JULIE COLLEGE LIBRARY
STEVENSON, MD 21153

Preserving the Family Farm

Women, Community, and the Foundations of Agribusiness in the Midwest, 1900–1940

. . .

Mary Neth

The Johns Hopkins University Press

Baltimore and London

HN
79
. A14
N48
1995

© 1995 The Johns Hopkins University Press
All rights reserved. Published 1995

Printed in the United States of America on acid-free paper
04 03 02 01 00 99 98 97 96 95   5   4   3   2   1

The Johns Hopkins University Press
2715 North Charles Street
Baltimore, Maryland 21218-4319
The Johns Hopkins Press Ltd., London

Library of Congress Cataloging-in-Publication Data will be
found at the end of this book.
A catalog record for this book is available from the
British Library.

ISBN 0-8018-4898-9

To my parents,
Shirley and C. O. Neth

Contents

Illustrations

Maps
Following page 44:

Photographs
Following page 44:

5. Women produced an important part of the food supply in their gardens and supervised the work of young children. Haskell County, Kansas, 1941 (BAE, Community Studies, Record Group 83-G, National Archives, Neg. 44000).

6. A farmer husks corn, Grundy County, Iowa, 1939. Photograph by Arthur Rothstein (FSA Photographs, Library of Congress, Neg. LCUSF 34–28869-D).

7. Farmers often continued to use horses even after they purchased tractors. Shelby County, Iowa, 1941 (BAE, Division of Economic Information, 1939–42, Record Group 83-G, National Archives, Neg. 44261).

Following page 160:

8. Nellie Kedzie Jones, leader of the University of Wisconsin's extension service educational program, 1920 (Iconographic Collections, State Historical Society of Wisconsin, WHI [x3] 43460).

9. "Pen of top hampshire hogs" at the Farmers' Union Livestock Commission pens at the Union Stock Yards, Chicago, 1927 (BAE, Record Group 83-ML, National Archives, Neg. 15631).

10. River Falls Cooperative Laundry, River Falls, Wisconsin, 1928 (BAE, DFP&RL, Record Group 83-G, National Archives, Neg. 17867).

11. Signs of the "modern" farm community illustrated in a 1929 advertisement (detail) for the *Farm Journal* (N W Ayer Advertising Records, 1889–1972, Archives Center, National Museum of American History).

12. Rural Electrification Administration photograph of family at dinner surrounded by modern electric appliances (Office of the Secretary of Agriculture, Historical File, 1900–1959, Record Group 16-G, National Archives, Neg. REA S-2605, n.d.).

13. Federal Extension Service photograph portraying the radio as an entertainment for the nuclear family. Champaign County, Illinois, July 1937 (Federal Extension Service, Farm and Rural Activities, 1906–42, Record Group 33-SC, National Archives, Neg. S22870C).

14. "Mrs. Ole Thompson, wife of a farmer, carrying food to the table." Nesson Township, Williams County, North Dakota, October 1937. Photograph by Russell Lee (FSA Photographs, Library of Congress, Neg. LCUSF 34–30787-D).

Acknowledgments

In the many years I have worked on this project, I have incurred debts too numerous to acknowledge adequately in a few pages. I must first thank the farm people who told their stories to oral historians and donated their papers to historical archives. I hope I have done justice to their lives. The members of the staffs of the archives that contain this material shared their time and their knowledge of the region and their collections. I thank those who assisted me at the State Historical Society of Wisconsin, the Iowa State Historical Society, the North Dakota State Historical Society, the University of North Dakota Archives, the North Dakota State University Archives, the Iowa State University Archives, the Steenbock Library Archives at the University of Wisconsin, the National Museum of American History Archives and Library, the Library of Congress, and the National Archives. In particular, I thank Dale Trelevan, then oral historian at the State Historical Society of Wisconsin, not only for his excellent oral histories, but also for suggesting that someone who grew up on a farm should write about rural America—a novel idea to a beginning graduate student.

This project could never have been completed without the financial support of a number of institutions. The National Endowment for the Humanities funded a crucial year's leave from teaching duties. The Virginia Foundation for the Humanities provided a semester residency at the Virginia Center for the Humanities, which gave me not only the time to rethink my dissertation, but also a creative and supportive environment of scholars and staff. The College of Arts and Sciences and the Department of History at Virginia Tech provided critical research grants. The dissertation from which this book developed would not have been possible were it not for a Smithsonian Predoctoral Fellowship at the National Museum of American History. In addition, research trips throughout the Midwest were funded by a Woodrow Wilson Women's Studies Predoctoral Research Grant and a travel grant from the University of Wisconsin. I am also deeply indebted to the Guaranteed Student Loan Program, though not so deeply as when I first finished graduate school. The following journals generously gave permission to reprint material that appeared as "Leisure and Generational Change: Farm Youths in the Midwest, 1910–1940," *Agricultural History* 67 (Spring 1993): 163–84, and "Gender and the Family Labor System: Defining Work in the Rural Midwest," *Journal of Social History* 27 (Mar. 1994): 563–77.

This work is the fruit of what I have learned from many scholars. I would like to thank John Hopper and Patricia Van Dyke, who inspired my interests in history and literature and taught me to research and write as an undergraduate at Northwest Missouri State University. Early in my graduate career, I was privileged to work with and learn from Daniel T. Rodgers, Barbara Melosh, and David S. Lovejoy. Paul Boyer, Allan Bogue, and Diane Lindstrom shepherded my work in its first rough drafts as a dissertation. Pete Daniel shared his knowledge of sources and his enthusiasm for rural history. His continued support and encouragement contributed much to this work. Many others offered important comments on parts of this work as it appeared in a variety of forms; I want to thank William Andrews, Jo Blatti, Midge Eisele, Jesse Gilbert, Anne Golovin, Linda Gordon, Kathleen Hilton, Joan Jensen, Jack Temple Kirby, Gerda Lerner, Barbara Melosh, Mary Lee Muller, and Rebecca Williams. I would also like to thank series editor Deborah Fitzgerald for her helpful suggestions, and Robert J. Brugger at the Johns Hopkins University Press for his attention to matters of style and his desire to make this book the best it could be. My thanks also go to Jane Lincoln Taylor for her careful and skilled editing and her enthusiasm for the project. I am especially indebted to Susan Smulyan for tackling a longer draft of this manuscript with both a critical eye and a friend's support. I am deeply grateful for the time and attention Nancy Grey Osterud gave to several versions of this manuscript. Her keen grasp of theory, the rigor of her analysis, and her respect for the people who make up this story improved this book immeasurably.

In the years it has taken me to complete this work, I have been a part of many communities, and many people have helped me be both a scholar and a human being. I want to thank the community of graduate students who provided social and intellectual camaraderie while I attended the University of Wisconsin, including Ed Agran, Lisa Fine, Bill Trollinger, Steve

Kretzmann, Kathy Tinsley, David Lewis, Janet Oldenburg, and Charlotte Borst. The scholars and farm women who participated in the American Farm Women in Historical Perspective Conferences have reminded me of the significance of my work, stimulated me to think beyond the geographic and time limits of this study, and kept me honest. I especially want to thank Lorna Miller, Wava Haney, and LuAnn Jones. For making the demands of those first years of teaching at Virginia Tech seem a little less like work, I would like to thank LeeAnn Whites, Anastasia Sims, Tom Howe, Doug Flamming, Tom Howard, Joy Harvey, and Ann LaBerge. Many other friends have enriched my life by sharing theirs, and I want to thank Jonathan Cooper, Sharon Locken, Rebecca Williams, Charlotte Fairlie, Gayle Trollinger, Donna Peckett, Bruce Walker, Diane Jensen, Judy Taylor, Viola Hoffman, Teri Stangl-Walker, Lori Greenberg, Cynthia France, and Linda Endlich.

Finally, and most importantly, I thank my closest friends and family. Marshall Neth, Zachary Neth, and Jessica Muller-Pearson continue to remind me of the wonders of growing up, while Mike and Shelia Neth share with me the rituals of kinship. I thank them for helping tie me to my roots in the past and the future. Jane Brinkman has been a friend since we were first thrown together as college roommates, and I thank her for the continuity of that friendship. Without Mary Lee Muller, I would not have survived graduate school, and I thank her for her dependable emotional and intellectual support through good times and bad. Kathleen Hilton has graced me with her humor and compassion, in addition to sharing her knowledge of teaching and introducing me to the world of computers. I thank her for being a 911 in computer and other emergencies. Midge Eisele has shared the gift of her stories, the expanse of her intellect, the sharpness of her wit, and the depth of her understanding of the human spirit. I thank her for her friendship. In the end is the beginning. I want to thank my parents, Shirley and C. O. Neth. Their wisdom and love sustain me.

Preserving the Family Farm

Introduction

"The Farmer in the Dell"

The farmer in the dell, the farmer in the dell,
  Hi-ho the derry-o, the farmer in the dell.
The farmer takes a wife, the farmer takes a wife,
  Hi-ho the derry-o, the farmer in the dell.
    The wife takes the child . . .
    The child takes the dog . . .
    The dog takes the cat . . .
    The cat takes the rat . . .
    The rat takes the cheese . . .
    The cheese stands alone . . .[1]

This children's rhyme replicates the hidden history of farm women. "Farmer," the term that designates one who works on the land, refers only to an adult man, even though women and children worked on family farms and also were "farmers." The language and ordering of the game suggest hierarchy, a chain of being that reflects the patriarchal structure of agriculture. Men controlled the land. A woman's access to land depended on her marrying a farmer. Women's ties to the farm have been as wives.[2]

Although the lyrics of this song reflect one reality of agriculture's structure, the physical map of the game more closely represents the daily relations of the farm. The game's players form a circle with an individual farmer standing in the middle. The farmer takes a wife, who takes a child, and so forth, with each joining the farmer in the center. The outer circle from which the participants come could be the farm neighborhood, while the farm family itself congregates in the middle. That family builds and the game progresses only because of the ties between the inner group (the family) and the larger circle (the neighborhood). At the end of the game, the cheese stands alone, but becomes the farmer in the dell for the next game, and the game continues its circular form. These circles create relationships that undercut the hierarchical order of the selection process. Historical narratives, farm policy, and agricultural institutions have been created with similar assumptions of patriarchal order—farmer as principal actor and male head of household—and have ignored the circles. This book looks beneath these assumptions to uncover the circles, placing gender, family, and community at the center of the story and using them as a lens to reexamine agricultural history and policy.

The first insight that emerges from examining circles is an awareness of the interconnections between social and economic ties, and the bonds among family, neighborhood, and work. The mythic resonance of the family farm has hidden these ties. "The family farm" suggests a unified interest, the family, which operates in an isolated environment, the farm. But, in fact, the individualistic farmer is dependent on women and children, and the family is a relational institution whose members do not always have identical interests.[3] The family farm was not isolated, but part of a web of community ties that connected farms and families in rural neighborhoods. Farm people understood their lives through these social relationships, created by social interaction and by the labor that dominated their lives—farming.

The study of midwestern agriculture offers an opportunity to explore the connections between patriarchal family structures and capitalist development and to break down the walls that separate, in much historical analysis, the spheres of public and private life. Focus on the workplace leads immediately to the family. The rural Midwest does not easily fit into any existing narratives of women's or labor history. Industrialization in urban America included a separation of spheres into the wage workplace and the unpaid domestic household. Such a model cannot match the realities of a rural labor system rooted in unpaid family and community-exchanged labor for both women and men.[4] Nor can the concept of separate spheres illuminate a system in which the physical organization of work integrated the emotional home, domestic work, and agricultural labor. Private and public were intimately connected.

Family farm agriculture depended economically on the labor of families and neighbors. Farm people did not simply sell products for cash; they also produced goods that could be used directly on the farm or by the family or could be exchanged to meet the needs of entire neighborhoods. Profits from cash markets were unpredictable because prices and weather were beyond the control of farm people; profits of production for home use and neighborhood exchange were more stable and helped assure survival.

These family and neighborhood survival strategies guaranteed rewards only because farm people shared cultural values and social obligations. The legal and customary hierarchies of patriarchal families shaped these social obligations, but success required the cooperation of all family members. Women and children could mitigate their dependent position through negotiation because of the crucial role they played in rural survival. Women, in particular, increased their share of farm resources through community building, home production, and making do, and through their activities they emphasized the mutuality of kin and community. As they did so, they increased the communal resources available to farm men as well. In times of crisis, farm people relied on these informal local relations for security.

The focus on circles of family farming leads to a reconsideration of the process of economic change. Families and neighborhoods were crucial in agricultural production; changes in the broader economy depended on significant changes in the private relations of rural society. In rural America, the development of industrial capitalism directly collided with a family-based labor system. Historians who have examined the development of capitalism in America have generally used rural America as a static jumping-off place for an examination of the seemingly more dynamic changes of urbanization and industrialization. Only recently have historians begun to examine the countryside itself as a place transformed by capitalist economic developments. Focusing on the eighteenth and nineteenth centuries, these historians have traced the participation of farms in the market economy. Their work addresses primarily the public side of agricultural production (marketing, credit), leaving the other half of the equation, the way the labor process itself was organized, largely unexamined. Although the "household mode of production" is a crucial term in this debate, it is generally used in an abstract way rather than being explored fully as a set of social and gender relations.[5]

By the twentieth century, midwestern farms specialized and produced for the market, yet household and unpaid family labor remained crucial to their functioning; the farm, family, and community continued to supply much of their own sustenance; and economic transactions were often regulated by the practices of kinship and neighborhood as much as by the market. Viewed from this social perspective, particularly focusing on the work of women, the transitions of the eighteenth and nineteenth centuries seem much less complete, and new questions emerge. In the early twentieth century, midwestern agriculture underwent its own process of industrialization. Machines replaced human labor and agricultural industries were consolidated, but farm labor, unlike urban industrial work, does not lend itself to an assembly line. The natural cycles of agricultural work must be completed sequentially; slack periods follow periods of intense labor. Tasks cannot be divided and performed simultaneously.[6] The flexibility of unpaid family labor complemented this cycle. How, then, was work and production in family farming transformed by the development of industrial capitalism?

This question forces a reexamination of the period known as the golden age of agriculture. If farmers were incompletely integrated into the market economy in the nineteenth century and modern agribusiness became dominant by the post–World War II period, then a crucial transformation occurred in the first half of the twentieth century. The so-called golden age is usually viewed as a prosperous period sandwiched between the economic and political crises of the 1890s and the 1930s. The period seems a time of prosperity, stability, and peace in America's rural communities, especially those in the midwestern states, untroubled by either the turbulent race relations and poverty of the rural South or the labor unrest of urban, industrial America. A textbook description would expand on the ability of farmers to buy new consumer goods that eased the drudgery of farm women, to travel in newly purchased automobiles, which ended the curse of rural isolation, and to farm more efficiently with tractors.

But separating the golden age of agriculture from the years of crisis that surround it hinders an understanding of the more constant, and contested, evolution of American capitalism in the countryside. Between 1900 and 1940, the foundations of modern agribusiness in the United States and the models for agricultural development policies abroad were laid. In this period one can trace the beginnings of the patterns that would plague twentieth-century rural communities. Mechanization and increased production costs outran farm incomes. Government policies promoted increased production despite growing overproduction. Farm people replaced home production with consumption, despite the inconsistency of farm incomes. The depopulation of rural America began. In these years, the strategies farm people had used since the frontier era to lessen the risks of unpredictable weather and markets began to be less effective.

As agricultural policy in the early twentieth century is reconsidered from this perspective, the attempts of government agencies to alter rural living take on new meaning. In order to change rural production patterns, the circles surrounding the farmer in the dell had to be removed, leaving the farmer and the nuclear family isolated but prosperous, practicing modern agricultural production techniques and buying middle-class consumer goods. Agricultural institutions used gender hierarchy to promote class stratification and to weaken rural neighborhood ties.

In the early twentieth century, the state took an increasingly active role in promoting changes in production and rural ways of living. Using urban industrial models of capitalist production, newly created government agencies hoped to increase agricultural efficiency by introducing more technology and larger production units. Yet implementing these policies was difficult because many farm families, not a few corporations, controlled the means of production. To gain control of agricultural production, the government promoted farm consolidation. Larger farms would be operated by a small class of men, progressive farmers, who shared industrial goals and whose families would assist economic growth by purchasing consumer goods and leisure products. Farm consolidation resulted in rural depopulation. The success of this reorganization required replacing labor with technology and displacing farm labor, including farmers on small farms, tenants, hired workers, and unpaid women and youths.

Modern agriculture, in theory, dissolved the practices of interdependence that characterized rural society. Rather than seeing themselves as parts of neighborhoods and families, some farm men had to put strategies that emphasized capital and production ahead of those that emphasized labor, family, and community. Because farm women were crucial to building gender and community interdependence and mutuality, agricultural policies asserted a new patriarchal structure that created a gendered division of economic and social concerns. Structurally and ideologically, these policies placed family and community needs into a separate "women's sphere," and then devalued them by subordinating social and family concerns to economic production—the "business" of farming. Modern farmers made decisions about production for business reasons, to increase efficiency, rather than to meet family or community needs. In addition, the separate women's sphere lowered the status of women and children as workers and economic contributors to agriculture and expanded their role as consumers of manufactured goods and mass culture. By definition "efficient" farmers deserved to replace "inefficient" farmers, and women and children were no longer agricultural laborers but consumers. With such an ideology, policymakers could easily dismiss those who were being displaced from agriculture's future.

As the government attempted to reorganize agricultural production, it confronted farm people accustomed to distrusting the marketplace and to using family and community resources to overcome the inequities and hardships of capitalist agriculture. For rural people the golden age of agriculture was not separate from periods of agricultural depression; the stories of hardship were never further away than the tales of their parents or grandparents. Their culture elaborated on the strategies of making do that had been necessary to build and preserve small family farms. Even though farm people might alter their way of living during the good times, patterns of dealing with scarcity, never completely gone even in the best times, reemerged easily in the bad.

Policymakers did not simply impose changes in agricultural production, nor did farm people merely resist these changes. Instead change came through an interactive process in which farm people adopted, adapted, and resisted new practices, and government policies both created new conditions and reacted to the choices and actions of farm people. Capitalist agriculture and family farming intersected in complementary and contradictory ways. Farm people often welcomed the advances of scientific agriculture and a consumer society. During this period, they gained access to some of the hallmarks of modern living. Contrary to historical interpretations that paint farm people as eager to abandon the "backwardness" of rural life for city living, many farm people blended the modern and the rural and were satisfied with the modified country way of life. But many did not believe that such changes required the farm consolidation and depopulation that professionals in agricultural agencies envisioned.

Although government policies and economic change may have increased some options for farm people, they nevertheless limited farm people's choices in significant ways. Gradually, rural social and economic life changed. New patterns decreased the need for labor, increased the need for cash, and broadened the geographic scope of community social life. These patterns and policies undermined neighborhood and family survival strategies. Capitalist development promoted neither more patriarchal nor more equitable gender relations, but it changed the context in which families negotiated these relations. The separate spheres of modern agriculture could in practice be either more patriarchal or more egalitarian. The stress of economic hardship could shake patriarchal families and propel dependents into a more independent economic status in the wage economy, or require more sacrifices and increase oppression within the family. But when women or children on smaller farms had successfully used family survival strategies to build mutuality within farm families, these policies undercut their position, threatening entire families of small-farm owners and tenants, as well as dependent workers, women, and youths within stable farm families. By 1940 rural communities of small family farms still existed, but the rules of the game had changed, disrupting both the circles and the hierarchy.

This study explores these changes in the Midwest. The midwestern region can be distinguished from the rest of the country in three ways. First, the midwestern landscape consists of prairies and plains that have shaped its agriculture. Second, unlike the East, the region was settled primarily in the mid- to late nineteenth century and developed in the context of an increasingly consolidated market economy. A third characteristic of the Midwest is the agricultural dominance of small family farms. Historians have largely assumed the presence of family farming in the Midwest and have rarely analyzed how it has shaped the region. The relationship of families to agricultural production needs more careful analytic attention. Families were crucial to all forms of agriculture. Both the planter's house and the slave quarters contained families, but slavery organized the relationship of these families to work. Sharecropping in the South grew from a very different social system than tenancy in the Midwest. In the West, ranching, highly mechanized and capitalized farming, and migrant labor molded the work of families who lived on the land. In New England and the Middle Atlantic states, the development of industry within relatively close proximity created alternative strategies for farm families much more than in the Midwest, especially its western sections. Even though small family farms existed in all these regions, farming organized around the labor of a family, supplemented by hired labor or exchanged labor, usually coming from other family farms, characterized midwestern agriculture more than that of other regions.

My study includes states in the western Midwest—Wisconsin, Illinois, Missouri, Iowa, Minnesota, Kansas, Nebraska, South Dakota, and North Dakota. The western Midwest was identified by Theodore Saloutos and John Hicks, in their study of farm politics, as the area of "agricultural discontent" between 1900 and 1940, the period of this study. Except for Chicago, this region had less of an industrial base than did the eastern Midwest, and its industry was largely agricultural. Throughout this period, the farm population was a more dominant portion of this region's total population than it was in the eastern Midwest. In 1920, the percentages of people residing on farms in the states I have studied ranged from 35 percent to 61 percent, except Illinois (17%), compared to a range of from 19 percent to 31 percent in the eastern Midwest. Even in 1940, farm populations in this region were between 25 percent and 50 percent of the states' total populations (again with the exception of Illinois). For the eastern region, none of the states' farm population was above 25 percent of the total.[7] In examining published materials and government records, I have used this regional base.

Within this broader regional perspective, I have focused on three states, Wisconsin, Iowa, and North Dakota, to provide a comparative perspective across the major twentieth-century commodity specializations of the region—dairy, corn and livestock, and wheat. I have examined documents recording the voices of farm people themselves, such as diaries, oral histories, and reminiscences, in archives in these states. Together these states illustrate the agricultural and geographic diversity of the Midwest, from prairie to plains to woodlands. Each commodity specialization had its own labor demands forming different rural work cultures. Income also varied for these specializations during the period. Although this comparative perspective is important, most farms in the Midwest were still general farms that organized work in similar ways. In addition, each state consisted of communities of small farms, and the social organization of rural life across the Midwest followed similar patterns. An examination of both the diversity and the commonality within these states helps complete the picture of change in twentieth-century agriculture.

The settlement of the western Midwest took place throughout the nineteenth century, with some parts of the western Great Plains and northern dairy states being settled in the early twentieth century. Most of this settlement followed the building of railroads and was clearly tied to the development of regional and national markets. The settlement of the Midwest was crucial to national development in terms of both economic growth and the expansion of the nation-state. Conquering the land of the Native Americans required the peopling of the region and assurance of those people's ties to the expanding northern economic system. To do this quickly, government policies promoted the family form of settlement and the small homestead (in the context of large land grants to railroads, which promoted household settlement for their own purposes). The family farm system met the needs of expansion and economic development.[8]

The people who settled the land came in families. The relationship of their migration to the development of capitalism, however, is complicated; the migration did more than merely fulfill the goals of market and national expansion. Many settlers left areas of the Northeast or Europe that were being disrupted by the development of capitalism. They considered the move a way of preserving family goals and community values, as much as a way of using the market to get ahead economically. Although much of the literature on capitalist development in the countryside sees the presence of the household mode of production as an earlier stage of development existing in opposition to capitalism, feminist scholars have begun to examine how patriarchal family structures also complemented capitalist development. In the settlement period, the family goal of gaining land largely complemented the development of the market. Patriarchal families, capitalism, and national expansion went hand in hand.

But the symbiosis was never completely without conflict. Once they entered the market, farm people had little control over the prices they would receive for crops. For those purchasing agricultural produce and reselling it in other markets, the easiest way to increase profits was to keep the initial purchase price low. As in other parts of the nineteenth-century economy, horizontal and vertical integration soon led to oligopolies and monopolies in agricultural industries. Railroads spurred development, but they also controlled the only transportation routes to increasingly central- ized markets. When farmers took their goods to market, railroads set their transportation costs, and distant purchasers, centralized in the late nine- teenth century in Chicago, including the Board of Trade for grain and the Meat Trust for beef and pork, set their prices. Even as other cities began to challenge Chicago's market control in the late nineteenth and early twentieth centuries, they did so through their own process of centraliza- tion. For example, in 1876 seventeen firms owned twenty flour mills in Minneapolis. By 1890 four corporations controlled more than 87 percent of the milling capacity in the city. Those who dominated seats on the exchange in the city often had interests not only in the mills, but also in railroads and the elevators that lined their routes.[9] In a much less direct way, corporations controlled the incomes of farmers as much as those of urban laborers.

Farm people reacted to centralization and changing markets in several ways. Farm organizations such as the Grange promoted state regulation of railroad rates as early as the 1870s. Farmers also adjusted their production to take greater advantage of changing markets. In older wheat-growing areas of the region, farmers began to alter their crop specializations. In Illi- nois and Iowa, farmers moved from frontier farming practices to speciali- zation in corn and livestock production, responding to the growth of meat packing in nearby Chicago. In Wisconsin, farmers shifted to dairy pro- duction, an industry that served largely local and regional markets and that would not undergo the centralization process until World War I. With these changes, farmers in these areas were able to avoid some of the worst dislocations of the 1890s. Farmers in the western areas, whose wheat pro- duction had led to the shifts in production in the eastern parts of the re- gion, were hardest hit by natural disasters and the collapse of prices, and consequently participated most fully in the economic and political pro- tests that culminated in the Populist movement.

These reactions, however, are the best-known part of the historical story—production for the market, economic cooperatives, and political action. When the daily lives of *all* family members are considered, how- ever, one sees additional strategies. Most farms remained general farms, despite their specializations. For example, in 1900 only about 17 percent of Wisconsin's farms were so specialized that more than 40 percent of the value of their crops was concentrated in dairy products.[10] Diverse prod- ucts and family labor were crucial rural strategies for survival. Commu- nity exchanges to save labor costs remained significant to rural life even in the twentieth century. Making do, saving money through the use of labor or simply doing without, was crucial to surviving hard times, and hard times were continuous for farm families with few resources. On more market-oriented farms or farms with means, making do often underwrote expansion. However, by the turn of the century, the goals of farm families and their traditional means of meeting those goals came increasingly into conflict with the industrial development of agriculture.

Agricultural industries, which continued to grow and consolidate, and newly created government agricultural institutions defined agricultural progress in terms of the expansion of production and consumerism on America's farms. Increases in farm size and decreases in the number of farms and the farm population lay embedded in this ideology of progress and in the structure of these institutions. Even though promoters proclaimed that such change would lead to greater prosperity for farm people, such goals directly conflicted with the system of small family farms promoted in the nineteenth century.

Although agricultural institutions proclaimed the inevitable direction of "progress," the first forty years of the twentieth century were in fact a period of flux. In many ways the rural Midwest of 1940 resembled that of 1920, or even 1900.[11] The midwestern region did not follow a steady pattern of mechanization, farm consolidation, and decline. Farm people migrated in and out of the rural economy, responding to both agricultural and urban employment cycles.[12] Migrations were specific responses to immediate conditions in the rural economy rather than an inevitable long-term trend. Farm consolidation also did not proceed rapidly. Over this period farm size increased by fewer than four acres in the prairie states and by about fifty-three acres in the plains.[13] Between 1920 and 1940, the number of farms in the nine states declined by 32,679, only 2 percent of the total number of farms in 1920. The number of farms in 1940 was only 3,942 less than the total 1900 figure, though clearly there were shifts across the region in farm location. Prosperity and technology, the automobile, and the "lure of the city" did not immediately send midwestern farm people cityward or alter the basic composition of rural society. Most of the patterns that would characterize post–World War II agriculture—drastic declines in farms and farm population, decreased tenancy, and increased farm size—had just begun to appear by 1940.[14]

Instead, between the agricultural depression of the 1890s and that of the 1930s, the crucial economic transformation of the rural Midwest was its social reorganization. The most prominent change in this period was a decline in farm population. The number of farms did not decline so dramatically; this indicates that internal household patterns, the social reorganization of family labor, preceded a reorganization of land ownership. Between 1920 and 1940, the farm population declined by more than six hundred thousand people, or nearly 9 percent of the 1920 farm population. The percent of decline from 1935 to 1940 was almost double the population loss during the post–World War I economic downturn (1920–25). Between 1940 and 1945, the rate of decline in the rural population more than doubled.

Although these data partly reflect the demands for labor in the armed forces and industry caused by the beginning of World War II, the farm population never returned to pre-1940 levels. Population loss has generally accompanied the maturation of frontier communities, but the loss of population in the Midwest in this period was more than just a stage of post-frontier development; it was the beginning of the restructuring and consolidation of agricultural production, the period when machine power replaced both animals and people, and the last vestiges of home production began to be absorbed into the market economy. The continuous consolidation of food production and the decline of the community system of family farms began at the close of this era.

Midwestern farm people faced the economic fluctuations of this period with incomes that usually did not meet middle-class, urban standards, and with increased pressures to spend cash for new farm technology, consumer goods, and recreation. Even though the period from 1910 to 1914 was notable for the equality between what centralized markets paid for crops and what farmers paid for manufactured goods, this condition was an aberration from the patterns of both the late nineteenth century and the first half of the twentieth century. At the edge of the Great Depression, farm incomes at best matched the cost of living and, at worst, fell far below it. The Great Depression was particularly devastating for farm families.[15] The uneven agricultural economy diminished the economic position of poorer farm families and dependents within farm families. As wealthier farmers adopted laborsaving technology, they removed important resources from the rural economy. Patterns of exchange, interdependence, and mutual assistance and obligation diminished, as did wage opportunities for rural youths and poorer farm families.

Simultaneously, increased needs for cash pushed family members toward wage labor, to supplement incomes from cash crops and home-produced goods. As wage-earning opportunities declined in agricultural communities, farm youths sought work in nearby towns. This transition occurred first for farm daughters, whose agricultural income-earning ability was most limited by the unpaid family labor system, but it increasingly became true for farm sons in the 1930s. Although, during this period, the home-production and community-building work of farm wives remained crucial for farm survival, they, too, began a search for wage-earning work after World War II. As farm families became more deeply enmeshed in the cash economy and as the nature of agricultural work changed, the rules of negotiation within families altered and the survival of the farm unit itself became more problematic. Women and children had to negotiate in a system that increasingly redefined the ways in which they could contribute to the farm economy and threatened the resources of their family and community bases.

Gradually, the system of small family farms eroded. As farming became more capital-intensive and living became more consumer oriented, cash incomes from the sale of products, home production, and neighborhood exchange rarely met farm and family needs. The Great Depression slowed the pace of change in some ways and accelerated it in others. The market provided few resources for farm people during this period, and survival depended on intensifying traditional strategies. However, the Great Depression also drained rural resources, and for many, survival strategies were not enough. New Deal policies supplied important relief to many of the poorer farm people, but the most long-lasting programs continued to promote capital-intensive agriculture among the wealthy farm survivors. Adopting new technologies enabled these farmers to farm more land, consolidating land previously farmed by owners or tenants of smaller farms, and decreased their need for labor, further hurting both exchange opportunities and rural employment for poorer farm people. As World War II provided jobs in urban areas, farm youths, tenants, and displaced owners sought these economic opportunities.

Between 1900 and 1940, farm people responded to a shifting economy with strategies for survival that had developed from the circles of gender, family, and community relations inherent in the system of small, interconnected family farms. *Preserving the Family Farm* describes these strategies and this struggle, the attempts of farm people to adopt, adapt, resist, or create change. These strategies ended in success for some families, failure for others. But gradually, as the elements of modern agribusiness were set in place, these particular survival strategies, based on labor-intensive practices and social connections, became less effective. Increasingly, farm families left the land.

The problem of rural life became a question of public policy in the early twentieth century and continued to be one through the crisis of the 1930s, but the massive depopulation of rural America that followed World War II did not engender an equal debate, because the groundwork for this change had been laid in the preceding four decades. Just as the demise of the Populist party ended the potential for democratic political answers to rural problems, alternative social policies for agriculture were lost at the end of the Great Depression. Although the loss of rural population was a crucial policy issue in the first half of the twentieth century, by the second half it was accepted as one of the costs of "progress." Only in the farm crisis of the early 1980s did the social future of rural America return to prominence as a subject of political debate, and national concern about it disappeared from the covers of national publications, even though farm people continued to lose their farms in the 1990s.

The family farm system of agriculture, long idealized as the essence of America's spirit—part of its "heartland"—was transformed by capitalism's development as much as were cities. Industrialized by the use of capital-intensive technology, increased commodity specialization, absorption into consumer markets, and a reorganization of labor, family farming was no longer the same, even for farms that were still family operated. These families had to develop new survival strategies in the world of modern agribusiness. The continued crisis of families struggling to preserve their farms, the instability of the agricultural economy, and the environmental dangers of modern agricultural practices are part of broader, worldwide problems, a sign of the heartland's full integration into a capitalist economy. The roots of both policy and crisis can be found in the first forty years of the twentieth century. In these years, many voices debated the future of America's agriculture, but the power of government and agricultural corporations and the hegemony of the social and economic ideal of progress overwhelmed alternative voices. The problems of modern agriculture underscore the need to understand the human dimensions of the historical development of contemporary agriculture. By focusing on the women's side of agricultural policy and rural social structures and by listening to the voices of farm people themselves, one can better understand the historical process of capitalist transformation in the countryside and begin searching for new policies that may rebuild communities, promote mutuality and equal access, and create a more democratic system of land control and food production based on an integrative view of nature, work, and human needs. I hope this book helps us see the circles.

Family Farming as a Social System

CHAPTER I

The Farm Family

Survival Strategies and the Family Labor System

Family farming, one often hears, is a way of life, not just a business. To those Americans who have never lived on family farms, this phrase may seem nostalgic, a romanticized view of living on the land. To be sure, family farming has undergone continuous change as the capitalist economy has developed. Yet the romantic view also reflects a reality—that family farming means organizing work in a way fundamentally different from urban-based industry. Indeed, people living on family farms see their values and history as lying outside the cultural and economic mainstream of industrialization and urbanization. In 1923, a midwestern farm woman described her sense of this distinctiveness:

You don't think of your home on a farm . . . as just a space inside four walls. The feeling of home spreads out all around, into the garden, the orchards, the henhouses, the barn, the springhouse, because you are all the time helping to produce live things in those places and they, or their products, are all the time coming back into your kitchen from garden, orchard, barn or henhouse, as a part of the things you handle to prepare for meals or market everyday.[1]

On the family farm, there were no separate spheres for women and men. The industrial division of wage and domestic work, between production for market and production for family use, had less meaning on a family farm.[2] Family space joined economic space. Market and home production served the same purposes, sustaining the family farm enterprise while providing resources for each family member. Family farming did not separate the jobs of men, women, and children; it tied them together.

This family labor system exhibited a tension between the interdependence inherent in the labor and goals of a family farm and the patriarchal power relations of the family and society. On the one hand, the labor of all family members was crucial for the economic survival and prosperity of small, family-owned farms. Because the vagaries of weather and markets made farm income highly variable, farm families compensated by designing labor-intensive strategies that met many of the needs of the farm and family, and saved cash. Family members' return for their labor came not through an individual wage, but through a share of the living the farm provided and an assurance that the farm would be a resource for the family's future. Farm people viewed their labor not as an individual effort but as part of a group effort, related to the work of the entire family. On the other hand, the authority structures of agriculture and family gave power to the male head of household, who represented the family in the larger political and economic world. Men controlled resources and economic decisions, and thus families were dependent on men. Except in rare cases, women had access to the most critical resource of farming—land—only through their relations with men.[3] These patriarchal structures made familial relations hierarchical, not mutual, and created the potential for an unequal distribution of labor and rewards within farm families.

As in other labor systems, the structuring of work and the division of resources were subject to negotiation and conflict; however, in the family labor system this negotiation process took place in a context of kinship and marriage. Managers and workers had personal relations beyond their work roles. Although the structure of agriculture favored men, the practices of family farming not only made men dependent on their families for success, but also encouraged them to define their success in familial terms. By emphasizing the cooperative and joint nature of the farm enterprise, members of the family could define their work in ways that undercut the traditional and legal definitions of patriarchal power. Women, who had the least legal and customary claim to family resources, had the most to gain within the family by emphasizing the mutuality of family labor and the farm enterprise. So long as the family goals of producing a family income and transferring the farm to the next generation depended on family labor, the strategies that gave dependents the ability to improve their position in the family ultimately were also those that helped maintain the family farm system itself.

Although the work of men, women, and children was interconnected on family farms, families divided their work according to the characteristics that distinguished family members—sex and age. However, despite ideological separations between "masculine" and "feminine" work, the reality of the family labor system often prevented such clear demarcations in the actual performance of work. Families expected that everyone would help out in whatever venue was most critical at a given moment. Children, especially, performed a variety of tasks that crossed gender lines, although their labor became more gender-defined as they approached adulthood. Children learned expectations and labor skills based on gender; they also learned an obligation to the farm and family that superseded such definitions.

The customary sexual division of adult labor grew from the physical layout of the farm. Women's labor centered on the house, men's work on the fields. The two met in the barnyard, where divisions were less clear. Farm people defined household work almost exclusively as female labor. When men participated in it, either they were helping out or no women were available to do the work. A woman's responsibilities included maintaining the house, supplying food and clothing for the family, caring for children, and supervising the work of those who helped her. In 1920, a federal government survey of women's work in ten thousand farm homes in the North and West assumed that all women performed housecleaning duties. Researchers did not ask whether women cleaned, but only the number of rooms for which they cared. Household and family maintenance clearly was women's work. In the central states, more than 90 percent of farm women washed clothes, sewed family clothing, and baked their own bread.

The feminine realm of labor also extended to areas immediately surrounding the house. Women tended to poultry flocks and oversaw egg production for household use or for trade in local markets. Women gardened, primarily to provide food for their families; sometimes, however, they specialized in vegetable or fruit production for local markets. Women procured heat and water for the household. None of these outdoor tasks was reserved exclusively for women; however, a United States Department of Agriculture (USDA) survey shows how frequently women performed them. In the central states, 89 percent of the farm women surveyed cared for poultry, 68 percent carried water, 54 percent carried coal or wood for heating purposes, and 67 percent maintained a garden. The actual percentage of farm women performing outdoor chores was probably higher than that given in the survey. The extension service and the county Farm Bureaus, which conducted the survey's fieldwork, usually reached the more prosperous and "progressive" farm homes, which often had a more restrictive gender division of labor.[4]

Working with animals was a chore less clearly defined by gender. The USDA survey showed that women were active in dairying; 66 percent made butter and 45 percent milked cows, while even more women washed pails (93%) and separators (75%). Men more often cared for other types of livestock. Only one-quarter of farm women in the survey reported doing nondairy livestock work. Men also marketed livestock more exclusively than dairy products. Judging from photographs, women rarely attended cattle auctions, but oral histories and photographs often show that women took products to creameries and cheese factories.[5]

Field work and farm management were the most explicitly masculine arenas. Women who performed field labor often described it as "helping out," in the same way that men described their household labor. Only 22 percent of the women in the survey indicated that they worked in the field, although this figure is probably low because of the biases in that study. Men supervised and assigned family work in the field, just as women did in the household, henhouse, and garden. Men had primary responsibility for the development and use of farmland and the marketing of field crops. They also purchased and repaired machinery. Although, according to the 1920 survey, one-third of farm women in the central states kept the farm accounts, men controlled the financial and land resources and had both legal and customary control of management decisions on the farms.

Supervising work on the farm not only kept the farm operating smoothly, but also trained children for their future work lives. Through work, parents introduced children to the different work cultures of women and men. Children learned skills that they could use to earn an income when they became adults. But children, in most farm families, also learned a dedication to the work of the farm that superseded gender norms. Work gave children a sense of responsibility to the farm and family, because they knew that their work was necessary, not superfluous. If the work of the farm could be done with family labor, help did not have to be hired, and therefore cash expenditures could be held down. Children's labor could increase home production, which lessened expenses, or increase the amount of goods produced for cash sale, which enlarged income. Economic necessity countered the ideological gender definitions of labor.

"Helping out" defined the work of young children. Tasks were assigned to farm children as young as five. Tasks in these early years were not segregated by sex. Children worked in the home or barn, and women took responsibility for teaching these chores. Young children milked, brought in wood, helped in the garden and with chickens, herded cows, and did errands, such as taking drinking water to field workers. Between the ages of eight and twelve, children began to take on more serious and skilled chores, and some gender divisions began to occur. Girls, but only an occasional boy, learned home tasks, such as baking, caring for children, cleaning and filling lamps, sewing, and housecleaning. Work outside the house remained similar for young boys and girls. Girls and boys worked in the garden and took greater responsibility for milking and livestock care, such as pumping water, feeding, and cleaning the barn. Field work increased as well, particularly in less skilled but more labor-intensive tasks. Children of both sexes pulled weeds in the garden, planted and dug potatoes, set tobacco, picked berries, harvested garden truck, drove teams, and raked hay. Few children, however, did year-round field work at this early age.

Increased work skills signaled progress toward adulthood. Farm parents expected farm youths, by the age of twelve or thirteen, to work at more closely gender-defined tasks. Boys took on full-time crop work and operated field machinery. Plowing in the spring, a job that was rarely done by girls, was a boy's first adult responsibility. Girls learned new skills such as canning and churning, but like their mothers, did not necessarily restrict their work to the house. As boys moved permanently into the fields, girls and younger boys took over livestock, garden, and dairy duties. While older boys moved further from the "female" types of work they had done at younger ages, parents did not restrict girls from field work, but their role continued to be seen as "helping." Because of their increased physical strength and maturity, all older children, girls and boys, took on new field tasks, such as shocking wheat, stacking hay, cutting thistles, and husking corn. All children, and often adult women, provided a reserve field labor force that did chores regularly in busy seasons. Families expected farm children of fourteen to sixteen to work hard at home or on neighbors' farms for exchange or hire.[6]

As children moved into adulthood, the farm became not just an obligation but a resource. Even so, gender increasingly shaped farm youths' opportunities. On more prosperous farms, sons were given assistance in purchasing land when they married, or worked with their parents until inheriting the family farm. In contrast, parents usually gave daughters goods or cash assistance to start their households at marriage or paid for an education. On less prosperous farms, families depended on children's wages from off-farm labor. Youths began working away from home in their teens. Boys worked on farms or as unskilled manual laborers. Girls did housework, or, if they were better educated, taught, worked in clerical jobs, or entered nursing. Canneries in rural areas sometimes provided wages for youths. Although this work helped the young people buy necessities, cutting farm expenditures, parents expected some of the wages to go toward the farm enterprise. Apparently, few young people questioned or resented these obligations. Most farm people later remembered their contributions as simply a matter of fact.[7]

The diary of North Dakota farmer W. B. Siebert shows how the labor and wages of children were important to farm families in times of economic crisis, how the farm provided a resource for children as they moved into adulthood, and how opportunities differed for girls and boys. The diary reveals the family work of nine children on a North Dakota farm in the 1930s. Boys' opportunities and work came in agricultural labor on or off the home farm. Most New Deal work programs targeted males and provided another source of jobs for the Siebert boys. The youngest son, Sonny, still attended school and worked only on the family farm. The two older sons worked on the home farm and did manual labor and farm work in the region. Louis's off-farm work included exchanging labor with neighbors and doing road work for the Works Progress Administration (WPA). Lester exchanged work, traveled around the region with threshing crews, worked in construction, and participated in the Civilian Conservation Corps (CCC).

The six daughters had fewer opportunities to work in agriculture, but they also both helped on the family farm and got assistance from it. The girls could not work for the government, and they found jobs in towns more often than in rural areas. They also traveled farther for work than their brothers did. Bertha became a schoolteacher but returned home every summer to work on the farm. Louella attended a nurses' training school for a brief time but primarily worked on the home farm and for neighbors. Irene and Ruth worked in Minot, the largest city in the area. Alice did housework in nearby Mohall, until she married Phill. Katherine married a farmer, Matt, in nearby Kenmare. Marriage provided new resources for the family and did not end the children's obligations. Katherine boarded Sonny when he started high school in Kenmare. Lester helped do field work for Katherine and Matt and also worked for Phill's uncle. In the Siebert family, the children worked on the home farm whenever possible and always returned there when other jobs ended.[8]

Although a gender division of labor existed on most midwestern farms, it varied across the region. Even on individual farms, women and men divided tasks flexibly, defining and redefining work assignments to complete the work of the farm. The cycles of nature and the different labor needed for different crops and products shaped family labor strategies. So did the economic resources available to farm families and communities, and the composition of families and their life cycles. Some factors encouraged more flexible or integrated patterns of family labor. Others pushed toward a more strict separation of gender roles. The changing nature of families and of farm work encouraged flexibility, leaving room for negotiations that could recognize different divisions of labor based on ethnic values, personal backgrounds, and individual skills and talents.

Some commodity specializations permitted divergent definitions of appropriate gender work. For example, in the hog/livestock belt, diversified farming patterns enabled farm families to create different crop balances, to spread labor demands more evenly throughout the year, and to divide labor according to ethnic values or family needs. In this area, some women were extremely active in field and barnyard work while others restricted their work to household and poultry labor. Because labor demands were easily altered, farm people could restrict and separate the work of men and women more completely. Consequently, other factors, such as economic conditions or ethnicity, played a larger role in determining these divisions.

Labor-intensive specialties, on the other hand, required more family labor and led to less restrictive definitions of women's work. For example, dairying required work on a daily basis. It also demanded seasonal work in grain or hay crops. Women on dairy farms more likely worked in the field and in the barnyard than did their counterparts in either the corn or wheat belts of the Midwest. The labor intensity of tobacco farming in Wisconsin also dictated that women and girls work in the fields, as they did in tobacco crop production in the South. These commodity specializations encouraged gender integration of tasks and often took precedence over the other factors that shaped the gender division of labor.

Wheat production entailed intense seasonal labor demands that individual families could rarely meet. Consequently, wheat-farming families shared work with neighbors or mechanized their farms. Although women and children worked in the fields at particular stages of the harvest, men needed less family labor, particularly that of women and girls, in the fields.[9] However, women in these areas took responsibility for barnyard chores, particularly milking, which was done primarily to provide milk for family use (although some surpluses were sold). The family of Anne Burke, who farmed in North Dakota and kept a diary between 1907 and 1942, illustrates how wheat specialization might remove women from the fields but not restrict them to the house. The Burke children consisted of four boys, who did most of the field labor, and two girls. The family operated the local threshing rig and cook car, and exchanged and hired help during peak harvest seasons. Although women in the Burke family rarely worked in the field, they actively marketed "women's crops" and produced food for home use. They raised turkeys and chickens, selling birds and eggs, had large amounts of garden and fruit produce, canned extensively, and traveled in the cook car at threshing time.[10] These activities not only used family labor effectively in slack periods, but also provided year-round income to supplement the once-a-year payments for wheat.

Within crop specializations, the size and prosperity of farms was the most crucial determinant of the sexual division of labor. Although smaller farms in all commodity regions relied primarily on family labor and thus had to be more flexible in assigning tasks, wealthier farm families could purchase technology or hire help and thus maintain a stricter gender division of labor. The diary of Elmer G. Powers, who farmed in Iowa and kept entries in the 1920s and 1930s, reveals a combination of factors leading to gender-segregated labor. Powers, a "progressive" farmer, bought new technology as soon as possible, shared work and technology with his brothers and father, who also had farms in the area, hired help regularly, and had a son who was the oldest child. These factors, combined with plentiful male labor, meant that women in the Powers family rarely worked in the fields. However, flexibility became important when times were hard. In the 1930s, Powers's daughter stayed home from high school to assist with corn husking and other field work. Prosperous farm families did not have to use labor to cut costs as a survival strategy, and thus needed less work from women and children. Prosperity ultimately shaped the labor strategies chosen by farm families.[11]

Although class and commodity specializations formed the general outlines of the gender division of labor, the composition of the family altered work assignments. Families could not control the sex or the birth order of their children to fit any abstract notions of a gendered division of labor. Older children began working in the fields whether they were boys or girls, and younger children performed whatever chores their older siblings' graduation left behind. Families divided tasks in similar ways no matter who performed them. The person who assumed the role of father worked in the fields with the assistance of the "oldest son," while the "mother" worked in the home with the assistance of the "oldest daughter." Younger children did daily chores and smaller tasks. One Iowa woman's story shows how changing family composition altered the gender definitions of work. When her father died, the family worked the farm with her mother's bachelor brother or a hired man. As the oldest child, she took on the role of mother and cooked, washed, ironed, and cleaned. Her mother assisted in the fields, fulfilling the role of the oldest son. As the children grew older, the family ran the farm without adult male assistance. Her mother had primary field responsibility, planting and plowing, and she began to disk and drag the fields. The younger children milked the cows and fed the hogs. This flexibility in gender roles continued until the "boys got older" and took over such work as picking, husking, and scooping corn.[12]

Each family also went through its own periods of growth and change. The stage of the family's cycle had particular importance for women's time commitments. In the early stages of a family's life, women were particularly burdened by the shortage of family labor. When children were young, women had primary childcare responsibility, which tied them to the home, but because less family labor was available, their work in the field became more valuable. A study of the labor and leisure time of farm women and men concluded that women's work loads were affected most by the age of children, while the type of crop had a larger impact on men's work loads.[13] The diary of Wisconsin farmer Frank Krueger illustrates the effects of changes in the life cycle for gender-defined work. In 1900 and 1901, when the children were young, Ida, Frank's wife, contributed extensive labor beyond childcare. During busy times, Ida planted and dug potatoes, hauled stones, harrowed, cut oats and corn, and hauled oats and wheat, as well as doing garden work and churning butter. In return, Frank assisted her in the garden and churned butter, and sometimes helped with laundry and childcare. Frank's brother, who farmed nearby, and his sister, who taught school, also shared the farm work, particularly in busy seasons. Nevertheless, Ida added "male" tasks to her "female" ones.

As the children grew older, they significantly augmented the labor of the farm, but also increased family living expenses. Because of the extra labor available, adult women could specialize either in household work or in field work, depending on the sex of the children and the mother's preference. In 1919 and 1920, the three Krueger sons replaced Ida in the fields, while Ida and her daughter, with some assistance from the men, expanded milk production and spent more time picking berries and growing garden truck. As the family matured, home production increased because the young adults ate more food, spent more for clothing, and had increased education costs; the Krueger children attended high school and college. Women's labor furnished many of the family necessities and paid for many of these personal expenses.[14]

The flexibility needed when a family relied primarily on its own labor created room for negotiation in the division of farm tasks. The backgrounds of families and the personal preferences of individuals shaped these family decisions. For example, definitions of appropriate work for men and women often differed by ethnicity. Women of German and Norwegian backgrounds worked most consistently at what might be considered male labor, participating in barnyard and field work. The gender division of labor for women of English or Scots background differed greatly, with some doing field or barnyard work, some working in poultry, egg, and garden production, and a few working only in the house.[15]

Women sometimes could assert their personal preferences in this negotiation process. Childhood experiences often influenced the work women chose to do as adults. One Iowa farm woman recalled that, as the oldest child, she was "Dad's chore boy." While her sister helped her mother with household and garden chores, she drove horses, disked, and put up hay. After her marriage, she continued the full spectrum of farm work, including milking cows, caring for poultry, trading eggs, gardening, and driving the tractor. Her husband accepted this division of labor, and even stated proudly, "She can drive anything that will run." Another Iowa farmer, Myrna Bogh, never did field work as a girl because she had three brothers. When she married, rather than hiring an extra man, which would increase her household duties, she decided to drive a tractor. She found the field work "very easy to do" and realized she would "rather do that than be in the house."[16] Although such factors as class, commodity specialization, and family composition shaped farm women's work, the family labor system provided some room for women to define and control their own labor.

Women's ability to control their labor depended on male cooperation. The negotiations took place in the context of patriarchal familial and economic structures. Family relations could stress hierarchy and control as often as mutuality. The needs of the farm, as defined by men, could take precedence over the needs of the family, as defined by women and children. The distinction between men's and women's labor often meant that men's labor was seen as crucial and women's as peripheral. "Flexibility" usually meant women doing the work of men, not the reverse. However, women and men shared much in their work lives. Farm people could use these shared patterns to create more cooperative styles of gender relations.[17]

Wages, the factor that devalued women's labor in the market economy, did not define the value of work on a family farm. Work was a part of the process of living. Daily, periodic, and seasonal tasks structured farm work and connected the rhythms of human needs to those of nature, the needs of the family to those of the farm. The daily chores, the heart of farm work, had to be completed and repeated every day to keep the farm and the family running smoothly. Daily tasks—starting fires, preparing and cleaning up after meals, carrying water—maintained the family; other tasks, such as feeding poultry, cattle, and pigs, milking cows, and gathering eggs, were necessary in caring for animals.[18] On farms that emphasized dairy or livestock as a primary commercial product, the daily routine increased in importance, but almost all farms had cows or chickens to meet family needs, and horses for field work.

In the performance of daily chores, all family members were equal. Because the daily chores were integral to every farm family's day, farm people rarely described them in diaries, except for an occasional general reference or when some part of the daily routine or task assignment was altered. Farm people rarely described or seemed to value the work skills needed for daily chores, except on dairy farms, where the speed of milking could be a source of pride for women, men, and children. Every member had the discipline of daily work, and this work gave each person a sense of place in the family and a responsibility to the family and the farm.

A pattern of regular periodic chores that were performed once or twice a week or every two weeks distinguished women's work. Primarily the responsibility of women, assisted by older girls and younger children, these tasks maintained the household and family, though some, such as churning, could be commercially oriented as well. Women added these weekly chores to their seasonal and daily work. Women throughout the western Midwest organized their workweeks in remarkably similar ways. Monday was laundry day. On Tuesday, women ironed and usually did another task such as baking or churning. Wednesday and Thursday were the most flexible days of the week. Some women baked; others did housework, sewing, or mending. On Friday and Saturday, women swept and mopped, baked cakes and pies for use on Sunday and the following week, churned butter, or went to town to shop. Although women still did daily chores on Sunday, they usually reserved it as a day for attending church and visiting. Sunday provided a break from the weekly routine.[19]

Since weekly patterns did not structure men's work, men often did not recognize the subtle differences in the daily work of women. Men's diaries ignored women's weekly chores just as they did all daily chores. Men only noted this labor when it affected their own. For example, men acknowledged that washing clothes was a labor-intensive task, and honored it as the only weekly women's work they regularly mentioned in their diaries. Men sometimes assisted with the wash by hauling water or carrying tubs. Even if men did not take part in the work of washdays, the demands of washing frequently changed women's performance of their other daily work and consequently shaped the men's days as well.[20] Otherwise, the regular weekly routine of women's work, particularly that which was centered on the house, was invisible to the men of the farm.

Household labor, the most distinctive form of women's work, was also culturally devalued. Although rural culture often praised a woman's ability to do men's work, it ridiculed a man doing women's work. Nellie Kedzie Jones, a home economist and extension service leader, recalled having a hired boy who had once worked in a city restaurant and liked assisting her with dishes. This lasted until the other hired help "poked fun at him." Farm boys learned lessons of female "inferiority" at an early age. Boys who took on the housework of women and girls usually chafed at the lowered status. One North Dakota man recalled staying home to help his grandmother after his mother's death in 1907. He cooked, did dishes, and baked bread, and as he described it, "I was the girl." He described this work as restrictive, and he resented missing all the action in the fields.[21] As in the rest of the society, farm women's household labor was valued less than men's work.

Although daily and weekly chores were the core of farm labor, seasonal tasks gave farm life its rhythms and diversity. Daily and weekly tasks were continuous and routine. Seasonal tasks provided variety in work, though still in a patterned and expected way. Farm people described the weather first in their diary entries because it affected the seasonal task for that day, the conditions under which that work would be conducted, and the success or failure of each crop season. Although daily and weekly work maintained the family, household, and livestock, plant production, whether for cash crops or for farm or home use, dominated seasonal tasks. Plowing, planting, cultivating, harvesting, marketing, and preserving filled the busy seasons of spring, summer, and fall, the specific routines depending on the types of crops. In winter farm people worked less, but still kept busy with such tasks as butchering animals, preserving meat, hauling and chopping wood, sewing, and doing odd jobs such as fence mending, equipment repair, and barn cleaning.[22]

Seasonal work united family members; seasonal change set the pace of rural life, and the demands of crop production often required the work of all family members. Women entered the fields for haying, shocking wheat, picking corn, and planting or harvesting tobacco and potatoes. The limited time available to complete these seasonal tasks made family labor necessary for success.

Because crop production dominated seasonal work and farm people defined field work as male labor, the seasonal demands of these crops reinforced the hierarchy of work. Natural cycles rarely set time limits on women's weekly tasks, making them seem less crucial. Unlike men, who failed to recognize women's weekly routines in their diaries, women recorded the seasonal work of men whether they actually assisted with it or not. Women could not ignore the labor of men in the same ways that men could the household tasks of women, because women's work might be disrupted by a call to work in the fields. In addition, women's daily work, such as meal preparation, had to be timed to accommodate the work of men. Men did, however, record garden work, probably because it paralleled their own seasonal work routines. Despite the recognition of women's seasonal labor, men's cash-crop production still took precedence over women's garden production when labor needs overlapped in busy seasons.

Women's work in the male arena of crop production did not necessarily lead to loss of status as did men's performance of housework. Competing definitions of "womanhood," most often based on class status though also influenced by ethnic traditions, existed within rural communities. Some women viewed their work in ways that seemed to approximate urban standards of domesticity. However, leisurely ideals of domesticity were not the model, even for farm women whose work most closely resembled urban, middle-class norms. Some farm families did not view barn or field work as respectable women's labor. For example, Lucille Hucke's father "didn't want to see women around the barn." Nevertheless, as a girl Hucke still gathered eggs and corncobs for cooking, even though her mother had a hired girl. Emma Henderson did not "help with regular chores very much," though she recognized that many of her friends did chores because there were no boys in their families. "I think we felt sorry for them." This, however, did not mean that women did not work. As Emma's husband Walter quickly pointed out, "There was more women's work at that time. . . . It took more help in the house than it does to-day."[23] Labor was a virtue for farm women even when it was restricted to the "less important" realm of the house and yards.

Other farm women's attitudes toward female labor clearly contrast with the domestic ideal. These women embraced all their work on the farm, including that which might be deemed men's work even by their own definitions. Many of these women explicitly said that they enjoyed working in the fields or barns and that they chose this labor. Anna Phillips, an Iowa farmer, described her own and her daughters' varied work, including milking, separating, and churning; caring for eggs and poultry; feeding pigs and doing other livestock chores; shocking oats and picking corn; cooking and baking; housecleaning; and raising children. When an interviewer commented, "Sounds like you and your daughters were busy," she replied, "Yes we were, but we didn't think so then. You know you just sort of enjoyed doing it."[24] Often a farm woman described her positive view of work in the context of family oral traditions of hardworking pioneer women. Husbands also accepted these alternative models of womanhood, and often looked at their wives' "male" work with pride. Although gaining value by performing male work tasks reinforced the hierarchical ranking of male over female labor, it nevertheless increased the importance of women to the family economy and often led to greater mutuality between men and women.

Another factor that supported the hierarchy of male over female labor was that the primary market commodities on most midwestern farms were the product of "male" tasks. Consequently, "men's work" led most directly to cash income. Even on dairy farms, where work in the barnyard was as traditionally female as male and the labor of commodity production was the most gender-integrated, an increase in production for the market often led to an increase in male control of the enterprise. However, farm people's valuation of work did not rest entirely on the direct exchange of labor for cash. In the family farm economy, production for market was not completely separated from production for home use. Laboring to produce goods for use on the farm was a crucial family farm survival strategy. "Women's work," such as managing home production, meeting family needs, and controlling the budget on a daily basis, created income indirectly by decreasing expenditures. Although the sexual division of labor emphasized that men's work increased cash income and women's saved it, in reality, men also decreased expenditures and women earned cash income. The economic importance of household production, the continued participation of men in nonmarket activities, and the significance of self-sufficiency in cultural traditions of family farming encouraged all farm people to value women's labor as integral to the farm family economy.

Farm people esteemed saving money as a real economic contribution, and women's labor made these survival strategies possible. "Making do," a term applied to the practice of making use of the goods at hand or doing without, was an economic necessity, a rural tradition, and a custom valued by farm people. Because most farm income came only at certain times of the year when cash crops were sold, and it depended on the vagaries of nature and the market, farm families developed work strategies that compensated for these ups and downs. Making do was a practical response to conditions of frequent shortage and inconsistent income. Although they were tied to commercial markets and credit systems, farm families were basically self-sufficient with regard to food, prized conservation, and condemned waste. These economic strategies reduced cash expenditures and helped keep the farms in the families.

Families who farmed through several generations understood the value of making do, and integrated stories of hardship and labor into oral traditions of family strength and survival. The oral history of a North Dakota woman illustrates this aspect of frontier life. The woman's parents rented forty acres of land in the Minnesota cutover area, where she was born in 1890 and remained until 1904, when the family moved to Mountrail County, North Dakota, to take advantage of free homesteads. She recalled the hardship, remembering that they "did as best we could." Her family kept fifteen head of cattle and produced its own milk, cottage cheese, butter, and vegetables. After working at a restaurant for several years, she married in 1908 and moved into another North Dakota shack, thinking "here we go again." She used the skills she had learned as a girl, milking, making butter, canning and smoking meat, and expanding the garden, concentrating on vegetables that would keep in a root cellar. In the years after her marriage, she recalled both good and bad crop years until the 1930s, when everything "dried up." Fortunately, the family had a good well, and her garden played a large part in the family's ability to endure. She carried her parents' skills of survival in hard times on newly settled land well into the twentieth century.[25] Although this frontier heritage is particularly clear in western North Dakota, where settlement came relatively late, similar family histories appear in other regions of the Midwest. Though adapted over time, strategies of making do remained vital to farm families throughout the first half of the twentieth century.

The value placed on making do reinforced the importance of women's labor to the family farm. Men appreciated this form of women's work because men also performed tasks that were not market oriented, such as raising feed for livestock and work animals and making or repairing tools and equipment.[26] In addition, their sense of the farm as a family enterprise, designed to meet family needs rather than just make a profit, enabled them to value the work of women. Women, likewise, saw their labor as integral to the farm enterprise rather than separate from its more market-oriented operations. Women and men viewed home production as crucial to family farming. When asked in the 1970s how his family had survived the 1930s, one North Dakota farmer replied that his wife was very "handy" and "then she was a Rutney [her maiden name] and they never threw away any money." His wife added that being self-sufficient was "the measure of a good wife, too, you see." She went on to add, "My daughter-in-law out there, I bet you, she couldn't even save you $200 or $300 a year on groceries alone. Got the money, so you use it." Reducing expenditures could mean survival in hard times or cash to invest in other farm operations, education, or consumer goods in good times.[27]

Most studies of agriculture have paid little attention to women's labor, but it proved crucial for improving farm families' standards of living. Women balanced family budgets daily through home production, sales, or trade, and controlled waste by making do or "making over." Food production constituted a major contribution to farm incomes. Studies done at agricultural experiment stations in the Midwest in the late 1920s and early 1930s show that the farm furnished a large percentage of a family's living, including fuel, food, clothing, and housing. Most of these studies show that about 50 percent of food value, and about 30 percent to 50 percent of all living costs, came from the farm. A study of 147 Iowa families between 1926 and 1929 found that these families produced three-fifths of their own food, including 95 percent of poultry, milk, eggs, and cream; 81 percent of meat (mostly pork and beef); and 43 percent of vegetables. Women cared for chickens, producing meat and eggs. From the dairy, they provided milk, cream, and sometimes cheese or butter. They canned and smoked meats and sometimes fished in nearby rivers. Work in gardens and orchards provided fresh fruits and vegetables in season and a winter food supply stored in root cellars, canned, dried, or made into jams and jellies.

This pattern of self-sufficiency through the work of women prevailed at most income levels. A 1929 study of nine hundred Wisconsin farms in seven counties found that the amount of furnished goods remained fairly stable on all farms and for all income levels, ranging from 39 percent

($317) at the lower incomes ($900), to 29 percent ($867) at higher incomes ($3,000). When incomes fell in the 1930s, these same Wisconsin families dealt with the crisis by cutting back on purchased food and increasing their use of farm products correspondingly.[28]

Besides furnishing food for the family, women sold and exchanged their products in local markets to increase cash income. Women as well as men earned cash for the farm. Most often women's income paid for family necessities, including groceries and clothing. This saved the cash from other parts of the farm enterprise to be used for investment in the farm. The connection between women's income and its use for family purchases appears almost universal. In the accounts of the Krueger family, who lived near Watertown, Wisconsin, egg money approximately equaled grocery expenditures, and the two were often listed together. Wisconsin farmer Percy Hardiman recalled that in the 1910s and 1920s his family had four hundred to five hundred chickens and "they always bought the groceries," while the money from ten acres of potatoes was used to buy ready-made clothes and to supplement income in midwinter. A North Dakota farmer recalled selling milk door-to-door in a local town and peddling eggs in the regional center of Manden in the 1930s, to get cash to order shoes, overalls, and fabric from Sears. Women's labor and women's products proved vital sources of income as well as income-savers for family farms.[29]

In the Farmer's Wife, the only magazine from this period targeting an audience of farm women, letters to the advice column in the 1910s and 1920s frequently solicited information about how to reuse things, how to use things for many different purposes, and how to cut down on expenses. (In this column, farm women answered each other with suggestions of their own methods of making do.) For example, farm women sewed; they made their own patterns and copied the latest styles from pictures in catalogs. Flour and sugar sacks were made of white muslin; when the lettering was bleached out, farm women could use them for underwear, diapers, pillow cases, sheets, shirts, or dresses. This kept down clothing expenditures and balanced cash-short budgets.[30]

Farm women could use the economic importance of their labor to negotiate greater equality within legal and economic systems that were essentially patriarchal. Recognition, however, did not come automatically because of the importance of women's work. Women's historians have often assumed a link between women's "productive" labor and the status of women in the household—that if women's work was crucial to the family economy, or if women earned income, or if women participated in higher-prestige male labor, this was a sign of a more egalitarian family structure. Other historians have argued that male control of land and the legal system led to authoritarian households where women had little influence or power. In fact, power relations in families, as in other systems of labor organization, developed through a process of negotiation. When families are the organizers of labor, personal ties become the basis of economic life. Farm women's work and their evaluation of that work are inexorably linked to the relations of family and kin. Although many factors shaped the division of labor on family farms, the status of women and children within the farm family economy often rested on the quality of their relationships with the men who controlled farm resources. Promoting mutuality was a strategy that encouraged farm survival and improved the status of dependents within farm families. By emphasizing work flexibility, shared responsibilities, and mutual interests, farm people limited the conflicts created by the patriarchal structure of the family and agriculture and created strategies for the survival of family farms.

Styles of authority relations converged with the other factors that shaped the gender division of labor, particularly class, to create divergent patterns of mutual or hierarchical gender relations. If a woman principally did house and poultry work, she could be marginalized and excluded from knowledge of the rest of the farm operation or she could take a more equal part through keeping books, sharing in decision making, and dividing profits, with investments in the house approximating those in the farm operation. On the other hand, when women were crucial to the labor force throughout the farm, exploitation would take the form of unending work with little reward. For women in these households, making do might mean doing without. Egalitarianism could come with an active and balanced partnership in which resources, work, and decision making were shared. Class status did not lead to either egalitarian or patriarchal family relations, but it shaped the expressions of these authority relations.

The intersection of gender and class can be seen in the forms of mutuality negotiated in the married lives of two Wisconsin farm women, Anna Pratt Erickson and Isabel Baumann. These marriages exhibit patterns of mutuality, but class differences structured these patterns. Both women had worked extensively on small general farms as girls, Erickson primarily in vegetable and fruit production, Baumann in tobacco. Erickson met her husband while assisting her brother and sister-in-law during the birth of their first child. Erickson married in 1904 at the age of twenty-one. She and her husband, Conrad, rented or managed farms for a number of years until they moved onto their eighty-acre farm near Athens, Wisconsin. Baumann met Dan McCarthy when she was teaching school in Sun Prairie, Wisconsin. Baumann married McCarthy in 1928 at the age of twenty-two and moved onto a large, specialized dairy farm. Both widowed young, Erickson at thirty-four and Baumann at thirty-six, the two women took divergent paths.

Erickson and her first husband, Conrad, developed reciprocal work patterns, sharing tasks rather than maintaining a strict gender segregation of labor. Although each had control of traditionally gender-defined work, they frequently helped each other, particularly after they moved to their "own 80" near Athens, Wisconsin, and operated the land as a family unit. The farm combined the commodity specialization of dairying with extensive gardening, eventually expanding into market production of vegetables and fruit. This enterprise seems to have been defined as Anna's and grew from her work experiences as a girl. Anna also participated in dairy production, frequently churning, cleaning the separator, and going to the cheese factory. In her diary, she rarely mentioned barn chores or milking, except when her oldest daughter was sick or when Conrad was out of town or busy with other work. At these times, she "did horse barn work and watered the stock." Conrad frequently assisted Anna with berry picking, laundry, childcare, churning, and garden and vegetable production. Anna assisted Conrad with haying, shocking wheat, and other field tasks that demanded more labor. The two worked side by side, closely coordinating all the labor on the farm until Conrad's death in 1917.

This mutuality contrasted sharply with her second marriage, to Joe Mauritz (1922–26). Joe primarily did field and machine work. Although Anna continued to work in the field during busy times, Joe rarely helped with fruit or garden produce, laundry, or housework, even when Anna was pregnant. Although Joe usually worked when the crop cycle demanded it, Anna perceived Joe as always "bumming," going to town or to his parents' farm while she was left to do the garden and berry work with only her children's assistance. Although in many farm homes both parties might have accepted this division of labor, Anna did not consent to it and resented Joe's absences. Comments on Joe's "bumming" first signaled that Anna's marriage to Joe was not a happy one. Later, problems intensified. Anna commented on Joe's "mean spells" and his "mean mouth," which, along with "bumming" in the evenings, was at one point in the diary associated with drinking. Though she never stated it in the diary, the verbal abuse may have escalated to physical abuse, because Anna had Joe arrested twice. They were divorced in 1926, and Anna legally took back the name of her first husband.

Although Erickson's actual work assignments changed little between the two marriages, Joe's lack of flexibility clearly changed her perceptions of her work and the family enterprise. The hard labor of a small dairy farm and her own skills with vegetables and fruit determined the type of work Erickson performed. However, the interdependent nature of work on a family farm and the patriarchal structure of family farming made the quality of the marital relationship crucial in defining her work and her ability to negotiate greater control of her own labor and that of other family members. Erickson's independent control of land as a widow gave her the economic resources to continue farming without a husband, and the labor of her children and neighbors enabled her to keep operating the farm until her son took over following World War II.

The McCarthy dairy farm differed significantly from the Ericksons' small general farm and the one on which Isabel Baumann grew up. Baumann's first husband, Dan McCarthy, farmed with his brother and father. They owned 160 acres and rented 80 more, and specialized in dairying with some hog production, selling directly to Oscar Mayer in Madison. With the labor of three adult men and additional seasonal hired help, the farm clearly did not require Baumann's work in the barn and field. Although Baumann described the extent of these operations, her words do not carry the sense of participation or mutuality that women who worked throughout their farms brought to their descriptions of the farm enterprise. Because of the farm's prosperity, Baumann's work was less crucial to farm survival, although it clearly improved the family's standard of living. Commercial specialization and a middle-class prosperity were expressed through a more gender-segregated division of labor.

Unlike urban, middle-class women, farm women could add income-earning work to the domestic activities that were common to both urban and rural women. Baumann renewed work traditions she had learned from her mother by developing a thriving egg and poultry business. Within this gender-segregated commercial farm, poultry production was Isabel's domain. Under a contract with a hospital in Madison, Baumann's operation produced four cases of eggs a week (with thirty dozen eggs per case). Although the farm subsidized her business with feed, Baumann controlled the income it created and used it to provide household furnishings, rather than household necessities. Baumann's sense of egalitarianism within the McCarthy farm came not from a mutuality of work in the farm enterprise, but from her control of this independent income. Baumann clearly viewed her poultry business with pride and a sense of accomplishment. She described it in ways that connected it to the farm but still kept it an individual project.

Other signs of equality within the McCarthy marriage also reflect the farm's prosperity. These included the willingness of the men to pair investments in the farm with improvements in the house—for example, putting water and electricity into the barn and house simultaneously—and Baumann's freedom to pursue activities in the community and in farm organizations, including becoming a leader in women's affiliates of the Farm Bureau and participating in a farm radio show in Madison. It is unclear whether Isabel shared in investment decisions. In one case her husband installed a new bathroom without her prior knowledge, though she appreciated the surprise and did not resent having been kept in the dark. This equality of consumption was a class-oriented expression of egalitarian gender relations, since poorer farms could not afford such investments. Clearly, the family shared the resources of the farm, but it is unclear whether this also meant shared power or decision making.

When Baumann was widowed in 1942, she pursued activities that took her out of farming. She briefly returned to teaching and then worked in an agricultural laboratory in Madison, because she felt she "had to be doing something." She married August Baumann in 1947. Baumann, unlike Anna Erickson, did not attempt to stay in farming, but rented the farm to a married couple.[31] Baumann's training as a teacher, her organizational and leadership experience, her lack of familiarity with the farm business, the farm's organization as a male partnership, and the absence of children contributed to her decision to leave farming. Although Erickson probably had few other job options that would have supported five children, she, in contrast to Baumann, continued to farm at least in part because she had been an active farm partner in labor as well as in sharing resources. Baumann's experiences of the class and gender systems in agriculture gave her more opportunities outside farming, while Erickson's increased her ability to remain in farming.

Although class differences shaped women's work and the expression of familial authority relations, class alone cannot explain the nature of women's labor on family farms. The lives of two North Dakota women, who had a similar class status but different gender relations with their husbands, underscore the importance of relations with male family members in determining the work of rural women. The labor of these women was crucial to their family farms. Ida Craft's story shows that hardship, poverty, and intense work demands did not necessarily lead to the specific exploitation of women. While Craft's oral history illustrates how patterns of mutuality enabled families to survive difficult economic times, the story of Cecilie Nelson illuminates the extent of patriarchal control possible in rural areas. Although some families developed unity through patterns of sharing in the farm enterprise, some men demanded "unity" through their sole control of resources and labor, and their insistence on familial subordination.

Ida Johnson Craft was born in Minnesota, just before her family moved to Mountrail County, North Dakota, in 1903. She married Oscar Craft, a Norwegian immigrant, sometime in the late 1910s or early 1920s. Oscar Craft bought a quarter-section of land near Stanley, North Dakota, in 1919. Interviewed simultaneously, Ida and Oscar each participated in the storytelling, filling in each other's gaps, presenting their perspectives even as they discussed the experiences they had shared. Most of this interview focused on the couple's married life together, particularly on the 1930s. The hard times required hard work from both Ida and Oscar, and each recognized the contributions of the other to the farm's survival. During the drought that devastated this region, Ida sold butter and eggs to pay the grocery bills, while Oscar worked for the WPA. She "raised a little bit" in her garden "when it wasn't a-blowin'" and remade clothes until she had "nothing more to patch." Throughout their marriage, the couple worked in the fields together, she driving three horses on the sulky plow while he drove five on the gang plow. She preferred this outdoor work, because she was "raised that way" and loved horses. He said with pride that his wife's work was "just as good as any man['s]," while she countered with a humorous story about him flying off a horse into a manure pile. The two also milked cows, but switched to raising beef cattle to cut down on their work load. They shared the tragic death of a daughter in 1934 (they had one other girl and a son), a passion for the Nonpartisan League (NPL) and the Farmers' Union, and an active community life, including barn dances and a ladies' aid group connected to the church, which was not just for "ladies" but for the whole family.

These shared experiences, of course, did not necessarily mean a complete lack of conflict or an absence of some signs of male prerogatives. Oscar sometimes told stories of extreme hardship that seemed to negate the value of Ida's contribution. However, when one of his stories did not reflect her reality, she felt free to correct his exaggerations and oversights. For example, he said that he spent sixteen dollars to join the NPL even though they did not have anything to eat; she disagreed, saying that they did have enough food to survive. Overall, she never described her participation in all the work on the farm as a burden, and they remembered surviving the hardship of the 1930s as a cooperative effort.[32] Despite the inequities of a patriarchal system, this couple negotiated a work relationship that they described in egalitarian ways.

In contrast, the oral history of Cecilie Nelson of Mountrail County, North Dakota, illustrates the extremes of male domination possible with the general economic control that was granted to men. She was born in 1888, married Nels Nelson of Wisconsin in 1911, and began homesteading. In her reminiscences, she described her husband's mismanagement of the farm and his absolute control of farm decisions and farm income. Although she was a knowledgeable farmer and was accustomed to the dryer western sections of the state, her husband never took her advice on farm matters and the crops rarely prospered. Her own labor was extensive, including rearing five children, raising and marketing chickens and turkeys, feeding calves and pigs, milking cows, separating cream, making and marketing butter, baking, gardening, canning, digging potatoes, and sewing. Although Nelson worked very hard for her family farm, the labor was not part of a cooperative effort.

This is most evident in Nelson's descriptions of financial decisions and the use of income. From the beginning of their marriage, Nelson's husband controlled the use of money in an authoritarian way. Nelson recalled that the five hundred dollars she brought to their marriage to buy household goods was spent by her husband in the first two weeks of their marriage to pay men on the threshing rig. Although in more egalitarian farm households such a decision might have been accepted by farm women as one made for the greater good of the farm, Nelson felt she had little influence on the decisions about the farm enterprise. The money she earned by raising turkeys and chickens and selling butter was not used for household items or to pay farm debts, but was spent by her husband on other things. Her husband was "awfully worked up on tractors," and if he had a million dollars he would have spent all of it on tractors. He told her not to write checks, and she "never wrote a check on him." Her lack of control of even her own income led to a sense of helplessness within the marriage. When asked why she did not leave him, she replied, "but what should I do, I didn't have no money." When he died in 1940, he left her more than thirty thousand dollars in debt.

This woman's oral history is filled with tales of abuse of women in her own family and others. Her family did not deem medical attention important for women. During one of her pregnancies, her husband "finally sent for the doctor" when the baby "came backwards and double." The doctor told her she would need an operation within the next two years. Fourteen years and four births later, she had that operation. Her interview is filled with stories of physical abuse by men and overwork for women. A few representative phrases convey her view: "Woman nothing but a slave to them." "That's the way the old men was them days." Some men "have a lot to answer for."[33]

Clearly the need for women's productive work in the farm enterprise did not necessarily lead to a mitigation of patriarchal control or abuse. Those families that did develop a general equality within family farm operations made choices that emphasized sharing rather than control. These choices did not alleviate all family conflict or result in total equality; however, they did lessen the worst abuses of patriarchal control and increase women's agency within the family.

The structure of family farming contained within it seeds of both hierarchy and mutuality. Family labor was necessary for farm survival. The economic and legal structure gave adult male heads of households the power to control resources and the labor of dependent family members.

The realities of working the farm gave considerably more influence to women and children in shaping their own work. Outside the most authoritarian family relations, women and children could use the need for their labor and the ties of marriage and kinship to gain greater control of their lives and decisions on the farm. Strategies emphasizing the mutual enterprise of the farm and the sharing of its labor and resources not only benefited dependents on the farm, but benefited the farm itself. Flexibility of task assignments, commitments to home production and making do, the willingness to sacrifice for the good of the farm and the family were all economic survival strategies that were most successful in an enterprise of shared interests rather than one of hierarchical dominance. Although gender inequities existed even within the most cooperative family farms, laboring together in a joint enterprise encouraged farm men, women, and children to view their lives and interests in relational terms. The good of the individual was inherently linked to and balanced with the good of the family and the farm.

Building a Rural Neighborhood

Although the family was the basic economic and social unit of the rural Midwest, farm families were far from isolated. Most farm people were part of well-developed neighborhoods. More than a mere geographic designation, neighborhood meant a set of social relations. In a series of articles published in the *Country Gentleman* between 1912 and 1916, Nellie Kedzie Jones, who grew up on a farm, created the home economics department at Kansas State Agricultural College, and became a leading educator in agricultural extension at the University of Wisconsin, advised a fictional young woman from town on ways to be accepted by her new rural neighbors. The first rule of the "country code," she wrote, was that borrowing and lending were good. It was "neighborly," not "nervy." This exchange had to be rooted in friendliness. The young woman needed to know all her neighbors. Jones recommended that she learn to recognize horses and dogs so she could know teams on the road and greet passengers by name, even when they were bundled up for winter. Hospitality and favors built an easy familiarity. If you passed someone walking on the road, you should always offer a ride. Jones summarized her advice by saying that a person should not fear to be "under obligation." Neighbors did not tally exchanges, nor view them as taking turns. If you had something nice, you should simply send it to a neighbor. If you needed something, you should always ask for favors, too.[1] It was important that a good neighbor request assistance as well as provide it.

Neighboring extended the patterns of mutuality formed in families to create a system of reciprocity that went beyond the ties of kinship to larger community groups.[2] As Jones's advice suggests, the shared rules and assumptions of behavior in neighboring made the distribution of economic resources possible. Since it was equally acceptable to ask and to give, and since all neighbors were expected to do certain types of favors, this code assured a general equality of exchange. Neighboring placed economic exchanges within social relationships that often overshadowed their economic nature. By emphasizing a friendly attitude of giving and helpfulness rather than a sense of direct obligation that balanced debts and credits in a mechanical way, neighboring created a flexible system of mutual assistance that met emotional as well as economic needs.

Neighborhoods mirrored the organization of the family labor system. Some neighborhood networks grew from the gender division of labor, and separated men and women. However, farm people reconnected these networks through social events that included all family members. Although both men and women participated in these events, women organized much of the informal social life of a neighborhood. The resources created by neighborhood sharing were particularly important to women. Through interpersonal relationships, women gained control of resources that helped offset their lack of legal or customary control of resources within the family.[3] These resources also assisted the farm itself, increasing women's contributions to the family economy. Like internal family survival strategies, community-based survival strategies not only helped preserve family farms but benefited farm women within the family's unequal structures. Women and men both needed the economic and social sharing of community ties; however, their needs differed because gender defined access to the resources of agriculture and divided the labor of the farm.

Informal patterns of interaction cemented farm people together in rural neighborhoods. Farm people described informal visiting and exchange prominently in their diaries. In oral histories, they almost always remembered the importance of neighbors and elaborated on the sense of loss caused by the passing of the old neighborhood and the sharing that neighboring involved. Although sociologists preferred to measure strong communities by the persistence of institutions, such as schools or churches, their observations forced them to acknowledge the importance of informal social life, which was more difficult to measure. For example, in 1933, Wisconsin sociologist J. H. Kolb noted the importance of neighboring, socially and in work exchanges, stating that it was "often the ingredient which actually makes the primary factor [institutions] potent." By the time of his 1941 study, two of the six factors he found most significant for neighborhood stability were "visiting" and "work exchange."[4] The cultural expectations of neighboring were more institutionalized than sociologists believed. Although these interactions were informal, their repetition gave them predictability and consistency.

The term *neighborhood*, as I will use it, corresponds less to a place than to supportive systems of repeated exchanges and social interactions. A neighborhood begins with a core of people whose interactions are most frequent and builds outward to include those who share consistent, face-to-face interactions. The term *community* describes the furthest extensions of these circles, including people who would be recognized as residents of the community, but not necessarily be included in neighborhood visiting or exchange. With these definitions, the term *community* more closely fits the geographic locale.[5] In practice, most rural neighborhoods did connect farm family units living in specific sections of the open country, but geographic proximity cannot be equated with social closeness.

The diary of Anna Pratt Erickson illustrates the process of rural neighborhood formation and its relation to the larger rural community. The diary provides an excellent example, both because it is a consistent record kept over a long period of time and because Erickson was a farm wife and a farmer at different points in her life. Erickson was born in Illinois in April 1883. She began her diary in 1898 and continued with daily entries until her death in 1959. In 1903, she went to Athens, in north-central Wisconsin, to help her brother Charles and his wife, who were having their first child. While with them, she met Conrad Erickson, and married him in 1904. After living in several places in Wisconsin, they settled permanently on an eighty-acre farm in Johnson Township, near Athens, in 1912. They had five children between 1905 and 1917 (Orma, 1905; Dorothy, 1908; Fay, 1911; Lois, 1913; and Morris, 1917). Erickson continued to operate the farm on her own after Conrad's death in 1917, except during her brief (1922–26) marriage to Joe Mauritz. Although Erickson's experiences and record are unique, the general process of neighborhood formation she portrays can be found in many other sources.[6]

The Erickson farm was located in Marathon County, part of the cutover region of north-central Wisconsin. The lumber industry dominated the region's development, but began to decline around 1910. As lumbering declined, developers turned their attention to promoting agriculture. The Ericksons' community in Johnson Township consisted largely of small farms, although the Rietbrock Land and Lumber Company still controlled significant amounts of land as late as 1920. Most of these families, like the Ericksons, owned eighty acres, but a few owned smaller (40-acre) or larger (120- to 160-acre) farms. Early agricultural production in the county included hay, potatoes, peas, oats, rye, barley, and wheat. By 1907, production of fruit, including apples, plums, cherries, blackberries, and strawberries, increased. Dairying began to predominate in the early twentieth century. By 1905 the county contained seventeen creameries, and by the early 1920s, there were sixteen cheese factories within a six-and-one-half-mile radius of Athens.[7] As was common in the area, the Erickson farm specialized in dairying and fruit production.

Between 1900 and 1920, the rural population of Marathon County increased by more than 50 percent. Most of the immigrants to the region were German and Polish, but by the 1930s the county's population was quite diverse, including significant Norwegian, Irish, Dutch, and Bohemian settlements. As in urban areas, rural settlers often moved in groups or settled where family, former neighbors, or people of similar backgrounds lived. Ethnic settlement patterns played an important cohesive role in rural communities. For example, a study of South Dakota done in 1937 described the concentration of ethnic groups in specific counties, and in 1937 the patterns of original settlement were still maintained.[8]

However, the Erickson neighborhood was not connected by the more obvious factors that usually linked rural people, revealing that neighboring was a matter of human choice as much as an obligation of kinship or ethnicity or simply a result of geographic proximity. The families that composed Erickson's social neighborhood were not all immediate neighbors, and not all her immediate neighbors were part of her social network. Some families, such as the McKinnons, the Flessings, the Lehmans, and the Kulases, appeared in the diary before the Ericksons moved to their own farm, and remained family friends despite the greater distances between their homes. Other families who lived further away, such as the Aderholds, shared membership in the Presbyterian church. Those families who were both geographic and social neighbors were not homogeneous, ethnically or religiously. Those who lived in the community but did not participate in social exchange had equally diverse characteristics. The Ericksons' geographic neighbors included Catholics (the Kulases, the Zettlers, and the Weigands), Presbyterians (the Browns), Lutherans (the Zubkes), and Evangelicals (the Brehms). The community did not share ethnic or religious ties, dense kinship networks, or unified neighborhood institutions.[9]

And yet Anna Pratt Erickson's neighborhood was very stable. Ethnic ties, kinship, and institutions alone did not lead to the perseverance of the system of small family farms, as sociologists of the time suggested. Instead, endurance came from the patterns of exchange and assistance that farm people built with each other. Social and economic sharing was not just an assumed obligation of kinship, ethnicity, or religion, but was an economic survival strategy and social system that farm people consciously chose to build. In many cases these exchanges did reinforce ethnic, kinship, or religious links; however, the Ericksons maintained the diversity of ties formed in the settlement process even as they built outward from them. The growth of Erickson's social networks paralleled both the maturation of her own family and the maturation of the region as it moved from frontier conditions to become a settled agricultural area. As the plat maps indicate, the Ericksons' social networks became denser and more widespread between 1912 and the 1930s (see maps 1 and 2). This diverse neighborhood maintained a relatively secure tenure status at least into the 1950s, and several of these family names remain in the region today. Informal social networks played a large role in building this community and helping it persevere during the first half of the twentieth century. Erickson's diary reveals how neighboring integrated the social and economic activities of men, women, and children, and how these flexible social networks met the needs of the community's members and helped maintain a system of small family farms.

Farm people created informal neighborhoods in four ways: visiting, exchanging work, exchanging products, and sharing life events. The social practice of visiting underlay all rural economic exchanges. Visiting was the primary means of rural socializing, and it occurred throughout the Midwest.[10] When a neighborhood had stable tenure, social contacts could stretch through many years. The Erickson neighborhood included six families (the Underwoods, the Browns, the Zettlers, the Kulases, the Flessings, and the Lehmans) who were mentioned in Anna's diary from 1912, when the Ericksons settled permanently, through the 1930s. Another three (the Zubkes, the Aderholds, and the Streamers) appeared consistently after 1917, and five more families (the Beckers, the Weigands, the Heindles, the Schneweisses, and the Peckers) after 1920. Because neighbors visited and built emotional ties with neighbors, trust and shared values could emerge from the consistent repetition of friendly interaction. The bonds created by patterned and stable social sharing enabled economic exchange to be more flexible, but still guaranteed relatively equal reciprocity.

The patterns of visiting reflected the social and economic purposes of the family labor system. Visiting integrated economic and social life, followed the gender division of labor, and reaffirmed family connections. Patterns of visiting flowed from the work demands of agriculture. During the week, visiting blended with work and trade. For example, a social visit might also include asking a neighbor to chop wood. In Wisconsin, oral histories described daily trips to the local creamery as occasions to stop and visit. Work exchanges held a social component, and socializing also included work.[11] For example, Erickson's closest friendship seemed to be with Mrs. Kulas. Their friendship developed not only through shared business interests, including purchasing strawberry plants together and

1. Women joined men in the fields during harvest seasons. "Putting up alfalfa by the 'Armstrong' Method, five tons per acre, Aurora, Missouri, July 1909."

2. Operating a threshing machine, Missouri, 1915. Men feed the machine from a stack at the right, grain empties down a chute in the center to be bagged, and the straw moves out the blower at the left where it is stacked.

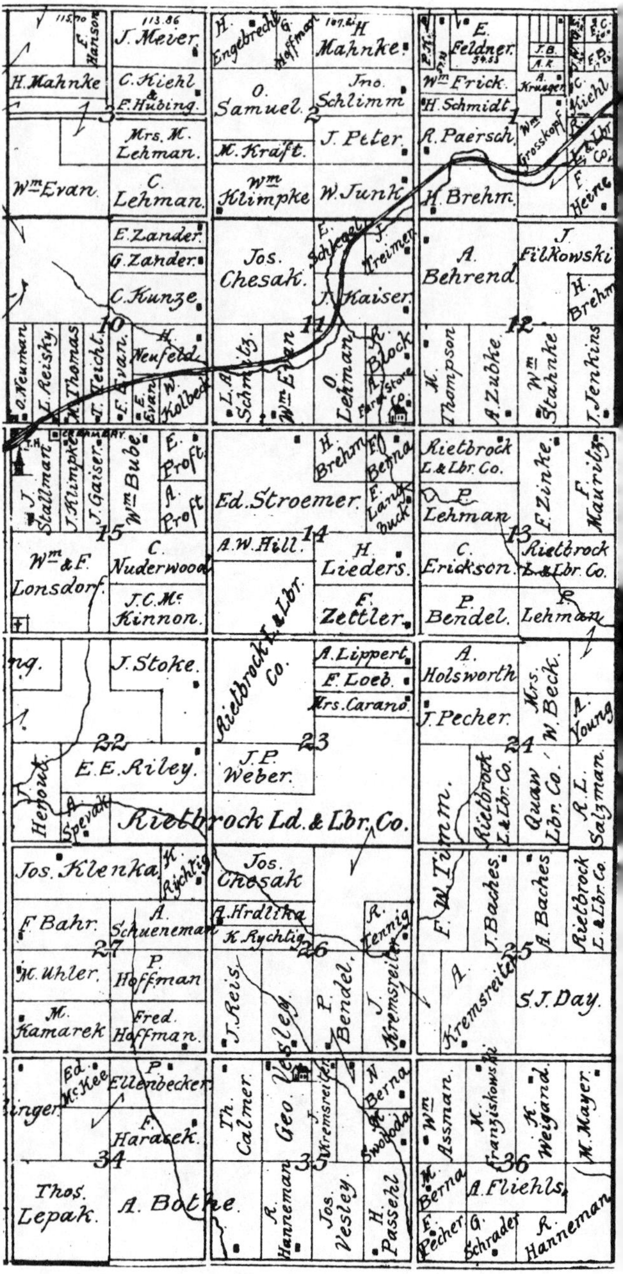

Map labels (township plat):

- 115.70 | 113.86 | 107.2
- L. Hanson | J. Meyer | H. Engelbrecht | H. Mahnke | E. Feldner 3633 | J.B. A.K.
- H. Mahnke | C. Kiehl & F. Hubing | O. Samuel | Jno. Schlimm | Wm Frick | A. Kruger | C. Kiehl
- H. Schmidt | Grosskopf | F. Heine
- Mrs. M. Lehman | M. Kraft | J. Peter | R. Paersch | Wm
- Wm Evan | C. Lehman | Wm Klimpke | W. Junk | H. Brehm
- E. Zander | G. Zander | Jos. Chesak | E. Schkopp | J. Treimer | A. Behrend | J. Filkowski
- C. Kunze | J. Kaiser | H. Brehm
- 10 | O. Neuman | L. Reisty | J. Feichtl | H. Neufeld | 11 | Wm Evan | O. Lehman | R. Block | M. Thompson | A. Zubke | Wm Stahnke | 12 | J. Jenkins
- J.F. Evan | W. Kolbel | L.A. Schmidt | Ferd Stroemer |
- CREAMERY | J.H. | E. Proft | H. Brehm | E. Berna | Rietbrock L. & Lbr. Co.
- J. Stallman | J. Klimpke | J. Gaiser | Wm Bube | A. Proft | Ed. Stroemer | E. Lang | E. Lehman | F. Zinke | W. Mauritz
- 15 | C. Nuderwood | A.W. Hill | 14 | H. Lieders | C. Erickson | 13 | Rietbrock L. & Lbr. Co.
- Wm & F. Lonsdorf | J.C. Mc Kinnon | F. Zettler | P. Bendel | Lehman
- ng. | J. Stoke | Rietbrock L. & Lbr. Co. | A. Lippert | F. Loeb | Mrs. Carano | A. Holsworth | Mrs. W. Beck
- J. Pecher | W. Young
- Herbort | 22 | E.E. Riley | J.P. Weber | 23 | 24 | Quan Lbr. Co. | R.L. Salzman
- Spevah | Rietbrock Ld. & Lbr. Co. | F.W. Timm | Rietbrock L. & Lbr. Co. | A. Baches | Rietbrock L. & Lbr. Co.
- Jos. Klenka | H. Richtig | Jos. Chesak | J. Baches
- F. Bahr | A. Schueneman | A. Hrdlika | R. Tennig | 25 | Kremsreiter
- 27 | K. Rychlig | 26 | A. | S.J. Day
- M. Uhler | P. Hoffman | P. Bendel | J. Kremsreiter
- M. Kamarek | Fred Hoffman | J. Reis | Geo. Vesley
- Ed. Mc Kee | P. Ellenbecker | Th. Calmer | J. Kremsreiter | N. Berna | Wm Assman | M. Franzishowski | H. Weigand | M. Mayer
- inger | F. Harasek | 34 | 35 | J. Swoboda | 36
- Thos. Lepak | A. Bothe | R. Hanneman | Jos. Vesley | H. Passerl | M. Berna | F. Pecher | G. Schrader | A. Fliehls | R. Hanneman

Map 1. The Erickson neighborhood, Johnson Township, Marathon County, Wisconsin, 1912. The Erickson farm is in section 13.

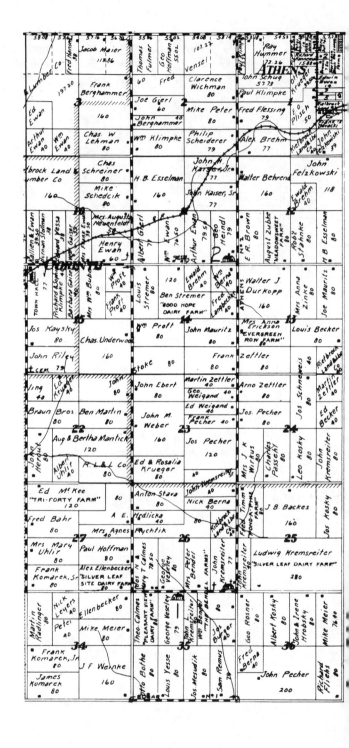

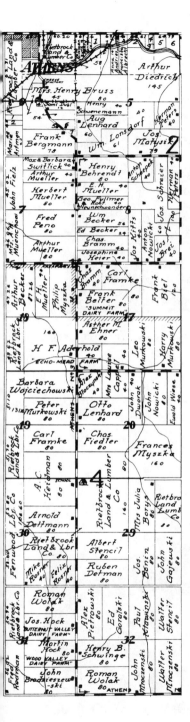

Map 2. The Erickson neighborhood, Johnson Township, Marathon County, Wisconsin, 1930. This map shows both the expansion and the persistence of Erickson's social and exchange networks.

3. "Lunch break in the field" for a threshing crew, Cross Plains, Wisconsin, 1915.

5. Women produced an important part of the food supply in their gardens and supervised the work of young children. Haskell County, Kansas, 1941.

Facing page:
Bottom: 4. Combining wheat, Kansas, 1921. "Grain chute extending to right with grain running into grain barge; this combine furnished traction for itself and the grain barge. When the barge is filled it is hauled away and another barge substituted at the combine. One team and teamster is thus kept busy hauling away grain and bringing back empty bags. This method of harvesting and threshing reduces the use of man and horse power to a minimum."

6. A farmer husks corn, removing the ear from the husk and throwing it against the "bang board," which guides the ear into the wagon. His son drives the wagon. Grundy County, Iowa, 1939.

7. Farmers often continued to use horses even after they purchased tractors. Shelby County, Iowa, 1941.

exchanging gifts, produce, and labor at picking time, but also through frequent social visits in the afternoon or evening, for evening or Sunday meals, and for trips to Wausau, the largest nearby trading center.

The integration of visiting with the daily routines of farming is best seen with the arrival of out-of-town guests. Visitors became a part of the family, sharing in its work, trade, and visiting. The columnist and home economist Nellie Kedzie Jones recommended that farm guests not cause a "domestic upheaval" but a "simple expansion of the usual family routine." This indeed is the practice revealed in most farm diaries. Erickson recorded the arrival and departure of visitors, but merged the rest of their stays with routine daily entries. For example, Earl, Anna's uncle, visited for an extended period after Conrad's death. Anna noted his arrival and departure, but many days she did not mention him at all. His name appeared only when he did certain work ("Earl and I haul hay") or made a special trip to town (Earl took Anna to the train in Wausau).[12] Visiting did not upset routine; it blended in with daily activities.

Because visiting blended in with the labor of farming, the division of labor between men and women created distinct male and female friendship networks. However, gender networks existed within larger patterns of family and neighborhood exchange. For example, Erickson often referred to her visitors by using the plural form of their last names.[13] Sometimes the family name referred to the household, but it might also mean just the household's women. During two separate weeks in 1928, Erickson referred to an individual name rather than the plural form of the last name only twice. Both occasions were work related and show the separation of male and female work. Frank and John Pecker came to work on a pump house, and Mrs. Aderhold brought produce. Other work occasions, such as a visit to the Lehmans' to sew, probably only included women even though Erickson used the family name. Other work-related visits may have been either gender-integrated or gender-segregated, such as two separate trips to the Zubkes', one to return scales and the other to get eggs.[14] Friendships between women or between men were important in visiting patterns, but farm people's gender networks existed within more-inclusive family visiting patterns.

Family networks emerged most clearly when visiting was not connected to work. Breaks from weekly work routines occurred on Saturdays and Sundays, and visiting on these days usually took on more symbolic forms. Because farm people organized their workweeks in similar ways, visits to trading centers on Saturdays became informal yet ritualized farm community gatherings. One Mountrail County, North Dakota, resident described Saturday nights as social events in which "families used to sit in the store and visit until 10 or 11 o'clock at night"; a second reported it as midnight or 1 A.M. The stores stayed open, they observed, as "long as there was anybody around."[15]

The most ritualized and family-centered visiting occurred on Sundays. Sunday visiting rarely included errands or work and often involved the entire family. In two Iowa townships, more than 60 percent of about two hundred families surveyed in 1920 reported that they visited often on Sundays, while another 10 percent said that they sometimes visited on Sundays. Almost every Sunday, Anna Pratt Erickson went visiting or received visitors, often more than one in a day or even at one time. These visits were rarely prearranged; neighbors simply arrived, "visiting" and "staying for dinner." Because the visits were so regular, they were clearly expected even if unplanned. On the rare Sundays when there were no visitors or visits, Anna continued the practice of "visiting" by writing letters to relatives, especially to her daughters when they were older and had moved away.[16]

Farm people chose to connect networks based on age and gender to networks that united all family members. For example, some people integrated children's friendships into larger familial networks. Most often children's friends were the children of neighbors (in Erickson's case, the Schneweiss, Kulas, Weigand, Brown, Becker, and Underwood families). But children participated in visiting and work exchanges as part of the family and even built individual ties to adult neighbors. The Erickson children would visit adult neighbors without their parents, sometimes attending school or town functions and spending the night. When children made friends outside the neighborhood, farm people brought those friends into their families and even connected the two families by bringing parents into adult visiting networks. For example, Margaret Copple was a friend of Anna's second daughter, but was not a resident of their neighborhood. Margaret and Dot spent the night at each other's homes. Eventually, Margaret and her mother visited the Ericksons, and Anna and Margaret's mother exchanged gifts and visits. Even after the daughters left home, Margaret and her mother still visited Anna and maintained the family connections.[17] Visiting patterns reflected the age and gender divisions within families but also recreated the family as the principal unit of rural organization.

Although visiting provided the social basis for the sharing of economic resources, work exchanges reveal the primary economic resource shared among farm families—labor. Crop cycles often required more intensive seasonal labor than a family could provide alone. Exchanging work expanded an individual farm's labor force without adding the cost of hired workers. The organization of community labor exchanges followed both the gender segregation of work and the gender integration of women and men in families. Exchanges took on a more familial, gender-integrated form when only a few families who were connected through social visiting participated. When labor needs expanded, particularly for seasonal field work, the work was more gender-segregated and the terms of economic exchange more defined. Nevertheless, farm people gave these exchanges social content, integrating women and men as they did in Sunday visiting rituals. While men's labor organized the economic side of these exchanges, women's work created their social component.

Work exchanges occurred throughout the first half of the twentieth century and in all the midwestern agricultural regions, though the type of work exchanged varied. A study of Boone County, Missouri, in 1920 indicated that families exchanged work frequently, and this was a "tangible expression of neighborhood life." Researchers recorded four incidents of "old time" community gatherings: tobacco stripping, corn husking, wood chopping for an injured neighbor, and a "sugaring off" party, and numerous smaller exchanges for hog butchering, threshing, corn gathering, and pond cleaning. In Geneva, Nebraska, in 1923, work exchanges varied in frequency for different tasks. One out of fourteen farmers exchanged work at corn shelling, one out of seven at haying, and more than half at harvesting; the practice of exchange at threshing time was "practically universal." Later studies indicate the persistence of work exchange in some areas into the early 1940s. In Dane County, Wisconsin, surveys done in 1941 indicated that families exchanged work with an average of six other neighborhood families. In eastern South Dakota, surveyors found in 1940 that seven out of ten families regularly exchanged work with at least one neighbor, while four out of ten did so with at least two.[18] Although the type of work and the size of the group needed to fulfill labor needs varied, farm families throughout the Midwest exchanged work through the 1930s.

Because a gender division of labor organized rural work, women and men exchanged labor in separate networks. For example, Anna Erickson recorded little information about the ways in which men organized their work while she was married to Conrad. The arenas for male exchange did become apparent when Anna took over Conrad's work after his death. Men arranged to exchange work or equipment when they visited, marketed their products, or attended organization meetings, such as the Equity cooperative or "cheese meetings" that Erickson's second husband and son attended. Similarly, women's exchanges flowed from women's visiting and work patterns, including gardening, caring for children, making clothing (sewing, quilting, exchanging patterns), trading and marketing women's products, and attending women's organizations, such as Anna's community club and her daughter Dot's Ladies' Aid. Men and women had separate arenas for exchange that reflected the gender division of labor on farms.

But labor exchanges also reflected the family organization of rural social and economic life. The women who exchanged labor were married to the men who exchanged labor. This was particularly true when families developed intensive patterns of exchange with a few other families, whether these families were extended kin or unrelated neighbors.[19] These networks can be followed through Erickson's diary by observing exchanges for butchering and processing meat products.[20] The task involved intensive work: preparing and heating water, preparing and handling the animals, butchering, preparing the meat, grinding it, rendering lard, and making sausages and head cheese. As within a family, the smallest informal exchanges were marked by a gender division of labor but were still coordinated and viewed as a shared venture.

These patterns of exchange particularly characterized communities of small, family-operated farms. In the early years of Anna and Conrad's marriage, Conrad managed other farms. Because of their frequent moves in these years, the Ericksons did not participate in established neighborhood networks, and they exchanged work less frequently and with less social content. During these years, Conrad and Anna butchered alone, or Anna did not mention it. When she described butchering, Anna primarily recorded her own work, mentioning rendering lard or cooking for men. She did not record the male work of butchering or the names of those who did it. The absence of detail from these early entries illustrates the separation of male and female work roles for farm laborers and how the absence of community ties could increase gender segregation.

When the Ericksons finally settled on their own eighty-acre farm in 1912, butchering appeared more frequently in the diary. They now owned a small family farm and became part of an established farm neighborhood. During the Ericksons' marriage, butchering remained principally a family task, but now Anna recorded both male and female work, seeing it more as a joint endeavor. The most detailed description occurred in the winter of 1916, and it revealed a total reliance on family labor. On 23 December, Conrad butchered a pig. From the 26th through the 29th, Anna and Conrad (who probably helped because of Anna's advanced pregnancy) ground pork, made sausages, and put one shoulder into a two-gallon jar. During her second marriage, the family butchered principally with labor from their own household, but her husband's brother assisted.

When Anna operated her farm independently, neighborhood exchanges took on an increasingly important role. In the years immediately following Conrad's death, Anna used family and hired help at butchering time. Generally, Mr. Gore, a neighbor who worked frequently for Anna, butchered while Anna and her older daughters prepared the meat. By the 1920s, Erickson had developed denser exchange patterns and depended on close neighbors with some additional hired help. Throughout the 1920s and 1930s, neighbors Joe Schneweiss, Edd Weigand, and Bill Bernea butchered; they hired more distant neighbors (but probably friends of her children), Constantin Rychtik and Mike Rosnover, to help. In preparing the meat, Anna primarily relied on the assistance of her daughters, but occasionally exchanged work with close neighborhood women, Mrs. Zubke (1924), Ruth and Caroline Lehman (1926–28), and Mrs. Weigand (1930). As this indicates, work was gender-separated, but related through patterns of family exchange. For example, in 1930 the Ericksons and Weigands exchanged butchering. The men, Edd Weigand and Bill Bernea, butchered, while the women, Anna and Mrs. Weigand, ground or canned the meat and made sausage. These close neighbors became part of an extended "family" labor force that reflects the gender-integrated patterns of family farming.

Feelings of reciprocity shaped these exchanges. The boundary lines between cash payment, exchange, and neighborly reciprocity were often blurred. Generally, when butchering took place, meat was the principal product of exchange. For example, in June 1928, Anna's daughter Dot went to the Weigands' farm to help Edd and Bill Bernea butcher. In the next few days, Anna and her daughters prepared meat for their own use, which indicates that they had received it in exchange for Dot's help. But exchange also involved other types of labor or products. In 1934, the Ericksons traded beef for pork with a neighboring family, the Zettlers. Anna "repaid" Caroline Lehman for some work by sewing her a new dress.[21] Often Erickson did not mention the payment for work, and "payment" might not have occurred in any direct sense; rather it would have been part of the give-and-take of long-term neighborhood interactions. Gift, exchange, and payment varied from year to year depending on a family's ability to pay or exchange. Women and men participated equally in this sharing of resources, and saw their own work in relation to that of others, even if the work itself was gender-segregated.

Larger work exchanges were more gender-segregated and formal than smaller ones, but farm people created rituals to make them more gender-integrated than they might otherwise have been. Seasonal work required large numbers of workers, and farm people flexibly expanded their neighborhood-building patterns to include more-distant neighbors. Because larger exchanges occurred most often for field work, men organized them. Seasonal work often required labor or machinery that could not be repaid easily in labor or exchange. Farm people balanced these exchanges, particularly for those outside the routine exchange networks, with cash payments. Despite this more direct economic content, women labored to make larger exchanges into ritualized social occasions. Although women's household work was subordinate in economic importance during these work exchanges, women provided large meals that made work an exchange of hospitality as well as labor.[22] Women's participation brought the social forms of family visiting to these formal work exchanges, creating a neighborhood feeling. By keeping exchange in a social context, farm people helped assure that work would be completed with minimum dependence on outside sources of labor or machinery and with a minimum cash outlay.

Erickson's diary illustrates how patterns of exchange kept farm costs down. The primary seasonal neighborhood work exchanges for Erickson were wood chopping, threshing, and in the late 1920s and 1930s, silo filling. These involved "rings" in which members would gather and, moving from farm to farm in turn, do the required work for each of the members. When these rings included only those within the core neighborhood, the exchange was direct. For example, Anna's son Morris cut wood for the same families—the Mauritz, Schneweiss, Weigand, and Zettler families— who cut wood for the Ericksons, and all were close neighbors. In contrast, those neighbors who rarely exchanged work or visits were much more likely to be paid in cash. For example, between 1934 and 1937, after Morris's graduation from high school, only two names appeared in threshing contexts and no others: Weber, who paid Morris cash for his work, and Stauke, who was being repaid for a previous threshing bill.

Social ties and year-round exchanges helped farm families compensate for a lack of resources or inequalities in exchange. Because much of the threshing work was "men's work," the most direct exchanges in the operation of a threshing ring appeared in Erickson's diary when an adult male participated. The consistency of work exchanged during these years suggests an equality of available resources that was not apparent in the years when the Erickson family had no man's labor to exchange. When farm families did not have equal resources, the exchange of work throughout the seasons could help balance these inequalities and share the neighborhood's labor and capital resources. Between 1934 and 1937, the Ericksons primarily provided labor and a team of horses at threshing time, and labor at silo-filling time. Other neighborhood farmers provided equipment. Zettler and Heindle cut the oats and barley with their binders, and in 1937, the Ericksons used Zettler's threshing machine. Morris then threshed and helped fill silos for these neighbors. The only direct payment mentioned in any of these exchanges was for the use of the threshing machine, which was the most expensive to buy and operate.[23]

Although they were organized to assure some economic equality, most exchanges also contained a social meaning for the participants. Women's work created this social context. Like threshing, the erection of new buildings demanded significant work exchanges. As time progressed, such events became less frequent than in the settlement period, and increasingly, farm people hired noncommunity labor. Nevertheless, barn raisings still included neighborhood exchanges and community ritual. In 1920, Erickson had a barn raising. The family skidded logs for several winters, preparing for the event. Neighbors hauled logs for pay, and also hauled back loads of lumber for their own use in exchange. In April, the "hewing men" stayed for several days, and Anna paid them and also "had to give them lunch twice." Because these were paid laborers from outside the community, Anna saw the meal preparation as a burden. The family and Joe Mauritz picked and hauled stones for the foundation, which was laid by neighbors. A crew of ten men from outside the community built the frame, and four to six hired men completed the work after the raising.

Although the preparatory and finishing work reveals a combination of family, community, and hired help, a community group of forty-one men raised the barn. The Ericksons "paid" these men with an elaborate meal and social occasion, creating a larger community ritual. Only the immediate family performed the earlier stages of "women's work," but neighborhood women contributed work for the barn raising. Herb Aderhold butchered for Anna, and four neighborhood women, Mrs. Zubke, Mrs. Aderhold, Miss Cameson (the local teacher), and Mrs. Lehman, helped her in the house.[24] Rural work exchanges like this barn raising blended social and economic content. Although specialized labor from outside the community was hired, family and neighborhood labor made it economically possible to complete the barn, and the gender-integrated nature of the raising increased the social content of work that was principally "male."

Farm people exchanged not only work, but also the products of their labor. Although by the twentieth century, small general farms usually specialized in some commodities to sell to larger markets, most farms continued to produce other goods to be exchanged locally. Like labor exchanges, the exchange of goods ran the gamut from monetary exchange to barter to borrowing and gifts, and it reflected the gender division of labor on family farms. As the economic and legal head of the family, a man generally controlled his family's entrance into the marketplace. Men often sold their products in larger, more impersonal cash markets. Women sold their products in local markets or exchanged them through community networks. While men controlled cash and land for their families, women gained control of economic resources through neighborhood exchange. Women's exchanges were as crucial to the system of small family farms as was specialized commodity production.

The Erickson farm produced goods for a variety of markets as well as for neighborhood exchanges. The farm's principal commodity operation was dairying. The Ericksons sold dairy products to local factories, which then sent their products to larger markets. Erickson's crop specialties included raising berries, garden produce, and potatoes. The Ericksons marketed all these products outside the local neighborhood to earn cash. They "peddled" or "traded" garden produce and berries in nearby towns or sold them to specific buyers. For example, the Ericksons sold carrots to Dr. Frick's fox farm for several years. Traders and individual purchasers also came to the farm to buy the Ericksons' products, particularly berries and fruit. In the 1920s and 1930s, all these crops, especially potatoes, became cash crops marketed in local trade centers.[25] These activities, in addition to the dairy operation, provided cash for Erickson's family.

The Ericksons also traded all these farm products, except for dairy products, in the neighborhood. Neighbors exchanged specialties for money, bartered them for other products, borrowed and lent them, and gave them as gifts of friendship. The rules of these exchanges are not clear, but Erickson's use of language suggests several levels of exchange. When money changed hands, Erickson sometimes recorded the amount. She used the term "borrow" to indicate the short-term use of equipment that did not require any direct payment. Erickson generally borrowed more expensive equipment, such as drills, trailers, and disks, but sometimes borrowed smaller items, such as kettles for butchering, quilting frames, and a meat grinder. Erickson used the word "give" to suggest nonpayment or no expected return. Her use of the term "gets" is more vague. It generally suggested a future payment in return, but the form that payment would take is unclear. When the primary purpose of a visit was social, Erickson described exchanges as "gifts"; she used the term "gets" when the exchange was the primary purpose of the visit. In either case, social visiting always accompanied an exchange.

Within local markets, Erickson most often exchanged products for cash when the products were closely linked to the money economy. Although men generally took more responsibility for cash crops, distinctions between men's and women's involvement in the market economy were not often apparent in Erickson's diary. Dairying and growing fruit, potatoes, and garden produce had strong traditions as "women's work," and frequently these jobs drew women into cash exchanges. In addition, Anna Erickson operated the farm independently for many years, and her oldest children were girls. Consequently, often no men were available to act as go-betweens in the market economy. In Erickson's case, strong traditions of "women's work" associated with the cash commodities of dairy products, fruit, and potatoes, and the absence of adult men, increased her participation in cash exchanges.

When Erickson exchanged products most directly related to the cash economy, the exchange generally included a direct cash accounting. Such exchanges often took place with male neighbors. For example, Erickson recorded her payment for cow breeding (associated with her primary source of income, dairying) at the end of most years, even though the payments were made to close neighbors: Zubke, Zettler, Bernea, and Pecker. Erickson generally paid a small cash amount or made a direct exchange, such as sewing a dress. Erickson suggested the monetary nature of these exchanges with her language. She went to "see about" an exchange with a neighbor, and later would go to "settle up" with him or her, which suggests a formal arrangement. However, within this general pattern there were exceptions, particularly with neighbors who belonged to Erickson's core neighborhood. When close neighbors, such as Edd Weigand and Herb Aderhold, got seed potatoes from her, Anna seldom recorded cash amounts at the time of exchange. The use of cash and ties to a larger market did not remove completely the exchange, or men's participation in exchange, from a social context.[26]

Informal exchanges occurred most often among women. Although husbands might accompany their wives during these exchanges, the products exchanged were those of women. Sometimes women traded goods simultaneously, which suggests that deals had been made. On 26 September 1926, the Aderholds exchanged swiss chard, six cabbages, a pail of onions, six squash, and eight peppers for parsley, green tomatoes, and a harness. On 10 October 1928, the Underwoods brought six pumpkin pies and got a bushel of carrots and onions. Sometimes exchanges were less direct and suggested complementary neighborhood specializations. For example, Anna often gave berries to Mrs. Kulas and Mrs. Zubke, and, in a different season, got poultry in return. While borrowing and giving did not require exchange, they did suggest reciprocal favors. A few days after Erickson borrowed a drill from the Zettlers, Mrs. Zettler came to get sweet corn. Anna's daughter Dot helped Agnes Hanson (probably as hired help) during a busy season, and shortly thereafter Agnes "gave" Anna tomato plants. Sometimes "gifts" not only reflected reciprocal neighborhood bonds of exchange, but also feelings of close personal friendship. The gifts between Erickson and Mrs. Kulas were the least tied to immediate reciprocity and were so frequent throughout the entire period that there seems to have been no accounting at all.[27]

Women's neighborhood building through exchange created a "social security" system for families on small farms. When people had a crisis, experienced hard times, or had some unusual need, they could rely on those neighbors who were part of exchange networks. For example, after Conrad's death, Anna's neighbors extended even more gifts than usual, particularly gifts of eggs and poultry. When a neighborhood consisted of farmers with secure tenure, they balanced these exchanges and favors in long-term, sometimes lifetime, exchange. But while this system worked best when exchanges occurred among specific neighbors or extended kin, the familiarity with and acceptance of the rules of neighboring could extend to include an ever-shifting group of neighbors. For example, when Anna did not have a car, she received rides from her neighbors (Mrs. Brown and the Streamer, Meyer, Ebert, and Underwood families). When she did get a car, many years later, she gave rides to a similar but slightly differing group of neighbors (Mrs. Brown and the Brickmeier, Streamer, Zubke, and Staube families).[28]

The flexible system of labor and product exchange was economically crucial for small family farms. The long-term opportunities for repayment and the many optional forms of repayment made it possible for neighbors to feel an equality in exchanges and to feel that exchanges were freely made between neighbors, not in an economic trade relation. In some ways these attitudes were marked by gender. Women in both labor and product exchanges were more clearly tied to the local, social meanings of trade. They gained control of resources only through these informal activities. Men, as their families' legal representatives in the larger world, were more tied to the wage and cash economy and gained their status from these ties.

However, in both labor and product exchanges, women and men were integrated as families and were tied to neighbors as friends. Although women benefited from local exchange more individually because of their unequal position within their families, both men and women benefited from the economic safety net and resources these activities provided for the farm and for the neighborhood. Men as well as women understood the importance of these ties. As one Wisconsin man said in an interview, when people needed help "nobody was particular about an hour" and you did not have to "carry a checkbook."[29] Work and product exchanges, the flexibility of cash, barter, and gift forms of "payment," and the values and codes of neighboring enabled rural people to share resources, minimize cash expenditures, and maintain some local self-sufficiency. Neighborhood economies and strategies of cooperation were vital for maintaining the system of small family farms in the rural Midwest.

Although visiting, work, and product exchanges linked people through the patterns of daily life, the sharing of transitional life events built ties that crossed generational lines and extended these patterns into the historical past and the future. Farm people interpreted their daily lives by taking a holistic view that connected rather than separated, and emphasized stability and continuity rather than change and distinctiveness. In a practical sense, sharing life events created both social rituals of neighborhood unity and economic security, which helped them survive the transitions of birth and death. Men and women built these aid networks by doing the kinds of tasks they did on the farm, but women organized the symbolic social rituals. In doing so, they created community-based and gender-integrated events, emphasizing the shared interests of women, children, and men in the larger community. This integrative character of neighboring, which was expressed in the meaning given to events and in symbolic social rituals, enabled farm people to make links with others that went beyond kinship ties and beyond geographic proximity.

Farm people gave meaning to life events by connecting them to both the routine of daily life and the history of their families and communities. Diarists suggested this continuity; for example, Anne Burke recorded the births, deaths, and marriages of those in her community in a direct style similar to her recordings of other more routine daily events: "Dr. Walker's baby buried." Burke suggested an increased level of intimacy by including the time of the event. "Grandma died at Moose Jaw at 7: a.m." "Edna baby girl at 4:30 p.m. at Drayton." In this way, Burke connected these personal events to the experiences of her neighbors and to her own daily life, but still distinguished their importance.[30] The small variations suggest emotional attachments without disrupting the pattern that connected the event to the rest of the day's routine and to the events described throughout the lifetime of the diarist.

The integrative view suggested by the style of some diaries was clearly articulated in the diary of Pauline Olson. Olson's diary reveals with particular clarity the connections of place and past, community history and personal experience.[31] Between 1926 and 1940, Olson recorded the deaths of the pioneer settlers of the region near Bottineau, North Dakota. She often paired these deaths with discussions of the history of the immigration to and the early settlement of the area. She then tied the deaths to the aging of her own grandparents and parents: "Also Olaf Vinge died of Stroke today. one of our first pioneers to come up to Bottineau County was Grandpa's (Kroger) best friend. It seems like the pioneers don't grow very old."[32] Later, recording another pioneer's death and including a history of the settlement experience, Olson moved naturally to revealing a personal crisis: "Also try to set Grandpa Kroger's leg today found out he had cancer in the leg and hip and bladder (a bad day seems to one)." She also tied these life transitions to the natural world and to the question of the future survival of the farm, the family, and the neighborhood. Olson described the passing of the pioneers and her own relatives in the context of dust storms and economic crisis: "I wonder to myself can I sometime in the future be able to look back on these impossible years and laugh and say yes we got over that to [sic]. Everybody seems blue."[33] In these ways, Olson integrated her personal experience of illness and death with the similar experiences of her neighbors and connected both to the history of her family and the community.

Just as diarists recorded the weather and work in the same entry style in which they recorded births and deaths, interviewees recalled their past by weaving together work, farm conditions, and personal and community experiences. In oral histories, dates of events or economic developments are often recalled by their proximity to personal events; an event might be described as happening the "year before our silver wedding." In one oral history from Mountrail County, North Dakota, a couple reflected on their experiences in the 1930s. They discussed the hard times—drought, feeding thistles to cattle, poor prices, getting by on butter-and-egg money, and receiving relief (what they called "welfare"). In discussing the driest year, 1934, they recalled the death of their daughter. As the wife described the incidents that led to the girl's death, the husband's comments repeated the emotional experience of death by connecting it to the conditions of the land. They were "bad years," or it was the "driest year we ever had." They linked the death to their poverty and the frustrations of events beyond their control. The doctor's bills took every last penny; they were "clean broke." If you had money to pay the doctor's bill, he said, you "got a show of it," but if "you have to beg your way by God, you haven't got a heck of a lot of show, that's about the end of it." The flow of memories connected the "dry year" to the personal tragedy.[34]

This integrative view of shared personal and communal life events provided the basis for a communal economic security net. Life transitions, such as births or deaths, often required economic assistance as well as emotional support. Neighborhood and kin networks provided this support, with men and women participating in gender-marked ways. Childbirth, obviously, principally involved women's networks. But these female networks integrated kin and neighbors and crossed generational lines, connecting adults and youths. In addition, women included neighborhood men in the ritual of birth.

Examining the births of Anna Erickson's five children illustrates the importance of female networks for both economic and emotional support during childbirth. Female kin of an earlier generation, Anna's mother (a few weeks after the birth) and her mother-in-law (immediately before and after the delivery), attended the birth of Anna's first child. Neighborhood women shared her other pregnancies, though all were attended by a doctor, and housework was occasionally done by Conrad (continuing the patterns of mutuality established in their daily work relationship), a hired girl, or, in the later years, her older daughters. The next two children, born in 1908 and 1911, were delivered in places where the Ericksons did not stay long. Although neighborhood women attended these births, the networks were not the persistent ones of a settled neighborhood. The Ericksons relied more on hired help in these two years. The final two births occurred after 1912, when the Ericksons had settled near Athens. Erickson's closest friends, Mrs. Kulas, Helen Flessing, and Ruth Lehman, all shared childbirth experiences, exchanging visits and work during pregnancy and sewing baby clothes for each other.

The births of Erickson's last two children illuminate the work sharing and social interaction involved in the birth process itself. Younger girls did chores that were not directly connected to the birth, but were still necessary to aid the pregnant woman. Erickson's fourth child, Lois, was born on 26 November 1913. Erickson's oldest daughter, Orma, learned to bake and clean in early November. On 23 November, the Ericksons hired a girl, but when she had a "bawling spell," they sent her home only five days later. Viola Zettler, the daughter of neighbors of the Ericksons, came the next day to do the washing and housework. The Zettlers also cared for the other Erickson daughters while Viola was working. On 19 December, Anna repaid Viola's service by sewing a dress for her to wear when she spoke at the school Christmas program. When Viola left, Conrad and Orma did the baking, housecleaning, and laundry.

Although a hired girl or a neighbor's daughter did the housework, washing the baby seemed a more ceremonial event, and an older neighborhood woman or a close friend did this chore. Mrs. Beck and then Mrs. Brown cared for Lois until Anna was able to do so in mid-December. In 1917, at Morris's birth, Helen Flessing performed this job. The importance of this task appeared first in the diary when Anna attended her brother Charley's wife, Mae, in 1904. Anna stated that she "did all the washing of the baby, my first baby washing." The comment suggests a pride in the accomplishment, a sense that this was a duty and privilege that had responsibility and meaning and was, perhaps, a sign of maturity. It marked a graduation from the girl's usual role of doing the housework, and was a social ritual experienced only by women.

The entire neighborhood welcomed the birth socially. The work that needed to be completed during a woman's pregnancy and delivery was firmly within "women's domain," though in marriages such as that between Anna and Conrad the husband often took an active role. However, social interactions that were not associated with housework or childcare were gender-integrated and paralleled more formal, Sunday visiting patterns. Soon after the birth, neighborhood families (in Anna's case, the McKinnens, Becks, Browns, Underwoods, and Zettlers), both men and women, visited.[35] Even though the childbirth experience most directly linked women with women and girls, the larger community, acting as families, also shared the experience.

The work associated with other life transitions was less female centered, and men's participation in networks of community aid is easier to see in these instances. The death of Conrad in 1917 illustrates how neighbors, both men and women, shared work and gave emotional support during illness and death. Conrad became ill on 18 December and required constant care until his death on 26 December. During that time, neighborhood men were the primary helpers both in completing Conrad's work and in assisting Anna. Neighbors Edd Brown, Bert Lorendorf, and Fred Longbecker did chores. Although historians have generally labeled nursing a part of women's sphere, two men, Edd Brown and Fred Flessing, relieved Anna of her nursing duties so she could sleep.[36] Edd Brown was with Anna when Conrad died.

While men most actively helped during Conrad's illness, when he died the women became the primary helpers. Men still performed some duties; Edd Brown sent telegrams to relatives and Herbert Aderhold did chores. Gender and family networks were clearly connected, because male and female helpers were often husband and wife. Mrs. Brown was the first to stay with Anna. Helen Flessing washed Conrad's clothing and bedding, did housecleaning, and cared for the Erickson children at her home. Mrs. Zubke washed and ironed. Mrs. Longbecker and Mrs. Zettler sat up with Anna after the embalming. Mrs. Beck and Mrs. Longbecker cared for the youngest children during the funeral.

In times of crisis, networks of assistance expanded to include kin, members of the core neighborhood, and other, more-distant neighbors. These were family networks, but men and women followed the "rules" of the gender division of labor. On the day after Conrad's burial, a group of neighborhood men cut and hauled stove wood. At various times during the following months, female neighbors, Helen Flessing, Mrs. Brown, and Mrs. Beck, helped with household chores. Relatives also played an important role. Earl came and did chores from 28 December to 19 February, and the oldest daughters, Orma and Dot, increased their share of the work. Neighborhood aid continued throughout the seasons when Erickson began to farm alone. For example, when Edd Riley, a more distant neighbor, helped haul hay in the summer, Anna noted that "Edd wouldn't charge me anything."[37] Neighboring during crises like these not only united people through shared experience, but also gave them the security of knowing that when bad times hit, neighbors would be there to help.

Life transitions were not always times of crisis; they could be times of celebration. Celebration rituals were largely the work of women. Women's reliance on social networks as a resource for exchange encouraged their elaboration of social bonds through gift-giving rituals. Women's practice of gift giving celebrated life's passages, building ties between neighbors and bringing children into adult support networks. For example, women shared those events that marked the growth of their children. Erickson planned and attended birthday parties, made graduation presents, attended weddings, and visited when the children of neighbors gave birth to the third generation. The Kulas and Erickson families shared these ties. When Anna's daughter Dorothy was married in 1933, Lucy Kulas helped Anna prepare a kitchen shower that thirty-seven neighborhood people attended. The Kulases also attended the wedding; they were the only friends outside the two immediate families to do so. In 1937, Anna and Morris attended the wedding of Lucy, and in 1938, Anna made a slip as a graduation present for Leone Kulas.[38]

Women also used ritual gift giving to maintain kinship ties. Birthdays, Christmases, marriages, births, and other special events were times for exchange. Women generally made the gifts, which, for Anna, included fancywork, aprons, postcard boxes, wreaths, and fruitcakes. Erickson listed Christmas gifts given and received almost every year in her diaries. The primacy of women in these traditions is suggested in two ways. First, Erickson gave gifts to Earl and Charley, but did not receive gifts in return. Second, when Anna's sisters or daughters married, the name of the female relative was listed alone in Anna's diary. When Anna listed gifts given to her married brothers or son, their wives' names also appeared. Gift giving as a means of maintaining family ties was primarily the responsibility of women, and these exchanges, along with extended visits, increased emotional and economic ties between women within more general kinship networks.[39]

Gift giving cemented ties between women kin and neighbors and integrated children into community networks; women also organized events that linked men, women, and children. By creating events that included men, women emphasized the familial and communal meaning of agriculture and encouraged men to view themselves in relation to the whole rather than as separate from it. In the history of a tenure-secure neighborhood, these rituals also linked the past and future through repeated celebrations that neighbors shared with neighbors and then shared with neighbors' children. One example is the chivaree. Although a wedding might be a small family affair with perhaps a small dinner following, the chivaree extended the wedding celebration to the entire neighborhood. At some point after the wedding, neighbors would congregate at night and try to surprise the couple in their home. As one farmer in Correctionville, Iowa, described it: "They surround the house and make noise and when you figure they've made enough to earn their treats you open the door and let them in. You introduce your wife and you'd better have some treats or they made it rough for you. Candy and cigars." Because a chivaree could be expected, the couple was generally prepared. If they were not, they could pay money or the chivaree could go to town and charge the treats to the couple. In some areas, celebrators brought treats rather than the couple providing them.[40]

In 1922, Anna Erickson married Joe Mauritz in a small ceremony witnessed by the Aderholds. They then had a family dinner, and later the Profts and Mrs. Schneweiss and her family visited and stayed for supper. At ten o'clock, neighbors came to chivaree, and Joe paid them twelve dollars. In 1938, another chivaree was held, this time for the next generation, Lydia Martin and Ralph Schneweiss. Ralph was the son of Erickson's neighbor Mrs. Schneweiss, had worked for Erickson, had escorted her daughters to various events, and was a friend of her son, Morris. The "bunch gathered here," Anna recorded, "and went to Martins to chivaree Ralph." They then had ice cream and cookies at the Gaurkes' house.[41] In this way, a small wedding became a neighborhood event, and generations of neighbors could be connected through reciprocal celebrations of their own and their children's rites of passage.

Many rituals paralleled core social networks; others linked broader groups throughout a geographic area or across geographic areas. Larger community rituals were often institutionalized in neighborhood schools and churches, and in some cases church, school, and informal neighborhoods overlapped.[42] Although community institutions primarily united groups in formal ways, they could also provide a center for informal gatherings and rituals that symbolized neighborhood solidarity. The formal organizations of school and church separated men from women and also adults from youths, providing important cohort networks for young people.[43] However, women also used these institutions to organize activities that integrated women, men, and children to symbolize the unity of the community.

In the Erickson neighborhood, informal social ties did not correspond directly to church or school.[44] Nevertheless, women used institutions to enact neighborhood rituals. Two important annual ritual events for the community, an annual Sunday School church picnic and a Christmas program, took place at the church in Erickson's neighborhood. In the latter, children would speak pieces and receive candy at a Christmas tree. Anna participated in this event as a girl, which is recorded in the early part of her diary, and all of her children did the same as they grew up, despite being in different communities and belonging to different churches. The continuity of this activity over time and across religions suggests its importance as a community event as much as a religious rite. The school sponsored occasional lectures and programs that the Ericksons attended and, like the church, sponsored a program at Christmas, with a similar format. The school also held an annual picnic on the last day of school for the entire neighborhood, and Erickson attended it regularly, bringing food to share. The community significance of the school is evident in that even after all her children were out of school, she and her son Morris still took part in functions at "our school." These rituals, organized by women, integrated a larger community than that which participated in most other types of exchange, and provided important symbolic links between members of the larger geographic or religious community.[45]

The ability of social rituals and patterns of neighboring to link farm people across geographic boundaries is further illustrated in the ways Erickson maintained kinship and neighborhood ties with distant relatives and friends, particularly with those in the Illinois neighborhood of her youth. Anna's ties with the members of her family who remained in Illinois had to be maintained in ritual forms because visits were so inconsistent. A 1912 visit illustrates how work, visiting, and gifts helped maintain family connections. Anna and her three daughters arrived on 13 June and stayed through 17 July. Activities that had shaped her life as a girl filled her visit. The family shared the work of berry picking, and Orma, the oldest daughter, became part of the family tradition by participating. They went to church, visited neighbors (all familiar names from the early parts of the diary), and attended a quilting party for a neighbor who was marrying. The two families exchanged gifts. Anna had a picture taken of the girls to leave with her mother, and her mother shipped jars of fruit to Anna's home. In this way, the families linked the new generation to the earlier ones through work traditions, and the older people to the younger with a family photograph.[46]

Erickson kept connections not only with kin but also with a place and a neighborhood. For Erickson, Illinois was not just where her mother lived. Even after her mother's death, Anna maintained ties with the Illinois neighborhood through letters and visits. In 1928, she, Morris, Earl, and her sister June met in Illinois at the home of her former neighbors Bill and Ada. They visited old friends in the neighborhood and went "to the old home place." The importance of place and neighborhood also appeared when relatives visited Anna. When June or "Mother Erickson" visited Anna, she always introduced them to friends and included them in the local neighborhood life.[47] In later visits, their ties grew not only with Anna's family but also with the place and the people who made up her daily life. In this way, they integrated past and present lives, shared experiences, and created continuity, minimizing the distances separating relatives or old friends. They created a larger community, linking neighborhoods beyond geographic boundaries through practices that ritualized the sharing of daily work and visiting patterns. People could use the practices of neighboring to build ties that were both intimate and ceremonial and that could connect people across distance because of the shared values that created rural neighborhoods. The ability to create bonds across gender lines, between generations and families, and beyond geographic limits provided crucial resources not only for farm women, but for entire communities.

The practices of neighboring created emotional bonds between farm people that facilitated economic exchanges and built a safety net to help them survive hard times. Neighborhoods, like the family farm system itself, connected families. Social networks, however, expanded and contracted to include smaller, more intimate networks based on gender, age, or core family friendships, and larger community groups that shared more ritualized social and economic exchanges. While men organized exchanges revolving around their work, women took a more active role in creating the social bonds of intimacy that linked neighbors and the social rituals that built communities. These informal exchanges made it more possible for economic exchanges to occur outside a direct cash or wage economy. Women benefited from these exchanges by gaining control of economic resources, but the atmosphere of shared interest also benefited the entire system of small family farming by increasing the availability of economic resources for all people in the farm neighborhood. Just as women's work in farm families encouraged men to see their interests as tied to those of their wives and children, neighboring created cultural values and a social system that enabled farm people to see their own good in ways that related to that of their neighbors. Neighboring allowed farm people to create ties across boundaries of age, sex, family, ethnicity, religion, and geography, increasing the resources available to each family farm and to the entire system of small family farms.

Communities Divided

The Limits of Rural Neighboring

The farm families of Orange Township, Iowa, according to a 1918 sociological study, created a cohesive and stable neighborhood. The thirty families at the community's core had lived in the area since 1878. They shared a German heritage and a religious faith, the Church of the Brethren. The families had intermarried and had a similar economic status. Most tenants were even related to their landlords. In 1915, the Church of the Brethren organized a committee to devise a system to regulate the sale of neighborhood land in order to keep out "undesirable" people and provide land for young men in the community.[1] Although mutuality characterized this community internally, exclusion characterized its relation to newcomers and outsiders. Cooperation and exclusion could go hand in hand.

Through neighboring, farm people could build ties that transcended differences, or they could create an intimate core of families separate from the rest of the community. The rural Midwest was neither homogeneous nor free of conflict. Length of residence, economic or tenure status, ethnicity, religion, and race often created barriers that farm people did not attempt to cross. Neighbors pooled local resources, and neighboring helped people preserve their family farms. But this localism, while sustaining its members, often made it more difficult to organize broad coalitions, and excluded more-marginal farm people. Those who were not part of neighborhood networks and those whose networks had few resources had more difficulty remaining on the land. Nevertheless, farm neighborhoods, by incorporating various levels of intimacy and cooperation, could overcome at least some of the barriers that divided rural midwesterners.

Tenure and economic status were principal divisions in rural America; however, in contrast to the South, where tenancy was almost universally an indicator of rural poverty, tenancy in the Midwest did not necessarily correspond to a certain income level.[2] Midwestern farm tenants sometimes worked the best land and the largest farms. For example, in 1925, the value of land and buildings on tenant farms was greater than on farms owned by farm operators in all but three of the midwestern states.[3] For much of the first half of the twentieth century, tenancy rates were highest and increased most in some of the richest sections of the Midwest. In these areas, tenants could be the most mechanized farmers with the most highly capitalized farms and could have higher incomes than farm owners with less acreage or poorer land in other regions.

The meaning of tenancy and ownership may have been changing in the first half of the twentieth century. Economic studies published in the late 1930s and early 1940s argued that tenancy was a more efficient way for a farmer to get a return for his labor and his capital investment. With similar capital resources, a tenant could earn a much larger income than a farm owner, they argued. In contrast, standard-of-living studies published in the 1920s and early 1930s indicated that farm owners had a higher standard of living than tenants or wage laborers. Farm owners were able to control and improve the quality of their homes, and they invested in better education and other "advancement" items more often than tenant families did. Some of these differences can be explained by the generally younger ages of tenant farmers. Most farm tenants were saving money to purchase farms. Although the returns for their labor might have been greater, tenants still aspired to farm ownership because of the insecurity of short-term leases, the possibility of frequent moves, and the inability of tenants to control the quality of their housing and living conditions. If economic profitability indicated that farmers should rent rather than own land, social and familial values pushed farmers toward the greater security of farm ownership.[4]

Following World War II, ownership and tenancy began to merge. Many farmers owned some land but rented significant portions of their total acreage. Although farm families continued to own some land, outside landowners' need for profits increasingly influenced their decisions. As these families enlarged the size of their farms by renting, they began to replace family and community labor with investments in technology and other, more capital-intensive farming methods. Ultimately, this shift encouraged an out-migration of rural families and a decline in the community system of small family farms. This modern organization of capitalist family farming only began to emerge in the period between 1900 and 1940. Before this larger process can be fully understood, many more historians will have to do local studies of the economic shifts in rural America in the twentieth century. However, the erosion of the community practice of sharing resources was part of the redefinition of farm management and contributed to class differentiation and the further development of capitalist agriculture.

Tenancy had the potential to hinder neighborhood exchange. The sharing of resources depended on repeated acts of reciprocity taking place over an extended period of time. A core of farm families with relatively secure tenure and economic status provided resources that increased the adaptability of a farm neighborhood. Owners, if they were free of debt, had a more stable place in a community than tenants did. Measuring community cohesion by institutions and membership in formal organizations, most rural sociology studies of the period found that higher tenancy rates hurt rural communities. However, institutions and membership in organizations did not always correspond with informal exchange. When tenants had fewer resources, they also needed economic exchange most. A Nebraska study covering the years 1911 to 1920 concluded that tenancy did hurt the stability of a community, but showed that tenancy did not limit exchange and socializing. While tenants participated slightly less often in organizations than owners did, they visited slightly more often than owners and exchanged work much more frequently.[5] Although rural institutions and organizations depended on a stable and prosperous farm population, informal neighboring practices flourished among those who were neither stable nor prosperous.

Stability in a neighborhood and economic need both increased farm families' participation in neighborhood economic exchanges and social life. These characteristics, however, did not correspond exactly to tenure status. Instead, stable owners of small farms, like poorer tenants and owners, used neighborhood sharing as a strategy. One South Dakota study done in 1937 revealed that debt-free owners who had the most tenure security (type I) were most likely to participate in informal neighborhood exchanges. Those whose economic need was greatest and whose tenure was least secure, including debt-free tenants with short-term leases, owners with heavy debt, and Farm Security Administration (FSA) clients, also participated in exchange and neighboring practices in large numbers. Neither land ownership nor tenancy alone determined whether a farm family would participate in neighborhood exchanges.

Those who were least likely to participate in the sharing of neighborhood resources chose different strategies for farm survival. This group crossed boundaries of tenure status, including families who were debt-free part owners (those who both owned and rented land), full or part owners with light debt, and long-term debt-free tenants (type II). These farm families had the greatest economic resources and had more acreage than the type I operators, even though they had no long-term right to work or live on the land. According to the study, these farmers were "more concerned with making money and achieving a high degree of security in control of their farms and therefore tend[ed] to slight community and neighborhood activities."[6] They chose to gain security not through a community base of exchange and support, but through increases in acreage and investments in equipment. Both tenants and owners could choose communal and neighborhood strategies or individualistic and capitalist strategies of farm management.

Type II, or "progressive," farmers chose strategies of wealth accumulation; type I farmers chose community strategies, which provided a relational security that tied them to other small family farms. Those who had less security and less economic prosperity, and those who were content to own less acreage or did not have the means to expand their operations and remain free of debt, tended to rely on the security developed through work exchange and visiting. The reasons for participation in systems of neighboring consisted of economic need, geographic stability, and commitment to community above strategies of expansion. Thus neighboring was not only an economic survival strategy, but also a support mechanism for the entire system of small family farms. As capitalist agriculture developed, neighboring and household strategies of making do increasingly became cultural and social expressions of class that indicated the economic status of farm people as much as owning or renting land did.

Those who rejected communal strategies often looked down on their poorer tenant neighbors. These attitudes are remarkably similar to the ways in which many middle-class urban residents viewed urban laborers. Like some urban progressives, some rural progressives, who practiced capital-intensive and individualistic farm management, attempted to help their poorer neighbors. This aid took the form of uplift; it did not reflect the relative equality of neighborhood exchange practices. In her advice column addressed to farm women, Nellie Kedzie Jones advocated respect for the rights of hired help and tenants, but she also assumed that their way of life needed to be improved. She recommended a subtle encouragement of refinement, better manners, cleanliness, and good habits rather than a "missionary effort." Jones suggested working through the children, taking them to church and training them by example, rather than telling their mother that her habits were "slovenly." Jones's advice seemed to carry over into her treatment of her own hired help and tenants, as shown in the letters of her husband, Howard Murray Jones, a minister, educator, and gentleman farmer.

Class uplift was intertwined with the Americanization of immigrants. The Joneses found immigrants or second-generation ethnics less satisfactory as help. At one point Howard and Nellie expressed relief that their help was gone: "Nellie finds the work even easier than when Mrs. Kungs was here for we have meals when we like and have what we want. The hired men wanted meat and potatoes three times a day and meal by the crock or they were cross and anyway they did not like the things we do as they are German." The Jones family acted cordially toward its help, but maintained clear boundaries and always tried to "improve" their behavior. Howard told a story that revealed this relationship. Herman, a hired man who was a German immigrant, invited the Jones family to a party celebrating the birth of his second son. Nellie, a Women's Christian Temperance Union (WCTU) member, accepted the invitation and agreed to provide ice cream and cake on the condition that there be no beer at the party. Although Herman already had purchased the beer, he agreed to keep it in the cellar until the Jones family, the only non-German guests, had left. After all the guests sat at the table and said grace, Herman brought out wine for Nellie. The story became a family joke: "We guyed her a good deal on impressing Herman with the fact that she was too 'tony' for beer—wine suited her station of life. I do not think Herman yet has got one glimmer of WCTU gospel." Although the two families shared this event, Herman's serving wine and Jones's desire to "improve" the immigrant worker illustrate their ideas of social station and distance. The Joneses finally found the perfect tenants in December 1916, a middle-aged couple from Illinois who had farmed for years and were "steady, temperate and experienced." They were also white, Protestant, and the Joneses' neighbors before they became their tenants.[7]

While some progressive and wealthy farmers promoted uplift, others simply rejected neighborly requests for assistance, especially from the "poorer sorts" of neighbors. One Wisconsin farmer, a Farm Bureau leader, recalled that his community ostracized two neighbors who supported the radical labor and farm workers' union, the Industrial Workers of the World (IWW). He recalled that these families underwent hard times, surviving only on apples and potatoes. The farmer blamed this on the families' own inadequacy and their failure to accept the progressive ideas that had led to his own success. They "didn't want to follow progressive things in agriculture to make life better and to earn more money." They were stuck because of "old habits," he believed, not because of a lack of resources or community support.[8] Such attitudes made economic barriers paramount. Since most poor farmers could not afford the capital-intensive practices of progressive farming, they could never become a part of this rural "community." In addition, progressive farmers often replaced hired or exchanged labor with technology, removing important resources from their poorer neighbors.

However, it was not just the practice of progressive farming that created divisions between owners and poorer tenants. Barriers often existed between economically stable owners who participated in the system of neighborhood exchange and poorer tenants whose tenure and place in the community were insecure. While stability of tenure and economic resources made neighborhood exchange easier, they also made it easier to exclude some groups from social and economic networks. Because neighborhood exchange was, in part, based on an assumption of long-term reciprocity, owners, whether wealthy or poor, could see tenants as a drain on valuable resources. Differences in tenure, when paired with economic distinctions, could set limits on the sharing of resources, and often removed crucial economic support from those at the bottom of rural society.

Some stable owners condemned tenants for their failure to live up to neighborhood values of reciprocity. For example, in 1927, Elmer Powers, an Iowa farmer who wrote a diary for submission to *Wallace's Farmer* in the 1930s, clearly found tenants wanting as neighbors. Powers generally relied on his brothers for assistance and, in good times, purchased modern farm equipment. He practiced both progressive farming and neighborhood exchange. When Powers did turn to his neighbors for aid, he found that reciprocity was not working: "I remarked to D.L. [his son] that we had sawed wood for Jack Lamb [a neighbor and tenant] and had not been paid for it yet, that he helped Walter saw and that we loaded the saw for Schuttler, but did not get our own wood sawed." Powers faulted the tenants for this failure of neighboring. When Lamb came to borrow a mower, Powers reflected, "I have loaned a lot of machinery and helped a lot of tenants on that farm and they move away without returning any favors." Powers saw that tenure insecurity created problems for tenants but continued to blame tenants for their tendency to move away and for their failure to reciprocate favors.

Ten years later, Powers assessed more clearly how tenancy hurt his neighborhood. The land to the west was owned by a publisher, to the south by a grain dealer, and to the east by the owner of a flour mill: "I do not have an owner-operator neighbor. I wish I did. These tenant farmers are alright [sic] in a way, but they cannot take the place of owners for neighbors." Powers believed that neighborhood reciprocity depended on stability and equality of exchange over time, and that ownership encouraged these practices.[9] Tenants could not live up to his expectations of what neighbors should be. However, his expectations no longer fit the economic realities his community faced in the 1930s. Tenancy hurt not only those who rented, but also those owners who were reliant on community systems of exchange and resource sharing.

Although Powers interacted with his poorer neighbors, some communities split into distinct neighborhoods based on class. In these cases, other characteristics of difference, especially length of residence, reinforced economic divisions. Such divisions ultimately hurt poorer neighborhoods that did not have sufficient internal resources. Three communities in the cutover area of northern Wisconsin studied in 1938 reveal how economic and social divisions kept the marginal from being part of more economically secure neighborhoods. The first, "Little River," was a highly integrated neighborhood with few divisions, but thirteen relief families, new to the area, remained in an isolated enclave of poverty in the community because long-term residents perceived them to be "poorer types." Ethnicity coalesced with economic status and length of residence to create separate neighborhoods within a geographic community. In the second community, "Polandville," the long-term, prosperous residents were Polish. In 1932, the Poles formed a mutual-aid society, the Farmers' Club, for relief, but it only helped those within its own group. Nonimmigrants, the majority of relief clients, saw the Poles as "successful farmers" who were "clannish" and "uncooperative."

Length of residence, family ties, and religion reinforced economic divisions in the third community, "Scandenburg." Kinship linked about eighty families who resided in the community's eastern area. Younger families lived in the western area, and half of them were on relief. Three-fourths of these families came from one "stem" family, and most married into other relief families. The two groups also attended different churches (the eastern group was German Lutheran; the western was Methodist) and different schools. The more prosperous families enforced a segregation that went beyond geography. The study reported: "Some children [of the relief families] had to walk more than two miles to an overcrowded school, although they lived next door to one that had less than a normal enrollment." In all three of these communities, strong neighborhoods were not inclusive, and mutuality did not extend to all who needed assistance. Depression conditions may have increased the fear of an outsider's inability to reciprocate aid and, paired with localism or intolerance, may have increased such exclusions; in any case, established systems of neighborhood reciprocity did not expand to aid impoverished newcomers.[10]

The lack of long-term reciprocity systems affected not only the way owners viewed tenants but also the way tenants and wage laborers experienced rural communities. The greater mobility of poorer tenants inhibited the development of neighborhood bonds for these families. The history of Andrew Vekkund, a resident of Traill County, North Dakota, illustrates the failure of neighborhood systems to help poor or landless people. When Vekkund's father arrived in eastern North Dakota in 1895 all the land had been taken, so he worked for other farmers. At the Vekkunds' first residence both parents worked for twenty dollars a month and had to feed themselves and their four children. They soon moved, hoping to get a more profitable place, but their new landlord was "impossible to work for." They got advances from him for groceries but did not record what they got. At "settling up" time the landlord said they had no money coming, although the family was expecting two hundred dollars. As tenants, this family clearly did not qualify for "neighborhood reciprocity." After another difficult tenant situation, the family moved to Mayville, where the father used his team for hauling jobs, particularly at the local mill.

Andrew's life closely paralleled that of his father; it was filled with short-term jobs, tenancy, and mortgages. During his early years he held a variety of jobs, working for a livery and for the railroad for a dollar a day. He hauled water for a steam engine during threshing season for seven years. Although the work was seasonal, Andrew's pay was seven dollars a day, and he "liked the job." Then came a series of tenant farms. Andrew spoke of "a lot of tough days" with little money. He rented one farm for nine years; "then he [the landlord] sold the farm so I had to get off it." He then rented from owners in Minneapolis who later sold the section (640-acre) farm to Vekkund in 1933 for twenty-two dollars an acre. In the Great Depression, he avoided foreclosure only through federal assistance.[11] Andrew Vekkund's story reveals a lack of security and permanence, even though there were long periods of residence lasting seven to nine years and most of his moves were within the same general area. His interview contains few examples of the neighborhood interaction found in other interviews, and there is little indication that he felt himself a part of any integrated neighborhood. Vekkund was single; his isolation may also have stemmed in part from his lack of a wife, who might have helped him build a network of family and friends. It is possible that he did not marry because of his poverty and lack of permanence, but the oral history did not address these issues. Economic instability, even when a farmer stayed within a geographic area, limited the use of neighborhood techniques for survival.

Although neighborhoods could exclude and isolate poorer farmers, the practices of neighboring did not necessarily exclude tenants or laborers. In fact, because neighborhoods expanded for work exchanges, they created possibilities for contact across barriers. While these contacts could, and often did, remain at a social distance, the ritual forms of contact were similar to those that led to more-intimate social bonds. Initially distant neighbors could become closer merely by increasing the number of their contacts. Although farmers who were poor rarely could become progressive farmers, there was at least a possibility that they could become good neighbors.

The experiences of hired hands illustrates the distancing and inclusion of poor farm people in social interactions.[12] Families who owned farms integrated hired workers into daily family life but often maintained social distinctions. Hired laborers entered farm neighborhoods without the benefit of owning a farm, which would have established them as residents and neighbors. They took their place in farm families as workers. John Seltvedt, a hired man in Traill County, North Dakota, summed up the treatment of hired men by saying that it "depended on who you worked for." His requirements for adequate treatment did not seem particularly high. He felt he was lucky and had always worked for nice people: "They'd always talk to me." A statement in a Cedar County, Iowa, survey suggested that even talking was not necessary for adequate treatment: "I don't talk much to the hired man, so we get along all right in that way." According to Seltvedt, a hired man ate at the same table, had his own place to sleep in the house, and could go to town or church with the family. However, Seltvedt preferred to go to town with the other hired men, and he recalled that this made his situation better than most.[13] While this social organization gave marginal farm people some place in the community and mitigated conflict or hostility in the workplace, it did not lead to a sense of equality.

Nevertheless, the interaction of owners, tenants, and hired laborers in a community allowed personal relationships to cross class boundaries and become more equal. Neighbors most often overcame class divisions when they shared other attitudes or characteristics. For example, tenants and hired help could be the children of neighbors; in such cases the owners and employers considered them equals within a farm neighborhood. While class differentiated families whose children had to work for wages from those who hired them, familial connections or shared ethnicity led to these workers being treated in more inclusive ways than other hired help. Margaret Segerstrom started working outside her home at the age of fifteen in 1918, but stayed in the Wisconsin neighborhood in which she had grown up. She worked for relatives and other Norwegian neighbors, all of whom were "pretty nice." Her pay was small—a dollar a week plus room and board—but she felt it was adequate. She was able to clothe herself and also help clothe her younger brothers and sisters.[14] The hiring of the children of neighbors redistributed resources within an entire neighborhood. For Segerstrom and others, tenancy or wage labor was merely a stage of youth. Their kinship, ethnic, and neighborhood connections kept them in neighborhood assistance networks despite their status as tenants or wage laborers.

In some communities a stable core of families could be flexible in accepting new neighbors, just as others could be exclusive and reject outsiders. The neighborhood of Anna Pratt Erickson generally accepted newcomers. New neighbors moved in and out of the Ericksons' area quite easily. As Anna's diary indicates, when new people appeared in the neighborhood, the Ericksons readily welcomed them. When neighbors left, they were given farewell parties, and the families often kept in touch. In this community, ethnicity, length of residence, and religion did not reaffirm economic divisions. The ethnic and religious diversity of the community probably discouraged exclusivity, and the relative newness of the settlement encouraged openness. Because the settlement was new, tenants and owners faced similar economic conditions and needed the assistance of others to build their farms and gain economic security. Such practices also seem to have been traditionally acceptable in this region. When the Ericksons moved frequently in the years before they purchased their own farm, they consistently became a part of neighborhood networks. As temporary tenants and managers, the Ericksons were not able to develop most of these relationships into long-lasting reciprocal ties; however, visiting, work exchange, and helping with childbirths occurred despite the family's mobility.

When the Ericksons became farm owners, they continued to develop neighborhood ties with tenants and wage laborers. After the death of her husband, Erickson hired a local tenant named Gore. Gore operated a farm similar to Erickson's in size, and Erickson needed labor. Consequently, their economic conditions were fairly equal despite the differences in tenure. Erickson paid Gore for his work, but this did not introduce social distinctions as it might have in other neighborhoods. Gore not only worked for Erickson but also came for purely social visits. Gore left his farm in 1922; however, he visited Athens and stopped at the Ericksons' farm in 1930. At the end of her diary, Erickson kept obituaries of close friends and neighbors. One of these was Gore's, suggesting that the work relationship with Gore was also a friendship.[15] A series of families rented or owned the Gore farm after 1922. Erickson integrated each into neighborhood exchanges and visiting networks, but none became so intimately connected to the Ericksons as Gore had. This illustrates the personal nature of social ties in rural neighboring practices and the continuum along which exchanges took place. The same practices of work exchange and visiting that ultimately led to close ties between tenant and a neighboring owner could also stop short of these ties.

For interaction to move from socially distant exchanges based primarily on necessity to more intimate cross-class social ties often required a shared sense of condition and a relational view of one's place in a community of small family farms. In the case of poor farm people, economic need and neighborhood exchange meshed, and it is difficult to distinguish between economic and community reasons for the support of neighboring practices. Farm people who had the economic resources to choose other strategies clearly reveal the existence of communal values. These farmers saw their own success as related to the success of their neighbors. Their acceptance of the values of neighboring provided an important resource for poorer farm people. While inequalities of wealth could lead to hierarchical social relations, values that emphasized sharing placed unequal exchanges into an egalitarian value system.

One example can be found in the oral history of a Wisconsin farmer whose family owned a forty-acre farm in Pigeon Township, a community that had strong ethnic bonds. After purchasing the farm in 1927, the family had a string of bad luck. In 1931, their barn burned, destroying all their machinery and livestock. In cleaning up afterward, the father got blood poisoning and had a long hospital stay. Because of the Great Depression, they could not get a bank loan. Instead, they went to a wealthy neighbor who was active in local cooperatives and the Farmers' Union. He lent them five thousand dollars at 5 percent interest. The son recalled how the whole family would walk to the neighbor's house when the interest payments came due, and remembered "my dad apologizing for not being able to make any payment on the principal." Despite the inequality suggested by such indebtedness, the two farmers still had rousing political discussions. The son described the neighbor's philosophy: it was awful that "money and capitalism were so powerful in our nation."[16] Unlike other wealthy farmers, he did not blame his poorer neighbors for their own economic difficulties, but emphasized their common problems as farmers. Though the interviewee laughed at the incongruity of a wealthy farmer feeling he had the same problems as a poorer one, it was an indulgent laugh that showed fondness, not resentment, for someone who might be considered an eccentric man who had moderate wealth but condemned the "capitalist." In this neighborhood, the wealthy and the marginal were linked by ethnic ties, neighborhood reciprocity, a common political view of the farmer's plight in the general economy, and a belief in the need for cooperation among neighbors. These links provided important resources for poor farmers, if not total economic equality with their wealthier neighbors.

Economic instability divided rural communities. Farm families that had stable tenure built ties that were reinforced by the very fact of their continued residence. The stability of these families enabled them to accrue resources that, when shared, enriched the entire community. Less wealthy farmers and tenants who entered such neighborhoods might be accepted or excluded by those who were long-term residents. Other factors such as religion, ethnicity, and race contributed to the exclusivity or openness with which residents met poorer newcomers. Whether included or excluded, these poorer families needed to build exchange networks to increase their resource base. They either entered existing networks or created alternative ones with families who shared their economic or outsider status. In contrast, wealthier owners or tenants had more flexibility and could choose to enter or avoid neighborhood exchange networks.

The practices of neighboring operated along a continuum from intimate friendships to more distant ties. Such contacts could lead to closer, more egalitarian bonds, but more often enabled wealthier or more stable farmers to accept poorer workers, tenants, or owners in a cordial way without necessarily including them in intimate networks or considering them an integral part of the neighborhood's survival. In this way, the social organization of rural neighborhoods often excluded the very farm people who most needed economic assistance. Although farm people could use the flexibility of neighboring practices to cross economic barriers and share economic resources, the localism of farm neighborhoods also created barriers to economic cooperation among farmers.

The rural Midwest, particularly the areas that were settled last, contained a variety of ethnic groups. Often these groups settled in self-contained communities, living in separate geographic areas side by side with little contact or conflict. In this case the face-to-face character of neighboring practices reinforced these ethnic, racial, religious, and geographic boundaries. Sometimes, especially in areas settled during the twentieth century, different ethnic groups lived side by side in internally diverse communities. In these mixed communities, direct contact should have encouraged interchange, but ethnic, religious, or racial divisions still limited cooperation. Sometimes neighboring practices allowed farm people to cross these boundaries and challenge the exclusiveness of ethnic, racial, or religious identities. Social contacts across these dividing lines operated along a continuum running from distance to intimacy. When face-to-face contact blurred divisions, farm people either overtly had to assert ethnic, racial or religious exclusivity in order to maintain them, or develop attitudes that accepted the blending of groups.

Settlement patterns created strong ethnic identities for rural communities throughout the Midwest. Often ethnic groups homesteaded land in the same regions, linking ethnicity and geography in their neighborhoods. A 1920 letter from a Minnesota researcher described the area between

Crookston, Minnesota, and Grand Forks, North Dakota, as having distinct "racial differences," with Norwegian Lutherans to the west and Germans to the east. A 1934 study of Hodgeman County, Kansas, located separate settlements of Russian-German Mennonites, German-American Lutherans, Irish Catholics, and African Americans. In such situations, the members of one ethnic community rarely knew those of another. Ethel Groh Fosberg described the settlements near Reynolds, North Dakota, with Norwegians to the east and Germans to the west, and added that she knew nothing about the latter. A man in Pigeon, Wisconsin, said 90 percent of his community still spoke Norwegian in the 1930s, and although there were Poles and Germans in the surrounding area, he was unable to give any details of their lives.[17]

This ignorance and lack of contact sometimes led to hostility and conflict. In North Dakota, early Norwegian settlers and later German-Russian immigrants seemed hostile toward each other. One 1927 study observed that Norwegians were "aloof" and "felt superior" and that German Russians disliked them. The sociologist recommended that schools in these districts hire German or American teachers because they created less conflict than Norwegians. One North Dakota woman recalled the arrival of German Russians in the Tappan area in the early 1900s in a "there-goes-the-neighborhood" tone, pointing out how "suspicious" and "clannish" they were.[18]

Hostility or suspicion did not generally erupt into open conflict until controversial issues provoked it. For example, British and German settlers coexisted in Dane County, Wisconsin, until 1921, when the Germans wanted to open a saloon and the British Temperance Emigration Association fought the opening. During World War I, hostility to German immigrants exploded in many parts of the rural Midwest. In Iowa, the members of Bertha Gabelmann's church debated whether to continue German services or change to English ones. To counter criticism, they alternated languages and issued a "patriotic proclamation." An Iowa Quaker said that he was "rubbed pretty hard" for taking a stand against bond issues during the war, but remembered that Germans "had it worse." A friend of his sister had to raise her hand in school because her teacher wanted everyone in the class to know who was German. He also recalled vigilante groups who painted the buildings belonging to opponents of the war yellow and harassed both Germans and Quakers.

Even within ethnic neighborhoods, tensions arose because of the need to adapt ethnicity to a new "American" identity. Although ethnic identity supported neighborhood unity, these neighborhoods still had to define their relationship to the dominant culture. Maintaining cultural traditions while becoming "American" was difficult for communities whose sense of neighborhood was strongly linked to ethnicity. Prejudice often made the development of a hyphenated ethnic-American identity more difficult. During World War I, the general hostility to anything German increased conflict within German communities and hurt the neighborhoods that had German ethnic bases. Clara Jacobs's isolated German community in western North Dakota kept its ethnic code of dress, morality, and traditions until World War I. Jacobs remembered being ashamed to be called "pro-German." She stopped speaking German at school and refused to answer her parents in German at home at the young age of seven.[19] When societal prejudice made it difficult to maintain an ethnic identity and become "Americanized" at the same time, generational conflicts often developed within ethnic communities.

In less hostile times, ethnic communities wanted both to maintain their ethnic identities and to enable their children to be successful in their new country. Ethnic identities met "American" culture in neighborhood schools. The school became a cultural crossroads, and teachers played an important part in transcending ethnic boundaries in rural America. For example, Alida Goodman first entered school speaking only Norwegian. She learned to speak English because the teacher forbade Norwegian in the classroom. In 1926, Goodman took her first teaching job in a Bohemian Catholic community: "I was scared stiff to tell the truth. It was only forty miles from home but it could have been 400 because they didn't allow you to go home weekends and I couldn't have even if they would allow it." The isolation was not only physical, but also cultural. She attended the Catholic church because "in my thinking, they would think more of you as a teacher that would participate," but as a Norwegian Lutheran, she had one question to ask before going:

I said okay my Mother used to tell me I don't know if this is true that if a Lutheran came into a Catholic church, when the Lutherans went out, they'd wash the pews that they didn't want Lutherans in there. So I asked her that, I said I don't want that to happen if I go with you to church. Oh my goodness no, she said, we don't do that.

Daily contact could undermine ethnic stereotypes and build personal ties among members of different ethnic communities.

Ultimately, however, the schoolteacher's role was to introduce the children of immigrants to "American culture." Goodman, like her own teacher, refused to allow the children to speak the language of their parents in school, and her pupils learned English just as she had.[20] The school, part of an ethnic enclave that was secure in its identity, enabled children and the community to begin to develop new ethnic-American identities. As a neighborhood institution, the school perpetuated the neighborhood and educated children within the neighborhood environment. But because education also prepared children for life in an English-speaking country, it encouraged the crossing of boundaries and made maintaining a pure ethnic identity difficult for members of the younger generation.

Although geographic separation often complemented cultural divisions, communities that were ethnically, religiously, or racially split internally had more diverse patterns of interaction. Some groups maintained separate neighborhoods despite sharing geographic space. People who shared religion, economic status, or length of residence, like people of the same class, crossed ethnic boundaries easily, particularly in the early stages of the settlement of a region. Economic need clearly pushed people across ethnic divisions, particularly through work exchanges. These work exchanges could expand to social visiting and increased intimacy. In other cases people maintained social distance by reaffirming ethnic distinctiveness and minimizing social contacts. Crossing ethnic barriers was most difficult when economic, religious, or racial differences reinforced ethnic differences.

The most complete segregation occurred when racial prejudice caused people to define ethnic differences in racial terms. Even when whites and blacks shared geographic spaces their neighborhoods remained the most completely separate. Studies in Missouri and Kansas reveal that blacks and whites developed distinct informal neighborhoods and formal institutions. In many areas, racial differences intensified economic distinctions of wage labor and tenancy. Whites developed hierarchical relationships with blacks rather than blending cordial contact with social distancing. White residents and white researchers viewed blacks as separate. Although researchers might note that blacks lived within a predominantly white community, they only detailed African Americans' work for white residents, not their neighborhood life. In a 1920 study of the Ashland community in Missouri, the hired help was described as "almost universally negroes who, with few exceptions, live in tenant houses on the place." However, the researchers went on to call the neighborhood "homogeneous" and "prosperous," which omitted blacks from their definition of "community."

Relations between blacks and whites in the southeastern parts of Missouri reflected the southern construction of tenancy and poverty rather than resembling tenancy as it existed in most of the Midwest. One researcher described the effects of poverty on isolated racial neighborhoods in Sikeston and New Madrid, Missouri, in 1920. "Capitalist investors" controlled the newly drained land in the area. Whether their hired help was black, as in the cotton country of New Madrid, or white, as in the wheat and corn area of Sikeston, there was "no such thing as a neighborhood in these rural districts and the hired men's houses are stuck around anywhere on the farms." These workers lived in poverty: "For instance, we can get a picture of a hog house which is so good in comparison with the tenant houses on the same farm that I imagine the hogs feel like feudal lords." The researcher's bias probably made him conclude that a black "neighborhood" did not exist, but the conditions of these African Americans set them apart from their white neighbors. These workers' lack of economic resources, their dependence on landlords, and their lack of connection to more stable, prosperous neighbors prevented neighborhood support systems from providing much real security for them.[21]

Racial prejudice also separated black from white neighborhoods in areas that did not have such drastic economic distinctions. Although tenancy rates in southern Missouri were as high as 80 percent, African-American tenancy rates in Boone County, in central Missouri, mirrored those in the rest of the Midwest. Despite the relative prosperity of this African-American community, racial divisions still predominated. Blacks had their own neighborhoods and organizations. Eighty-nine black families, many of them farm owners, lived in the open country, creating four black neighborhoods in the county.

The issue of education reveals the effects of racial prejudice on these black communities. The black communities of Boone County centered on churches and lodges, not schools, because white taxpayers controlled the operation of and funding for black schools. Legally, whites did not have to support a separate black school if there were fewer than fifteen black children in the district; therefore, whites "discouraged" blacks with children from staying. As one researcher stated, "there were already ten [families] in this district and [white] property owners were on the alert to prevent the entry of others." Whites would not give money for a school building until they saw the "permanency of the negro settlement." African Americans reported that this lack of school control was the most important reason for them to migrate to the nearby city of Columbia. Three of the four neighborhoods were losing population.[22] Although these African Americans were prosperous compared to those of southeastern Missouri, their neighborhoods still faced obstacles that other ethnic European-American neighborhoods did not. African Americans created their own neighborhoods, but because of their legal status and the pressures of white prejudice, they had less control over the conditions of their neighborhoods, from the tenant housing of southeastern Missouri to the schools of Boone County.

Racial prejudice and legal restrictions also separated Native American communities from European-American communities. The reservation system clearly introduced a legal separation that reinforced racial and ethnic prejudices. Although this book does not directly examine Native American "neighborhoods,"[23] several North Dakota oral histories describe how whites viewed their relationship with nearby Indians. White hostility to Native Americans often prevented cooperation or interaction between groups. White comments such as "half-breeds are nothing but scum" suggest the extent of racial prejudice.

But other stories indicate that whites and Native Americans could share cordial social contacts and yet retain social distance in much the same way that members of different white ethnic groups did. Jake and Clara Jacobs of Van Hook, North Dakota, lived near Indian reservation lands that had been opened for settlement to whites in the early twentieth century. Jake's family settled there in 1906, when Jake was four years old. Jake recalled that he had been scared of Indians when he first arrived but later had "many Indian friends." He remembered Indians, like others, standing around the stores and talking. His description assumed differences in language and custom, but did so to recognize similarities. He pointed out, for example, that Native Americans were well educated and spoke "good" English. His description is not hostile—indeed, it is even friendly—but it does not suggest any closeness in these relationships.

Clara left her isolated German community and went to Van Hook in 1931 to teach. Because she was an outsider, curiosity shaped her view of Native Americans. Her attitude was sympathetic, but still distant. When she first arrived in Van Hook, she went to the cemetery and read the names on Indian headstones because they were so different, and she "liked that." She recalled seeing Native Americans at the Shell Creek Church, suggesting that some whites and Indians shared religious institutions. This does not necessarily suggest close interaction. Clara observed that after mass, Indians met in their own groups and smoked "peace pipes." The same pattern of limited sharing and ultimate distancing occurred at dances. Clara said that young Indian men went to all the dances. The "younger generation" of white girls danced with them, and she noted that the Indian boys were "swell dancers." Indian girls never went to dances. Clara explained that they would go to school and dress quite fashionably; however, when the Indian youths returned to the reservation, the girls returned to the "old, traditional clothes" and the boys would dance the traditional Indian dances.[24] Although the Indians retained their own primary community and culture, they frequently shared institutions and socialized with others in the geographic community. Like other ethnic groups, Native Americans formed hyphenated American cultures, though their very different history placed this process in a completely different context. While Native Americans and their European-American neighbors crossed some cultural barriers, they rarely created intimate patterns of sharing and exchange.

When only a few families in an area shared an ethnic or religious heritage, they had to cross boundaries to build a community. Such mixed neighborhoods provide an interesting view of both the ability of farm neighborhoods to accept diversity and the limits of that acceptance. In mixed neighborhoods, farm people crossed boundaries when they had to, particularly in work exchanges or in community institutions such as schools. Sometimes these patterns expanded to include visiting and assistance in crisis. An Iowa Quaker described his work exchanges with neighboring Lutherans and Presbyterians. Even through World War I, when tensions against pacifists ran high, the Lutherans and Presbyterians "still neighbored with us." Christ Larson in Mountrail County, North Dakota, described a Scandinavian neighborhood that included Danes, Norwegians, Swedes, and a few Finns, but all attended the same Lutheran church. The Jacobses' neighborhood included Italians, Irish, Swedes, Norwegians, Germans, and Native Americans. The Jacobses butchered with other Germans, threshed with Norwegians and Swedes, and danced with Native Americans.[25]

Clusters of families sharing an ethnic heritage or religion but living in mixed communities found it difficult to maintain a separate ethnic or religious identity and still cooperate with neighbors of different ethnicity. They accepted these neighbors during work exchanges, but rejected more intimate social ties. However, contact at work or in community institutions often led to greater intimacy. Youths, for example, often met potential marriage partners at work exchanges, school, or church. Ethnic or religious groups often perceived intermarriage as a threat to ethnic identity, and this made them cling more fiercely to their distinctiveness. Those who remained within ethnic communities almost always described intermarriage in negative terms. Joe Cvancara lived in a "tight" Bohemian settlement near Ross, a primarily Norwegian community. When asked to describe relationships between the groups, Cvancara said that they "never got together." Nevertheless, when questioned further, he revealed that both he and his brother worked for neighboring Norwegians and that his brother had married a Norwegian neighbor (probably in the 1920s). The marriage apparently created tensions in the family, and Cvancara noted that he had married a Bohemian girl.

Asserting the centrality of ethnic or religious distinctiveness did not always preserve an ethnic community. Mixed-nationality neighborhoods encouraged Americanization, cooperation across ethnic lines, and intermarriage. On the other side of Cvancara's Ross neighborhood was a Syrian settlement. Charlie Juma recalled that at the first school he went to, he was the first Syrian to attend, and that other pupils "looked down on" him because he did not speak English. His move to a more ethnically mixed neighborhood made him feel less of an oddity, eased the transition to English, and enabled him to identify with others outside his ethnic group. At this school, three older Syrians and more Bohemians also could not speak English. The Syrians in Ross both maintained their own culture and cooperated with others. They shared work with neighboring Swedes and Norwegians but kept their own neighborhood and mosque. In the 1910s and 1920s, single men headed many of the sixty households. The lack of single Syrian women increased pressures to marry outside the neighborhood. By the early 1930s, the ethnic community had begun to dwindle. Economic pressures forced many to leave the area, and the single men in the community began marrying Scandinavian and German women.[26] Small ethnic neighborhoods, particularly in economic hard times, had difficulty sustaining themselves and their distinctive ethnic identities. They needed to cross ethnic lines to survive economically, but such contact often led to interethnic social ties that many ethnic rural people viewed as a threat.

On the other hand, intermarriage did not always mean loss of ethnic identity or fissures in family connections. Intermarriage, particularly among Christian European Americans, became increasingly common in the 1920s and 1930s. Oral histories reveal the mixed ethnic heritage of many rural midwesterners. For example, Wisconsin farmer Isabel Baumann was the daughter of an English father and a Norwegian mother. Because she lived in a predominantly Norwegian and Lutheran neighborhood, she "always felt Norwegian." After graduation from high school, Baumann moved to another rural community to teach. This neighborhood was predominantly German and Catholic. When she married a Catholic farmer, she decided to convert to Catholicism. She felt it was easier for her than for her husband to convert because they were living in a completely Catholic community. Her parents, despite their shock, accepted her choice. Her mother said she would "rather see you do that than not go to church at all."[27] Such intermarriages gradually became more common as farm youths took on identities that were more "American" than ethnic and as contacts between ethnic groups increased in larger community arenas such as schools, work exchanges, and dances.

One of the most detailed descriptions of social interactions in an ethnically mixed rural neighborhood is Era Bell Thompson's autobiography, *American Daughter*. Her perspective is particularly rare because Thompson is an African American. Thompson's experience in a largely European-American mixed neighborhood tests the ability of neighbors to cross divisions, particularly the most strict boundaries of race, and illustrates how neighborhoods drew social boundaries. Thompson moved with her family from urban Iowa to rural North Dakota in the early 1910s. Because

North Dakota was still in an early stage of settlement, the residents of Thompson's neighborhood generally shared the economic status of small farm owners or tenants and needed the economic assistance of their neighbors. The neighborhood consisted principally of immigrants from northwestern Europe; the only other "black" family in the neighborhood consisted of Era Bell's uncle (a half brother of her father), his Irish wife, and their two children.

While neighbors viewed the Thompsons' arrival with curiosity, they quickly took the family into the neighborhood's work and social life. The earliest contacts with neighbors centered on work. Era Bell's brother Tom soon earned a good reputation as a worker and as a horseman, helping give him a place in the community. In addition, the wild horses belonging to the Thompson family became legendary and provided a social event for the community. "Every Sunday the yard was filled with the wagons and buggies of those who came to watch and help us break our horses. In the house jolly farm women opened baskets of food, while Mother made pot after pot of strong coffee for the inevitable lunch that followed the show." The Thompsons soon became close to neighboring families: the Olsons, whom they visited on Sundays; the Nordlands, who felt "close to us" because they were also from Iowa; and Old Gus, a "drunken bachelor." Thompson recalled, "The farm people were kind and friendly to us, encouraging and advising, offering the use of their tools and machinery, even bringing a pig or a chicken to help us get started. Old Gus offered fresh milk." Work exchange soon led to gift giving, economic assistance, and social visiting, despite racial differences.

The Thompsons' participation in neighborhood economic security networks and social interactions indicate a more intimate level of inclusion than work exchange. When the Thompsons had no money and no food in the first season on their rocky, drought-ridden farm, "Big Carl" Brendal, a German widower who "lived in the tiny speck of a farm to the northeast," happened to stop by at mealtime. The Thompsons, with rural hospitality, invited him to stay for dinner, but he refused, seeing their bare table. When he returned from town, he brought sacks of food, flour, and sugar, and said, "I vant no money. Ven you git it you pay me if you vant. I got money, I your neighbor, I help you. Dot iss all." The Thompsons later reciprocated. At the end of the threshing season, the Thompsons used their first returns to repay Brendal. Era Bell's brother Harry also worked for Brendal "as long as he was needed." As the Thompsons became part of neighborhood social networks, Era Bell and her brothers also made friends. The cultural diversity of the community added interesting dimensions to their friendships. Brother Harry began to give pets names in an odd language they called "Negrowegian." Era Bell made friends with the Koch girls who herded cattle nearby. She taught them "to shoot gophers and tin cans with a .22" and in return they taught her to swear in German.[28] The practices of neighboring led to social tolerance and cultural interchange among these diverse groups.

Nevertheless, whites in the community often viewed blacks as an oddity, and the Thompsons sometimes felt like outsiders. Because Thompson's memories are those of childhood, adults may have shielded her from many racial conflicts. However, Era Bell encountered her own problems at the major cultural mixing point, the school. On her first day in school, other pupils stared at her, and the teacher interrogated her. Her cousins were very light skinned and had both white and black physical characteristics; the children called them "skunks," clearly showing community hostility to her relatives' interracial marriage. With her family's arrival, she said,

Now, suddenly without warning, here were two studies in brown, not quite like the pictures in the geography or funny papers, but near enough to be identified. They were the first bona fide Negro children she [the teacher] or the pupils had ever seen. . . . Every eye was upon us. One or two little girls snickered; a boy pushed another against me and grinned.

At recess her cousin's friends, she said, "felt of my hair" and "stared at the white palms of my hands, and I closed my fists tight until they hurt. For the first time I began to wonder about the soles of my feet and my pink toes, and I was glad she couldn't see my feet where the color ran out." The other children's curiosity about difference blended with prejudice to make Thompson self-conscious about her distinctive features.

Eventually, these initial reactions gave way to friendships, but, despite the generally humorous and upbeat tone of the autobiography, Thompson occasionally reveals her essential isolation in the community. At one point, children played a "hate" game. Different coalitions would form, and children would attack each other with gossip. One day they would talk about Lena, who "thinks she's smart and her clothes are Old Country." But when a new coalition formed, Era Bell found she was being attacked. She was called "black" and "nigger" and unlike the others, she "was alone in [her] exile." She decided, "I could not afford the luxury of hate, the little game was not for me."[29] While generally her playmates accepted her, underlying racial prejudice could always come to the surface, separate her from friends, and place her outside their groups.

The Thompsons' essential separateness from their neighborhood and the desire for the acceptance provided by shared racial and ethnic identities caused the Thompsons to seek out other black farm families. When Era Bell and her mother joined the men of the family in North Dakota, the mother's first question was "But aren't there any colored people here?" Uncle John calmed her fears by mentioning the Williams brothers, who lived north of Steele, about three miles away. The families did not visit on a regular basis, but they did get together occasionally. At one Christmas, the Thompsons visited the Williams families. Although they did not share a geographic community, the bonds were strong. Era Bell noted that the fifteen people in the three families made up 4 percent of the state's entire black population.

> Out there in the middle of nowhere, laughing and talking and thanking God for this new world of freedom and opportunity, there was a feeling of brotherhood, of race consciousness, and of family solidarity that I have never since felt. For the last time in my life, I was part of a whole family, and my family was a large part of a little colored world and for a while no one else existed.

Although the Thompsons shared much with their white neighbors, they only felt totally accepted and part of a "family" when they visited the Williamses.

This small black community could not sustain the family on its farm. For the black community, as for other ethnically or religiously distinct groups in mixed neighborhoods, staying in that neighborhood suggested intermarriage and threatened ethnic identity. Racism made this threat even stronger. Law reinforced prejudice; interracial marriage was illegal in North Dakota. Thompson does not examine white attitudes toward inter-racial marriage, but her father disapproved of the interracial marriages in his family. As Thompson's brothers grew older, they became increasingly restless. They tired of the hard work, the poverty, and (though Thompson does not mention this directly) the lack of possible marriage partners. While both cousins traveled to Minnesota to marry whites, where there were no bars to interracial marriage, Thompson never mentions her broth-ers dating or visiting young women in the neighborhood. Although the farm had been a place to raise boys and keep them out of mischief, it did not offer enough to keep them satisfied as adults. By the time the family purchased its own farm, only Era Bell was happy with it, and she was still a schoolgirl.

While her older brothers longed to be part of a larger black commu-nity, Era Bell appreciated the security and safety of the bonds built by rural neighboring. When her brother Dick wrote from Chicago in 1919, he asked, "How can you folks stay out there in that godforsaken country away from civilization and our people?" As Era Bell read the copy of the *Chicago Defender* that Dick had enclosed, she saw "civilization" as race riots in the North and lynching in the South: "I wanted never to leave my prairies with white clouds of peace and clean blue heavens, for now I knew that beyond the purple hills, prejudice rode hard on the heels of promise and death was overtaking." She saw the farm neighborhood as a haven. Despite incidents that reminded her of her essential difference, the small neighborhood world provided community and insulated her from more violent forms of racial prejudice.[30] That her older brothers felt restless in this secure world showed its limitations.

While their neighbors accepted the Thompsons into work and social exchanges, they did not accept the family's children as an integral part of the future community. The Thompsons' isolation also made it difficult to retain ethnic traditions and identity. Ed Smith, a friend of Era Bell's father who operated a pawnshop in Bismarck, described the trade-offs. Smith liked Bismarck's small black community and wanted to see it grow and prosper. He was a "race man" and liked seeing his people "decent and respectable." His wife, however, disliked raising their children in such an isolated area and wanted to return to the South; she "don't want to bring the kid up ignorant of his own people. Junior, he's only seven but he thinks he's white." Although this attitude might be echoed by many minorities isolated in mixed neighborhoods, the hostility of whites increased the difficulty of blacks' choices. Despite the disadvantages of living away from a large black community, Smith preferred North Dakota: "Don't want him [Smith's son] to learn to run from white folks."[31] In rural North Dakota, the Thompsons found a place where their white neighbors accepted them on a daily basis. They also avoided the more violent forms of prejudice found in areas of the South or North where the black population was significantly larger. But maintaining a separate black neighborhood was difficult because of their small numbers.

Thompson's story illustrates the flexibility of rural neighborhoods and their potential for crossing boundaries of difference. Despite the racism in the culture and laws of the United States, the Thompsons exchanged work and visited with their predominantly white, European immigrant neighbors and were included in neighborhood economic security systems. Although they felt more intimacy with other blacks and although their lives were not free of prejudice, they were in many ways still accepted by their white neighbors because the Thompsons shared the values and practices of neighboring. In neighborhoods like Thompson's, farm people had to cross ethnic lines to maintain the social and economic advantages of sharing resources among farm families. Ties with their neighbors, however, did not meet all the family's social needs, nor did they eliminate the boundaries of race.

Rural communities, like their urban counterparts, were divided by economic class, ethnicity, religion, and race. The practices of neighboring frequently reinforced these divisions, focusing farm people's sense of interdependence on those in their immediate neighborhood who shared ethnic, class, religious, or racial characteristics. For these people the potential benefits of neighboring lay in sharing resources. The practice provided a buffer, for those with resources, or a lifeline for survival, for those without resources, in facing the uncertainties of nature and the agricultural economy. The diversity of rural America encouraged reliance on these homogeneous, intimate social connections as the primary strategy for survival.

When communities were ethnically or economically heterogeneous, neighbors more frequently crossed these boundaries. A second potential benefit lay in neighbors' ever-expanding circles of exchange and their ability to meet needs and create larger community ties even while maintaining the intimacy and primary social identity of a core group. Farm people could ritualize these exchanges to maintain a social distance from those considered essentially "different," or could expand ties to create a shared sense of values and responsibility despite these differences. Neighboring could be used to unite larger groups of diverse farm people around shared values or needs and yet enable them to maintain local identities. In the twentieth century, as agriculture became more complex, the crossing of boundaries was essential in organizing economic or political groups with significant grass-roots support. While the diversity of rural America made such coalitions difficult, neighboring nevertheless made them possible.

Agricultural Policy and Community Survival Strategies

Defining the Rural Problem

Social Policy and Agricultural Institutions

In the early twentieth century, business and government made plans to develop agriculture in ways that increasingly conflicted with the traditional organization of agricultural production. Beginning in the nineteenth century, state and federal governments established institutions to develop new scientific methods and technology that would stimulate the growth of businesses related to agriculture. By the twentieth century, government had expanded this mission, creating agencies that would teach farm people to use new agricultural and consumer products. This new approach viewed farm life as a problem, and saw farm people who failed to adopt modern techniques as "backward." "Progressive" farming meant that farmers would adopt the scientific methods, new technology, and consumer goods developed and recommended by experts. Like the progressive reformers of urban America, those who hoped to reform rural America privileged the knowledge of experts and aspired to change society, using the language of progress and efficiency.

Fundamentally, the goal of this progress was to increase agricultural production for commercial markets. Professionals in these institutions measured efficiency by production standards: higher crop yields per acre, more milk per cow, the replacement of human labor with technology. In this ideology of progress, promoters assumed that increased production would give farm people higher incomes and help them purchase consumer goods. Yet the profitable application of the technology of progressive agriculture often required larger farms, more specialization, and higher capital investment. The notion that purchased technology would reduce labor costs rested on the assumption that farm people hired the labor they used. In fact, becoming a progressive farmer required more cash. Yet higher production levels lowered agricultural prices, a side effect that could be borne by large farms, but not by small ones. If people on small farms were to increase their cash expenditures to practice progressive farming and living, agricultural prices would have to go up, not down. The ideology of progress hid these contradictions and assumed that farmers who followed progressive practices would increase their profits and raise their standards of living. For those who believed this ideology, farmers who did not practice progressive methods failed not because progressive practices could not help them, but because the farmers refused to become modern.

When Theodore Roosevelt appointed the Country Life Commission in 1908, the federal government made solving the problem of farm life a priority. As the name of this commission indicates, its goal was to alter not simply agricultural production but country life itself. This created divisions within government agencies. As rural society became a national issue, professionals and social reformers concerned with the quality of rural life gained positions in agricultural institutions. While the primary purpose of these agencies remained the promotion of the business of agriculture and the technology of scientific agriculture, social reformers focused attention on the social impact of rural economic change. Because they advocated that farm people share the economic benefits of industrialization, they were potentially at odds with the production orientation of these institutions. Indeed, such reformers could have allied with grassroots farm organizations as easily as with agricultural business interests.

In general, this did not happen. First, social reformers shared the ideology of progress that linked the interests of the public (in this case farm people) with those of agricultural businesses. Second, the structures of agricultural institutions hindered professionals from challenging the direction of agricultural change. As agricultural institutions matured over the course of the twentieth century, the economic conditions of farm people became a social issue that was structurally subordinate to the business and production goals of agricultural development. By the 1920s, the activists' goal of helping farm people no longer fit professional criteria. By 1940, professionals who proposed solutions to the "social problem" of farm people that criticized development policy rarely maintained secure places in these institutions.

From their inception, government agricultural institutions promoted the commercial development of agriculture. In the late eighteenth and early nineteenth centuries, powerful landholders organized agricultural societies and printed agricultural journals. These "gentleman farmers" linked rural and urban commercial development because they were also merchants, bankers, lawyers, and politicians. Unlike the vast majority of farmers, these men had the financial resources to fund experiments, take the financial risks that experimentation required, and develop commercial markets for their products. By the mid-nineteenth century, new agricultural businesses such as implement manufacturers and seed stores reaped the benefits of these societies' efforts. They joined the landholders in these societies and demanded state and federal funding for agricultural development. Their efforts led to the creation of public agricultural institutions. The Morrill Act of 1862 authorized and funded the land-grant college system, which encouraged agricultural research. The USDA, created in 1862, promoted commercial farming and the settlement of the West. The Hatch Act of 1887 led to the founding of the state agricultural experiment stations to conduct scientific research.[1]

In the early nineteenth century, the alliance of agricultural institutions with agricultural business interests provoked little public response, but the consolidation of the agricultural economy in the late nineteenth century made the role of these publicly funded institutions more controversial. By midcentury, a growing number of corporate powers, including railroads and the newly consolidated grain and livestock exchanges, had emerged to challenge the interests of smaller agricultural businesses and farmers. Industrial consolidation undermined any unified interest in agricultural development. This changing economic landscape also led to a proliferation of farmers' organizations, from highly commercial commodity associations to political organizations of smaller farmers, such as the Grange and the Farmers' Alliance. In addition, the institutions themselves contained a new class of agricultural professionals whose interests did not always correspond with those of either agricultural businesses or farmers' groups. The role and purpose of public agricultural agencies were caught in the middle of the political controversies arising from industrial consolidation.

Many agricultural voices made demands on public institutions and debated the uses of the knowledge they gathered. "Farming interests" seemed unified in their demand that colleges provide a "practical" education, including training in "business principles, the use of technology, or accounting and farm management." In fact, this demand often served different economic interests. Grass-roots farmers' organizations, particularly the Grange and, to a lesser extent, the Farmers' Alliance, demanded that the colleges be accessible to farm people and pressured the colleges to meet the needs of a broad spectrum of the farm community.[2] The Grange and the Alliance paired these demands for greater responsiveness to farmers' needs with a critique of the concentration of power in the hands of corporations. These groups wanted access, along with regulation, in order to balance the power gained by incorporated businesses. When the farm press or agricultural businesses demanded that institutions educate farmers in new techniques, they wanted the education to promote their products and interests. In this case, access supplemented the consolidation and rationalization of commercial agriculture rather than opposing it.

Ultimately, agricultural institutions became most responsive to those groups that had the greatest political and economic clout. This does not mean that the institutions did not serve broader public interests, but they tended to define public interests in ways that promoted corporate agriculture or the concerns of organized commercial farmers and small businesses. For example, regulation of the fertilizer industry in 1886 occurred only when the newly formed National Fertilizer Association, like many other industries of the period, saw that rationalization and regulation could serve its own interests. While farmers demanded regulation to keep fraudulent products off the market, the fertilizer industry also benefited because research conducted on fertilizers helped industries develop new products and national standards aided the industry in rationalizing its business practices.

Although battles continued among commercial agricultural interests, the twentieth century began with agricultural institutions closely tied to commercial supporters. In general, the colleges educated "commercial farmers," the wealthiest farmers in their states, to appreciate the value of scientific research and, in return, received the political support of their organizations. Those farmers who had the capital to adopt innovations made up the constituency of these agencies. Agricultural agencies also developed close ties with editors of agricultural journals, country bankers, insurance agents, merchants, implement dealers, railroads, grain exchanges, and meat packers. In contrast, those farm groups that led the political critique of the consolidation of the agricultural economy in the late nineteenth century were rarely part of these coalitions. As agricultural institutions stood at the brink of further expansion at the turn of the century, their primary political and economic support came from large agricultural corporations, associations of smaller agricultural businesses, and commercial farmers and their organizations.

In the nineteenth century, agricultural institutions had primarily focused on research into methods of increasing agricultural production. With the success of these programs, a new problem gained priority at the turn of the century. Proponents of agricultural change were frustrated by the failure of farmers to adopt new techniques. To those promoting agricultural development, agriculture seemed to lag behind industry in efficiency and productiveness. While exposing farmers to scientific agriculture and modern technology was their chief goal, professionals in agricultural institutions also sought to explain the reasons for farmers' reluctance to adopt the methods of progressive farming.

In the nineteenth and early twentieth centuries, agricultural institutions, business interests, and farm organizations experimented with diverse educational tactics. Between 1906 and World War I, these efforts became institutionalized and nationally funded. Early agricultural societies promoted education by publishing journals and organizing agricultural fairs. Agricultural businesses, which wanted to promote their products, and farmers' organizations, particularly the Grange, which wanted access to the latest information on farming techniques, demanded greater educational efforts. Land-grant colleges joined agricultural and commercial businesses to organize and finance short courses, in which farmers went to the colleges for several weeks of training, and Farmers' Institutes, in which speakers on agricultural topics traveled to rural communities for several days of exhibits and lectures. The colleges and the USDA also printed pamphlets and bulletins to make the latest information available to farm people. Nature education entered elementary schools and agricultural education spread to secondary schools in the late nineteenth century. The Smith-Hughes Act of 1917 extended and formalized agricultural education in secondary schools by providing federal funds.

Agricultural businesses also played a large role in developing agricultural extension, which became the government's primary form of farmer education. In the extension service, people trained and coordinated by the USDA or the land-grant colleges resided in farm communities. These representatives, eventually called county agents, educated the farmers, demonstrating the latest farming methods developed by the colleges. Business interests—railroads, machinery manufacturers, the farm press, mail-order houses such as Sears—and commercially oriented farm organizations financed early extension experiments at the local and state levels. In many ways, salespeople for agricultural products were the models for county agents. Businesses assumed that county agents would continue to promote their products as necessary for modern farming and living, and lobbied for the passage of the Smith-Lever Act. Passed in 1914, Smith-Lever coordinated the extension efforts developed in various states and pushed them into states where they did not exist, supplied funding to assure stability for the program, and thus established the county agent system as the best outreach method.[3]

Smith-Lever made county agents employees of the government or the land-grant colleges. Despite the extension service's language of independence, other interests continued to influence county agents. Each county raised funds to sponsor an agent. Organizations of commercial farmers, called Farm Bureaus, often raised these funds, and, consequently, expected the county agents to serve their needs. Many agents also had close ties to agricultural businesses; they used the information the businesses provided and promoted their new methods and technologies. Farmers demanded that county agents help counter the control of local buyers by, for example, testing the fat content of milk to challenge the accuracy of the tests of commercial creameries,[4] or assisting them in organizing farmer cooperatives. When county agents entered rural communities, controversy often followed. In some states, such as Iowa, ties between agents and Farm Bureaus became formalized; in other states, such as Wisconsin, agents attempted to be more independent and serve all farmers' groups. Although detailed histories of this contested terrain in the Midwest have yet to be written, it is clear that ties among agents, commercial farmers' organizations, and agricultural businesses persisted, at least unofficially.

As these educational methods were being developed, a national effort to understand and alter the causes of farmers' "backwardness" also got underway. A progressive social reform movement began in 1908 with Theodore Roosevelt's appointment of the Country Life Commission. In both its mission and its membership, the commission and the country life movement that followed united business and social issues. The Country Life Commission report detailed the deficiencies of rural life that stood in the way of agricultural progress, and established the need for social reform. The report supported economic measures to promote scientific and efficient farming; educational efforts, including the funding of extension services; and social measures to increase rural prosperity and survey the conditions of rural living. Farmers' economic conditions could only improve if agricultural production became more efficient, more centralized, and more technologically sophisticated.

The country life movement's membership further linked production to prosperity. The movement was a loose coalition of groups, dominated by representatives from various commercial farm interests and by professionals in the new agricultural institutions.[5] Business interests (including merchants, bankers, implement manufacturers, mail-order houses, railroads, chambers of commerce, and boards of trade), commercially oriented farmers, agricultural scientists, elected federal officials, and civil servants, particularly those in the USDA, each had a direct economic stake in the development of a more centralized agriculture. Other agricultural professionals in the movement, such as some county agents, USDA officials, and professors at the colleges of agriculture and agricultural experiment stations, did not gain so directly from commercial development. Service professionals (social workers, ministers, and educators, representing such groups as the National Education Association and universities and normal schools) and reformers from women's clubs, village improvement societies, church organizations, and the YMCA and YWCA also participated in the country life movement. These professionals brought a concern for the economic and social conditions of farmers into agricultural policy debates. However, they worked within the ideological and institutional framework of economic reorganization that had been promoted by commercial agricultural interests and government agencies since the mid-nineteenth century. Like the urban progressive reform movement, rural progressivism paired social reform with economic restructuring and efficiency.

This new group of middle-class professionals that emerged from the country life movement and the movement for farmer education began to define their fields and claim expertise during the Progressive Era. They faced numerous problems in asserting their status. Their struggle for professional legitimacy within agricultural institutions shaped public policy and separated professionals from the majority of farm people. Professional concerns and ideology limited the ability of these experts to speak for farm people's needs in regard to government policy.

All agricultural professionals worked in new institutions and had to establish their academic credentials in the context of more established, classically based institutions of higher learning. In the nineteenth-century view, the land-grant college idea was an amalgamation of technical education and "higher learning." Opposition to the colleges often focused on the supposed absurdity of this combination. Many scholars and educators believed that technical education in farming best belonged in common schools, and that combining it with academic subjects either denigrated academic standards or added a frippery to a practical course of education. Critics in academia derisively labeled the land-grant schools "cow colleges." Professionals working in land-grant institutions were immediately placed in a professionally suspect position within the realm of higher education.

To defend their professional status as academics in these "lesser" institutions, agricultural professionals stressed the importance of research. Academically, the abstract pursuit of general knowledge garnered more prestige than did applied knowledge. For professionals, particularly scientists, in land-grant colleges this presented a conundrum. To establish their credentials academically, scientists had to stress the importance of pure science, but to maintain political support and public funding, their work had to have public or applied uses. The growth of these fields rested on their ability to blend scientific research with the economic interests of commercial agriculture. The wedding of science and industry gave land-

grant colleges increased social prestige, because they served broader industrial goals, and improved academic credentials, because they pursued
pure research.

Ultimately, science, scientific methods, and research became the preferred modes of academic respectability. Scientific research and economic
growth merged in a vision of progress that made efficiency a priority and
defined it as increased production. Progress and production became the
dominant goals of public agricultural institutions. The fields of education
and extension could not meet the research criteria for institutional, academic, or professional prestige. As the country life movement indicates,
education and extension gained importance because they implemented
scientific and economic goals in agricultural production. Consequently,
education, extension, and social issues gained the attention of the important economic and political supporters of agricultural agencies only when
these fields met the needs and priorities set by the merging of science with
industrial growth.

This criterion limited professionals' ability to speak for a diversity of
farmers and often gave their mission a politically conservative agenda. As
social policies developed in the twentieth century, they were rooted in an
ideology of progress that was essentially based on class because it made
commercial development a priority. Agricultural professionals sought to
create a prosperous class of farmers who would practice the tenets of scientific agriculture and modern farm living. They assumed that farmers
would agree with and accept these values. Because the Progressive Era was
relatively prosperous, reformers believed that wealth was available to
farmers if they abandoned the old ways and became efficient businessmen. The keys to success lay in education and efficiency. The professionals assumed an identity of interest between themselves and all farmers.
Progress, middle-class standards of living, and scientific, commercial agriculture benefited everyone.

But this unity of vision ignored economic and political differences in
the countryside. Reformers believed that an empowered group of middle-
class farmers would not only balance the urban dispute between capital
and labor, but also stabilize the countryside itself. Political movements
such as the Populist revolt of the 1890s, the early cooperative movement,
and the growth of the Nonpartisan League and other groups that tried to
ally farmers and laborers potentially undermined the goals of commercial
agriculture. An increase of immigrants in rural areas, growing tenancy
rates, and other economic changes disrupted any chance for a homogeneous farm population. Although in some states the country life movement worked with the growing cooperative movement, at the national
level and in many states it led farmers away from alternative political and

economic activity and assumed that the same economic and production policies could help any farmer.

The mix of empowerment through education and political conservatism can be seen in a 1917 novel that promoted extension, *The Treasure of the Land* by Garrard Harris. In the novel, a teacher attempts to change the production techniques of a rural neighborhood. Farmers resist these changes because they believe learning better farming from books is useless as long as corporations retain economic power over agriculture. The book ridicules the Populist-inspired critique by placing it in the dialect of an "ignorant" farmer: "I am in favor of specialized readin'. F'r instance, the farm boys and girls should be taught how the farmin' class of people is oppressed an' discriminated against; how the trusts and combines and the plutocrats of th' money power of th' East is grindin' the farmer into the very dust." The teacher counters this argument by pointing to two successful farmers and accusing the unsuccessful farmer of laziness.

I do [have sympathy for the "farming class"], but not with those who are trying to lay the blame for shiftlessness or lack of enterprise on somebody or something else. . . . The trouble is farming has not progressed. Every other calling under the sun has gone forward, and the average farmer is just where farmers were two thousand years ago. . . . Of course they [the two successful farmers] are [exceptions]. They have studied farming as a science. They are specialists — and successful, aren't they?

The teacher implies that all farmers could be successful if they just worked and practiced the new methods.[6] If farm people were willing to be educated, they could become successful. The author, and other reformers, assumed that personal adjustment to the new economic system, not political action that criticized it, was the proper road to progress for farmers. If, when exposed to the knowledge of reformers, farmers did not change their methods, their continued poverty was their own responsibility, not that of an inequitable economic system.

Progressive Era reformers assumed that political action was unnecessary for farmers; those of World War I and the 1920s perceived it as dangerous. Agricultural professionals' fears of farmer-controlled political organizations increased with the Russian Revolution in 1917, the labor and farm radicalism in the United States during the war, and the Red Scare. Farm activism, particularly in the upper Midwest and Great Plains, had been steadily increasing in the late 1910s in political groups such as the Nonpartisan League and the Farmer-Labor party, economic cooperatives such as the Farmers' Union and the American Society of Equity, and labor organizations such as the IWW. These organizations tried to form economic alternatives to corporate-controlled agricultural markets and polit-

ical alternatives that would unite urban workers and small farmers to oppose corporate influence on political parties.

Such activism caused even reform organizations to move in more conservative directions. For example, the Interchurch World Movement (IWM),
an interdenominational religious reform organization founded in 1919
and funded by John D. Rockefeller, often cooperated with the USDA in
rural survey work. It supported regulations that benefited poor farmers,
tenants, and laborers; however, its support for such issues grew from a
belief that national leaders needed to initiate corrective measures before
farmers acted for themselves. Its credo expressed a paternalistic view by
comparing farmers to children and using child psychology to analyze
rural people. The farmer was the "sensory child" who

broods and suffers inward distortion and silent degradation of spirit. His maladies
and madnesses are of a subtle and horrible nature. Freudian analysis let us in on
some of the awe-inspiring results of suppressed ideas and desires. This is what the
farmer has most terribly. The vociferous, organized and frankspoken city wage
laborer has and is a social problem. He is the motor child of the situation. But the
brooding discontent of the farm population is that of the sensory child. Peasant
uprisings, whenever it has come to that point, have been the most brutal and un-
imaginatively awful of history.

Although it worked with noncommercial farmers' organizations, the IWM
nevertheless distrusted these farmers' groups and preferred uplift through
the safe leadership of churches, commercial interests, the YMCA and
YWCA, public agencies, and employers.[7] The merger of social issues with
commercial farming and political conservatism prevented most professionals from working with grass-roots political organizations or speaking
for poorer farm people who could not gain economic success through the
methods they promoted.

Other professional and cultural considerations further separated rural
social reformers from the interests of farm people. The professionals in
education, extension, and the new social sciences who studied rural America not only took second place to scientific professionals within agricultural institutions, but also faced obstacles within their own disciplines.
Progressive reform in these fields favored urban-oriented activism. As the
"cow college" nomenclature suggests, association with farmers was a sign
of lower status. As the intermediaries between science and industry and
the rural population, these service and social-science professionals had
more contact with rural people than the scientists did, and shared the low
status of their clientele. To improve their professional status, rural reformers either distanced themselves from the culture of rural America or
worked to alter that culture to fit urban, professional standards.

Unlike their urban counterparts, rural middle-class professionals lacked a middle-class constituency. Farm people throughout the first half of the twentieth century did not have easy access to the services, consumer goods, education, and cultural advantages valued by the dominant middle-class culture. They did not share in the economic prosperity of the nation, and agriculture was becoming less important to the national economy as commerce, manufacturing, and service industries grew. Farmers' disadvantages, like those of the urban working class, were partly due to lack of income, but even when farm people had resources, their thin population distribution made access to advantages such as high schools and libraries more difficult and more expensive. Agricultural professionals, who often came from rural backgrounds, hoped to raise the living standards of more prosperous farm people to meet urban, middle-class standards.

In addition to these measurable economic and social disadvantages of farm living, ideological and symbolic uses of rural life created negative stereotypes of farm people in the dominant culture. An urban/rural dichotomy strongly organized perceptions from the mid-nineteenth to the mid-twentieth centuries. The city represented corruption, evil, and social disruption, but also adventure, progress, opportunity, and the future. The farm symbolized honesty, virtue, and social stability, but also stagnation, backwardness, decline, and an out-of-date past. Although an idealized farm past existed, real economic and institutional power emanated from the urban half of the dichotomy. The future of the nation was clearly urban; the past was rural. The values of progress held that the modern world developed with a transition from rural to urban that was both inevitable and beneficial. Professionals in the country life movement hoped to create a modern countryside that would replace the one that was doomed to disappear. From the perspective of these forward-looking professions, those concerned with rural life labored in a cultural and economic backwater.

In defending the importance of their work, these professionals did not criticize this urban bias. As modern professionals, they believed that rural people and rural institutions were indeed backward and inferior. Their mission was to change that status by changing farm people and their institutions. The educational and religious leaders of the country life movement both criticized the backwardness of local rural professionals and looked to them as the implementers of farm reform. National and state leaders proclaimed the training of rural professionals woefully inadequate. Few teachers or ministers had as much college training as their urban counterparts, and country life movement experts declared their methods "backward." Rural teachers relied on memorization rather than modern pedagogy, and ministers were more concerned with theology and salvation than with using the church for community reform.[8]

The negative view of rural institutions and those who chose to work in them dominated the service professions even in the predominantly rural states of the Midwest. When Olga Peterson, a North Dakota teacher, enrolled at the normal school in Valley City for her teacher education in the 1910s, she encountered two problems:

I got lost in the buildings, and I discovered I was enrolled in the rural department. Now that I was becoming educated I didn't want to be rural. I brought my problem to Julius Meyers, a frightening, bombastic man in the math department. I must have felt he was my friend so I told him my troubles. He said nobody was to make me rural and took me to the office. I wasn't labeled rural anymore, although I think I continued in the same subject.[9]

Being rural and being educated were contradictory in these professions, and the prefix "rural" immediately implied professional inferiority to "urban." Because farm people generally had fewer resources, rural schools paid less and required less education of their teachers than urban schools did. Because rural schools had fewer pupils, they could not experiment with the modern methods of teaching nor follow the practices of graded schools. Consequently, educators viewed rural schools as merely a training ground for new teachers, who, with experience, would, of course, move into the superior and better-paying town and city schools. To identify with or defend local rural institutions or communities led to a marginal status within the service professions.

Although leaders of the country life movement considered local rural professionals to be inferior to their urban counterparts, they nevertheless viewed them as superior to other rural residents. With proper training, they would be the local leaders who would implement the reform goals of the country life movement. These leaders charged teachers, ministers, and county agents with a mission of uplift, and many of them accepted the mission "to spread the propaganda"[10] with fervor. In 1912, the first publicly funded county agent in the United States wrote to his former professor at the University of Wisconsin using religious terms to describe his work. Alfalfa, corn, and silos were "our three graces," "our religious trinity." He did not mind the long hours, he added, because "this is my religion. So I can work it on Sunday."[11] Indeed, the jobs of local organizers, teachers, ministers, and investigators took great energy and dedication. For those who identified with the new professional standards of these institutions, the critique of rural institutions and rural professionals did not apply. They believed in the superiority of their professional values and identified with their professional groups and institutions rather than with rural people and their community institutions. The search for professional authority contributed to policies that ran in opposition to rural community structures and values.

All these indicators of professional status—science, research, production, and separation from rural communities and values—coalesced with the assertion of gender hierarchies within these new professions. Agricultural institutions grew quickly, creating a vast need for trained professionals. College-educated women, limited in their participation in most professions, provided an available and cheap labor pool. The land-grant colleges and other agricultural institutions employed women in the sciences, social sciences, and service professions. Because the existing definitions of "professions" rested on male dominance and the exclusion of women, the movement of women into these careers threatened their professional status. These institutions and professions developed new forms of gender hierarchy and segregation in order to increase their own status, maintain male economic privilege, and yet use the training of middle-class women.

During this period two types of professional gender hierarchies developed from the struggles of women to secure a professional definition of their work, the struggles of men to defend their professional status, and the institutions' needs to expand their programs. First, the professions developed a distinction between "professional" and "technician" and between "professor/researcher" and "teacher/instructor." As institutions hired women as technicians and instructors, men continued to dominate the higher-paid positions, maintaining male definitions of "professional." Second, the ranking of fields established a gender hierarchy by extending nineteenth-century notions of "separate spheres" to the definitions of significant subject matter. Science, business, and production questions became "masculine"; social issues, the economics and science of households and communities, became "feminine." The field of home economics, for example, segregated women professionals and simultaneously denigrated studies that focused on family issues. Nutrition research depended on biology and chemistry, but its designation as female and home-centered masked and denigrated its scientific content. This process had wide implications. The feminization of some fields and types of positions affected all disciplines concerned with community and family issues. Those who studied "larger" economic issues, agricultural development and production, had more professional status than those who studied the "social" issues, the "lesser" economic needs of farm people. Thus, gender ideologies were integral to the separation and subordination of the study of rural communities and farm families to the goals of business and production.

The field of rural sociology illustrates the impact on rural social policy of the struggle for professional legitimacy and the structural marginalization of social fields within agricultural institutions on rural social policy. Early rural sociology developed from social reform movements and, in particular, from the social gospel, which combined theology with social action. Although women played an important role in the development of social reform and were accepted into early sociology and social work, rural sociology was dominated by men. Nevertheless, in nineteenth- and early-twentieth-century terms, religion was part of "women's sphere." Rural sociology's roots in religious reform also defined it as an applied rather than an abstract academic subject, a charge that was still being leveled against it in the 1970s.[12] Consequently, rural sociology was less than a profession because it was applied rather than abstract, it was rural rather than urban, and it concerned a feminized subject matter, rural communities, rather than a masculine one, production.

The career of Charles Josiah Galpin parallels the development of rural sociology and shows rural sociology's relation to the land-grant colleges and the USDA. Galpin was one of the first professionals to teach a college course on rural life, the first to do a field social survey of rural institutions, and the first head (1919–34) of the Division of Farm Studies in the USDA. Like many early rural sociologists, Galpin had a rural background and his career began in religious reform.[13] Although Galpin was born and raised in a small New York town, his parents were children of farmers and almost all his aunts and uncles lived on farms. After teaching in a rural academy, Galpin did postgraduate work at Harvard, Colgate, and Clark Universities, studying philosophy, religion, and sociology. In 1901, Galpin quit teaching; he then held a series of jobs, including living on a farm in Michigan, helping a brother set up a milk-processing plant in Wisconsin, and becoming a pastor to university students in Madison. Gradually, he became aware of the problems of the rural church and rural social life. His concern led him to the state country life movement.

Before World War I, rural sociology was only beginning to develop as a specialized field and to get a foothold in public agricultural institutions. While the country life movement increased interest in the need for more efficient marketing and better standards of living for farmers and farm communities, agricultural colleges and the USDA generally emphasized production techniques and science in their programs, not economics or social issues. One exception was the University of Wisconsin. Social reform movements often spurred the inclusion of these new issues and the social sciences in the curricula of agricultural institutions. In contrast to the national country life movement, Wisconsin had a locally active cooperative movement that influenced progressive reform in the state and at the university. In 1902, the University of Wisconsin became the first college to establish a Department of Agricultural Economics. This department focused on marketing rather than production, because for farm organizations, as for cooperatives, marketing promised to increase farm income, while production only led to overabundance and declining prices.

The study of the social side of farm life grew as an adjunct to agricultural economic reform and paralleled the growth of sociology and agricultural economics as academic disciplines. Galpin met Henry C. Taylor, the founder of agricultural economics at the University of Wisconsin, through the country life movement. Nine years after the introduction of agricultural economics, Taylor asked Galpin to develop a course on rural social problems. Farm life studies began at the university in 1911. For the next eight years, Galpin taught at the University of Wisconsin.[14]

As rural sociology entered agricultural institutions, its position remained marginal, even at a progressive land-grant college such as Wisconsin. Rural sociology as a discipline did not fit wholly into either sociology or agricultural economics. As a result, it was marginal to the success of either department. In addition, the reform origins of the discipline oriented it toward outreach rather than academic research, further marginalizing its importance. A logical home for rural sociology might have been in the growing extension field, but that program was dominated by the production and science disciplines rather than the economic or social ones. During the Progressive Era, the study of rural life introduced new problems to agricultural discussions but still struggled to get a foothold in the institutions designed to establish and implement agricultural policy.[15]

World War I provided new opportunities for agricultural social scientists and legitimized the study of agricultural economics. County agents coordinated agricultural production during the war, and the war effort increased the need for agricultural planning and more centralized marketing to meet emergency food needs. As the USDA became interested in marketing issues during the war, agricultural economics once again provided the entering wedge for rural sociological studies. In 1918, Henry C. Taylor was chosen to head the new USDA Office of Farm Management and asked Galpin to go to Washington and create a farm life division. Galpin used his position at the USDA to coordinate the work of rural sociologists throughout the land-grant system. Although state colleges had begun to add agricultural economics and rural sociology to their curricula, Galpin's efforts still met with indifference at schools that had no rural sociology offerings. His efforts aimed to increase the viability of rural sociological study. Galpin's work in this period described existing rural conditions and provided a statistical base for future policy recommendations. As head of the Division of Farm Studies, he encouraged the gathering of information by coordinating field studies at various agricultural colleges and experiment stations. He also established the separation of rural farm from rural nonfarm statistics in the federal census to study the conditions of farm life more accurately.[16]

Despite the increased interest in marketing issues during the war, agricultural economics remained subordinate to production within agricultural institutions. Food shortages and new markets abroad meant that production was still a high priority, and domestic labor shortages further encouraged mechanization. The postwar agricultural depression also led to realignments within the coalitions that supported agricultural institutions, and began to unveil problems in the production orientation of agricultural policy. Agricultural interests, particularly commercial farmers' organizations, turned to the field of agricultural economics to find remedies for the post–World War I crash in farm prices. They desired more coordinated and controlled marketing to counter the negative impact of overproduction. The Republican administrations of the 1920s failed to respond to the crisis, and the coalition between industrial and commercial agricultural interests, which had shared goals in the more prosperous Progressive Era, faltered. Coolidge and Secretary of Commerce Hoover opposed even the most conservative proposals of these agricultural interests, even those supported by Secretary of Agriculture Henry Wallace.

In this political atmosphere the Office of Farm Management did not prosper, and Galpin's Division of Farm Studies fell to the bottom of the priority list. Consigned to a single basement office, the division had one staff member and one secretary-clerk. By 1921, Galpin faced the constant threat of budget cuts, because the opposition in Congress saw no practical use for studies on such topics as the farmer's use of leisure time. The political problems slowed Galpin's zest for reform. When Carl Taylor, Fred Yoder, and Carle Zimmerman submitted a study of southeastern Missouri that revealed "violent contrasts" between the living conditions of landlords and tenants, Galpin refused to publish it because he was "averse to risking my Division's life over such an issue."[17] Despite the problems of overproduction and inequitable distribution of wealth within agriculture, which were starting to gain attention in the 1920s, the study of such issues remained subordinate to economic and production policies that favored consolidation, new technology, and a cheap food supply.

As rural sociology's ties to social reform became politically embattled from the outside, rural sociology continued to struggle to assert its professional credentials. The move toward a more scientific approach and away from the reform roots of the field encouraged its political institutional security and professional legitimacy. Sociology divided into narrower specializations, and rural sociologists had to justify their discipline as a legitimate academic field. New scholars criticized older ones for their lack of objectivity and their reform impulses. In the scientific stage of the 1920s, sociologists purposely moved away from reform and from applied sociology toward a broader search for theory and abstract principles.

The search for science distanced sociologists from contact with farm people or identification with their needs. As Galpin reflected on his scholarly work, he recalled:

Probably I overdid the rural contact part of my theory. I should have possibly paid more tribute to abstraction. . . . limits to the value of first-hand contact: fatigue, incapacity to abstract, struggle with doubt about the value of anything but *living out life*, doubt of cogitation itself, no long periods of getting up to the point of imaginative ignition.

As rural sociology at the University of Wisconsin developed its academic credentials, it moved away from its role in extension and in organizing local community groups. E. L. Kirkpatrick, one of Galpin's successors at the University of Wisconsin, stated in 1933 at the Third Purnell Conference, "The idea of personally feeling out each locality as to their desires, wants, ideas, and ideals seems to the writer a worthy procedure (on a short-term basis, particularly) but it is subject to question as to its being research." Abstraction demanded a search for the laws of economics and rural societies—generalizations that had much more in common with the goals of industrial development than with the study of their impact on farm people.[18]

The move toward science and legitimacy also required a strict assertion of gender boundaries in personnel, disciplines, and policy. Agricultural economics largely relegated women to the lower positions of statisticians, but women were crucial members of the early staff of Galpin's Division of Farm Studies. Emily Hoag, who wrote pieces on rural women and community organizations, and Veda Larson, who worked with statistics, made up half the division's research staff in its early years. Women who did research or organized projects in the Division of Farm Population and Rural Life, however, received less money and less encouragement than their male colleagues and constantly had to defend the wider significance of their research. Correspondence between women staff members and their supervisors in the Division of Farm Population and Rural Life often show conflict over such things as salaries, organizing tactics, and failure to have male extension personnel approve projects. Female personnel also occupied lower-level field positions that had continued contact with farm people. Because many state and county extension services resisted spending funds for female agents, women field agents in the USDA often filled the gap by organizing and coordinating women's clubs. Such activism led to criticism from male heads of state extension services, and reminders from Galpin that their work was to be investigative only.[19]

Women agents also were pushed into separate, low-status fields address-ing women's issues. When male field agents asked Galpin for suggestions on how to advise young women who were interested in rural sociology, Galpin replied that women would be excellent for standard-of-living stud-ies because the "information would be obtained from the women of the house," and home demonstration agents would be likely to need "socio-logical training" as the field developed. Galpin clearly relegated women to home economics and household studies, their "appropriate" realm. The farm and the home were separate professional disciplines. Galpin also be-lieved that this role was subordinate to that of men. For example, in 1922, Galpin wrote that the role of farm women in the economic crisis of agri-culture was to "stand back of the farm man in holding the fort on the farm. . . . [her national role was to] maintain the home and farm family." Although the division he headed was closely tied to social and domestic concerns, his interest in "women's work" was so slim that he admitted that he had never read a "household page in a farm journal."[20]

Galpin's assertions did not go unchallenged. Anna Clark, an agent in the division, responded to Galpin's statement that a woman's role was to stand behind the farmer by saying, "I quite agree with you that she has an enormous task to perform, but I think she also has a plus task in commu-nity and national affairs."[21] Although female agents battled to continue activism and for the recognition of the significance of women's issues, the professional and institutional structures limited their effectiveness. Rural sociology included women and examined issues of community and fam-ily; male professionals could only assert their status by disconnecting their own work from women's and connecting what might be considered women's issues to the male realm. Since the male realm of the farm was production, gender hierarchies further encouraged the subordination of the economic and social issues of farm families and communities to the goals of scientific farming and increased production.

To maintain their professional status, male professionals needed to sep-arate rural sociology from home economics and connect it to production. They also needed to reestablish the importance of sociology to commer-cial development in order to appease their political opponents. The re-search agenda of the Purnell Act accomplished this feat of balancing. Following the difficulties of the early 1920s, the Purnell Act institutionally stabilized agricultural economics and farm life studies in 1925. It allocated funds for the study of rural economic and social problems and reorga-nized the agencies. The Office of Farm Management became the Bureau of Agricultural Economics (BAE), and the Division of Farm Studies be-came the Division of Farm Population and Rural Life. The BAE emerged from the political battles of the early 1920s with the support of significant commercial agricultural interests, particularly commercial farmers' organizations and commodity groups. In some ways, the BAE pursued a reform agenda. Its focus on agricultural planning and coordinated marketing set it at odds with the conservative administrations of the era and some agricultural interests. For example, those in the business community who handled agricultural goods and the United States Chamber of Commerce opposed government organization or coordination of farmers' cooperatives, even those connected to the more conservative farmers' organizations. To continue its marketing agenda, the BAE needed to show its compatibility with industrial development.

The Purnell Act authorized social research on two topics. The first, standard-of-living studies, successfully related the study of social issues to production and industrial growth. The "male" part of these studies centered on the income of the farm family. Standard-of-living studies argued that farmers' incomes needed to be comparable to the cost of manufactured goods. They believed that farm prices should have parity with the prices for manufactured goods, and looked to the prosperous period from 1909 to 1914, when, they believed, these were roughly equal. In this way, they related farm income to farm prices and farm production, since farming efficiency, increased production, and marketing were crucial to improving farm families' income. This focus separated male rural sociology from female home economics, which more narrowly studied the household uses of farm income.

A concentration on farm income also served the greater economy. Farm people would use their larger incomes to increase consumption, creating new markets for urban-manufactured consumer goods. By showing that farm people could become consumers, professionals won the support of urban manufacturing interests for their agricultural marketing reforms. To gain conservative political support for reform, agricultural professionals limited the broader reform goals of the Progressive Era. The task of improving farm people's lives became increasingly individualized and subordinated to the interests of the industrial economy. It was not the farm community that needed aid, but the farmer as consumer, and consequently it was the urban manufacturers who benefited from increased sales. Farm social policy became a form of advertising for urban manufacturers.[22]

The second area of research funded by the Purnell Act, population studies, reflects the continued class-based focus of sociologists. The loss of farm population was a major concern of agricultural institutions throughout the first part of the twentieth century. From the Progressive Era through the 1920s, professionals believed population decline hindered the growth of a prosperous farm middle class, because the "better" farmers often left the country for the "advantages" of city living. This analysis underplayed

the ways in which commercial agriculture restructured the rural community and displaced poorer farmers. Although the declining rural population troubled the professionals, they were only troubled when those leaving were the prosperous. The division's studies of population decline
showed that between 1919 and 1927, 38 percent of those leaving the farm
left because of economic distress. Less than 3 percent chose to leave for a
better standard of living, and only 11 percent for better schools. Yet, in
their analysis of the problem, this defection of the prosperous was described as "a loss which overshadows the importance of other losses.
Farming can absorb its share of the inefficient persons of the nation, if it
can adjust its social organization so as to retain a fair share,—its own
share—of the efficient, the prosperous, the wealth-producing and wealth
conserving persons." Those concerned with farm social policy in the
1920s defined the farm problem only in terms of relatively prosperous
farmers.[23] All the problems of farm life could be solved by giving efficient
farmers the advantages, incomes, and standards of living of urban dwellers. Those who did not fit this image were inefficient and had no place in
agriculture's future.

With the crisis of the Great Depression, rural sociologists could no
longer ignore the problems of poor farm people. Nevertheless, the New
Deal institutionally separated programs that met the needs of smaller farmers from those designed to help agriculture, as an industry, recover. To a
large extent agricultural policymakers defined the new social problem as
an emergency rather than viewing it as part of a long-term restructuring of
agriculture that resulted from changes these agricultural institutions and
industries had promoted.[24] Even as these problems became paramount,
agricultural institutions continued to exclude poor farmers and small family farms from their vision of agricultural development.

The economic crisis and New Deal experimentation did make agricultural planning more acceptable and boosted the role of agricultural
social scientists, particularly in the Bureau of Agricultural Economics.
BAE economists originally designed the major New Deal plan for industrial recovery, the Agricultural Adjustment Act. Although the BAE was the
only USDA agency to incorporate social issues into its research agenda,
the Agricultural Adjustment Administration (AAA) adopted business and
production goals divorced from concerns about their impact on the social
structures of agriculture. Although business and some agricultural interests initially opposed the AAA, the county agent system, controlled at the
local level by agricultural institutions and influenced by commercial agricultural interests, eventually administered it.

The AAA continued the approach initiated by standard-of-living studies. Its goal was to assure agriculture's equality with other industries and

to increase farm income. The AAA programs enhanced agricultural prices by establishing parity prices based on the golden age of agriculture, 1909–14, and by controlling production through acreage-allotment programs. The AAA hoped to increase farm income, but it was not designed to keep small farmers or tenants on the land. By increasing incomes for moderately wealthy and wealthy farmers, the AAA increased the purchase of machinery and encouraged land consolidation. In the Rural Relief Studies and Rural Problem Reports of the BAE, researchers often commented that AAA payments led to less work for farm laborers and marginal farmers because farm owners used payments to purchase machinery.[25] As the United States entered World War II, the Roosevelt administration switched to an agricultural policy that favored increasing production for the war effort. This change fit the overall designs of the AAA and the dominant wings of the agricultural institutions. The AAA was largely absorbed into the structure of the USDA and became the base of post–World War II agricultural policy.

Although industrial recovery was closely coordinated with existing agricultural institutions and interests, rural social policies were initially part of general relief activities conducted by the Federal Emergency Relief Administration (FERA). FERA was an emergency agency, not a permanent one. When relief policies changed to work relief with the WPA, government officials separated rural relief efforts from general relief and paired them with long-range land-use planning in the Resettlement Administration (RA) in 1935. This tied the agency to the interests of agricultural economists and rural sociologists. Likewise, the BAE in the 1930s coordinated its economic plans with a broad social picture and included the work of educators, rural sociologists, anthropologists, and home economists.[26] The number of rural sociologists in the BAE alone tripled in the late 1930s. The new climate and employment opportunities of the 1930s led to an increasingly reformist orientation among these professionals and a new interest in rural economic inequities. A critical, reform-oriented rural sociology developed within these government agencies, and, for the first time, the existing social policies of agricultural institutions were called into question from within. As an agency, the BAE had feet in two camps—the first tied to issues of industrial planning and commercial agricultural interests; the second connecting these issues to rural social problems, the home of rural relief.

Critical rural sociology found a home in the Resettlement Administration and its successor, the Farm Security Administration. Pairing long-range social planning with relief work made the RA controversial, and agricultural institutions and commercial agricultural interests attacked it. The controversy led to its demise. The FSA was then created, but this agency had no long-range planning purpose and was housed within the

USDA. Both agencies addressed the problems of the rural poor. The FSA attempted to relieve the immediate suffering of farm people, develop ways to keep them on the land, and provide them with a decent income. The FSA hoped to return farm people to stable conditions on the land, when possible, or resettle them if they were on submarginal land that could not support farm families. The FSA's programs included relief grants to help farm families meet immediate needs for food, clothing, and other living expenses; loans for feed, seed, and other farm operating costs; debt readjustment assistance; loans for tenant purchase of farms; and some resettlement communities where land was acquired by the agency to accommodate displaced farmers.

The FSA provided an alternative voice to that dominant in agricultural institutions, but its marginal status caused the agency numerous problems in meeting its goals. Because the original program was a temporary relief measure, the agency never received full congressional political support or funding to cover the tasks it hoped to perform. Except for the BAE and sometimes the Soil Conservation Service, which had similar land-use goals and also provoked hostility from the production-dominated agricultural interests, the FSA was never able to find allies within the Department of Agriculture or among commercial agricultural interests. Its support came from outside agriculture—for example from the National Association for the Advancement of Colored People and the major labor unions, or from less powerful, alternative farm organizations such as the Farmers' Union, which was just beginning to grow in power, and the Southern Tenant Farmers' Union, whose low-income membership gave it less clout. Although the FSA hoped to have a long-range impact on agricultural policy, it never had the resources or political power to change the direction of that policy.

Because the FSA was underfunded and housed within the USDA, it also had to rely on local administrators and agricultural professionals who frequently shared the views of commercial agricultural interests and did not want to reach the rural poor. The conservative ideology of rural social policy in the 1920s continued and limited the FSA's effectiveness. For example, E. L. Kirkpatrick was the coauthor of numerous standard-of-living studies in the 1920s and pleaded for improvement of farm people's living conditions. In the 1930s, however, his studies of the cutover areas of northern Minnesota and Wisconsin reflected a changed attitude toward those needing better living standards. The report complained that the home economics representatives wanted Polish relief families to have iceboxes. "Imagine these people using ice boxes and other house conveniences foreign to them." He believed that giving Indian families aid equal to that given to whites was ridiculous. "Anyone who has seen Indians live, will recognize the absurdity of this policy." Despite his past arguments for the parity of rural and urban living standards, he now argued that town people on relief deserved more than farm families did because it was necessary "to give them better clothing so that they may maintain their status in the community." Improving standards of living for moderate-income farm people in the 1920s was an issue quite different from raising living standards for the rural poor, especially those of different ethnicity, with government assistance in the 1930s. Many agricultural professionals, even those who administered relief, staunchly opposed the organization of farm people into groups that demanded relief, better farm prices, and new agricultural policies that would assist small family farms and farm tenants.[27]

By the 1940s, commercial agricultural interests and congressional political opponents attacked those relief agencies that served the poorest and smallest farmers. Professionals in the FSA began to look for arguments to preserve its life and the role of small producers in the future. Attacked for its support of inefficient farmers who could not meet production needs or repay loans, the FSA had to defend its policies on the ground that small producers were efficient, and on a traditional financial credit basis rather than on the basis of social need or an equitable distribution of agricultural resources. The gap between the vision of agriculture promoted by the AAA and that of the FSA narrowed. By 1942, funding for the FSA had been cut dramatically and in 1946, the government replaced it with the Farmers Home Administration, which operated more like a private financial credit agency and did not challenge commercial agricultural interests.

Even the more established BAE came under attack. While some political interests protested the BAE's economic planning, it was most vulnerable for its studies of the inequities of agriculture. It produced a study of capitalist agriculture in California that proposed limits on farm size in order to promote family farm agriculture, and one of sharecropping in Mississippi that criticized southern race relations. In addition, organized commercial farmers, such as those belonging to the American Farm Bureau Federation (AFBF), criticized BAE programs that promoted farmer participation in the development of planning policies. They viewed this as a threat to their own political influence and they increased their attacks on the agency. Ultimately, Congress cut the BAE's budget and reduced its role to the gathering of statistics rather than economic planning. When the BAE proposed policies that could assist and be controlled by the existing agricultural institutions and commercial interests, such as the AAA in its early years, it retained support. When its policies promoted an extension of services to other farmers, greater farmer participation in policymaking, or critical studies of social inequities within agriculture, it was no longer acceptable.

By 1946, Congress abolished funding for "social surveys." This created a chilling effect on critical rural sociology. The agencies that employed reform-oriented professionals had their budgets and staffs cut, or were eliminated altogether; to remain employed, these professionals had to return to the land-grant colleges or the extension service. With the McCarthyism of the 1950s, most universities discouraged reform-oriented research and activist approaches to rural social problems. For example, at the University of Wisconsin, rural sociology had its own department and funds, but it ended its role in outreach and community leadership training. Rural sociologists might study rural conditions, but the departments and most of the practitioners in the field no longer advocated change or had direct ties to the rural communities its founders had hoped to serve. By the end of World War II, the "purification" process was complete.[28] Rural sociology was a science whose studies did not disrupt the direction of agricultural development or critique the production orientation of agricultural science or the corporate control of agricultural production.

By the 1930s, two views of agriculture appeared in agricultural institutions. The BAE and the FSA envisioned farm people within a larger community. They photographed the economic diversity of rural people, placing the rural poor in the context of entire rural communities in need and an agricultural system reeling from natural and manmade destruction. In their images and programs, these agencies attempted to address economic issues of agriculture with social policies that would keep people on their farms and still improve their economic condition.

In contrast, the AAA pictured the future of agriculture as embodied by an idealized, prosperous farm family. The images emphasized production and removed the farm family from the rural community. The AAA image of the farmer always placed him in control of a tractor. The farm wife reigned over a modern kitchen with the latest appliances, all running on electricity. Farm youths went to agricultural colleges and returned to teach their parents the latest farm and home techniques. The AAA's policies and imagery ignored the dislocations and suffering caused by the restructuring of agriculture. The future the AAA promoted did not address what was to become of the farm people who could not benefit from price supports based on acreage reductions.[29]

The complete separation of these two visions and the dominance of the latter emerged from the professional struggles within agricultural institutions and with the consolidation of commercial agriculture that was completed after World War II. But during the first half of the twentieth century, this vision was contested territory. Economic policy attempted to alter the production techniques and consumption patterns of farm people, and social policy attempted to change the parts of rural life that stood in the way of these changes. Agricultural production and consumption were inextricably linked to the social organization of rural communities and farm families. Consequently, those who hoped to improve rural life also held values that opposed the community and family strategies that farm people used to maintain small family farms. As agricultural professionals educated farm people, farm people adopted, adapted, and resisted these new methods, reshaping policies even as policies shaped their choices.

Reorganizing the Rural Community

Contested Visions of Community

When Charles Galpin looked at rural communities, he saw a people isolated, more in touch with animals and plants than with other human beings. Farm people, he argued, did not have the skills for social cooperation. Their limited social circles led to "inbreeding" and stagnation. He thought that "knowing" everyone in a neighborhood was "too shallow," and "visiting" was simply not enough for an "adequate exchange of important ideas." Independence and small intimate neighborhoods had been of value in the old days, but to assure progress and stability, farm people had to reorganize beyond their immediate surroundings. Galpin called this need to increase ties between towns and country "rurbanism." Believing the farm neighborhood to be on the verge of extinction because of its backwardness, Galpin and other social reformers proposed "rurban" organizations as a way to preserve old farm communities by making them more like "progressive," urban America.[1]

This rurban vision ignored the strengths of rural neighborhoods. Social critics saw isolation rather than the neighboring practices that often protected small farms economically or provided a basis for political activism. In the Progressive Era, social reformers attempted to end the cultural isolation they felt blocked acceptance of new farming techniques and modern living, but they still promoted organizations that reinforced rural communities. Following World War I, professionals no longer fostered community-based organizations. The new organizations segregated men from women, giving priority to the business interests of men and reducing women's activities from community organizing to running the household. By weakening community ties, agricultural experts gained more control of these organizations and encouraged farm people to replace community exchange with modern farming and increased consumption. When these programs entered the countryside, they did not meet an institutional or social vacuum as Galpin believed, but interacted with the existing social and economic organization of rural communities. Farm people sometimes adapted the new organizations to reflect their own needs and values, but they also could reject efforts to reorganize their patterns of living, or create alternative organizations that articulated a very different view of rural communities.

Progressive Era social reformers promoted a new type of rural community that formalized institutions and linked farmers and townspeople. They believed these ties would strengthen farm communities and help them gain the advantages of urban, middle-class living. This urban ideal glossed over the idea that town and country interests might not be identical or even compatible. However, in practice the organizations Progressive Era reformers encouraged remained based in local farm neighborhoods. In addition, reformers wanted farm people to voice their needs. Reformers assumed that farm people would demand the benefits they promoted, and often they did; but even if the farm people's demands were not identical to those of the promoters, farm people could adapt the Progressive Era organizations to meet their own needs.

Reformers advanced a middle-class modernity that included an abundance of consumer goods. Reformers believed that farm people, living far from urban consumer centers, not only had less access to consumer goods, but also did not understand their importance. Farm people needed to be taught where and how to spend their money. Such a program, not coincidentally, also promoted the business interests of some country life movement supporters. Competing for the rural market, small-town merchants, chambers of commerce, and mail-order houses advocated these reforms. Agricultural professionals promoted the local trade center as a rurban institution that would help farm people gain access to goods and educate them in middle-class tastes.

The rurban goals of the promoters of country life created forums for those who profited from the education of rural people. Local businesses, in conjunction with agricultural professionals, organized events to educate farm people to buy the advantages of middle-class status. For example, in Waupaca, Wisconsin, in 1918, merchants and high schools organized the "hustler plan," in which pupils and their rural schools would get points for academic achievement, personal grooming, bank accounts, and having homes with "recognized cultural standards," such as telephones and musical instruments. For five hundred points, an individual won twenty-five cents' worth of certificates to trade in town. Students who went to the best school attended free movies, also in town. In this way Waupaca businesspeople hoped to bring in business and cement trade loyalty between town and country.[2]

Although professionals believed that rurban institutions would benefit town merchants and farm people alike, farm people rarely saw merchants as allies. They distrusted rural professionals because of their close ties to merchants. For example, one county agent in Wisconsin did not invite businessmen to organizational meetings because "we want the farmers to get the notion that this is theirs." The participation of business interests in rurban organizations rarely led to an alliance of merchants and farmers. Although farm people sometimes had loyalty to local stores that gave credit, bartered, or provided good service or prices, they did not see the trade center as a fundamental rural institution. Neighborhoods and local crossroads continued to be their primary centers for socializing.

Although a diversity of businesses united behind reform, increasingly these business interests competed for the rural market. Small-town trade centers tried to use country life movement promotions to keep rural business, but farm people capitalized on the competition for their business to gain advantageous prices or credit, not to develop rurban ties. Farm people extended the range of their shopping beyond the stores in the open country, but did not develop buying allegiances to specific towns. Farm people made purchasing decisions based on convenience and economics, not on town loyalty. They shopped in larger towns and cities to buy better-quality goods, such as dress shoes or women's ready-made clothes. Most often, farm people went to the nearest local town (which might have a population of between a thousand and twenty-five hundred) for services, work clothes, groceries, credit purchases when cash was short, and entertainment. Farm people also purchased groceries, clothing, dry goods, supplies, and larger items from mail-order houses because their prices were cheaper than those charged by local merchants. Stores in hamlets and in the open country declined in numbers somewhat, but continued as "convenience stores" for quick or small grocery purchases.[3]

During the 1920s and 1930s, agricultural professionals abandoned the promotion of local trade centers as rurban institutions. By the 1930s, chain stores, national brands, and more centralized retailing took farm business from cities and mail-order houses. Agricultural professionals replaced the promotion of consumption as a way to build social institutions with a simple push to buy. One study criticized local merchants for their lack of efficiency compared to chain stores. Just as professionals had critiqued farm people for their inefficient social organization, they now favored consolidated retailing over locally controlled stores.[4] Although farm people rarely viewed local merchants as allies, in the long run this loss of local control would hurt both rural towns and the surrounding farm neighborhoods.

Progressive Era reformers also claimed that a modern education was crucial to middle-class status. To improve rural education, reformers worked to consolidate elementary schools in the open country and to increase farm youths' access to town high schools. Although farm people often battled to keep their neighborhood elementary schools, they rarely saw high schools as rural institutions. High schools more easily fit the goals of rurban institutions. Reformers believed that the high schools would broaden farm people's horizons, encourage their cooperation with towns, and enlarge their concept of community. High schools would educate rural youths to change production and consumption patterns, helping create a prosperous farm middle class.

High schools, unlike elementary schools, were always town and city institutions. For example, in North Dakota, where almost 60 percent of the population was still rural in 1935, 80 percent of farm children in grade school attended country schools. In contrast, less than 10 percent of all high schools were in the open country, and only 10 percent of farm children in high school attended country high schools. Before the 1920s and 1930s, few farm people attended school beyond the eighth grade. Sending a child to high school required significant economic sacrifices on the part of a farm family. Farm people often had to pay for tuition, transportation or board, books, and supplies, and they also lost the significant labor of older youths.[5]

For high schools to foster rural-urban cooperation, agricultural professionals felt they had to change high schools and farm people's attitudes toward them. Professionals wanted farmers to gain access to education and share power with town people. According to sociologists C. J. Galpin and J. A. James, "the monopoly of knowledge and the monopoly of social instruments are no longer the birthright of the city man." Despite their belief that urban control of high school administration hindered cooperation, they primarily blamed farmers' ignorance for this failure. Galpin argued that farmers had "elude[d] the responsibility of high school ownership and control" and needed to take on their share of the financial and managerial burden of high schools. Such patronizing attitudes limited professionals' effectiveness in creating cooperative high schools.[6]

Social reformers also promoted changes in high school curricula to better meet the needs of farm youths. High schools attracted the brightest farm youths from the most prosperous families, and professionals pointed to high schools as the main culprit in the losing battle to keep these children on the farm. They argued that town-controlled schools taught the superiority of town and city, neglecting the needs of farmers. Reformers attacked the urban-oriented curriculum; adding scientific agriculture and home economics solved the problem. Agricultural courses would "educate the farm boy and hand him back to the land as a permanent rural citizen" and create a "more remunerative, better organized and more contented countryside." Better-educated youths not only assured agriculture's future, but also improved present farming. Boys and girls would take their learning home and end their parents' pursuit of "independent ways of thinking and handed-down custom." High schools would build a farm middle class by changing rural production.

In practice, high schools met a number of the reformers' goals. In the 1920s and 1930s, farm people's access to education increased. For example, in 1920, 73 percent of farm men and 62 percent of farm women in Cedar County, Iowa, had no education past the eighth grade, but only about half their children of high school age did not attend high school. High school attendance in Wisconsin increased by a third between 1912 and 1923. In North Dakota, farm children's high school attendance increased 43 percent between 1921 and 1926, and by another 33 percent between 1926 and 1935.

Scientific agriculture and home economics were successfully introduced into high schools. By 1936, thirty-eight North Dakota high schools offered vocational agriculture and forty offered home economics. This was two more high schools than had offered home economics in 1928, and twelve more than had offered agriculture in 1926. In the same ten years, boys' enrollment in these programs increased 83 percent, while girls' increased 138 percent in eight years. Although these gains were significant, less than 20 percent of North Dakota farm children who were enrolled in high schools participated in these programs. The high school did, however, successfully link rural and town people. Studies in Wisconsin, South Dakota, and Missouri found that rural families who had students in high schools not only increased trade in the towns, but also expanded their social activities, particularly when the youths made friends in town through the high schools.[7]

Despite these successes, high schools did not meet all the goals of the social reformers. First, rurbanism did not necessarily lead to shared control of high schools by townspeople and farm people. Local high schools often resisted serving rural students. For example, in 1920, the superintendent of schools of Webster County, Iowa, would not introduce agricultural training "because it encouraged pupils to come in from the country and at present there was not room for them." In Wisconsin, when funding was tight, high schools denied enrollment to farm children and cut agricultural courses from the curriculum. School attendance remained expensive. In 1925, in Wisconsin, 25 percent of all high school students from farms still paid tuition. Even as village high school districts expanded to include rural areas in their tax bases, they rarely shared administrative control with farm people. In 1923, although 48 percent of district students in Dane County, Wisconsin (aside from the cities of Madison and Waupaca), were from farms, only 27 percent of the school board members were farmers. Even in 1933, according to University of Wisconsin studies, farmers still had no control of high school policies, whether they were in or out of town school districts.

Finally, the education of farm youth, despite its expansion, did not keep pace with that of urban or village youths. In North Dakota in 1928, only about 10 percent of all farm children of high school age were in high school, compared to 23 percent of town and city youth. In Wisconsin in 1936, 38 percent of urban youths ages fourteen to twenty did not go to school, compared to 56 percent for farm and village youths. When counting farm youths alone, the number climbed to 62 percent.[8] Although high schools may have successfully linked town and country, they did not overcome rural disadvantages, and rurbanism did not necessarily lead to equal power sharing or a larger role for farm people in the education of their children.

Reformers hoped to connect farm people to town-centered institutions such as trade centers and high schools; however, they also promoted community clubs, or farmers' clubs, which were based in the open country. Reformers hoped clubs would give farm neighborhoods an institutional social life, create broader ties to other clubs, and educate farm people about scientific agriculture and improved living standards. Often these clubs merely formalized informal neighborhood groups and complemented neighborhood social patterns. Community clubs had a local base and were gender-integrated, with membership open to everyone in a family. Such clubs reinforced local traditions even as promoters attempted to alter them.

Although community clubs existed before the country life movement, professionals played a large role in their spread and in the content of educational programs. In North Dakota, prior to World War I, the counties that had had county agents for the longest time also had the highest numbers of farmers' clubs. Extension services and land-grant colleges, in the 1910s, provided speakers for educational talks on the new scientific methods; increasingly, agricultural professionals, not local farmers, were the experts who spoke at farmers' club meetings. Agents also successfully melded new ideas with social traditions. For example, extension agents might link community-style picnics that included speakers, games, and contests with the newest advances for home and farm. Contests at agricultural fairs introduced experts' criteria for judging, promoting standardized products and increased specialization, such as purebred stock and improved seeds. A Wisconsin fair in the 1910s demonstrated self-feeders for hogs, quick egg separators, and power washers. Combined with carnivals, pageants, plays, plowing and corn-husking contests, and other entertainments, the demonstrations contributed to a holiday atmosphere and drew large crowds. Local trade-center merchants benefited from these crowds and often sponsored the fairs or supplied the money for prizes.[9]

Despite these successes, community clubs were never rurban institutions. Farmers dominated most clubs, which were likely to be in the open country or connected to rural towns with fewer than five hundred people. A study of North Dakota clubs in 1927 and 1929 found that the least successful clubs were those that included townspeople from villages of more than five hundred people. Community clubs sometimes sponsored picnics or fairs with other clubs in the area, but usually included only local groups. Despite the role of professionals in their promotion, farmers' clubs remained independent. In 1930, Illinois farmers' clubs and community clubs depended less on extension services for their programs and growth than did other farmers' organizations.[10]

Community clubs, though receptive to educational efforts, did not see the teaching of new agricultural practices as their main function. Farm people used community clubs primarily for social purposes; educational and community-service projects remained secondary. Social activities used local talent rather than professionals from outside the neighborhood. The Skillet Creek Farmers' Club began in 1905, in Sauk County, Wisconsin, just forty miles north of the University of Wisconsin. Although the Skillet Creek club was closely tied to the university and the Wisconsin country life movement, it nevertheless was primarily social and self-sustaining. An account of its activities reveals some programs on new agricultural practices, but also shows the importance of local issues and socializing. In its third year, 1908, the club sponsored milk testing for dairy herds; debated school issues; heard recitations by schoolchildren; studied local history, the legislative process, health issues, and agricultural topics; and held a "jollification" meeting, an ice cream social, a picnic, and a debate "for fun" on the members' use of slang. The members celebrated birthdays and anniversaries and gave flowers and consolation when deaths occurred. Such activities formalized informal ways of building community and mirrored the social community-building activities of farm women.

The club Mary Still belonged to also indicates the primacy of social life in club activities. In January 1911, the club was formed in Steele County, North Dakota, about seventy miles southwest of Grand Forks. The club did not merely connect those in Still's neighborhood, but paralleled broader networks of community exchange. In June 1912, Still reported meeting "a number who do not usually attend. Saw Mrs. Newell, the first time in four years." The frequent meetings that year were mainly social. Later in June, the Stills hosted a "strawberry social," which drew "about the largest [crowd] ever. Had twelve strawberry shortcakes and cream, besides sandwiches and coffee." Three weeks later, the club had a picnic.

July 13: Fine bright day. Started for the picnic at eight o'clock. Leslie went in a haystack load from Green's. Had our programme before dinner. I had the Club Paper. After dinner, races and a ball game, then supper and home. I rode home with Stewarts' in their auto, I got here at eight, the rest came at nine. Had a lovely day altogether.

Still's club facilitated community socializing and self-education. Still never mentioned the agricultural college. Her personal experience of the club was as a social, locally controlled community group.[11]

Progressive Era social reformers relied on education and organizing to move farm people away from local values and institutions, but their community-based approach complemented informal, local farm neighborhoods. High schools and trade centers, as well as churches, often did link farm people to townspeople, but farm people were rarely equal in rurban institutions. In contrast, community clubs promoted a social vision of local farm neighborhoods uniting for the improvement of self and community. Although experts guided these institutions toward changed agricultural and living practices, farm neighborhoods still controlled the clubs and used them to meet local needs. Despite professionals' assumption that all farmers needed what they and their business supporters were promoting, their method of organizing did, in fact, leave the power of choice to neighborhood farm groups.

At the same time that professionals were advancing community clubs, a growing number of farm people were organizing economic cooperatives, women's clubs, and gender-integrated cooperative and political movements. Since the nineteenth century, farm people had organized gender-integrated neighborhood-based institutions and political movements, as well as gender-segregated organizations that reflected the different work roles of men and women. For example, the Grange and the Populist party built from community-based local groups that included entire families as members. Men within these organizations operated economic cooperatives that paralleled their greater ties to commodity production and the market economy. Women organized educational and social activities, raised funds, and united the community behind these farm and political organizations. By the 1910s, cooperatives, women's clubs, and alternative political organizations had increased in importance in the rural Midwest.

In contrast, professionals were creating a new social agenda that more carefully matched the professional and institutional goals that developed in the late 1910s and 1920s. This agenda reproduced the priorities and gender hierarchies of agricultural institutions, including the male emphasis on production and the segregation and subordination of women and "feminized" issues. The new system of Farm Bureaus, Homemakers' Clubs, and 4-H Clubs, created by the extension service in 1914, individualized the farm family by isolating the interests of each of its members. They defined the interests of men as agricultural and those of women as homemaking, mirroring the specialties of most experts. These organizations concentrated on the work of individuals in the nuclear family rather than the family and its role in the farm community. This elevated male business concerns to the position of the principal community need, and subordinated and narrowed the view of women's role to that of homemakers, ignoring the crucial activity of women in organizing rural communities. This redefinition of community gave priority to male business interests and separated them from any rural community or family issues.[12] This social vision complemented the economic vision of centralized agriculture—large mechanized farms, whose residents were not dependent on neighborhood cooperation for either work or socializing, but were dependent on agricultural institutions, experts, "modern" production methods, and new consumer goods.

Economic cooperatives, like community clubs, did not originate with country life movement promoters. The first farm cooperatives in the Midwest probably grew from informal work exchanges. The first, a cheese factory in Jefferson County, Wisconsin in 1841, was called a cheese "ring," a term often used to describe a system of neighborhood cooperation. Men generally dominated the cooperatives, reflecting the market orientation of most male farm work. Cooperatives, prior to World War I, responded to local marketing conditions. An Iowa farmer described his father's participation in forming a grain-shipping cooperative in the early twentieth century. The five different elevator companies along the railroad in his region offered farmers the same price for their barley, a price well below the prices the companies would earn in Chicago. He heard of people shipping their barley directly to Chicago: "So he got in contact with . . . a man by the name of Dunn from Mason City. He was a cooperative man and he organized it. . . . Before long they were not only shipping their own grain, but their cattle and hogs. . . . So this became a very cooperative town." Cooperatives attempted to give a community of farmers greater power in the centralized economy of the late nineteenth and early twentieth centuries.

Local cooperatives dealt with a variety of commodities and community needs. In Orange Township, Iowa, between 1889 and 1918, farmers formed a telephone company, a cooperative egg-selling association, three cooperative threshing companies, six cooperative silo-filling companies, a cow-testing association, and a cooperative creamery. The earliest successful cooperatives in the Midwest were in the grain states. Thirty cooperative elevators operated in Iowa in 1904. By 1913, six of the nine states of the Midwest had grain associations. In Wisconsin and Minnesota, farmers started dairy cooperatives. In 1914, Wisconsin had 380 cooperative creameries, and by 1915, 718 cooperative cheese factories. Livestock-shipping associations did not grow until World War I, with organizing efforts peaking between 1917 and 1920. Even as cooperatives moved into larger-scale marketing during World War I, more than nine-tenths of the active associations remained local in 1921.[13]

Despite the cooperatives' local community bases, many affiliated themselves with regional or national cooperative organizations. In the late nineteenth century, the Farmers' Alliance linked economic cooperatives in the South and Midwest and eventually turned to politics with the Populist party. Many historians mark the decline of the Populist party in the 1890s as the end of large-scale farmer political movements; however, economic cooperatives continued to grow. Two organizations, the American Society of Equity (Equity) and the Farmers' Educational and Cooperative Union (Farmers' Union), continued to link local cooperatives into loose federations. Farm journalists, a seed-business owner, and owners of grain elevators founded the Equity in 1902, but farmers soon pushed it in new directions. They experimented with pooling crops, cooperating with labor unions to eliminate middlemen, promoting farmer-owned warehouses and grain exchanges, and, in some areas, sponsoring political candidates. The Farmers' Union also was formed in 1902; it was led by a former member of the Farmers' Alliance. The union sponsored withholding actions to get higher prices, but also encouraged education and pursued politics, lobbying for better farm legislation.

These affiliations brought both advantages and problems for local cooperatives. Larger cooperatives often did not inspire loyalty as local cooperatives did. They met infrequently and were less well attended than rural organizations. Although local affiliates remained meeting places for farm neighbors and provided a broad base of community support for national cooperatives, farmers' allegiance to the larger organizations depended not only on neighborhood affinity, but on an awareness of farmers as a type of worker or as producers of a particular commodity. Local cooperatives could only challenge local, privately owned grain elevators, shippers, or creameries. This may have reduced some of the farmers' costs by allowing them to avoid local prices that were lower than those at the market centers, but local cooperatives could not address the low prices or unfair grading practices in the large terminals, exchanges, centralized creameries, or milk-processing plants. Only affiliation with larger cooperatives could effectively challenge the increased centralization of agricultural businesses. When the 1914 Clayton Antitrust Act legalized cooperatives by exempting them from antitrust laws, larger cooperatives attempted to set up cooperative exchanges and get seats on boards of trade and livestock exchanges.[14] These larger cooperatives challenged corporate agricultural interests.

While the cooperative movement attempted to gain more control of prices for farmers through economic organization, parallel political farm groups organized to increase government regulation in hopes of eliminating the abuses of the shipping and marketing industries. The most radical of these, the Nonpartisan League, had its largest successes in the Dakotas, Minnesota, and Wisconsin, before and after World War I and again in the 1930s. Its programs attacked agricultural businesses and middlemen; proposed state-owned grain elevators, banks, and utilities; and promoted an alliance with labor unions. In other midwestern states in the 1910s, 1920s, and 1930s, economic cooperatives, such as Equity and the Farmers' Union, joined labor unions to elect progressives and Farmer-Labor party representatives who were more sympathetic to the problems of farmers than candidates of either major party. In 1922, such groups won electoral victories in Iowa, Minnesota, North Dakota, Nebraska, Wisconsin, and Kansas. These victories not only strengthened the Farm Bloc—members of Congress from predominantly rural states who lobbied for agricultural legislation—but also made it more radical.

Responding to the growth of these alternative, politically active farm cooperatives, agricultural institutions encouraged the creation of a national farmers' organization. The AFBF, founded in 1919, was closely allied to the interests of agricultural institutions and was less critical of corporate agricultural interests. Farm Bureaus existed before the formation of the national federation. Originally, local Farm Bureaus helped fund county agents and organized commercial farmers and businesspeople sympathetic to the goals of scientific agriculture. Like the extension service, Farm Bureaus had financial ties to businesses such as International Harvester, the Chicago Board of Trade, and Sears. Their membership primarily included wealthy landowners and substantial farmers. Agricultural experts from the land-grant colleges provided leadership. The first Farm Bureau was a division of a local chamber of commerce and was composed of businessmen who received money from bankers and railroads. Although before World War I local Farm Bureaus varied in their membership and outlook, by 1919 Farm Bureaus were closely linked to the county agent system and land-grant colleges.

During World War I, agricultural institutions became more interested in marketing issues. This interest was a response partly to pressure from commercial farmers in Farm Bureau organizations, but also to the growing power of cooperative movements critical of agricultural institutions and corporate agriculture. The newly created AFBF, the USDA, and agricultural colleges gradually added marketing to their educational and production concerns. They planned to create centralized marketing mechanisms that would rationalize agriculture, stabilize prices, ally farmers to business, not labor, and destroy agrarian radicalism. The AFBF began to organize farmer cooperatives, as historian Lowell Dyson noted, "in order to beat the NPL to the punch."[15] State governments often made state Farm Bureaus legal units. Government financial credit aided their foundation, county agents and land-grant college personnel organized them, and businesses supplied them with financial backing.

The AFBF saw agriculture as a business and farmers as businessmen. Its purpose was both politically and economically conservative. The AFBF did not demand more strict price controls for farmers or challenge the middlemen. Rather, it planned to educate members, improve the quality of merchandise, increase demand through advertising, and raise prices through marketing efficiency.[16] The Farm Bureaus' organization did not challenge the existing marketing system but hoped to include larger farm producers in the system. Even this relatively conservative plan challenged processors and handlers in 1923. Boards of trade, and, to a lesser extent, livestock exchanges sometimes denied seats to the Farm Bureaus, just as they did to other, more radical cooperatives. Eventually, other groups' radical proposals made conservative Farm Bureau programs, such as financial credits for cooperatives and tariff protection equal to that given other industries, increasingly acceptable. Radical and conservative farm organizations, cooperating through the legislators of the Farm Bloc, finally forced Republican administrations to introduce modest reforms in agriculture in the mid-1920s.

Despite this limited cooperation, the Farm Bureaus fundamentally countered rural community-based institutions. The social organization of the Farm Bureaus complemented the economic goals and the long-range policies of agricultural institutions. The Farm Bureaus were organized from the top down, at the county rather than the local level. In most states, their ties to county agents were direct rather than advisory, and the county agent often led the county Farm Bureau. The Farm Bureaus emphasized production and marketing, and their membership was limited to men. Unlike community clubs, Farm Bureaus had few ties to local farm neighborhoods and did not have to compromise with local interests. The Farm Bureaus emphasized business and education rather than socializing, and relied on outside experts for their programs. They constituted a business organization that lobbied for the preservation of agriculture as an industry, not for the preservation of small farmers or a system of small family-owned farms.[17] The AFBF became the official representative of the farmers, allowing agricultural institutions to ignore groups that challenged its policies. The AFBF could represent farmers without representing the diversity of the farm community.

The Farm Bureaus largely met the professionals' goal of organizing a prosperous middle-class constituency. Though its local membership could vary, in general, farmers who joined Farm Bureaus were relatively prosperous. For example, in the Illinois Farm Bureau owners joined more often than tenants or laborers, high school graduates more often than eighth-grade graduates, and stable (defined as having spent more than ten years on the same farm) more often than unstable farmers. These farmers had the stability and resources to use more capital-intensive farming methods and to increase spending on consumer goods.

The Farm Bureaus also had a regional appeal. They succeeded most in the corn-livestock belt of the Midwest, particularly in Iowa and Illinois. Though appealing primarily to substantial farmers even within these areas, their support was nevertheless widespread. This was due, in part, to the legal and direct association of the Farm Bureaus with extension services in these states. The programs of the agricultural colleges and the Farm Bureaus also suited livestock producers in the corn belt, who had made substantial capital investments and already practiced the diversified agriculture preached by the agricultural agencies. The farmers of the corn belt could also be more conservative because their livelihoods were less buffeted by the expansion and depression cycle of the World War I years, and they depended less on foreign markets than did the wheat regions to the west. In the Great Plains and the dairy regions, farmers were more likely to join alternative farm organizations, such as the Farmers' Alliance, the Nonpartisan League, Equity, and the Farmers' Union. In these regions, these groups were strong and their activism predated the creation of the Farm Bureaus. Consequently, the Farm Bureau programs clearly attacked the politics of these organizations and had little strength in the wheat region or the dairy belt. The Farm Bureaus grew somewhat in the dairy region during World War I, but declined in the 1920s and 1930s and did not regain strength until after World War II.

The Farm Bureaus drew more members than many farm organizations, but other factors make equating membership with full acceptance of their agricultural policies somewhat questionable. For example, studies indicate that Farm Bureaus had less active participation, less social attachment, and less commitment from farmers than did other farm groups. To participate in the larger statewide shipping associations or terminal markets coordinated by government agencies, farmers often had to join Farm Bureaus. Despite the significant number of farmers who were members of the AFBF, large landowners who had little sympathy for small family farms and agricultural professionals dominated the AFBF leadership.[18] The Farm Bureaus ultimately contained a broad-based membership, but the AFBF leadership and structure firmly linked the organization to the goals of production-oriented, centralized agriculture.

As agricultural institutions moved away from organizing farm neighborhoods and centered on farmers as businessmen, they also deemphasized women's community activities and concentrated more narrowly on their work as homemakers. In the Midwest, women's clubs, like community clubs and cooperatives, did not originate with the efforts of promoters. Church-affiliated ladies' aid societies, school-affiliated mothers' clubs, and informal women's networks were part of farm life before any government push to organize them. As in the informal farm neighborhood, these separate women's clubs both complemented and were integral to community farm organizations. Although women had separate organizations, they also participated in other community groups, especially in the grassroots farm organizations and even the community clubs promoted by the country life movement.

The growth of formal women's organizations in the late nineteenth century accompanied the women's club movement. It included such groups as the WCTU and the General Federation of Women's Clubs (GFWC). Although they participated in the women's movement, farm women had their own organizations and their own issues. When urban-dominated women's organizations, such as the GFWC and the YWCA, set up separate divisions to reach rural women as part of the country life movement, their attitude of uplift caused friction with farm women, just as it had between middle-class and working-class women in urban areas. In 1912, the secretary of a purely rural women's club in South Dakota described the conflict in a letter to the *Farmer's Wife*, the only journal published specifically for farm women in this period:

While we realize in some ways the lives of farmers' wives are circumscribed, we also realize our many advantages and we watch with interest the turning of the tide of thought among Federated club women to the "uplift" of our class of people. . . . We welcome every co-operative aid; but our lives are different and it may be that we have something of wealth to offer to our town sisters as they have to us. Is there no way for the two classes to meet without the appearance of superiority or patronage on the one side, and consequently humiliation on the other?

Despite attempts by urban women's clubs to include farm women and despite the existence of such rural federations as the National Farm Women's Congress, most rural women's clubs, like economic cooperatives, remained local and did not affiliate with larger organizations.[19]

Farm women's clubs, like community clubs, often formalized preexisting informal groups, and had a large social component. In general, they engaged in three kinds of activities: self-education, community service, and activities related to women's work. Women's clubs usually met in homes, often took on the work women had done informally, and showed flexibility in their structure. For example, the Alfalfameda Club in North Dakota operated as a community club during the winter season and a women's club during the summer. Before 1924, when it became affiliated with the extension service, the club helped neighbors with work in difficult times; assisted during illnesses, births, and deaths; and celebrated birthdays, anniversaries, and farewells. Women also used clubs for self-education. The 1916 and 1917 field reports from the USDA's Division of Farm Studies' "woman agent," Anne Evans, revealed that midwestern women's clubs studied such subjects as gardening, poultry, local and state history, state laws affecting women, the lives of famous women, Montessori education methods, and nutrition.[20]

Women's clubs also built community support, both emotional and financial, for local organizations and institutions. Church-affiliated ladies' aid societies raised money to pay ministers and to improve churches, and mothers' clubs collected funds for schools. Both staged important social get-togethers that added to community solidarity. Other women's clubs raised money and coordinated work with state and county agents to provide such things as "better baby" contests, which provided free health examinations for children; rest rooms for women in towns; apparatus for playgrounds; trees for churchyards; rural libraries and hospitals; and hot lunches and milk for schoolchildren. One club in Missouri provided a yearly scholarship for a girl to study agriculture, not home economics, at the state university.[21]

Finally, women's clubs attempted to improve women's working conditions and increase their contribution to farm income through sales or increased home production. The sexual division of labor unified farm women, and sharing work played a large role in women's clubs. Anna Pratt Erickson participated in a club that decreased women's work by sharing big projects, such as quilting, sewing bedding, and learning new canning techniques. Other clubs more actively marketed women's produce. During Evans's field trip for the USDA, she coordinated the sale of eggs, poultry, dairy products, and garden produce by making direct connections between rural women's clubs in Illinois and Missouri and urban women's clubs in St. Louis.

Women's clubs blended all these components, and their ventures often complemented male economic cooperatives. For example, the women's club of River Falls, Wisconsin, was formed in 1903. Its initial purpose was social: to "counteract the growing lack of neighborliness and the increasing sense of a kind of resigned discontent." Its members also educated themselves, but they did not study the domestic sciences, because they had been "studying them for years." Instead they studied history, literature, current events, conservation, politics, child-labor laws, and laws relating to women. When a local farm woman had a bee to demonstrate her new hand-powered washer, the club began to look for ways to decrease everyone's work on "Blue Monday." At a country life meeting at the University of Wisconsin, another member heard of a cooperative laundry in Minnesota. When she returned with the idea, the women canvassed door-to-door, and, with the cooperation of the town women's club, they started a cooperative laundry in 1915, using the facilities of the male-operated cooperative creamery. While other cooperative laundries failed due to competition from private laundries or individually owned appliances, the River Falls laundry succeeded largely because the nearby normal school sent its gym clothes, and its students eagerly used the facilities. By 1924, the laundry served 206 patrons a month, half of whom were from the country. The club expanded its connections beyond its local farm neighborhood in this economic venture, but it still continued its woman-centered self-improvement, its social and community functions, and its gender-integrated pattern of cooperation.[22]

Although the farm women's clubs of the Progressive Era carried out a number of diverse functions, extension services promoted much narrower women's organizations in the 1920s. The development of Homemakers' Clubs paralleled the development of the Farm Bureaus and the professionalization of home economics. As women in extension services defined the discipline of home economics in the conservative climate of the 1920s, they concentrated more on work in the home and in the nuclear family and less on the community service and activism that was a tradition in women's clubs. Like the Farm Bureaus, Homemakers' Clubs tried to change work practices, for example, by increasing consumption. The primary topics of club programs included clothing and textiles, food and nutrition, home management, child development, health, gardening and poultry, handicrafts, and cultural appreciation, such as music or art. Experts took a larger role in the new, more hierarchical organizations. They designed programs and gave their expertise on "proper" methods rather than having local women design their own programs.

But women's clubs, even Homemakers' Clubs, never lost their local character. Unlike Farm Bureaus, women's clubs continued to formalize more informal interactions. Anna Pratt Erickson recorded in her diary the names of the women who had formed a club; the names were familiar from informal neighborhood exchanges. Newspaper accounts and University of Wisconsin extension records indicate that this club was a Homemakers' Club affiliated with the extension service; however, none of the diary descriptions indicates this affiliation. Erickson did not even mention such noteworthy events as a visit from state leader Nellie Kedzie Jones. Most club entries simply list the names of the local people who attended, and thus fit into the patterns of other social visits. Unlike male county agents and Farm Bureau experts, who did not use other farm organizations, female extension agents continued to work with existing women's clubs. For example, the Marathon County, Wisconsin, agent organized clubs that were simultaneously church ladies' aid societies or Women's Auxiliaries of the American Society of Equity.[23]

Farm women's clubs retained their local character because home extension agents never received the funding that agricultural county agents received, and, consequently, could exert less control from the top down. Local clubs sent women to general sessions where they were taught the current lesson by county or college home economics professionals. These women, in turn, would share the lesson with other club members. Local clubs chose from a long list of possible topics, and the amount of time to be spent on the lesson and the acceptance or rejection of the ideas in it could be freely discussed within each local group. Groups had the freedom to pursue their own interests. For example, the Hamlet, North Dakota, club switched to charity work in 1926–27. Although county agents emphasized home improvements in their reports, the social role of clubs remained vitally important. As the Williams County, North Dakota, agent observed in the 1926–27 report: "The social side of really knowing each other and the service rendered each other not shown in reports is of much greater value to the members and to the community." Women's clubs remained based in the neighborhood.

Although Homemakers' Clubs did not destroy local autonomy, they did alter definitions of what was appropriate work for farm women. Affiliation with the extension service narrowed the range of activities women's clubs were likely to perform. In the beginning, Homemakers' Clubs were for farm women, but they eventually expanded to include town and city women. As they did so, some programs, such as those concentrating on poultry and gardening, lost importance. By the 1930s, club programs identified all women as homemakers and neglected the issues peculiar to agriculture and farm women. The Farm Bureaus and Homemakers' Clubs formalized the separation of men's business from women's homes, and operated against local traditions of integrating men and women in neighborhoods despite the existence of a sexual division of labor.[24] This separation discouraged women's traditionally active role in community groups and diminished the power they exerted in fund-raising and encouraging of neighborhood loyalty. It also lessened the need to balance an individual farm's business decisions with the needs of rural communities.

In the early twentieth century, agricultural institutions attempted to reorganize rural communities, attacking the informal structure of farm neighborhoods and the local character of rural institutions. During the Progressive Era, agricultural professionals hoped to guide farm people into the "new agriculture" through education and uplift. After World War I, a more conservative political climate encouraged policies that focused even more narrowly on prosperous, commercially oriented farmers. Community clubs may have appealed to more economically secure farmers, but all members of a neighborhood could benefit from parks or libraries. Only the more prosperous could benefit from lessons on the latest home appliances or farm machinery. These new groups discouraged organizing the whole community of small family farms by separating business interests from community interests and underfunding and neglecting farm women's community organizing. Earlier organizations whose primary purpose was social and whose base was local could include a greater variety of people. The new organizations had even fewer connections to the traditions of local farm communities and, in fact, hoped to alter them fundamentally.

Despite efforts to reorganize rural communities, farm people continued to build farm neighborhoods grounded in social and economic exchanges and the values of mutuality. These strategies could be adapted somewhat to modern production and modern living, but farm people continued to resist total reliance on a commercialized economy. Some isolated themselves by attempting to make their rural neighborhoods as self-contained and autonomous as possible. Others used neighboring practices to cross barriers and create alternative organizations rooted in the values of farm neighborhoods.

Farm organizations that were critical of agricultural institutions and centralized agriculture were not new in the 1920s, but the increased importance of the AFBF particularly angered some farm groups. The AFBF threatened these alternative farm organizations because it competed with them economically and politically. Alternative farm organizations disliked the Farm Bureaus' privileged relationship with agricultural industries and government agencies. The Farmers' Union, the strongest of the alternative farm organizations by the 1920s and 1930s, attacked the Farm

Bureaus' connection with business, arguing that the Farm Bureaus got their money from the business interests that exploited farmers, such as meat packers and boards of trade. By letting businesspeople join, the Farmers' Union insisted, the Farm Bureaus made the interests of farmers secondary to business interests. The Farmers' Union further objected to the Farm Bureaus' close ties with the federal government and the agricultural colleges. The union members believed this connection enabled the government to control and channel the opinions of farmers. The Farm Bureaus also gained unfair advantages over other farm groups because of their affiliation. County agents helped them recruit farmers at taxpayers' expense and often required farmers to join to get government information and aid. Finally, the union members criticized the slow political response of the Farm Bureaus and the government to farmers' economic problems and their late support for the cooperative movement. The Farm Bureaus set up large marketing groups to organize unaffiliated cooperatives, capitalizing, the Farmers' Union argued, on a local movement that the Farm Bureaus actually had opposed in their formative years.[25] They saw the Farm Bureaus as controlling reform rather than as cooperating with reform. The Farm Bureaus' ties, they charged, were to the political and economic interests who opposed reform for farmers, not to farmers themselves.

Although these critiques reveal the political opposition of alternative farm organizations to the Farm Bureaus, the differences between these organizations and the Farm Bureaus ran much deeper, existing not just in political ideology but in their organization and social vision. Groups such as Equity, the Nonpartisan League, and the Farmers' Union organized at the grass-roots level. Their organization was not top-down like the Farm Bureaus, but built from local neighborhoods. North Dakota farm people referred to the NPL organizers and speakers frequently, and they often expressed a personal connection to the leaders, starting their discussion with "I heard . . ." or "I knew. . . ." Others did not recall outside organizers but felt that local membership had grown because "a bunch of farmers got together." One farmer recalled that the NPL was organized "by talking." The organization epitomized self-help rather than experts uplifting ignorant farmers. A Wisconsin Farmers' Union leader said that the Farmers' Union differed from the Farm Bureaus because it went in and asked farmers what they needed and wanted, rather than telling them.[26]

In contrast to the Farm Bureaus, these groups did not ally themselves with town business leaders. Town businesspeople often opposed the NPL and the Farmers' Union. In North Dakota, merchants organized the Independent Voting Association (IVA) to oppose the NPL. One Wisconsin woman recalled that in the 1930s the local chamber of commerce forbade the Farmers' Union from meeting in the town of Menomonie. Learning that a local variety-store owner had said that "if farmers stayed home where they belong, they wouldn't be in the mess they're in," she confronted him at the store: "If all those farmers had stayed home, where would your store be today? [Who of] your rich friends who accompany you to Florida would come in your store, buy your ten cent articles? [They] have five or ten dollars to spend." Unlike the Farm Bureaus, whose ties to business and commercial interests were deep, alternative organizations represented primarily the interests of farm people.

Another significant difference between these groups and the Farm Bureaus was the alternative groups' family organization and the integration of men, women, and children. Reflecting the social base of farm communities, this structure gave organizations the benefits of women's community-building skills and kept issues of community welfare linked to the business interests of farming. Women created social occasions that gave these groups deeper meaning and made commitments stronger. According to a 1937 North Dakota State University report, the Farmers' Union locals were strong because "the local meeting of the Farmers' Union is the medium thru which the farmer member has the opportunity to discuss his problems with his neighbors, to make a study of matters of mutual interest and to meet his neighbors in a social way." A Farmers' Union leader in Wisconsin recalled that meetings often lasted until 1:00 A.M. and included a long coffee break at 10:00 for visiting. Women's activities, such as picnics, plays, and pageants, helped recruit new members and raised money. For example, a combination of cooperative sales, money from basket socials, and cooperative labor funded the creation of a Farmers' Union education camp in Wisconsin in the late 1930s.

In the Farm Bureau, the Homemakers' Clubs and 4-H Clubs had few direct ties to the business of men; in contrast, organizations such as the Farmers' Union included the whole family. All attended the meetings and anyone over the age of sixteen could vote. Although some Homemakers' Clubs did help organize local community support for Farm Bureaus, women in the Farmers' Union did not work in separate auxiliaries but within the organization. They were active members. As one man in Mountrail County, North Dakota, observed, a woman "can't keep her mouth shut long," and that was a "compliment." Women didn't "play politics" like men, who want to "lift their hat for everybody." In order to work for political change, one had to confront powerful people and "keep the hat down sometimes." Women would "always let the world know about it." Although men largely held leadership positions in the Farmers' Union, women often headed the education division, locally and at the state and national levels. The Farmers' Union saw education as central to its purpose and gave women an integral position of power within the organiza-tion.[27] These organizations mirrored local neighborhood structures and had a larger social vision of community welfare than simply promoting business efficiency.

Because of this vision, alternative organizations were economically more inclusive than the Farm Bureaus were. The NPL and the Farmers' Union appealed to families who owned small farms, those who were ten-ants, and those who were laborers. Where the Farmers' Union dominated, as in South Dakota, North Dakota, and Nebraska, more small farmers belonged to farm organizations than in states like Illinois, where the Farm Bureaus dominated. Organizations such as Equity, the Farmers' Union, and the Nonpartisan League believed in a community of small farmers. For example, the Farmers' Union operated on the Rochdale cooperative principle, including "one man, one vote," and limited the total amount of investment per member. Wealthy farmers had no more influence than poor farmers in the Farmers' Union, which reinforced the values of equality and cooperation found in local neighborhoods.

In order to succeed, these organizations moved beyond neighborhood identity to find an ideological vision that was inclusive of a larger commu-nity, the "common people." Members of these groups called themselves "poor" or "common" people, not "progressive" or "scientific" farmers, even if they used some of these methods. When asked by an interviewer if the NPL was socialist, one Mountrail County farmer replied that when farmers got something new, they were called "radical." The "poor man" would not always "take it the way it comes." Another replied that the NPL fought the "moneyed class" for the good of "the poor people." This identification crossed neighborhood lines and united farmers and "com-mon people" in urban areas. These farm groups allied politically with labor, not business.[28]

This broad perspective helped build bridges between these organiza-tions. These organizations often shared membership or built alliances, especially in the areas of their geographic strength.[29] Except for the Equity/Farmers' Union merger in 1926, Equity, the NPL, the Farmers' Union, and the Farm Holiday Association did not formalize connections. They did cooperate, however. In addition, many of the same people and the same families joined these groups successively as one gained and another lost strength. The connections could cross generations as well. For example, the Segerstroms were active local leaders in the Farmers' Union near Mondovi, Wisconsin. Their parents had supported Robert LaFollette, and they were involved successively with cooperative threshing rings, a cooperative creamery and lumber store, Equity, the Farmers' Union when it began to organize in Wisconsin in the 1930s, the Depression Era Farm Holiday milk strikes, and finally the Farmer-Labor party. In North Dakota, Oscar and Ida Craft recalled that they had been in farm organizations "all their lives" and that the people in the Farmers' Union, the NPL, and the Farm Holiday Association were "more or less the same."[30]

Although these alternative farm organizations politically opposed agricultural institutions, this does not mean that their members were "backward" or that they rejected all the methods or ideas of the "new agriculture." Even supporters of the Farmers' Union or the NPL in states in which these organizations were strong, such as Wisconsin and North Dakota, would sometimes support the affiliate groups of the Farm Bureaus. The number of Homemakers' Clubs increased steadily in North Dakota during the 1920s and 1930s, the same decade in which the Farmers' Union grew. The diary of North Dakotan William Siebert reveals that, even in the activist political climate of the 1930s when his family attended meetings of the NPL and the Farmers' Union, the children still attended 4-H. Harold Tomter, a Wisconsin farmer, was both a Farmers' Union junior and in 4-H. He saw no conflict between the auxiliary group of the Farm Bureau, which taught "how to make a living," and the Farmers' Union group, which was "attempting to get you a better living."[31] Even if members accepted practices and educational goals similar to those promoted by agricultural institutions, their very different social vision remained, rooted in the composition of the organizations' membership and its ties to rural neighborhood structures.

While these organizations actively promoted political alternatives to the economic and social visions of agricultural institutions, some farm people resisted change informally. Many historians as well as agricultural professionals of the time described this resistance as "backwardness," "individualism," or dislike of change of any type even when it was "obviously for the better." However, such cultural resistance, viewed from the perspective of farm people, was an attempt to maintain a valued way of living and working. Although reports from agricultural experiment stations and extension services tended to emphasize the positive reception of their programs in the countryside, the reports also contain signs of opposition. Statistics indicate that many farmers did not participate in any farm organization. In North Dakota, researchers found only 111 community clubs in 1926, which was the peak year for such clubs; 40 percent of the state's counties had no clubs at all. In 1923, a University of Wisconsin researcher found that even in an active county, "the enumerator could work for whole days without finding a farmer who would confess to membership in the movements." In 1942, a South Dakota researcher concluded that South Dakota farm families were not joiners, with fewer than four of ten families participating in any Grange, Farm Bureau, Farmers' Union, women's extension club, or purchasing or marketing cooperative.[32]

The reasons for this resistance lay in the local nature of farm communities and their reliance on neighbors for survival. These farm people were satisfied with their own local institutions and their informal social life. The features that gave neighborhoods their cohesion also supported their resistance — ethnicity, religion, length of residence, patterns of exchange. As in the formation of neighborhoods, these factors were often intertwined. For example, Traill County, North Dakota, was a prosperous farm region in the Red River Valley, reasonably close to the agricultural college in Fargo. It would seem a logical place, at first glance, for extension work. Nevertheless, Traill County continuously voted against hiring a county agent until 1936. The 1928 Extension Annual Report for the county suggested that this was due to the strength of the county's Norwegian identity and because the people "have achieved financial success through hard work and it is difficult for them to understand how anyone can come out and tell them how to farm." This suggests that residents preferred to rely on local work traditions and experience rather than on the advice of experts. Even in 1936, residents approved the county agent only by a narrow margin, with more support for the measure coming from towns than from the open country.[33]

Resistance did not rely solely on a strong ethnic or religious identity, but also reflected a hostility toward the class backgrounds and attitudes of uplift expressed by agricultural professionals. Conflicts appeared when interviewers and researchers went into the field to gather information. Resistance could be subtle or openly hostile. One researcher in Cedar County, Iowa, found that about 20 percent of the residents refused to cooperate in the survey, and that 5 to 10 percent wanted nothing to do with the Farm Bureau, county agent, state college, or government. Farm people often made the outsiders prove their sincerity. The work, for this professional in Cedar County, was more difficult than he anticipated: "Made hay one day in order to get information from an 'impossible' farmer, helped put a binder on trucks, got one covering of mud helping to lift a ford out of a rut, fifteen cussings from farmers and one dog-bite." He found some had no time, others considered it a "useless waste of time," and others thought it none of his business how much money they made. In the final report, one farmer's view represents many of these protests:

How in h. . . will this survey do any good? What will I ever get out of it? To h. . . with helping someone else. Too d. . . many of these fat white shirt guys setting around now. Let any county agent or Farm Bureau man come on my place to tell me how to farm and see how quick I'll kick the s. . . off. Got along without 'em when I was a boy and we can now. Feller's luck changes one will be lucky and then another. Nobody's G. . D. . . business how much I own.

The importance of class and work traditions, the value of practical results, and a hostility to the patronizing attitude of uplift all played some part in resistance to reform efforts.[34]

Cultural resistance, like alternative organizations, grew from a different social vision that allowed farm people to adapt new methods, but still define their choices to fit the needs of their communities. This social vision, less ideologically articulated than those of organizations, was at odds with the community reorganization proposed by agricultural institutions. The oral history of one Wisconsin farmer, Howard Brusveen, illustrates neighborhood resistance to reorganization, adaptation of new practices to fit local values, and the essential value placed on a community of small family farms by many farmers who, nevertheless, did not join alternative organizations.

Brusveen participated actively in few farmers' groups. He did some business with cooperatives, but this did not reflect an ideological commitment, because he also patronized private firms. His family maintained a small diversified dairy farm that was largely self-sufficient rather than expansive. The area had a strong neighborhood, with work exchanges persisting into the 1950s. While he participated in government programs and accepted some new techniques, he always adapted them to his small operation. Although he read some farm magazines and college bulletins, he preferred getting his agricultural knowledge by talking to neighbors during work exchanges or visits. Rather than expanding, he preferred to keep his farm small (eighty-one acres) because he never wanted to "be rich." He supported the New Deal and participated in soil-conservation and dairy-support programs, but had little other contact with New Deal agencies. He believed that both the Farm Bureau and the Farmers' Union profited from their members and offered very little in return.

Although he did not join farm organizations, this did not mean that he was apathetic or that he accepted the ideology or the restructuring of agriculture promoted by agricultural institutions: "We've heard our government talking about preserving the family farm for almost as long as I can remember but it's just cheap double-talk is what that is. There's never been any effort made to preserve the family farm." He opposed agricultural institutions, but did not trust farm organizations to help small farmers either. Instead, he used strategies that had always worked for small farmers. He could trust his own skill and his farm neighborhood. He resisted by keeping his operation small and largely self-sustaining and by participating in local social and economic exchanges. When his neighborhood no longer provided a social base of resistance by the 1960s and 1970s, Brusveen joined the National Farmers' Organization (NFO), a modern farm organization that opposed the point of view of agricultural institutions.[35]

Through their social communities and neighboring practices, farm people were able to preserve the system of small family farms. During the first half of the twentieth century, the social policies of agricultural institutions tried to alter these practices and restructure rural communities to implement the methods of scientific agriculture and to encourage a greater centralization of agricultural production. The creation of these programs had been a response to farm resistance, but resistance did not end with their implementation. Farm people used their neighboring practices to build bonds across community boundaries, creating alternative farm organizations that challenged agricultural institutions and businesses. These organizations resisted some change, but also adapted to a situation that required more than a local community response. These farm people retained neighborhood values but no longer identified with a local community alone. They were part of a "farming class," part of the "common people," which could also include urban laborers. In a sense, they built rurban coalitions to counter the power of agricultural institutions and centralized agriculture. But their rurban coalitions retained local values and grass-roots control, both in their ideology and in their structure.

Most farm people, however, did not participate in either the organizations promoted by agricultural institutions or the alternative farm organizations. Instead, these farm people chose to rely on neighboring practices as survival strategies. They did not organize to resist change, but resisted it through their daily lives. Like those farm people who formed alternative organizations, these rural people also used neighboring to adapt to new conditions and yet still retain local traditions and values. Much of what agricultural institutions promoted benefited rural people, and some willingly accepted these changes. Nevertheless, the reorganization of agriculture encouraged by agricultural institutions put increased economic pressures on small family farms. These pressures buffeted communities, but farm people continued a balancing act, resisting and adapting with the flexibility afforded by their neighboring practices.

Community Work and Technological Change

The Thresheree

A rural community sparked to life for the harvesting and threshing of small grains. The thresheree was a vital community work ritual. As Willa Cather described it:

Every morning the sun came up a red ball, quickly drank the dew and started a quivering excitement in all living things. In great harvest seasons like that one, the heat, the intense light, and the important work in hand draw people together and make them friendly. Neighbors helped each other to cope with the burdensome abundance of man-nourishing grain; women and children and old men fell to and did what they could to save and house it. Even the horses had a more variable and sociable existence than usual, going about from one farm to another to help neighbor horses drag wagons and binders and headers.

The thresheree was not only a means of sharing economic resources within a neighborhood, but also a vital sign of neighborhood unity. One North Dakota farmer exclaimed that you "worked like a son of a gun . . . but it was excitement."

Agricultural professionals perceived the thresheree through a different lens. They saw it as an opportunity to develop new technology that would eliminate the need for "hiring the high-priced and often unsatisfactory transient labor" and end the "inconvenience of exchange labor." Following developments in industrial manufacturing, professionals hoped to increase efficiency by decreasing or eliminating labor costs and introducing economies of scale, larger farms, and more-elaborate technology. They saw neither the cultural importance of community rituals nor the economic importance of labor-intensive strategies.[1]

During the first forty years of the twentieth century, most farm people chose to maintain practices and rituals that celebrated physical labor, work skills, community sharing, and gender-integrated social patterns. These rituals not only provided symbolic meaning and social unity, but also defined economic relations in the community. In contrast, some farm people chose more capital-intensive methods in the 1920s and 1930s and pioneered the use of combines, which mechanized the harvest and threshing, ending the need for exchange. This loss of work exchange signaled a decline in the importance of community social exchanges in meeting the economic needs of farmers and eliminated an important ritual that celebrated the mutuality of women's and men's labor. During the Great Depression, old work rituals persisted, but the new trends of harvesting that would dominate post–World War II agriculture also began.

The community work associated with harvesting and threshing small grains was in its golden age in the late nineteenth and early twentieth centuries. New technology in this period actually enhanced the community nature of threshing. In earlier periods, farm people threshed with hand flailing or horse treading. Family labor or work exchanges with a few neighbors allowed the work to be completed in small amounts throughout the fall and winter. The advent of threshing machines, both horse-powered and eventually steam-powered ones, meant that farmers would hire a custom thresher to do the work once a year. This telescoped the harvesting and threshing into a shorter period and increased the need for labor during that time. The farmers' exchange networks flexibly expanded to meet the needs of this new labor process. Threshing became not just one of a number of smaller exchanges between families, but a larger community event.[2]

In this period, the harvesting and threshing of small grains played a particularly large role in midwestern folklore and cultural traditions. The harvest appears in almost every oral history or literary account of the region. The threshing crew and the steam thresher were perhaps the most photographed images on midwestern farms. The arrival of the threshing machine brought a thrill to farm people not only because of its impressive size, but also because it signaled the arrival of neighbors, work crews, hard work, and socializing. Even in 1978, threshing retained its power. One Iowa farmer continued to raise oats for "nostalgic reasons—we like the threshing and we like the straw. . . . We threshed about twenty acres of oats, and my gosh, we pretty near had more help than we knew what to do with."[3]

Although nostalgia embellishes midwestern threshing lore, the power of the theresheree was apparent even when the hard work was real. In states where small grains were secondary crops, threshing blended with other rounds of work, such as haying, digging potatoes, and corn picking. Nevertheless, farm diarists recorded the arrival of threshing crews and the exchange of labor as a break in the usual routine. Where small grains were the primary crops, the harvest dominated farm diaries. Although farm people recorded the harvest in the same style as they recorded other work, they devoted more space in each entry to the harvest, constantly reported the wheat's growth and condition, and started each entry with an account of the harvest activities, which replaced accounts of the weather or daily chores.[4]

Why has the harvesting of small grains become such an important part of the oral tradition of farming while that of other crops, such as corn, has not? Although stories of corn-husking contests and oyster suppers to celebrate the end of the corn harvest do appear in oral histories, they occur much less frequently than stories of the wheat harvest, even in states where wheat was not the main cash crop. One reason for this is the urgency with which wheat must be harvested. The harvest of small grains is compressed in order to gather the maturing grain safely and prevent loss or damage. Wheat harvests occur in the middle or at the end of the busy summer season with other summer and fall tasks, such as haying and gardening, surrounding them. Farm people harvested corn in the fall as farm field work was winding down. Corn can be picked over a longer period without damage. Consequently, farmers could use family labor or small exchanges to harvest corn, though this was beginning to change by the late 1920s and 1930s as owners of larger, more specialized farms invested in corn-picking machinery and depended more on day labor. A photographic essay on rural life in Kansas in the 1930s noted that there was no "glamour" to corn picking. One simply followed the row, removing the ears and heaving them into a wagon, where one could "hear these ears banging against the high side of the wagons." Bad weather also hindered the possibilities for joyful celebration. One farmer recalled picking corn in frost and cold weather, commenting that "shucking in the snow wasn't a bit unusual."[5]

But the large numbers of workers and the total community involvement made harvesting wheat a vital ritual. The annual ritual of harvesting and threshing symbolized sharing and the unity of the participants. For farm people, the passing of threshing represented the passing of those local neighborhood bonds. Even as early as the late nineteenth century, Hamlin Garland used changes in threshing to describe a sense of community loss. Threshing time was "becoming each year less of a 'bee' and more of a job (many of the men were mere hired hands)." Garland felt a loss of community because his family moved from its close friendship and kinship networks in Wisconsin to the prairies of Iowa. He used the symbol of the harvest to evoke memories of intense community life, a sense of people and place. In oral histories, farm people linked the passing of the group harvest to the loss of neighborhood mutuality, the decline of rural communities, and the increase of selfish, individual wealth seeking.[6]

Although different technologies, crop selections, and labor resources shaped the thresheree, the general work rituals were similar throughout the Midwest. Three tasks make up the work rituals: the field work (harvesting the grain); the threshing (separating the grain); and boarding the crews (preparing the meals and lodgings for workers). Oral traditions of the harvest valued physical labor, skilled work, community sharing, and cooperation. These rituals expressed community ideals and articulated the community social order. They differentiated participants by skill, economic status, sex, or age, but they also reinforced the need for unity across these distinctions, emphasizing mutuality and interdependence.

To harvest small grains, farm people cut the standing grain, bound and shocked or stacked it, and hauled it to the thresher. During the first half of the twentieth century, farm people most commonly harvested grain with a binder, although by the 1920s farmers in the southern Great Plains used a header. The binder cut the grain and bound it into bundles, usually with twine, saving the labor of people gathering the stalks and tying them into sheaves. One person or sometimes two people operated a binder, with one person guiding the horses while the other ran the binder. Because of the small amount of labor required for this operation, the initial stages of the harvest could be completed with family labor.

Family labor, not community labor, cut the grain, so this stage of the harvest is not prominent in midwestern folklore. Although the binder required skill to operate, farm people did not value that skill so highly as those needed to operate a thresher, perhaps because binder skills were common among rural people. Diarists usually simply mentioned the task by noting that they had "cut oats" or "cut wheat." Pauline Olson, a North Dakotan who kept a diary from 1926 to 1969, described the work in some detail on only two occasions. In 1936, she commented that the binder was about to fall apart, and in 1935, she wrote, "Oh what a hot day. Seems impossible to be on the binder but I stuck it out." As this diary also indicates, women often worked in the early stages of the harvest. Field work, which was not part of community exchanges, could be flexibly assigned within the family. Public communal work, such as the threshing, conformed more closely to prescribed sexual divisions of labor.[7]

Shocking or stacking the grain was the next stage of the harvest. Stacking entailed workers hauling bundles from the field to the threshing site and carefully arranging them in large stacks that would repel water and allow the grain to dry. By the twentieth century, shocking had largely replaced stacking. To shock, the worker placed the tied bundles into smaller stacks (shocks) in the field, standing them so the air could dry the grain heads. Farmers shocked or stacked the grain several days or a few weeks before the threshing took place. On smaller farms that did not specialize in small grains, family labor or exchanges with a few neighbors could complete this work; however, on larger, more specialized grain farms, stacking or shocking became the first stage of community exchanges or required hired labor. Shocking and stacking took great effort and skill; consequently, this task had higher status in the harvest. A Kansas farmer noted that it "took a lot of know-how to make the stacks right, so they'd repel rain." Iowa farmer Brownie McVey found abundant help for his threshing in the 1970s, when it was seen as nostalgic, but he found fewer helpers willing to shock. McVey pointed out that many people could toss a few bundles, but only a few wanted to do the much harder work of shocking.

The third step of the process, hauling grain, initiated the excitement of threshing work exchanges. Because only men did this work, the values associated with it reflected the male work culture. This work culture was both hierarchical, in that certain skills had higher status, and communal, in that all labor was valued and crucial for the success of the harvest. The last step of the field work, loading the bundles onto racks and wagons and transporting them to the thresher, first reveals this hierarchy. When hauling, one man drove each wagon and one or two stackers or pitchers assisted for each wagon. The stackers had to stack the shocks on the wagon so they would safely make the trip to the thresher for unloading. This stacking required skill, and the stacker set the pace of the threshing. This crucial task carried a relatively high status.

The driver and the stackers on the wagons were assisted by spike pitchers, who stayed in the fields to help load all the wagons. Work in the field was hard and was respected as "manly" labor, but because it required less skill, it was near the bottom of the male hierarchy of threshing work. Most often, younger workers, inexperienced workers, and hired help worked in the field. Era Bell Thompson described her city-bred father's and brother's first encounter with this work in North Dakota: "The slick, round handle of the pitchfork galled their soft hands as they staggered under the burden of the golden bundles; prickly beards of wheat worked down their shirts and into their bodies to torture them, dry stubble cut through their thin city soles." Although these workers were at the bottom of the threshing hierarchy, farm people still valued good workers in these positions. Conflict occurred when workers did not meet the work standards of cooperation and effort. An Iowa farmer who worked on the wagons remembered: "Some of them [field spike pitchers] acting smart would loaf along and you never did get a rest, just moving from one load to the other. If they didn't do their part you had to be able to speak up for yourself. You could work too hard, in 90 to 100 degree temperature and kill yourself." Even those in the least-skilled threshing positions could disrupt the smooth operation of the workday. Shirking was the worst of harvesting sins because of the interdependence of all threshing tasks.[8]

Threshing lore lauded the power of the threshing machine. The ritual of threshing began with the arrival of the machine; diarists always noted its arrival. Oral histories and novels elaborate on the excitement the machine brought. In *RFD #3*, Homer Croy, a novelist who was raised on a farm in Nodaway County, Missouri, described the steam thresher:

Two weeks later was threshing time, that busiest, most exciting day of the year. The engine came down the road with its train of thresher and blower behind it, rattling and clanking to the unevenness of the road; behind was the water wagon drawn by horses, the driver humped up on the seat, one leg lopped over the other, contently smoking a corn-cob pipe. The procession swung in, the snorting and puffing of the engine echoing among the buildings. The engine turned into the hog lot, the great wide wheels with their iron cleats leaving behind a trail of broken corn cobs pressed into the ground. Turkeys went fluttering away, guineas flew screaming into the tops of the peach trees with ear-splitting protests.

The size of the machine impressed farm people, but its arrival also meant that that family was taking its turn hosting an event of that important season.[9]

The thresher loosened the grain from the straw, blew the straw out onto the ground, and dumped the cleaned grain. Early in the century, steam most commonly powered the thresher, but the use of gasoline-powered threshers increased by the 1920s and 1930s. Between 1900 and World War II, the binder and the stationary thresher were the primary harvest tools in the Midwest, and the basic work of the thresher, whatever the power source, remained the same.[10] The workers began by setting up the machine, stabilizing it in the ground, and attaching the belt. On the day threshing began, the operator of the steam engine arose first, usually as early as three or four o'clock in the morning, to get the engine fired and running by six o'clock. John Vaage, an engine man who had taken exams to become a steam engineer and was licensed in Canada and Minnesota as well as in North Dakota, recalled that in a good season, he would get little sleep.

The threshing crew consisted of eight to ten people, in addition to the haulers and stackers in the field. The crew included an engine man, who operated the power source; a separator man, who operated the thresher; people to unload wagons and feed the bundles into the machine; one or two people to sack or tend the grain; and one or two people to stack the straw. In general, farm people described threshing work positively. Christ Larson of Mountrail County, North Dakota, worked on threshing crews as a teenager. As the "firer" man, he put straw down the chute. Because he had to keep it full all the time, he had little time to relax. Despite the pace, he enjoyed the work and liked to listen to the engine puffing and watch the smoke. The only job that farmers described with less-than-fond memories was stacking the straw. This job exposed workers to the worst of the heat from the machine and, when combined with the itchy, irritating straw or the beard on barley, was not a pleasant experience. Arthur Wileden, recalling his boyhood Wisconsin farm, stated that the people who hosted the threshing built their own straw stack because it was the most "disagreeable" job. This neighborly courtesy assured that the job would be performed by all the members of a community ring.[11]

The men who ran the threshing machine sat at the top of the threshing hierarchy. The engineer and the separator man received the highest wages. Usually these men had special training or skills with machinery. Sometimes they also owned and operated the machine for custom (paid) work or for use in a community ring. Farm people valued highly the ability of these men to keep the machinery running, despite rather frequent breakdowns. Although much lore surrounds the power of the machines, they were clearly fallible. It took human, particularly "male," skills to operate them. Men who had mechanical knowledge and could improvise solutions when problems arose won high praise. Stories of men fixing broken machines in unusual ways—with coins, for example—appear frequently in oral histories. John Faul, a farmer from Wells County, North Dakota, described a time when his skill gained him new status in threshing work. The first time he used a gas engine to thresh, he knew nothing about it, so he hired a man named Charley to run it. When the machine broke down, Faul suggested putting water in it, but Charley insisted on taking it apart, losing precious workdays. When it still would not work, Faul took over. He poured water into the machine and it worked. Charley quit in anger. Faul's stories of breakdowns and quirky, simple repairs not only illustrate his pride in his ability to improvise and repair machines, but also point to the imperfections of technology and the constant need for human skill and common sense to operate it.[12]

Although farm men prized knowledge of machines, such knowledge did not replace physical skills, strength, and endurance as the central elements of male work values. Farmers who fed the machines had high status because their work combined many skills and set the pace of the threshing. In Homer Croy's novel about life in rural Missouri, the area's most respected farmer had a variety of skills, mechanical and physical. First, he checked the thresher to see that the operators had set it up correctly and that it was in good operating condition, clearly showing his superior knowledge of machines. When the threshing began, he fed the machine: "His arms reached out while he watched the crying cylinder; he ran his arms under the bundles, lifted them, gave them a half twist—the long heavy, yellow stalks slid off his arms in a well-calculated curve into the whirling teeth." The job required physical strength and fortitude: "His sleeves had been cut off at the elbow leaving exposed his hairy, thick-muscled arms, scratched and scarred from barbwire, kicks from horses, slashes from boars when he had been 'tusking' them. Such cuts meant nothing to him; he continued at his tremendous pace. . . . He was ready for his work as the most important man on the 'set.'"

Farmers did not assign these different tasks solely on the basis of skill, but also by community status. Community work reflected the rural social order. Farmers reserved the best jobs for those who were part of the community, those who exchanged work, rather than for the hired help. Hired men often did the least-skilled tasks, such as hauling bundles. Owners and neighbors more likely tended and fed the threshing machine. The hierarchy of jobs reinforced the important position of neighborhood men as heads of households, but the hired man who had special physical or mechanical skills gained higher status as a good worker or a man who understood machines. One North Dakota farmer liked threshing work because it was a social time and "[you] always had your place."[13] The event reaffirmed patterns; it brought the community together and assigned an order and use to every person in it.

Men's work ritualized handling the grain; women's work rituals centered on serving the workers. Women created the threshing dinner, the heart of the community threshing experience. Accounts of meals—both their quantity and their quality—enrich harvest folklore. The dinner served as a break from work and brought workers from all parts of the harvest—field, thresher, and home—together. However, the preparation of meals, as well as the readying of the home for any crew members who were lodging during the threshing, meant work for women. Women's labor was integral to the threshing production process, and transformed it into a cultural expression of community.

Women began preparing for the arrival of the threshing crew several days before the threshing. The woman who hosted the threshers planned the meals for crews of from eight to twenty-five people and coordinated the labor of other women who exchanged work. Careful organization was essential. Food was prepared in advance of the threshing. Nellie Kedzie Jones, in her advice column to farm women, recommended that cookies and piecrusts be baked three days before the threshing. On the day before, bread should be baked, a ham boiled and baked for sandwiches, and potatoes peeled, at least four for each man. Women also had to clean and ready space in the house or barn, if some members of the crew were lodging. Anna Pratt Erickson cleaned up the shed for lodgers before the 1919 threshing and baked twenty-seven oatmeal cakes. Women and children had other diverse duties. Often they ran errands for the threshers and field workers. For example, on the same day Erickson prepared for threshers, she went to a neighbor's home to get sacks for the grain. In addition, neighboring women often brought their children, and women and girls shared childcare responsibilities.[14]

The hosting woman's day, like that of the engineer, began before that of the rest of the crew. Since threshing or field work began at seven in the morning, women served breakfast as early as six, so cooking began at four or five. After cleaning up breakfast, women began preparing to serve lunch. The harvest ritual could include five meals—breakfast, morning lunch (at about nine), the noon dinner, afternoon lunch (at about three), and supper at the end of the workday, as late as nine or ten o'clock at night. Local workers usually ate breakfast and supper at home, but hired help, machine crews, and family ate these meals in the host's home. Some farms served an afternoon lunch and no morning lunch, and others recorded that if someone wanted a lunch he brought it himself. But generally, two lunches were the rule. Farm women often had a pitcher of lemonade constantly ready for the field workers, who would stop to visit and drink when they had finished bringing in a load to the thresher.[15]

Women served lunches in the field; a typical lunch described by one Iowa woman included sandwiches, cookies, cake, and lemonade. Taking the food to the field meant a chance to escape a hot kitchen, but, when wedged between cleaning from the previous meal and preparing the next one, it was a hectic task. An Iowa woman called it "running with the food." Serving in the field could also be awkward. One North Dakota woman recalled that, as girls, she and her sister had served the lunch. One held a pan full of cups while the other balanced the coffeepot and drove the wagon. Male farm workers enjoyed the breaks that food and drink provided. One Iowa farmer jokingly derided the so-called progress of modern farm technology: "Do the young folks think we are making progress? How about the five meals a day!" Meals united the work of women to the male work of the threshing, and food symbolized community sharing.[16]

The threshing dinner connected themes of community to the work of the harvest, and provided an arena where women's work skills were recognized. All the workers gathered; men and women rejoined the entire community. The meals were lavish. Women served the noon meal at the house, inside on expanded tables or outside on benches or improvised picnic tables. The threshing and field workers washed up at the kitchen sink or with washpails and towels set up outside the house. Although Nellie Kedzie Jones advised in her columns that women serve meals on paper plates in the fields, picnic style, most farm women resisted this change in their work. Transporting involved precious time, and paper or tin service precious cash, neither of which was in great supply before the harvest. In addition, serving the meal in the home with regular service emphasized the hospitality of the hosts and the cooperative nature of the work. Hosts treated workers like guests and offered the hospitality of the home. This hospitality marked women's accomplishments.

Women demonstrated their skills through their cooking. Dinners were huge, including meat (roast beef, chicken, or ham), potatoes, vegetables from the garden, salads, bread or rolls, several kinds of pie or cake, and coffee or lemonade. As a Wisconsin farm woman said, no one could expect that kind of meal every day. Following patterns of sex-segregated community work, only women and girls served the noon meal. In her advice columns, Nellie Kedzie Jones suggested that men help serve and clear dishes, but she admitted that this "was an unusual proceeding and most men would have botched it," suggesting that women valued their skills and knew men did not possess them. Both women and men judged women's work skills. Women "prided themselves in cooking" and valued men's appreciation. They enjoyed seeing a hungry crew "do justice to the meal." Farm people respected cooking skills, and both men and women told stories of harvest dinners. Bad cooks became the source of jokes, but the good cook was praised with lavish descriptions of her product and tales of the hard work and time involved in its preparation. As in male work culture, women's work culture valued hard work and skill. However, although men alone judged the work of men, women and men judged women's labor in a gender-integrated community setting.[17]

Because it celebrated the values of neighborhood unity and shared work associated with the harvest, the noon meal made women's work visible and crucial to the success of the entire threshing operation. The rest of women's labor did not share this gender-integrated community status, and closely resembled their daily chores. Women rarely mentioned cleaning after meals at threshing time and described it only in terms of the time it took, or as their least favorite task. The absence of folklore surrounding the evening supper also indicates the centrality of the noon meal. Supper, coming at the end of a long day rather than in the midst of the excitement, was rarely a shared community meal. Farm people ate a quick supper because another early rising and another hard day of work followed. Even at the end of one farm family's period of hosting, the next day brought another neighbor's turn, and the spirit of exchange obliged one to assist.

Sometimes farm people celebrated the end of the season, when all the threshing in a neighborhood or ring was complete, with a picnic, a "thrashing ice cream," or a dance;[18] however, most farmers still had other crops to harvest. In fact, farm people did not celebrate the end of work, but the work itself, and the sharing of that work among men and women. The threshing dinner symbolized the importance of women's work to the work of men and to the creation of the rural community.

Threshing rituals provided an arena both for showing off individual skills and for assuming a place in the community's social order. Stories of competition and rites of passage illustrate these critical elements of the threshing process. Farm people competed for status on the basis of work skills and games. However, shared cultural assumptions placed limits on this competition and individualism in order to maintain the event's cooperative purpose. During the threshing, youths claimed "manhood" or "womanhood" by taking on new roles that symbolized their adult status in the community. Threshing rituals supplied a way of establishing status within the existing social web of community relations.

Competition and contests took place in all phases of threshing work. One Wisconsin farmer recalled keeping yield-per-acre records to see who in the ring produced the most. Gerald Goodwin, an Iowa farmer, remembered another kind of competition.

And it was always competition in the loading to see who was going to be the last out and have to clean up the field at the end of the day. If I use some judgment whether to load heavy or lighter on a particular load, I could jockey my position. . . . Well, you either thought or you was the goat every time.

Both men and women competed. Fay Goodwin, in Iowa, and Clara Jacobs, in North Dakota, noted that hosting farm women always tried to outdo each other in their meal preparations. For men, competition during work carried over into contests and games after work. One farmer described racing horses when going home for supper. During the interview, his son joined in, saying, "we did that, too," and the two proceeded to reminisce excitedly about the good times. Competition and games provided excitement and fun, and the talented enjoyed status in the community.[19]

There were, however, limits to competition. If competition went too far, it could upset the sense of shared work and equal participation crucial to the harvest. The competition Gerald Goodwin described was not an all-out effort, but instead had rules of cooperation at its base: "You didn't mind taking your turn cleaning up, but if you got a couple of guys who were loading heavy or light every time, it got you mad after a while." Although they competed, everyone was expected to take a turn being the "loser." Farm people held their competitions to community standards of practicality and equality. For example, a woman who used a white table-cloth on an outside dinner table became a source of humor. Neighbors saw her as a "little more well off," and, the story implied, she was a bit pretentious in showing her wealth off in this way. For the rest of the neighborhood, a "new oilcloth" was a sign of "doing good," and using one was clearly the more acceptable practice. Clara Jacobs described not only women's competition in cooking, but also its limits. "Got so bad they were making cream puffs to send out for lunch. . . . Mother drew the line there." Always winning, showing off one's superior wealth, or pushing skills to a point that required too much work or an impractical effort led to neighborhood censure.[20]

As adults vied for status through cooperative competition, youths gained adult status by taking on new roles in the threshing. Although children had plenty of time to play, building rope swings from twine or getting in trouble for walking on straw stacks, they also had particular jobs assigned to them. A farm child might run errands, supply water for thirsty field and thresher crews, drive an extra horse for the binder, take lunch to the field, pass bundles, do odd jobs around the thresher, or, if the child's family owned the thresher, perhaps stoke the fire. Many of these jobs were not gender-defined but were assigned by age. Boys served water and took out lunch. Girls passed bundles and watched the engine. Everyone had a work role in the harvest.[21]

When children reached a certain age, their work began to change, taking on more gender-specific characteristics that signaled approaching adulthood. This was particularly true for boys, who became men as they gained the skill and physical strength to complete higher-status threshing jobs. In the late nineteenth century, before the advent of the binder, Hamlin Garland wrote that "binding on a station" was "man's work" and a "boy's goal." At fourteen, he became a stacker, and this "made a man of" him. In the 1910s in North Dakota, Era Bell Thompson's brother Tom "took the bundle wagon out alone. He was already a man." In 1938, Pauline Olson, a North Dakota farm woman, observed her son's new status in her diary: "Jack was out as a real man Spick [sic] pitching and held out every day to [sic]. not so bad at 15 years." The annual harvest ritual provided an opportunity for measuring a boy's ability to perform the skilled work of threshing and marked a transition to manhood.[22]

For girls, the road to maturity was less closely tied to work skills. Although girls clearly assisted in the kitchen and traded work with other women during the harvest, the credit for the meals went to the woman in charge of the household. Young, single women rarely took over cooking chores during the harvest. Winning praise for a well-baked pie may have been seen as a step toward adulthood, but it is rarely described in those terms. Most frequently, teenage girls appear in stories connected to court-ship. Young women often served the meal and used the opportunity to talk or flirt with single men: "The young girls always found this an excit-ing time waiting on the tables for there was sure to be some good-looking unmarried man in the crew." For young women, achieving womanhood centered on courtship and marriage; consequently, harvest folklore ritual-ized their interaction with men.

Boarding work did become a rite of passage for young women after their marriages. Farm mothers trained girls so that they could successfully organize the threshing. For example, Isabel Baumann, who grew up on a Wisconsin tobacco farm and then taught school after finishing her educa-tion, had little experience with the work associated with threshing. Then she married a Wisconsin dairy farmer. Her first experience organizing the cooking for threshers came shortly after her honeymoon. Her husband's cousin assisted the "greenhorn" teacher. This served as her introduction to the work skills necessary for organizing meals for twenty people. Girls' transition to maturity, unlike that of boys, was gauged less on the acqui-sition of specific work skills and more on their assumption of the duties of the manager of household labor, which usually came at marriage.[23] Communities valued women's work skills and girls clearly learned these skills, but farm people did not acknowledge womanhood based on these skills alone.

Threshing rituals recreated both the gender-segregated networks of la-bor and the gender-integrated social networks of community. Men de-fined themselves most through the former, women through the latter. Boys moved to manhood through their labor; girls gained status through their position within the family. Men's competitions in the fields set their status within the hierarchy of the male community; women's competitions and the evaluation of their work were ultimately tied to the evaluations of men as well as women. Men did value the gender-integrated social interactions of meals, and the meals solidified their place in the community as heads of households. In their tales of women's accomplishments, men valued the work of women and its connection to the success of the threshing. Young men might also hope to impress young women with their skills in compe-tition and work. However, women had a greater stake in gender-integrated community interactions because they had to rely on men for resources and for their place in families and the rural community.

Threshing was not only an important social event, but also a major economic undertaking. Harvesting and threshing made large demands on the labor and capital resources of a farm family and a farm neighborhood. Social rituals defined economic relations; through them farm people shared resources and kept cash expenditures low. Nevertheless, exchanges often did not provide enough labor or capital for equipment to complete a job. Farm people's economic transactions ran the gamut from gift to barter to cash, and threshing involved these same practices. Although farm people met their needs for labor and machinery in a variety of ways, they continued to invest even the more cash-oriented transactions with social harvest rituals.

The machinery for threshing required a considerable capital investment, much greater than most farmers could afford. Even small farmers could reasonably invest in a binder or header, but a farmer who purchased a threshing rig needed significant acreage to make up for the cost of investment and operation. Most farm people either cooperatively owned or custom hired threshing equipment. While cooperative ownership did not predominate, custom threshers often worked locally, keeping resources within a region. The arrival of gasoline-powered threshers in the late 1920s and 1930s made individual or neighborhood ownership even more common. Since gasoline-powered threshers were smaller than steam rigs, neighbors could purchase a small rig cooperatively and pay a local farmer who had a gasoline tractor to power it.[24] Even when farmers hired a machine for cash, they tended to pair this cash transaction with exchanges of labor within the neighborhood.

Cooperative ownership, less common than custom hiring, generally took place in communities with tight ethnic or religious bases or with clearly developed informal patterns of sharing and exchange. For example, Clara Jacobs recalled that her parents' small German neighborhood in western North Dakota owned a threshing rig cooperatively, while her husband, Jake, who lived in an ethnically mixed area in Mountrail County, North Dakota, recalled only custom threshers. The ring organized cooperative work and sometimes the ownership of machinery. The threshing ring was a group of farmers, usually from five to twelve families, that organized labor and capital to complete the harvesting and threshing of their grain. The group exchanged labor and moved from farm to farm until the threshing work was complete. Sometimes these rings purchased the threshing rig cooperatively. Such ownership often followed other cooperative enterprises. Wisconsin Farmers' Union leaders recalled that in the 1920s and 1930s, threshing was only one of many cooperative efforts, including silo filling, corn shredding, and marketing.[25]

Many farm neighborhoods adapted other methods of ownership to reflect community traditions. Individual ownership was common; however, this private ownership often worked within the traditions of the ring. One neighbor might own a machine, but he would thresh for all those in the ring. As with cooperatively owned machines, the thresher would start at one end of the ring and work to the other. Because more damage was

8. Nellie Kedzie Jones, leader of the University of Wisconsin's extension service educational program, "on the agricultural extension home economics circuit" in 1920.

9. Marketing livestock was almost exclusively a male preserve. This is a "pen of top hampshire hogs" at the Farmers' Union Livestock Commission pens at the Union Stock Yards, Chicago, 1927.

10. Farm women, like men, organized to sell their products or ease their labor. One example is the River Falls Cooperative Laundry, River Falls, Wisconsin, 1928.

Facing page:
Top: 11. Signs of the "modern" farm community are illustrated in this 1929 advertisement for the *Farm Journal*. The items portrayed in this advertisement are similar to those that were used by agricultural professionals to measure rural standards of living.

Bottom: 12. Differences of economic conditions are apparent in photographs of farm homes taken by different agricultural agencies. The Rural Electrification Administration promoted the success of its programs with photographs of families at dinner surrounded by modern electric appliances.

13. In the photographs of the Division of Farm Population and Rural Life, radio was a community event, but the Federal Extension Service portrayed the radio as an entertainment for the nuclear family. Champaign County, Illinois, July 1937.

14. The Farm Security Administration portrayed the other side of farm life during the Great Depression. This farm woman worked in conditions very different from those in the "modern" farm kitchens promoted by other agricultural agencies. "Mrs. Ole Thompson, wife of a farmer, carrying food to the table." Nesson Township, Williams County, North Dakota, October 1937.

possible the longer the grain stood in shocks or stacks, farmers assured equitable treatment in several ways. Sometimes they did half of each farmer's crop, and the thresher would work around the ring twice. Other rings would alternate the starting point for the ring each year, giving each farmer a chance to have his crop threshed first. Ownership of the rig did not guarantee the owner special treatment. John Vaage, a farmer in Mountrail County, bought his first rig when the neighbor, who owned the machine used in the community, decided that all his grain should be threshed first. "We didn't go for that," recalled Vaage.[26]

Farmers most commonly hired an itinerant custom rig, a privately owned rig that threshed outside the immediate neighborhood of the owner. Generally, however, these rigs worked within a small geographic area rather than following the harvest from south to north. Although machines traveled greater distances in the wheat belt of the Southwest (Texas, Oklahoma, and Kansas), in North Dakota farmers hired machines from within the state, or sometimes from Canada. Even when farmers custom-hired a thresher, a local neighborhood ring, rather than an individual farmer, contracted the rig. In Northwest Iowa, according to Gerald Goodwin, the neighbors "all voted on who we wanted to do our threshing. . . . He set his price and we all had a meeting and all agreed, that was it." Two men in the nearby town of Correctionville had machines, and "they always battled back and forth to see who'd get the choicest runs."

Farm people integrated the itinerant custom rig into local work traditions in several ways. Even when hiring a threshing crew, neighborhoods still exchanged work in the fields and in the house. Particularly in the wheat belt, regional crews employed the younger sons of farmers, who would thresh in their own neighborhoods and then go with the machine to other neighborhoods in the region. Daughters, too, sometimes found employment in the cook cars of these larger rigs in North Dakota. This increased links between regional crews and local communities. The owners of rigs often returned to the same runs every year, adding stability and friendliness to the event and helping integrate the financial transactions into local work traditions.[27]

Generally, the owners of threshers charged a certain amount per bushel threshed or by the hour. This covered the owner's costs for operating the machine and a fraction of his initial investment. Farmers in the ring supplied teams, rigs, and labor. Early in the twentieth century, in some regions, farms in a ring had roughly equal resources and acreage, guaranteeing a roughly equal exchange. As the twentieth century progressed, farm sizes became more varied, and farm people established more elaborate means of assuring equity in exchange. For example, Brownie McVey of Pocahontas County, Iowa, recalled that, at first, exchange was mostly informal, with larger farms providing more teams or labor, but no one really keeping track of bushels or hours. From the 1920s to the 1950s, farmers paid the thresher so much per bushel, and "if I had less oats and put in as many hours as the rest of them," said McVey, "then I would draw money back." The farmers used "belt time," the number of hours the separator ran, to estimate hours of labor, but this was not exact since time spent in field work did not correspond precisely to machine time. The person with the most oats became the source of cash. He paid into a kitty and others drew from it or added to it depending on the amount of acres they owned and the amount of labor provided.[28]

Although this represented a movement away from older traditions of exchange, it preserved cooperative ideas of fairness and compensated for increasing differences in farm size. The kitty, a community pot, allowed the farmers to avoid a situation in which the wealthier paid the poorer individually. It was a community harvest, and individuals worked for the group, not for one another. Despite the increased use of cash, the informality of the threshing system and the somewhat imprecise estimates of costs maintained the spirit of exchange and sharing, and helped balance out inequities among farm families who had different economic resources.

Farmers mobilized the labor for threshing in a number of ways, using family members, neighborhood work exchanges, monthly hired hands, and day labor hired specifically for the harvest and threshing work. In many farm neighborhoods, local traditions of family labor and work exchange made hired help, aside from the actual threshing machine crew, an unnecessary cash extravagance. Nevertheless, hired labor remained crucial to small-grain production, particularly in the wheat belt. Agricultural institutions believed that hiring labor was a major problem of the harvest, and argued that workers brought disruption to the countryside. In fact, hired labor was more often local than itinerant, and rural, not urban, in origin. The threshing gave poorer farmers and young farm men a chance to earn income to help support their farms.

Family labor was the backbone of the harvest. Family members cut and shocked the grain, particularly in regions that did not specialize in wheat or when wheat farmers had little cash for hired help. For example, W. B. Siebert described the 1937 harvest near Greene, North Dakota, as wholly a family affair. Siebert's father and brother Louis cut the wheat, while the youngest son and both parents shocked. Women labored in the field not only in emergencies, but regularly at peak seasonal times. Extended families also provided extra labor. Around 1900 in Door County, Wisconsin, Frank Krueger primarily exchanged work with his brother, Fred, who also farmed in the area.[29]

Most farm families could not rely on family labor alone to complete the threshing. Although all the families described above used family labor for harvesting, they also exchanged labor with neighbors for threshing and meal preparation. Exchanging work kept cash expenditures to a minimum while it cemented neighborhood bonds. For example, family and exchanged labor completed all boarding work. Farmers only rarely hired cook cars along with steam rigs to provide meals and spare the women extra work. A cook car added a one- or two-cent charge per bushel. Outside the wheat belt, most families relied exclusively on exchanged and family labor.[30]

However, larger farms and farms located in the wheat belt required extra labor at threshing time. Arguing from the perspective of larger, specialized farms, agricultural institutions labeled this need for hired help the principal problem of small-grain production and used it to promote the development and use of new labor-saving technology. Agricultural professionals described transients as a "social evil" that disrupted local life and introduced an unsafe element to the harvest. Lorna Doone Beers, in a 1925 novel that otherwise supported the radical farmers' political organization, the Nonpartisan League, portrayed a stereotypical itinerant worker:

Each spring there was an exodus from the cities all over the country—from the gutters, the cheap lodging houses, the saloons, the curbs, the shadowy doorsteps, the breadlines, the charity establishments, the filthy lobbies of bad hotels. These slouching figures, these tattered creatures are headed to the harvest fields. . . . They are reinforced as they go along by the ne'er-do-wells from the small towns.

Even H. Paul Douglass, whose Interchurch World Movement study exposed the problems and exploitation that migrant workers faced, defined labor as a problem and encouraged the introduction of machines to lessen the need for seasonal workers.[31]

Evidence does not support this portrayal of workers as itinerants, hoboes, and transients from cities. In areas of the northern Great Plains outside the wheat belt, farmers hired labor as monthly help throughout the busy spring, summer, and fall. These laborers came from nearby communities. Even day labor was more often local than itinerant. In his study of the 1919 wheat harvest, H. Paul Douglass estimated that only 20 percent of the total farm labor force was itinerant. USDA studies of the harvests in 1919, 1920, and 1921 revealed that 40 percent to 50 percent of even nonlocal transient workers worked in only one state.[32]

These transient workers, as USDA and IWM studies reveal, did not fit the negative stereotype. Eighty percent of the workers surveyed came from the wheat states and the tier of states immediately to the east. At least 55 percent of the itinerant workers were born on farms. The actual figure was probably higher since the USDA studies relied primarily on those who registered in its employment offices. Men from cities registered more often than local laborers who understood how to get threshing jobs. Of the itinerant workers born on farms, 42 percent still worked in agriculture, while the others did "common" or "semiskilled" labor. Of the transient workers, 69 percent had participated in a harvest before, and 38 percent had worked in four or more harvests. Of the workers interviewed (including local workers), 25 percent had worked in the harvest for more than ten seasons, and 78 percent had been in one or more harvests during the previous five years.[33] Although the workers interviewed did include large numbers of nonfarm laborers, these people had more connections to agriculture than critics implied. The work force had more stability than the words "transients" and "hoboes" suggest.

Even though agricultural institutions defined migrant labor as threatening and unreliable, local sources reveal both positive and negative attitudes toward hired help. Farm people's reasons for disliking seasonal help differ from the criticisms leveled by agricultural institutions. Although North Dakota might differ from other regions (for reasons to be described later), oral histories from that state show that local values shaped attitudes toward hired workers. Farm people most commonly criticized hired help because these people did not work the same long hours that farmers did, or lacked the necessary skills to do the work well. Farmers expected threshing workers to share their values of hard labor, although the wage workers did not receive the benefits of reciprocity that those in farm families gained from long hours. Clara Jacobs, for example, recalled that laborers who belonged to the IWW, a radical labor organization that had some success in organizing farm laborers in the 1910s, caused no trouble, but they did quit early and were "no good" with horses. Rain delays also led to conflict. Farmers believed workers should do chores while the farmer was providing board, but workers believed this was unfair since they were not hired to do chores. Peter Paulson noted that his father hired IWW men to work for the entire day, but they refused to hay to fill in the hours remaining after they had finished shocking, the job for which they were hired.[34]

Although some North Dakota farmers described problems with workers, particularly those who belonged to unions, many others remembered their hired help in more positive ways. The ultimate compliment for them, as for farm men in general, was to be called a "good worker." Despite Paulson's disagreement with IWW workers, he still remembered them as "good workers," if "independent." Farmers considered the best workers to be those with rural backgrounds. These men valued physical work and had the skills that could win respect. Although the Jacobses found city workers wanting in skill and desire, they praised their crews from Minnesota and Wisconsin as very good workers because they were "brought up that way." Others farmers had positive recollections of workers who were lumberjacks, railroad men, or farmers from the South. H. Paul Douglass reported that farmers favored men from Montana because they, too, were farmers, and the employers had sympathy for those whose crops had failed. He believed such favoritism grew from feelings of "class solidarity," as well as appreciation for the farming experience exhibited by these men.

Many farmers, particularly in a poorer state like North Dakota, understood the conditions of their workers. Alfred Berg remembered that his father got along well with organized IWW workers because he had been a "working man himself and knew what they had to put up with." They worked hard, and he liked to pay them decent wages. If they were talked to and treated "okay," they were no problem. Farmers often labored beside their workers, and many farmers had themselves worked in the harvest as young men; this could lead to cordial working relationships. Many crews returned year after year, and networks developed in which friends and relatives of workers returned to the same farms.[35] In these ways, farm people used neighboring practices to integrate workers into the harvest rituals, sharing neighborhood work values and skills and creating informal networks to maintain steady employment for workers and a reliable labor source for grain farmers.

Farmers did not view their workers as a "social evil." Even when the workers came from different regions, farm people often welcomed them as unusual visitors who had experiences and stories to share, adding to the excitement of threshing. One farmer noted that there were "no bad eggs." As a child, he had hauled lunch to the field and once overheard a worker tell a "woman story." One of the worker's peers immediately criticized the worker for telling the story in front of a child, saying, "I didn't think you was so raw." Ethel Fosberg remembered that workers from Kansas were used to "living rough" and often arrived "black and whiskered." However, she thought they were respectable because their first request was for hot water for a shave.[36] Even those with negative attitudes toward transients did not share the professionals' view of workers as a "social evil."

Farm laborers who worked on threshing crews within the region where they lived, for their part, also described the work of the harvest in ways that blended the familiarity of farm neighborhoods with the excitement of traveling and meeting new people. Farm youths, particularly in the northern plains, commonly worked on threshing crews to earn income. As an engine man from 1914 through the 1920s, John Vaage recalled that his crews always had the same run, the same crew, and a cook car, so it was "like a home." They were all single men and had a "good time." Jake

Jacobs worked for threshing crews and remembered playing poker until ten o'clock, when the boss would stop the game. His crew began in his local area, but also traveled. When working within the neighborhood the crew members boarded, maintaining neighborhood customs and sharing meals, but when outside the neighborhood they took a cook car. Hazel James of Wells County, North Dakota, worked in a cook car. She prepared meals for sixteen men in the very hot car, cleaned the car, and did the wash. She looked forward to the season, which lasted anywhere from two weeks to a month or more, because she was happy to get the three dollars a day and enjoyed meeting all the "nice guys" who came in for the harvest.[37]

These workers recalled being integrated into local traditions and welcomed as returning friends or "good workers," but workers from outside the region experienced more hardships. Outside workers did not have access to informal networks of employment and had difficulty following the entire harvest. The main problem for laborers was finding a consistent string of jobs that minimized layoffs between jobs. Boarding and lodging expenses during these layoffs ate up cash. Work could also be interrupted by rain, which increased costs and lessened the workers' income. Although the federal government set up employment offices, during and after World War I, to allocate labor and establish wages, the most common method of finding work remained going to regional centers and waiting for farmers to come to town and hire crews. Migrant laborers experienced hostility in these towns, where townspeople considered them disturbances and often hustled them out of town or charged exorbitant rates for food and lodging.

Workers were exploited in other ways as well. Some farmers and agencies overadvertised jobs, drawing too many workers. Workers might be promised a certain wage in an urban center, but arrive at a farm to find that local conditions dictated a reduction in their pay. Railroads charged high prices for passage, were not convenient for north-south travel, and were unreliable and unsafe. Because Nebraska and the northern harvest region needed fewer workers, many workers could not get a longer run by following the harvest north; if they did get jobs, the wages were lower in these states. With these complications, it is not surprising that most workers stayed in one state or worked only the spring wheat or winter wheat harvest, moving east and west, not north and south. These reports may overestimate the level of workers' contentment, especially given the success of the IWW in the 1910s, but in general, workers complained less about working conditions or problems on individual farms than about the process of finding work throughout the harvest. Although the work was physically demanding, workers generally felt satisfied with it, the board and lodging they received, and the way most farmers treated them.[38] Many workers, particularly those in regional networks, used the harvest to supplement their incomes from their family farms or from other seasonal or agricultural labor. When agricultural institutions studied the problem of the harvest, they did not evaluate the impact of agricultural technology on these workers' incomes or on their small farms.

As farm people organized the harvest, they could choose types of technology, labor organizations, and crops that preserved work traditions and neighborhood exchange, or they could make choices that relied on specialized crops, more expensive machinery, and transient day labor. Several factors affected farm people's choice of technology and labor organization. First, regional variations in climate and soil conditions, as well as the physical characteristics of individual farms, favored certain types of crop specializations and influenced the choice of technology. Economic conditions, such as the size of a farm, the amount of capital available, prices and markets, and the cost, availability, and suitability of technology also shaped farmers' choices. Social and cultural factors, although less often studied by agricultural historians and economists, played an equally important part in farmers' decision making. Farm labor and cash resources depended on family size and composition, as well as on the stage of the family's life cycle. Community traditions of exchange and cooperation and the general economic condition of a neighborhood were also important factors in farm management decisions. Finally, cultural attitudes toward work, technology, crop specialization, and family farm goals vitally contributed to the decision-making process. These factors created a complex web surrounding the central decisions of farm management, and affected the pace of agricultural change.

A comparison of two diaries kept by farmers outside the wheat belt illuminates the complexity of the factors shaping individual choices of technology and labor organization. Anna Pratt Erickson lived on a small farm (80 acres) near the town of Athens in north-central Wisconsin. Erickson's income came from dairy products, truck and garden produce, potatoes, and fruits. Elmer G. Powers farmed a moderate-sized farm (280 acres) in Boone County in central Iowa. He, too, followed a diversified farming pattern, but specialized in the products that predominated in the region, primarily corn and livestock. Small grains provided feed for Erickson's and Powers's animals, but Powers also sold the grain as a secondary cash crop. Erickson's region in Wisconsin did not have the richest agricultural land in the state, so there were few pressures for farm consolidation. Her neighborhood remained a stable one of small farms throughout the period from 1900 to 1940. Powers's farm was located on prime Iowa agricultural land, and his neighborhood changed considerably dur-

ing the period; it underwent increases in consolidation, outside ownership, and tenancy, particularly during the 1930s. Erickson encountered
the new agriculture within a local context, through the local high school
and her Homemakers' Club. Powers, on the other hand, participated in
the Farm Bureau and extension service, and even wrote a special diary in
the 1930s to submit to *Wallace's Farmer*. All these factors shaped the harvesting and threshing practices of these two farmers.

Although Erickson moved to Wisconsin in 1912, she rarely recorded
threshing details until after her first husband's death in late 1917. From 1917
through the 1930s, Erickson paid for custom work rather than purchasing
harvesting and threshing equipment. Except between 1922 and 1926, when
she was married to her second husband, Erickson hired neighbors to cut
oats, while she assisted with a scythe. Her second husband, Joe, also a local
farmer, owned a binder, and during their marriage he harvested Erickson's
land as well as his own. She also custom-hired a thresher. In 1918, she recorded paying eight dollars to thresh eighty-one bushels of oats. By 1934,
the Ericksons were threshing five hundred bushels of oats. When Erickson
hired technology for the harvest, she got it from other neighbors in the
area. These neighbors formed the backbone of work exchanges, as well as
providing the technology for harvesting and threshing.

To perform the work of the harvest and threshing, Erickson depended
on a combination of family and neighborhood labor, both exchanged and
paid. The amount of labor hired and exchanged depended a great deal on
the life cycle of her own family and the presence of adult male workers in
the household. In the years after her first husband's death and before her
second marriage (1917–22), Erickson's children were small, so family labor
provided only a small supplement. Erickson assisted in the harvest and provided the meals; hired men, neighbors who assisted her throughout the
year, performed the field and threshing work. During her marriage to Joe,
the family became more active in threshing exchanges, with Joe doing much
of the field and threshing work, while Anna exchanged boarding.

As her children got older, Erickson relied on them as field labor, especially after her divorce from Joe in 1926. While hiring a neighbor to cut the
oats with a binder, Anna and her second-oldest daughter, Dot, shocked.
Her oldest daughter, Orma, cared for the household and children. Although women could do the family-based field work, men did the community-based threshing. Her workers were part of earlier labor exchanges,
but in the later years Erickson probably hired the crew since she had little
male labor to contribute to the threshing. She and her daughters continued to exchange the gender-appropriate boarding work. By the 1930s,
threshing exchanges increased again as Erickson's youngest son, Morris,
entered his teens. Although she still hired harvesting equipment, Anna and

Morris now hauled, shocked, and pitched bundles. During the rounds of threshing, the Ericksons supplied Morris's labor, horses, and a wagon for exchange, much as had been done with Joe's labor in the 1920s.[39]

Erickson's farm organization, in short, relied on techniques that emphasized labor—family labor, neighborhood exchanges, and hired hands—and deemphasized capital investment in technology.[40] The stability of the farm neighborhood enabled her to rely on neighbors for technology and labor assistance even at peak times. Those who assisted her in exchanges and as hired help participated in the social neighborhood as well. Although her production of grain was minimal, she nevertheless expanded her output with neighborhood exchange and family labor as her children grew.

Powers, in contrast, relied to a much greater extent on capital investment. At least as early as 1922, when his diary begins, Powers owned his own binder. Powers described an established network of kin in the area, rather than neighbors, which supplied threshing technology. In the early years, his brother Dan owned and operated the thresher. However, by 1932, Powers reported that "[we] used our engine" to separate, suggesting the purchase of a smaller gasoline-powered rig. That year, Powers also owned a truck to haul grain to market. This technology became a resource for the community, with Powers and his son hauling oats for neighbors for exchange or hire. By 1937, Powers had entered the modern technological age through family investment. While he threshed 1,607 bushels in the "old way," his brother Dan combined 150 bushels for him with his new machine.

Although Powers relied more than Erickson did on capital investment to obtain technology, he, too, depended on various combinations of family, exchanged, and hired labor. His sources of labor did not come from a stable social neighborhood, but through a series of yearly arrangements with a changing group of neighbors and hired men. From 1922 through the 1930s, Powers hired one or two men—different men almost every year—to assist with the field work, shocking while Powers ran the binder. These hired men worked throughout the busy season, and sometimes one stayed even through the winter. From the 1920s through the 1930s, Powers also exchanged work with his brothers, Dan, Sam, and Walt, and one or two neighbors for threshing. By the 1930s, Powers's son consistently joined the work force for the grain harvest and threshing, and his daughter joined occasionally. In 1937, Powers noted a shortage of hired men, and the list of neighbors with whom Powers exchanged work grew from two to five. Powers and his son hauled oats for these neighbors; his hired men, Harold and Gus, performed field and threshing work for Powers's neighbors. Although exchange played an important part in meeting Powers's labor needs, the list of the workers kept changing. The neighborhood celebrated the completion of the harvest with a "thrashing ice cream," but these neighbors did not play an active role in other social or work exchanges.[41]

The differences between Erickson's and Powers's strategies were shaped by the capital resources available to them; however, the different constructions of the neighborhoods in which they lived also influenced their choices. The presence of tight social networks, like Erickson's, encouraged strategies that viewed technology and labor as community resources, whether exchanged or hired. Powers practiced more exclusive strategies that emphasized kin, technology, and hired labor. Though a truck might be hired or exchanged with neighbors, the gasoline-powered thresher was generally used within kin networks. By hiring workers rather than exchanging labor, Powers further removed his farm strategies from dependence on neighbors. Powers's preference, which was perhaps personal to him, for kin over community was reinforced by the high turnover and tenancy in his neighborhood. For Powers, resource sharing came with economic crisis rather than being embedded in a sense of community interdependence.

The similarities in Erickson's and Powers's strategies, however, are suggestive of the slow process of change in agricultural production despite technological innovation. They also illustrate the continued difficulties farmers faced as they struggled to expand or survive on smaller farms, or even to introduce new capital-intensive methods on more prosperous ones. Both farmers relied on neighborhood or kin networks to provide some technology and save money. In cash-short times, both farmers relied on exchanged labor as a method of improving income by keeping costs low. For Erickson such strategies were crucial for survival. For Powers, traditional survival strategies became more important in the crisis of the 1930s, at the very time he entered the new technological age of combine harvesting.

While an analysis of individual choices outside the wheat belt exposes the importance of community structure and family composition to changes in production patterns, a larger regional examination of the wheat belt reveals broader trends in the process of agricultural change. A comparison of three of the wheat states, Kansas, Nebraska, and North Dakota, drawn from a 1921 USDA study published in 1924, illustrates how choices varied despite similar available technology and labor sources. The farms in this study were much larger than average in Kansas and North Dakota, and slightly smaller than average in Nebraska. An examination of field technology, crop selection, thresher ownership, and labor organization indicates that some options promoted the capital-intensive farming of the new agriculture and a dwindling reliance on local work resources, while others emphasized local values of neighborhood work, family labor, and the survival of rural communities.[42]

Farmers in Kansas, according to the USDA survey, organized their work to specialize in one cash crop and hired technology and labor rather than relying on neighborhood resources. In Kansas, the primary crops were small grains, which took up 85 percent of cropland, and most of this was wheat. The almost total dependence on wheat created a short, intense crop-harvesting season. Kansas farmers harvested with headers rather than binders. The choice of a header shortened the season even more. The header could only be used after the grain had ripened, but before the grain shattered, a period of about fourteen to twenty-one days. The header removed the grain head from the straw and dumped it into a barge, which was then taken to the thresher. This eliminated the need for shockers and stackers, saving labor steps, but compressing the harvesting and threshing time into the same few days. This created an intense need for labor in a short span of time. Consequently, contracted threshers with full crews did 88 percent of the threshing. Farmers provided only teams and men to haul the grain. The large size of farms in this study, 537 acres compared to a 275-acre average for the state, probably overrepresents the capital-intensive nature of the harvest in Kansas by focusing on larger, more specialized farms. In the study, only 11 percent of farm families hired no labor for the harvest, but even their farms (which averaged 302 acres) were slightly larger than the state average.

On these larger farms, the use of headers and the specialization in wheat increased dependence on transient labor. Although family members provided almost 40 percent of the labor for the harvest, exchanged labor (which was not counted in this USDA study for any of the states) and monthly hired labor (less than 6 percent of the total labor used) did not sufficiently meet the demand. The short time span hindered exchange, and the short season and specialization decreased the need for long-term help outside the immediate family. Day laborers performed over 64 percent of the harvest work in Kansas. Because farms in Kansas were closer to urban centers, such as Kansas City, than were those in the northern plains states, Kansas farmers used city workers rather than relying on local townspeople and neighbors. Kansas farmers paid workers higher wages than were paid in other states, but the weeks for harvesting were much shorter, making it more difficult for workers to maintain a long run of employment. Kansas farmers needed more ready cash to complete the harvest and threshing than elsewhere. They used larger threshers, which could thresh about fifteen hundred bushels a day, and large crews of about twenty-two men, most of whom were day laborers. This made the cash cost of threshing about $116 per day. On these larger Kansas farms, threshing was capital-intensive and, although it used family labor, the practice did not lead to a sharing of community resources with poorer farmers by providing wages or exchanged labor within the state. Large Kansas farms best fit the profile of the problem studied by agricultural institutions.

In contrast, Nebraska's farmers developed strategies that were capital-intensive but emphasized family and exchanged labor and individually or cooperatively owned technology. Farmers in Nebraska, like those in South Dakota and western Minnesota, relied less on small grains as a cash crop (about 60 percent of the total crop acreage), and ran more diversified farms, with corn being an important secondary crop. Although the study did not discuss the harvest technology used in the state, Nebraska's farmers probably used both headers and binders. Individuals owned 16 percent of the threshers used, while another 11 percent were owned cooperatively. This contrasts with Kansas, where only 12 percent were owned by individuals and cooperatives. When Nebraska farmers hired custom machines (as 62 percent of Nebraska farmers did), the farmers provided most of the crew, hiring only two to four men, usually to operate the engine and the machine. Farm families boarded these workers, and women exchanged work.[43] Only 11 percent of the farmers hired a machine with a full crew, the method most Kansas farmers chose.

The choice of crops and technology allowed Nebraska farmers to rely primarily on family and exchanged labor. The family did 62 percent of the harvest work, and 44 percent of Nebraska farmers in the study hired no labor for the harvest. Generally, three to seven farm families would join together to buy a medium-sized thresher, and farm men acted as engineers, crew, and spike pitchers, while their sons and daughters or exchanged help did field work, shocked, and drove teams. There was little need for transient labor. Monthly hands who helped with the full season of work in all crops did 17 percent of the harvesting and threshing. Day labor did only 21 percent. In contrast to Kansas, more of the hired help in Nebraska came from local than from urban sources. According to the study, Nebraska farmers had adjusted their acreage to spread work over the entire season and had increased work exchanges to make up for labor shortages during World War I. They maintained the practice afterward. Although the practice was still capital intensive, since farmers owned machines, the system made up for this cost by decreasing cash expenses for labor. Diversification made neighborhood exchange and family labor much more important and preserved the local nature of the harvest.

In North Dakota, farmers used crop selection and technology to increase local autonomy and to use local labor sources, lessening cash expenses. Almost 79 percent of North Dakota cropland was planted in small grains, but North Dakota farmers raised less wheat than farmers in Kansas. Significant acreage was planted in barley, rye, and oats. Because these crops ripened at different times, the harvest and threshing season lengthened. The use of binders, more appropriate in the wetter climate of the northern plains, rather than headers also prolonged the season. Binders cut the grain while it was still green; then the grain ripened in shocks, expanding the time between harvesting and threshing.

North Dakota farmers obtained threshers through a number of methods. As in Nebraska, farmers owned a significant number of machines. Individuals owned 26 percent, and cooperatives owned just under 5 percent, a slightly larger combined total than in Nebraska. North Dakota farmers hired a large number of custom threshers with full crews (although not so many as in Kansas). Fifty-three percent of farmers in North Dakota contracted threshers with full crews, 35 percent of these crews boarded, and 19 percent of them provided a cook car. In contrast to Nebraska, only 16 percent of the farmers in North Dakota contracted with an engine crew only. Significantly, three-fourths of the contracted machines threshed from one to eight farms. Four to eight farms, the most common number, is about the size of one traditional threshing ring. Custom threshers in Kansas had to follow the harvest throughout the southwest to get a long run, but the variety of grains enabled North Dakota threshers to have a longer run within a small neighborhood.

The long season created by the use of binders and different types of small grains also made the demand for labor flexible over a longer period of time. North Dakota farmers could hire a few shockers to first harvest and then thresh, or could rely on family labor, which made up about 35 percent of labor used in the harvest, and exchanged help. Three to four farms could easily exchange labor, since only three to four people were needed to harvest the grain. Twenty-nine percent of North Dakota farms in the study did not hire any workers, and these farms are probably underrepresented because farms in the study were larger than the state average. However, North Dakota farmers employed more workers than Kansas farmers did. Monthly labor performed a comparatively larger percentage of total harvest work: 24 percent in North Dakota compared to less than 6 percent in Kansas. Day labor played a smaller role: 41 percent in North Dakota compared to 64 percent in Kansas. North Dakota workers garnered steadier employment for a longer period of time and did not have to rely so much on a succession of different jobs. The threshing crews in the spring wheat area of the northern plains consisted of neighborhood crews and local monthly hired help more than migrant day labor from other regions. By using smaller machines that would thresh twelve hundred bushels per day and employing smaller crews of about twelve men, farmers held threshing costs down to about fifty-one to fifty-four dollars a day. Because many threshers were locally owned, this kept much of the cash within the community.

Both Nebraska and North Dakota farmers used traditional community resources and exchange to decrease costs of production and increase income, while Kansas farmers chose the more modern harvesting equipment and increased income by working larger acreage. Kansas farmers could harvest more grain faster than those in North Dakota and Nebraska, and they specialized in wheat to make this profitable. They did not invest in threshing equipment, but hired custom threshers that traveled throughout the southwest plains. Their work crews were composed of transient, nonlocal labor. Nebraska farmers, much less dependent on small grain for income, used family and neighborhood labor much more than farmers in either of the two small-grain states. Although more Nebraska farmers purchased threshing equipment, their choice of technology enhanced their ability to use local and family labor rather than making them more dependent on outside labor sources. North Dakota farmers organized their farms to use local and regional labor and to keep cash costs low. The harvesting technology they used did not encourage larger acreage; it was most profitable on smaller farms. Their patterns of threshing-equipment ownership also emphasized a small region rather than itinerant custom work. Although changing practices in North Dakota and Nebraska hurt itinerant laborers from outside the region, they reinforced resource sharing and exchange within the immediate farming communities. The practices in these states blended with local threshing rituals and integrated newer technology with traditional practices.

Although the technology of the early twentieth century could be adapted to fit local community work patterns, the introduction of the combine in the late 1920s and 1930s challenged the very basis of community work. The combine both harvested and threshed the grain and required only an operator and one or two people to haul the grain from the field to the place of storage. Needing only a crew of three to five people, the combine eliminated the shared work of the harvest and threshing. Farmers used the first combines in the wheat regions of the Far West. These machines were large and needed up to forty horses or huge steam tractors to operate them. Combines could not be used in the dry regions of the southern wheat belt until smaller machines were developed around 1917. By 1926, 30 percent of Kansas wheat was harvested by combine. In wetter areas that same year, farmers were only beginning to use combines. North Dakota, for example, had only 27 combines. In 1927, combines numbered in the thousands in Kansas and Nebraska, while North Dakota and South Dakota had about 200 each, Illinois 300, Minnesota 11, and Iowa 27. By

1928, however, North Dakota had 1,172 combines. The number of combines increased dramatically throughout the United States during this period, from 4,000 in 1920 to 90,000 in 1937. Nevertheless, penetration was uneven. Even in 1938, only 25 percent of North Dakota's wheat was harvested by combine, a lower percentage than in Kansas twelve years earlier.[44]

The USDA and the land-grant colleges studied and promoted the use of combines with arguments that defined agriculture as a business, not a community enterprise. The first argument reveals how agricultural professionals viewed work. They believed machines should replace human labor. The combine was beneficial, they argued, because it decreased the need for extra labor and made the work less physically demanding. They also argued that the combine would lessen labor demands, decreasing the need for paid help and farmers' reliance on transients and the "social evil" they represented. Neither of these arguments meshed with local values of skilled physical labor and community work. To the experts, the physical labor of the harvest and the work of meal preparation represented drudgery that could be avoided with new technology. Promoters even argued that the combine would eliminate the "inconvenience" of labor exchange within a neighborhood. Clearly, to promoters, the social and community values surrounding threshing and the skills and sharing involved in it had little value.

The second argument used to promote the combine applied the economies of scale to agriculture. With a combine, more acres could be harvested per worker-hour than with other methods. As farmers put more acreage into production, the cost of producing would decline. Farmers could make more money, the promoters argued, as they increased the amount of land in production. With the combine, harvesting took less time, freeing the farmer for other work. It also freed the land faster, enabling the farmer to produce two crops in one year. For promoters, the key to successful farming was increasing production by decreasing labor, using more land, and using available land more intensively. These arguments for the use of combines illustrate the agricultural professional's economic and social vision of agriculture. The implementation of this vision replaced farm workers with machines and displaced farm families by encouraging land consolidation and capital-intensive farming.

Although professionals did not ignore the problems involved in switching to combine farming, they clearly underestimated these problems and did not even consider the devastating impact these developments would have on family farm survival techniques and local farm communities. Their studies based all estimates of decreased cost and increased income on large acreage planted in small grains. According to the USDA estimates, binders were more efficient when fewer than 110 acres of small grains were cut, headers on fewer than 175 acres, and combines only on larger farms that specialized in small grains. One study suggested that the need for larger acreage would convert marginal or semi-arid lands from pasture to wheat production. This became one of the major conservation problems of the 1930s. The combine also discouraged diversification because farmers transferred land from corn to small grains and decreased livestock. With a combine, straw was left standing in the field, adding nutrients to the soil, but when straw was cut with a binder, it was still green, keeping its nutritional value as feed. During the 1920s and 1930s, increased production and saturated markets made farm prices unstable. The idea of increasing production or increasing specialization to raise farmers' income was not necessarily economically effective.

In contrast, traditional practices increased farm income by decreasing cash costs, diversifying crops, and using more family and exchanged labor. The combine decreased labor needs but introduced fixed costs that could not be replaced, as labor costs could, with unpaid family or exchanged labor. These fixed costs included the capital needed for the initial investment in machinery. Interest on this machinery also had to be paid in cash. Combines required a switch to power farming, meaning farmers had to purchase a tractor. Horses could be fed with crops grown on the farm, requiring labor, not cash, but tractors had to be fueled with gasoline, available for cash only. Although many farmers had mechanical abilities, early tractors and combines broke down frequently, and bills for repairs and parts also had to be paid in cash.

Technical problems with combines, particularly outside the dry areas of the southern wheat belt, led to further innovations that continued to increase farmers' costs. One of the main problems of running a combine in wetter climates was green weeds. These weeds, when cut with a combine, increased moisture levels in grain. This required special storage or further separating, increasing storage costs. High moisture content also meant a lower grade and price for grain. Use of the combine also spread the weed seeds throughout the field. After World War II, herbicides were developed to solve this problem, creating another expense. Combines also demanded even ripening of the fields, increasing the use of improved seeds, another additional cost. Because combines were large, they were difficult to store and transport. This often necessitated new gates into fields, changes in fencing, and larger sheds for storage. Clearly the switch to combine farming was not easy to make, but required large investments and large farms.

Farmers' evaluations of the impact of the combine on work and rural communities are difficult to assess. Farmers and oral historians rarely addressed the question, because the changes are often masked by an assumed inevitability of progress. Very few comments about combines appear in diaries, though Elmer Powers observed that his brother's new combine "works very nice." Farmers discussed combines in oral histories from the perspective of contemporary agriculture. They associated the combine with the loss of farms and the unsteady state of contemporary agriculture. For example, Peter Paulson of North Dakota said that, at the time it came into use, he welcomed the combine because it made the farmer more "independent." By the 1970s, however, he had concluded that the trend had gone too far and that farms were simply too large. For him, the combine initially helped farmers, but it began a trend that he believed undermined them.

The most detailed reaction to the combine in the oral histories likewise emphasized the negative impact of combines on farm size and the persistence of small farmers. John Vaage had long used steam and gasoline threshers, and the new machine represented a significant change in his work. He saw his first combine in 1941 or 1942. His criticisms of the machine ran from the practical to the moral. He felt that threshing decreased the spread of weeds while combines spread them throughout the fields ("that's how the racket of spraying started"). Vaage thought that early combines wasted more grain because of spillage, particularly on uneven land. But, most important, he "didn't believe in 'em." He only bought his first combine in 1949 when he was unable to get help for bundle hauling. He admitted that many of the early combine problems had been solved, but he still rejected the large-scale farming that it introduced. It was unfair. The largest farmers "had money to buy it and the little fella didn't," he commented. Vaage firmly believed that limits should be set on the size of farms because there was "no sense to it [land consolidation and large farms]." Although farmers did adopt the new technology, they often resisted it, and their acceptance did not necessarily mean an acceptance of the farm reorganization that accompanied its use.

Farm people connected combine farming to the loss of community. Those who resisted buying combines often lived in tight, cohesive neighborhoods. Most of the farmers who discussed the importance of community work did not purchase combines until after World War II. North Dakota farmers purchased combines in the late 1940s or 1950s. In Wisconsin, not a profitable area for combines, Norval Ellefson exchanged work until the 1960s. At first, some farmers integrated combines into community patterns of sharing capital, through cooperative ownership or neighborhood custom hiring. Howard Brusveen first hired a neighbor to run a combine in the 1950s. Nevertheless, because combines decreased the need for labor exchange, there were fewer noncash means to pay for their use.[45]

Both men and women remarked on the loss of community sharing that accompanied threshing's decline. For men, the decline of threshing altered not only their work rituals but an important aspect of male community work culture. Women also missed the chance to share their labor. One Wisconsin woman noted that with the loss of community work "[you] needed something like a homemakers' group to get together or you just didn't know your neighbor." For women the decline of threshing rituals meant the loss of an important community event that recognized their work skills and integrated their labor with that of men. Without the ritual, their boarding work returned to being household labor, undervalued and invisible. However, the loss of community work meant more than changes in work patterns; it also meant the loss of a sense of interdependence. One Wisconsin farmer noted that, in the past, he and his neighbors worked as a community and cared for and helped each other. Now, he went on, the attitudes were those of "separatism." This loss was particularly difficult for farm women, who contributed to community resources to strengthen their own positions within farm families. As the economy altered, and the need for cash replaced barter and exchange, farm men worked in more isolation, and farm women needed to develop new resources and economic contributions with which to negotiate egalitarian family relations.[46]

As farm families adopted the combine, they did become more independent; they were no longer reliant on hired labor or on work exchanges with their neighbors. From another perspective, this was also a loss of interdependence, the ties of labor and economic needs that helped create social neighborhoods in rural America. From the perspective of long-range agricultural development, this decline in interdependence or increase in independence within farm neighborhoods meant, in fact, an increasing dependence on the larger cash economy. As farm production became more deeply enmeshed in a market economy, reliant on technology and cash, farm families could no longer rely on the buffers of community labor that had helped protect them economically from the vicissitudes of the market and their fluctuating incomes.

During the period from 1900 to 1940, threshing rituals celebrated both the alterations caused by the new technology, the threshing machine, and the preservation of the interdependence of men and women, neighbor and neighbor. Farm people adopted new practices and preserved old traditions, choosing technology to serve both their own farms' and their communities' interests. In contrast, government policies promoted technological innovations that opposed the interests of communities of small family farms. The technology they promoted encouraged capital-intensive farm practices, larger farms, fewer farms, and a smaller economic role for farm women. The Great Depression reinforced farm people's use of community exchanges, but it also eroded rural resources. As prosperity returned, New Deal policies continued to assist a wealthier class of farmers, and some farmers entered the technological revolution of modern agriculture by replacing community work with combines. Other farmers fled the economic hardship of farming and migrated to urban jobs. Those who stayed on small family farms used labor-intensive strategies as long as possible, but had to develop new strategies as they gradually found that there was no longer a community of small farmers with whom to share resources and labor.

Agricultural Policy and Family Survival Strategies

Consumption and the Isolated Nuclear Farm Family Ideal

Making Do in a Consumer Culture

As government policies promoted organizations and technology that reorganized and undermined community exchange and survival strategies, they also encouraged farm people to leave behind their strategies of making do and enter the mainstream of consumer culture. When consumer goods became an increasingly important part of the American economy, manufacturers and advertisers perceived farm people as a potential market. A 1921 *Country Gentleman* advertisement for a Pure-Bred Breeders' Association pictured a farmer who used progressive methods walking to greet the washing machine, piano, vacuum cleaner, automobile, radio, silos, and large, modern house and barn that were all "coming his way," walking on legs to join him.[1] Such consumer goods increasingly became the subject of agricultural professionals' research in the 1920s.

As this illustration indicates, rural advertising that promoted consumption, unlike its urban counterpart, directly linked changes in consumption with changes in production. Advertisers and policymakers envisioned a consumer-oriented farm family, isolated from community exchange. This ideal complemented farm consolidation and capital-intensive farming and conflicted with the survival strategies of people who operated small family farms. Agricultural institutions encouraged changes in farm and home production that increased a family's reliance on cash, decreased the possibility of community product exchange, and made farms less able to meet their needs outside the marketplace. In reality, farm people purchased new consumer items in a selective way that fit their values and economic resources. The purchase of new consumer items did not mean the abandonment of rural community life or the acceptance of the changes that agricultural institutions promoted as an inevitable part of modern agriculture.

In the 1920s, advertising became increasingly important to manufacturers of consumer goods and to the finances of magazines; however, early advertising generally targeted an urban, middle-class market. The farm press increasingly encouraged manufacturers to consider rural markets. Farm journals wanted to develop advertiser interest in farm consumers in order to increase their own advertising revenues. They promoted their magazines and the potential buying power of their readers. A 1929 *Farm Journal* advertisement boasted that the magazine "reaches 1,500,000 modern prosperous homes. . . . It has sought out especially the fertile acres where the real farm money is made. . . . with precision and without waste, it reaches the last remaining virgin market." This prosperity translated into consumer purchases. *Farm Journal* readers were "above average users of clothing, shoes, food, furniture, home equipment, automobiles, radios, silk stockings, face creams — everything."[2]

Social research into rural issues also increased the promotion of consumer goods in the 1920s. Although Progressive Era country life movement programs addressed the problems of the rural community, such as the poor state of schools, health care, and churches, they also promoted laborsaving devices, more and higher-quality leisure activities, and more consumer goods. Standard-of-living studies were common in urban social research in this era; the Purnell Act of 1925 defined the economic problem of agriculture as an industrial imbalance between manufacturing and agriculture and made the study of inequalities between rural and urban standards of living official policy. These studies, like the farm press, pointed out that prosperous farm people could become an important market for consumer goods. Professionals no longer studied what rural communities could build, but what farm families could buy.

Businesses interested in altering rural consumption patterns had played a role in the development of government agricultural institutions, and the farm press continued to have influence on and access to government resources. Sometimes government agencies actively and officially cooperated with the farm press in designing and studying farm income and standards of living. Magazines occasionally conducted their own studies of readers' desires for new consumer goods, but they shared the results with the agricultural institutions. The farm press also requested information and services from agricultural officials. For example, in 1921, the editor of *Farm and Home* wrote C. J. Galpin, head of the Division of Farm Population and Rural Life in the USDA, "What our Advertising Department wants, is a convincing article regarding the improvement in farm home

conditions, during the last few years, which will lay before manufacturers, the possibilities of the farm market." Galpin agreed that this was a
"good idea" and asked if payment could be made to one of his staff members to do the analysis "outside of government hours." Although government administrators wanted to avoid official ties to agricultural businesses,
the farm press was an influential constituent for agricultural institutions.[3]

In addition to official and unofficial cooperation, agricultural institutions and the agricultural press shared a language and symbol system,
defining a vision of American agriculture in a modern, capitalist society.
The items manufacturers hoped to sell matched the items considered essential to improve the farm family's living standard. The consumer goods
that walked out to greet the Pure-Bred breeder were the same advances government agencies measured in their standard-of-living studies. Although
these studies also measured other expenses and tracked education and leisure time, they usually assumed that consumption was the ultimate goal
of better education and increased income. Purchases increased leisure
time and indicated a more "fulfilling" way of living. These attitudes mir-
ror the dominant themes of urban-oriented 1920s advertising, which some
scholars have labeled "capitalist realism." Comparing advertising to "socialist realism," sociologist Michael Schudson argues that advertising, as
a form of propaganda, provided a "common symbolic culture" that represented the goals of a capitalist consumer culture and promoted capitalism
as a "way of life."[4] Standard-of-living studies shared this symbolic culture.

As in urban advertising, this symbolic culture was class based, but
agricultural advertising and standard-of-living studies tied new forms of
capital-intensive agricultural production to new consumption-oriented
standards of living. "Buying" meant purchasing farm implements and
products made possible by advances in scientific agriculture as well as consumer goods for the home. It included silos as well as washers, tractors as
well as radios. This unified vision of capitalist farming combined cultural
and aesthetic improvements, modern homes, laborsaving devices for farm
and home, increased income, and more leisure. These advances spiraled
forward, intertwining to form a steady line of farm progress. The economic side of being a progressive farmer was inextricably linked to the
social side of being a progressive farmer. This vision inherently excluded
large portions of the farm population. The USDA's sourcebook for standard-of-living studies done in the mid-1920s began its nationwide survey
to search for the "middle range" economic regions of the country. Although claiming to use a random sample, it excluded all blacks, all those
who did not speak English, and people with smaller incomes. The USDA,
the extension service, and land-grant colleges argued that the goal of
increasing farm income should be applied only to the few. Substandard liv-

ing implied inefficiency, and inefficient farmers were expendable, while efficient farmers needed to receive rewards equal to those received by the urban middle class.[5]

These studies adopted urban, middle-class values to create an idealized, nuclear farm family that would complement capitalist agriculture. Although farm households were generally nuclear in structure, they also were embedded in kinship and neighborhood networks. In contrast, this ideal portrayed an isolated, private nuclear family that had no extended kinship or community relationships. This isolated, nuclear farm family ideal separated home life from the work life of the farm, and associated this separation with class-based issues of taste and consumption. In most farm homes, the kitchen functioned as family and work center, and the house, yard, barns, and fields were physically connected, reflecting the integration of family and work and the work of men and women. When neighbors visited, they entered at the back door, exemplifying the integration of socializing and work and the informality and familiarity of social relations.

Lantern slides produced by the USDA, which were used for talks at Farmers' Institutes and other forums, illustrate how the ideal physical layouts for the farm home and grounds altered these practices. The slides depict large and elaborate homes with extensive yards and gardens, appealing more to an undefined public viewing the home than to the family that used the farm grounds. Neighbors did not see the home from the informal back door, but approached it through rows of trees planted along a curved driveway that framed the elevated farmhouse for public view. The ideal designs separated the farm's work from its home life by using trees and shrubs to hide the stable, yard, and outbuildings from the home. Separating work from the home paralleled urban ideals of the home as a sanctuary from the work world and stressed the division between the male and female spheres. The modern farm home no longer served as the site of agricultural production, but instead demonstrated class status and increased consumption altering rural patterns of work and socializing.[6]

Modern conveniences filled the ideal farm home. Agricultural professionals underestimated the significant costs of such improvements and assumed a particular class of farm people. Progressive Era reformers had promoted conveniences, but by the 1920s, the variety of conveniences and consumer goods had expanded greatly. For example, a University of Wisconsin study argued for the need for electricity to operate washing machines, electric irons, vacuums, churns, cream separators, sewing machines, pumps for house and barn, milking machines, motors to generate power around the barn, lights, incubators and brooders for poultry, and cooking and refrigeration equipment. The 1926 study estimated an initial

investment of $375.00, plus an annual charge of $68.51, a monthly charge of $5.71, and a 3- to 5-cent charge per kilowatt-hour used. This did not include the cost of purchasing any equipment or appliances to use the electricity. Although most studies saw costs as minimal when compared to labor saved, farms were usually short of cash, not labor. Farm people would not be prosperous enough to afford the conveniences that agricultural institutions proclaimed necessary in the 1910s and 1920s until after World War II.[7]

In the 1920s, the agricultural institutions' consumption-oriented definitions of minimal standards of living combined with the growth of advertising in the mass media and a consumer-oriented urban middle class to define existing rural standards of living as subnormal. Recalling the radio programs of the 1920s, one North Dakota farmer observed, "It seemed like everyone else was going through such a good time period, and it was only in North Dakota where people were poor." USDA photographs set new standards by contrasting the best houses, with modern conveniences and aesthetically pleasing detail, to those that needed some improvement and those that could not possibly be improved. Studies that applied these standards in the field encountered striking levels of substandard living. A North Dakota study in 1928 found slightly more than 40 percent of homes in good condition, 27 percent in fair condition, and almost 23 percent in poor condition, "shacks" and "very disorderly." When the researchers included the conditions of lawns, buildings, barnyards, and interiors, they categorized even fewer farms as in "good condition." These images connected substandard living with inefficiency. Substandard living could be improved by replacing inefficient farms with larger, more efficient ones and teaching efficient farm people to improve their living standards through consumption. The makers of rural social policy never debated the fate of the inefficient beyond their exit from farming.[8]

The modern farm family was to be an isolated farm family; this further obscured the fate of many farm people and that of rural communities as a whole. The ideal made leisure and consumption an individual rather than a community activity. Although other characteristics of the ideal farm have roots in the Progressive Era, this did not. For example, photographs taken for the Division of Farm Population and Rural Life, which are concentrated in the period between 1910 and the early to mid-1920s, pictured rural recreation in community groups. Community halls, picnic grounds, baseball parks, town bands, and farmers' club get-togethers dominated portrayals of rural leisure. Because early agricultural reformers defined rural isolation as the primary rural social problem, improved leisure had to be community centered. Recreation projects took neighborhood organization, and sometimes community money or labor. If a neighborhood built a hall or park, the community shared the costs and benefits. Even poorer farmers could attend a picnic or donate an hour of labor to community projects.

The portrayal of leisure in the late 1920s, 1930s, and early 1940s rarely included such community recreation; it focused instead on families using new consumer goods and establishing class status. Photographs taken for the Office of the Secretary of Agriculture, the Federal Extension Service, the Agricultural Adjustment Administration (AAA), and the Rural Electrification Administration (REA) displayed recreation as an event for the nuclear family. Farm people, these visual images implied, could best spend their leisure time in consumer-oriented pursuits that suggested middle-class status. Photographs portrayed the ideal farm couple, with one to three children, sitting in a comfortable living room, reading farm magazines, listening to the radio, or playing with toys. Other signs of middle-class status, such as electric lights, telephones, and musical instruments, were the backdrops for family-centered entertainment. Families played croquet or tennis in the yard; children had bicycles and electric trains. Family members worked together to keep their yards attractive and decorative. Community life and recreation rarely appeared in these photographs.[9]

In this ideal world, farm people spent their leisure time with family, not with neighbors. These positive portrayals ignored farm families who could not afford modern conveniences. Photographs delineated an ideal that did not recognize the actual standards of rural living or the diversity of the rural community. The only agencies that did not share this vision were the alternatives ones, the BAE and the FSA. The BAE, particularly in its community studies, did have similar images, but also continued to record community recreation as a vital part of rural life. The FSA photographs recorded community leisure as well as families in their homes. Because the families photographed by the FSA were poor, the photographs created a counterpoint to the images of the USDA, using similar poses to convey the absence of any signs of modern living, subtly critiquing the ideal.

Throughout the 1920s and into the era of the Great Depression, the dominant agricultural agencies fostered a class-based image of farm families that promoted new forms of capital-intensive farming and consumer-oriented living. These images glorified the possibilities of capitalism and consumption and ignored the actual lives of poorer farm people. Policymakers in agriculture hoped to alter the production and living patterns of rural Americans in ways that complemented the development of capitalist agriculture. Increased consumption was an integral part of these changes.[10]

Although promoters saw consumer goods as inseparable from modern capitalist agriculture, farm people viewed consumption differently. The economic realities of rural life prevented many farm people from being consumers even if that had been their goal. On the other hand, farm people of moderate incomes often lived frugally in order to gain more security by owning their land or to provide greater resources for their children. Although promoters believed that farmers could expand their acreage and introduce more capital-intensive farming methods simultaneously, many farm people found that expansion required saving, not spending, on household consumer items or other "advantages." Cultural traditions of community and work often conflicted with consumption. Finally, the professionals' attitudes of superiority led to local resistance and opposition. Farm people most often preferred their own values and customs to those promoted by outsiders, who neither understood nor appreciated the economic conditions and cultural traditions of farm life.

The primary reason farm people did not become model consumers was that their incomes were insecure. Much farm income came inconsistently throughout the year, and markets and weather made it uncertain from year to year. In response, farm people saved their money and carefully planned their expenditures. The conditions of agriculture in the 1920s and 1930s reinforced these conservative consumer practices. The fall in prices after World War I confirmed the need for caution even after some regions experienced recovery during the mid-1920s. According to standard-of-living studies conducted in the 1920s, farm families at all income levels kept their expenditures, and thus their standards of living, at approximately the same level from year to year. Even in the relatively prosperous state of Iowa, irregular income, the need to save money for security during lean times and to pay mortgages, and the desire to give children economic resources for adulthood led to modest standards of living. Farmers who had properties valued between twenty thousand and forty thousand dollars still said that they could not afford conveniences, because they did not have cash on hand and because property could not be converted easily to cash. Few farmers were willing to borrow money to improve their homes. Families whose homes were in the best condition had the benefits of long-term income accumulation, something many farm people had not experienced. Both survival and advancement required saving. [11]

Community values reinforced these economic realities. Moderate living standards visibly represented neighborhood equality and unity. Many rural communities displayed a level of consumption that was accepted by most of the community. North Dakota farm people interviewed in the 1970s frequently commented on the lack of local "class distinction" in the 1920s and 1930s compared to the contemporary period. As one put it, today "everybody wants a whole lot." In the past they were satisfied despite hard times; they "didn't know any better at the time. . . . Just the way we lived." Sometimes failure to meet local standards of living led to conflict. A report on

Meade County, Kansas, in the 1930s, found one rural community bitterly divided because those who still had jobs bought cars and new clothes, and those who had no work saw the others as "living high." But in another part of the county, there was a "stronger bond of sympathy among its citizenry and there was little ostentatious display." Many rural communities shared values that discouraged consumption and encouraged relatively homogeneous living standards.[12]

Some farm people saw consumer expenditures as extravagant, frivolous, or pretentious. When the author Hamlin Garland attempted to modernize his aging parents' home in West Salem, Wisconsin, his mother consistently disapproved. She saw his plan to build a dining room as "luxurious" and told him, "You better think a long time about that. . . . We're perfectly comfortable the way we are." Running water she thought "almost criminally extravagant." Whenever Garland suggested improvements, his mother would argue that they were unnecessary because all she wanted was a daughter-in-law and grandchildren, not conveniences. Generational continuity, not household improvement, was her goal.

Farm concepts of labor also shaped farm people's attitudes toward consumption. Farm labor did not turn directly into cash; products did. If farm families' labor furnished products for their own use, then they could save cash for those necessities or investments that could not be produced on the farm. Farm people did not accept that spending cash could easily substitute for labor, or that reducing labor automatically led to increased income. For example, in 1924, a county home economics agent in Williams County, North Dakota, compared the cost of making cheese to the cost of buying cheese and the price for selling cream. She found that unless a farm had extra milk that went to waste, it did not pay for farm women to make cheese. But "since nearly every woman said that they would do without cheese entirely before paying store prices for it," she decided that making cheese was better than doing without it. These farm women were accustomed to making cheese and did not believe that the labor this required was worth the cash it took to buy cheese at the store. Farm families needed cash for things that could not be produced on the farm and as security for lean years. It was not economically wise to spend on what could be made.[13]

As noted in chapter 1, farm women had responsibility for making do, and this was one of the most culturally valued parts of women's work. Although changing patterns of consumption affected the work of both men and women, farm people associated spending for the home most with the frivolity of consumption, which reflects the relative devaluation of women's labor. In general, farm people more easily justified investments in the barn or field because they would lead directly to increased production and more cash, whereas investment in the home seemed merely to save labor and increase expenditures because it did not lead directly to more products to sell for cash. Women could both win and lose because of the new values of consumption. They could gain ease from their labors and justify it as modern, but could lose a valued part of their work culture and status in doing so.

The importance of women in the transition to a consumer society took on symbolic significance in literary treatments of the conflicts of tradition and cultural change. In his 1924 novel, *RFD #3*, Homer Croy, a former Missouri farm boy, explored the new consumerism and its clash with rural values and community standards. He focused on the altered behavior of a farm daughter. The lead character, a teenage girl named Josie, hoped to escape rural poverty and labor, and her city-bred mother encouraged her. The neighbors pitied her father because of this. "No wonder Kirb Decker couldn't get ahead, they said, a city wife who didn't know how to manage and a daughter lolling in the hammock." Josie entered local beauty pageants, hoping to become a movie star, and many in the community viewed this as "vanity." Her father indulged her, but when Josie wanted to buy a sixty-dollar dress for a special beauty contest, her father balked because the best suit he had ever bought cost only twenty-two dollars. Making do, her mother sacrificed and saved to buy Josie the dress. Despite Josie's acceptance of consumer values, she still absorbed the value of making do. When Josie married a city man, she assumed it was her "wifely job" to be "awfully saving," and her husband had to tell her not to worry about spending money. The clash between the old values of saving and the new values of spending particularly affected women who, as managers of household budgets, were both the keepers of traditional values and the advance guard of the new culture.[14]

Despite the gendered meaning of consumption, farm men and women shared a culture that valued hard work. Since work was positive, spending merely to reduce it seemed wasteful. New laborsaving devices disrupted work practices and threatened the value of work skills. The conflict between old ways and new was often generational. Younger generations had fewer ties to older work traditions and accepted the new standards more readily than did their parents. One Wisconsin farmer built a silo and had water pumped into both the barn and the house. His father saw "no need" for "all that" and thought "they'd lost their minds completely" to be spending all that money on "such things" in 1936. Jean Long, another Wisconsin resident, recalled that her mother-in-law, whom she called Mrs. Long in the interview, opposed advances that would change her work. Mrs. Long would not let her daughter-in-law buy a washing machine and refused to use milking machines. Skilled at doing laundry and milking, Mrs. Long "washed better by hand than any machine." For farm people, raised in hard times, accustomed to hard work, proud of their work skills and their ability to make do, the new conveniences were both extravagant and disruptive.[15]

Finally, farm people resisted advances because agricultural professionals, merchants, and advertisers often patronized rural consumers and criticized their culture. Since the nineteenth century, the associations of wealth and readily available consumer goods with cities joined class bias to create an urban prejudice against rural life. Nellie Kedzie Jones described the impact of prejudice in a 1912 article: "Why should you feel apologetic when a guest comes from the city? Most of us do. We feel that the lack of certain luxuries which the guest has in her home will cause her to draw comparisons. . . . Too many of us country people assume or suspect a latent pity in the mind of the city-bred for the unfortunate who must make her home on the farm." Although Jones blamed the country person for imagining city people's feelings of superiority, most authors with rural backgrounds saw it as a real rather than an imagined prejudice. In a 1914 autobiographical novel about her early days on the prairie, Margaret Lynn recalled her city cousins' patronizing attitude. They delighted in "telling us about the things they had and we did not have." Trips to the city brought even more criticism. Lynn's uncle saw himself as a "beneficent and well informed fairy, showing off the city to us with urban toleration of our ignorance and amusement at our excitement. . . . we failed to wonder in the right place or we admired in the wrong place, and Arthur said over and over, 'Well, you certainly are queer kids.'" The absence of city advantages, though these were by no means even shared by all city dwellers, made rural living seem inferior, and many rural people resented this judgment.[16]

From the beginnings of the country life movement, agricultural professionals shared these attitudes, which persisted even in the 1930s, when the economic roots of farmers' social problems became obvious. Agricultural professionals continued to blame the "backwardness" and "stupidity" of farm people for their living conditions. A 1934 report on relief efforts in Oneida County, Wisconsin, concluded that rural people would "have to be trained to accept advice" from agricultural and home economics extension personnel. The author described one caseworker who had been told by several farm women that "they had been canning all their lives and needed no advice." The tone of the report reflected the assumption that these farm women were ignorant and did not understand how to improve their own standard of living, and worse, did not even know that it needed to be improved. Agricultural professionals saw this unwillingness to accept their superior knowledge as the cause of rural poverty and a justification for the decline in the farm population.

Although this attitude predominates in reports and studies undertaken during the Great Depression, one author of a 1934 study of Burke County, North Dakota, recognized, and was critical of, the prejudices of some agricultural-relief professionals. This report revealed the conflict between outside professionals administering relief and rural staff members and farm people from the region. One local staff member said the outside professional "jumped on all [those] asking for relief with both feet. He started rough, consequently causing antagonistic feeling among the people." A stenographer recorded the professional's random comments: "[it is] hard to deal with [people here]. . . . they seem kind of dumb. [On farmers not keeping accounting records:] I think that almost the whole group of North Dakota farmers just didn't have anything else to do and so they started farming." Unlike most authors of rural relief reports, this staff member sided with farm people (except the more radical and organized groups that demanded relief), and criticized the administrator: "The majority of the people in this area are asking for necessities only, and it's hard for them to accept anyone calling at their homes in a new car, well dressed, telling them what they should buy and how much, when their past experience has not been in their line." From the Progressive Era through the 1920s and 1930s, the goals of uplift and social reform did not reflect sympathy for rural conditions and values and condemned those who did not or could not readily accept consumption and progressive farming.[17]

Although promoters' ideas about consumption clearly clashed with many local rural traditions, farm people nevertheless did welcome some goods that were part of modern farm living. However, most farm families could not purchase all the necessities of a modern farm; they had to balance the improvements they made on the farm and in the home. General economic trends and regional conditions shaped these choices. The United States Census counted the basic measures of modernity on farms, including automobiles, tractors, telephones, radios, electricity, and running water. Farm people decided to enter the realm of modern agriculture cautiously, and the statistics reveal their choices.

Throughout the Midwest, farm people's purchases reflected a desire to increase their ability to communicate with others. Of the items counted in the census, farm people first bought telephones and automobiles. Both shortened the distances that separated farm people from neighbors, towns, and markets. In the 1920 census, telephones and automobiles led all other improvements, appearing in the highest percentage of farm homes in all the states of the western Midwest. Telephone ownership ranged from a low of 47 percent in North Dakota to a high of 86 percent in Iowa, and automobile ownership ranged from 31 percent in Missouri to 76 percent in Nebraska. All the other signs of modern life appeared in no more than

20 percent, and most often less than 10 percent, of farm homes in each of these states. Between 1920 and 1930, the number of households with automobiles increased to 80 percent or more in all midwestern states except Missouri. During this same time the percentage of farms having telephones decreased slightly in all midwestern states but Wisconsin, where it remained the same. Despite this decline, the increased presence of automobiles illustrates that transportation and improved communication were primary goals for farm people.

Variations in regional agricultural specializations affected farm people's choice of modern conveniences. Tractors increased in numbers most quickly in the wheat belt of the Great Plains. In 1920, tractors appeared on more than 15 percent of the farms in only two states, North Dakota and South Dakota. Manufacturers adapted tractors earliest to wheat production, and the large tracts of land in the Great Plains made the use of tractors more crucial than in other regions. This changed quickly; by 1930, only one state, Missouri, had tractors on less than about 25 percent of the farms. Nevertheless, the states of the Great Plains continued their lead, ranging from Kansas, with almost 36 percent of the farms having tractors, to North Dakota, with almost 44 percent. Nebraska roughly equaled the corn-belt states with about 30 percent.

In contrast, farmers in the dairy region lagged in the adoption of tractor technology, but led the way in electrification. By 1940, electricity had entered more than 30 percent of the farm homes in Illinois, Iowa, Minnesota, and Wisconsin, but less than 30 percent of those in Nebraska, Kansas, the Dakotas, and Missouri. Electricity had practical uses for milking machines, separators, and cooling tanks that made its introduction more vital to dairy farmers. Although farmers in the Great Plains states invested in tractors, fewer dairy farmers bought tractors. By 1940, Iowa and Illinois farmers owned tractors in the same numbers as farmers in the Great Plains, and they electrified their farms at the same rate as dairy farmers, equaling the region with the highest number for each convenience. Both states included significant dairy sectors, and manufacturers adapted tractor technology to production in the corn belt by the 1930s. Modern advances became applicable at different times for different commodity specializations, and farm people made choices that best suited the economic needs of their farms.

Both long-range and short-term economic trends also affected the adoption of modern advances. Long-term prosperity in a region led to a broader range of purchases than in more newly settled areas or states where incomes were more variable. Iowa's earlier settlement and relatively continuous prosperity led to a more consistent investment in both farm and home improvements than was evident in other states. In 1930, almost 30 percent of Iowa farms had tractors, 24 percent had running water, and 21 percent had electricity. In contrast, 44 percent of North Dakota farms had tractors, but only 8 percent had running water and 8 percent had electricity. Farm people settled North Dakota relatively late and had not had as long to accumulate savings. Wheat markets also recovered more slowly than corn, livestock, or dairy markets after World War I.

Short-term economic trends also had an impact on regional economies and consumer purchases. Before 1920 (1925 for radios), the southern states of the Great Plains, Kansas, Nebraska, and South Dakota joined Iowa and Illinois as the states with the highest percentages of farm homes having each of the six conveniences. However, wheat markets collapsed in the 1920s and did not recuperate, while both livestock and dairy prices recovered in the mid- to late 1920s and did not suffer as much in the 1930s. This gradually altered the states' relative standings in convenience ownership. By 1930, South Dakota had fallen out of the top categories except in tractors, and Wisconsin had become the state with the highest percentage of farm homes with electricity. By 1940, the dairy states again improved their relative standing in most categories. The availability of running water in homes increased between 1930 and 1945, from 13 percent to 21 percent in Minnesota and from 16 percent to 31 percent in Wisconsin, but in Nebraska it increased only from 30 percent to 31 percent and in Kansas from 17 percent to 23 percent. Although the lower Great Plains states had prospered earlier, poor prices and drought conditions hurt their region more than they did the dairy and corn belts. Although the middle-range states changed their relative positions, Iowa remained more prosperous than other states, and North Dakota and Missouri (with its southern regions reflecting the poorer economies of the cotton-oriented bootheel and hilly Ozarks) remained less prosperous in terms of most of these measures than did the others.

Despite these regional variations, the Great Depression had a strong impact throughout the western Midwest. The statistics of 1940 reveal the effects of the Great Depression. The percentages of farms possessing the two major advances made during the previous twenty years, automobiles and telephones, declined, although this varied by state. While the number of automobiles increased or stayed the same in Iowa, Illinois, Minnesota, and Wisconsin, it declined in the Great Plains and Missouri. Telephone ownership declined in every state—perhaps a measure of the strategies of saving necessary in hard times. Autos, once purchased, remained on the farm even when farmers had no gasoline to operate them. Farm families could remove phones and save the monthly expense. The percentages declined the least in states where the percentages were smallest in 1930, North Dakota and Missouri. They declined the most in the states of the

Great Plains, Kansas, and Nebraska, where the percentages had been highest. The loss of these advantages indicates the severity of the economic hardships in the Great Plains states and throughout the Midwest. Even in relatively prosperous Iowa, the number of farm homes with telephones declined from 84 percent to only 67 percent.

The methods of distribution and the assistance that was available for obtaining services also shaped the adoption of new technology. For example, telephone ownership declined in farm homes largely because of the changing structure of that industry. Access to telephone lines grew with the availability of independent phone-line companies and with industry-wide competition between 1900 and 1915. Access declined as American Telephone and Telegraph (AT&T) expanded its monopoly in urban areas and increased rates in or ignored rural markets, and as independent companies folded in the 1930s. AT&T again increased competition for these rural markets in the late 1930s and 1940s as the government debated adding telephone service to subsidies for rural cooperatives through the REA.[18] Electricity entered most farm homes only after farmers could get government assistance through the REA. In contrast, the provision of running water to homes was not an easily collectivized effort, and did not promise profits beyond the initial installation; no government programs helped farm people afford running water for their homes. Consequently, in every state of the region except Nebraska, fewer farm homes had running water in 1945 than had electricity in 1940.[19]

Finally, farm people balanced the adoption of different types of technologies. The automobile was a clear priority for farm families. Advances for the main productive activities of the farm took precedence over advances for the home. Running water was a low priority in farm homes not only because it was relatively expensive but also because it was the least tied to production and the most tied to women's household labor, the most devalued part of farm work. Although in 1930 more than 25 percent of farm homes had tractors in all of the midwestern states but Missouri, the percentages of farms with running water and electricity remained below 20 percent in 1930, except in Nebraska (running water), Wisconsin (electricity), and Iowa (electricity and running water), and even remained below 15 percent in all but another five (running water in Illinois, Wisconsin, and Kansas and electricity in Illinois and Nebraska).

Perhaps the most interesting balance occurred with the large increase in radios between 1925 and 1940. By 1940, radios were present in more than 70 percent of farm homes in all midwestern states but Missouri (59%). More farm homes in every state had radios than had telephones. In North Dakota, more homes had radios than had automobiles. Radios required only a one-time purchase cost rather than monthly bills, and a neighbor or family member could recharge batteries or do repairs. Farm people who could not afford the other advances could still afford this one modern form of recreation. In North Dakota, when running water (9%), electricity (15%), and telephones (28%) were scarce, almost 83 percent of farm homes had radios. Although they did not help production or reduce labor, radios, like automobiles, served the whole family, and their use increased dramatically throughout the rural Midwest in spite of the economic difficulties of the 1930s.

These statistics reveal that availability did not automatically mean adoption. The idea that tractors, electricity, or running water changed the majority of farm homes, even in the relatively prosperous Midwest, misrepresents the reality of technological change in rural America. Between 1900 and 1940, the only advances to be adopted by a majority of farm families in this region were the automobile and the radio. Although they accepted some signs of modern life, most farmers differed dramatically from those represented in the progressive ideal promoted by (and assumed to be the constituents of) agricultural institutions in the 1920s and 1930s.

Although census data indicate how general economic conditions and regional factors influenced the purchase of modern farm conveniences, they do not reveal how farm people viewed themselves as consumers, how and why they decided to purchase these items, or how they balanced purchasing goals with the reality of farm incomes. Despite the differences between the consumer culture promoted by advertisers, the farm press, and agricultural institutions on the one hand, and local rural traditions of making do on the other, many farm people wanted at least some of the new conveniences for their farms and homes. However, their acceptance of some parts of the new standards of living did not necessarily mean rejection of old values; in general, farm people bought new items for traditional reasons.

Farm people wanted conveniences for reasons that often did not mesh with the ideals of middle-class consumption. Even advertisers, who rarely distinguished campaigns by class in urban areas, developed different advertising strategies for rural markets. For example, when advertising telephones to urban markets in the 1920s and 1930s, AT&T emphasized status, portraying women dressed in stylish clothes organizing social gatherings or planning visits. Advertisements promoting phones for rural markets featured practicality: finding out the market prices for livestock, grain, produce, or poultry; calling doctors for medical emergencies; and saving time by calling ahead for shopping orders. When the audience was rural, advertisers even portrayed visiting by phone in practical terms, with use of the telephone substituting for travel over bad roads or in poor weather. In the 1920s, the Sears, Roebuck Company gradually changed its advertising strategies to promote increased consumption. Its advertising maintained a balance between the inexpensive prices and cheaper goods that were the hallmark of the company's rural success and the promotion of new, more expensive conveniences and higher-grade, fashionable clothing. The catalog gave the latter more space and displayed the "new," the "most modern," and the "best available" more prominently to indicate their desirability. This strategy kept the cheaper prices that first attracted rural customers, but also introduced new standards of modernity and status.[20] Advertisers hesitantly but gradually applied urban, middle-class values of consumption to their rural markets.

Farm people's consumerism blended with other parts of their lives and reflected their cultural values. If farm people recorded in diaries the parts of their lives they found most important, then both men and women on farms saw themselves as workers and members of communities and families, not as consumers. Although diarists noted trips to town, they rarely described in detail the stores they visited or the purchases they made. Shopping did not dominate diary entries as the work of the farm and the social life of the family and community did. Only the diary of Bertha Gabelmann, an Iowa farmer, recorded purchases in detail, and she wrote these in the same style as she did the work entries. Gabelmann's entry on 22 November 1912 listed the day's activities: her mother and father sold eggs, roosters, and cherries; the family butchered a calf; they went to town and bought flour, raisins, yeast, coconut, and cranberries; they went to singing school and brought the minister eighteen eggs and a sack of corn. The purchases were merely a small part of the day, and she integrated them with observations about work and community life.

Although routine shopping and spending did not receive much notice, unusual purchases and special trips to town did merit more attention, which indicates that consumption provided a break in farm routines. The types of purchases farm people made suggest the generally modest items that represented unusual purchases. For Gabelmann, trips to Charles City, rather than the family's usual trade center, Greene, and mail orders from catalogs resulted in longer entries. Nevertheless, she integrated even unusual purchases with local cultural experiences.

Saturday, September 14, 1918

Mother dug her early New Yorker potatoes. Father, Jake and Mina went to Greene, sold Tomatoes. to Mrs. O'Niel $1.60, Mina bought Hilda Brush and Comb had a set put in ring for her. Christine a dish. .10 cents. Bought a Glass baking dish 85 cts. it rained this noon Will was to Greene.
  Lydia was to Nashua bought Olga a hat $2.00 took Bertha's Films to have them Developed. Send Oscar a letter. Fritzel a Toy (Chinese shaving a man). Colored led

pencils. 6 cts. Postage. Send Sears Roebuck $2.06 for Tam O Shanters for Ruth and Rosa. Bought 2 lbs. Sugar. Interest for Liberty Loan $11.91.

Even though unusual purchases were events, they were still intertwined with family life (they might be given as gifts to kin) and with work life (they might come about because rain prevented the family from doing other work; tomatoes might have to be sold to get the cash for purchases). However, this diary entry also includes a special, modern purchase: a camera. The photographs that Gabelmann took with the camera show family, work, and community life, but also unusual purchases, such as cars and tractors. Although these signs of modern living were clearly important, farm people did not portray them in diaries or photographs as sharp departures; they placed them within traditional patterns of work and social life.[21]

The willingness of farm people to buy new consumer items also does not mean that they stopped spending money cautiously. Most diarists rarely recorded purchases, but the items they did mention were also the measures of the new standard of living—telephones, washing machines, tractors and other machinery, cars, radios, phonographs, and cream separators. When Pauline Olson, a North Dakota farm woman, bought a new stove in 1937, she noted: "brought out my new stove. had my other Monarch 22 years." The infrequency of the purchases also indicates that farm people did not rush into a consumer culture on credit, but planned and organized their purchases. For example, in the diary of North Dakotan Anne Burke, major purchases are clearly spaced. The Burkes purchased a new spring mattress in 1907, a cream separator in 1908, an electric washing machine in 1919, a telephone in 1938, and a tractor in 1939. Occasionally for one step forward there was a step back. During 1932 and 1933, Burke recorded doing the wash "by hand," indicating that either the washer or its generator was no longer operating.[22]

The diary of Anna Pratt Erickson illustrates how new living standards blended with patterns of saving and making do. In the early years of the diary, from about 1898 to 1925, she rarely recorded special purchases. In 1901, Anna bought a "new factory skirt," a major purchase for a girl who was accustomed to making her own clothing. She also placed orders from the Montgomery Ward catalog, though she never described in detail what she ordered. She had a sewing machine as early as 1913 and occasionally subscribed to a magazine. During the late 1920s and the 1930s, Erickson began to record more purchases, but she balanced them with other economies. During these years, she bought clothing; appliances, including a new stove, a telephone, a radio, and a pressure cooker; and machinery, including a drill and a hay loader. But during these same years, she had the phone disconnected, made clothing and linens from flour and sugar sacks, began to make her own soap, and canned immense quantities of food.

Erickson's children encouraged modern consumption. The generations who entered their teens and twenties during the 1920s and 1930s were more interested in conveniences and higher standards of living than their parents. Much of Anna's personal spending came after gifts of money from her children. For example, her daughter Fay, a nurse, gave Anna money for a new hat, a new coat, and two pairs of shoes in 1935. Children also introduced new conveniences to the household. Anna's daughter Dorothy, who farmed with her husband nearby, first used a pressure cooker for canning in 1934. Dorothy and Anna canned together until 1936, when Anna purchased her own pressure cooker. Erickson's son Morris, a high school student in the 1930s, brought a secondhand radio home in 1933 and bought a new radio in 1938. Even when Anna still had no telephone and was using sugar and flour sacks for cloth, she found money to purchase a new Maytag washer, for a total of $79.50 with $7.50 down, to give to Dorothy after the birth of her second child. She rarely recorded a credit purchase, probably indicating that she rarely bought items on credit. Although Erickson worked hard and made do, some of her children benefited from jobs with constant cash wages, and they encouraged and accepted new standards of living and increased spending for the home and farm.[23]

The different strategies farm people used to improve their farms, the differences in access to new farm and home technologies, and the differences in the ways farm people viewed their move into progressive farming and the consumer culture can be illustrated by a close comparison of two oral histories.[24] Percy Hardiman and Harold Tomter were raised on very different Wisconsin farms. Hardiman was born in 1909 and grew up on a hundred-acre dairy farm in Waukesha County, Wisconsin, near Milwaukee. The farm income came from milk, potatoes, wheat, barley (sold to Milwaukee breweries), sheep, and four hundred to five hundred chickens. During the post–World War I depression, when only four of eleven farms on their road escaped foreclosure, the Hardimans' farm survived. In the 1920s, they added peas to their specializations to sell to nearby canneries.

Harold Tomter was born in 1923 on a homestead farm, "a starvation patch," near Pigeon, Wisconsin, in the northwest part of the state. In 1927 the family moved, purchasing a forty-acre farm near Pigeon Falls. The Tomters, too, used a myriad of crops to earn cash. Besides selling milk from about a dozen cows, they rotated alfalfa, oats, and corn; raised and sold cattle; kept three hundred laying hens; maintained a garden and orchard; sold grapes and gooseberries; and grew a little tobacco as a cash crop in the 1930s. Although these farms were both diversified operations, the Hardiman farm was larger, more specialized, closer to markets for specialty crops, and had the benefit of earlier settlement and longer-term capital accumulation than did the Tomter farm.

As Hardiman and Tomter construct the stories of their families' farms, different patterns emerge. Hardiman's story is a linear tale of the progress of building the farm, expanding acreage, purchasing new technology, and improving the home. His narrative credits contact with the county agent and a willingness to "follow progressive things in agriculture to make life better and earn more money" with the improvements. In contrast, Tomter's story is constructed as a mixture of economic struggle and vibrant community life. Its narrative frame of reference is the fire that destroyed the family's barn, cattle, and machinery in 1931, and the neighborhood assistance that helped them survive. The story spins back and forth in time from this point. Tomter mixes accounts of technological purchases and home improvements with stories of struggle, community, and kin. In Tomter's story, a discussion of the team of horses used in the field soon expands to tales of using the team for visiting and trips to church, and stories about the large horse barn at the Pigeon Creek Lutheran Church. Hardiman also describes an active rural community with exchanges of work, church socials, and visiting, but he segregates it from his story of farm progress. Although consumption and improvements are the foundations of Hardiman's tale of building the family farm, they are incidental to Tomter's narrative—worth noting, but not the measure of success or meaning in his life.[25]

The Hardiman and Tomter farms underwent significant changes about twenty years apart. The Hardimans' steady prosperity enabled them to make major technological improvements and improve their home simultaneously. In 1918 and 1919, the Hardimans drained marshy land, built a new barn, and installed a coal furnace in the house. The latter was "a real luxury" because it heated the upstairs bedrooms, which was a rarity in rural homes. In 1920 they purchased a tractor. They had milking machines by 1923 and got electricity in 1925. The family installed a bathroom and sewage system in about 1929 and bought a rubber-tired International Farmall that could be used for cultivation in the 1930s. As these dates indicate, the Hardimans improved their farm and home well in advance of the majority of the farm population of the rural Midwest.

In contrast, the Tomter story is one of improvements constantly put off. Electricity was available through the REA in 1939, but the family could not afford the cost of wiring and the $3.50 minimum monthly charge until 1941. Tomter farmed with horses until 1948. Despite these delays, the Tomters also paired farm and home improvements when possible. When they got electricity they used it to light the chicken coop to increase production; to run an electric motor for the cream separator and water pump; and to light the house.[26] After 1945, Harold's father paid off his debts and bought milking machines and a refrigerator. Although both the Tomters and the Hardimans paired farm and home improvements, the Hardimans had more leeway than the Tomters did to improve their home when the advances—such as central heating, bathrooms, and indoor plumbing—were not connected to improvements in work. These did not directly increase income, and the cost was too high for poor families. Although this might seem to indicate that poorer families valued women's work less, women on smaller farms often did more tasks related to cash production and so benefited from farm improvements more than women on larger farms, who did less of the farm labor.

Although Hardiman's story focused largely on the work of farm men and their willingness to accept progress in farm techniques as the key to consumption, Tomter's story of getting "modern improvements" often highlighted cutting corners, the work of women as well as men, and participation in cooperatives and community groups. The family bought a 1923 Model T in the 1930s and subsequently used it to haul cream and thus increase their income. After the 1931 fire, the Tomters replaced the lost machinery with used machinery purchased at auctions. In contrast to Hardiman, who often mentions labor that was probably done by women but rarely discusses its importance, Tomter recalls that his mother was a good gardener and played a large role in fruit, dairy, and tobacco production as well as serving the entire community as a nurse. The community also played a large role in what consumption meant to the Tomters. In the 1930s, the family bought an icebox because there was a cooperative icehouse in Pigeon Falls that decreased the cost of ice. The Tomters had a radio in the 1930s, and Tomter recalled that they only listened when the family invited neighbors or relatives who did not have radios. The family considered listening alone or as a nuclear family "wasteful." That the Tomters used the radio as a shared community resource illustrates that farmers could use modern conveniences to reinforce community rather than simply to improve the nuclear family's standard of living.

The advantages available to the children on these two farms also differed. Hardiman, the youngest of three boys, attended high school and worked in a cannery to help pay for college at the University of Wisconsin, from which he graduated in 1932. The Great Depression altered his plans to become a teacher of agriculture. Because he could not find a teaching job in the 1930s, he bought a tank for his truck and hauled gasoline and oil until he was able to buy his own farm in 1940; he bought a second in 1944. He continued to expand his operations and rent additional land. In Hardiman's oral history, these improvements represent strategies of expansion and measures of success. Although he tells of the importance of home production in the early years and hard work as part of the family enterprise, for Hardiman progressive farm techniques, not saving, kin, or community, were the keys to success.

Tomter's education and adulthood continue the themes of making do and struggle that shaped his family's history. Tomter was the younger of two children. Tomter should have gone to high school in 1938, but the family could not afford the three dollars a month per child for the bus ride, so he waited until after his sister's graduation in 1939. He graduated from high school in 1943, worked as a hired man and taught agriculture for a brief period, and then became a soldier until 1946. He took over the family farm when his parents retired in 1947. In 1952, he rented a two hundred–acre dairy farm, but he was unable to get financial backing to buy the land. In 1968, he decided to leave farming.

Percy Hardiman's story reverberates with the vision of progressive farming promoted by the agricultural institutions; Harold Tomter's story indicates the perspective of farm people who were outside their constituency. Hardiman's story matches the standard-of-living studies and the advertisements that heralded the potential success of capital-intensive agriculture and increased consumption. In contrast, Tomter's move into farm and home consumption does not resemble the ideals of agricultural progress. The growth of consumption and the changes in agricultural practices were tempered by the rural traditions of his community and the realities of his economic class. Struggle and making do remained crucial to Tomter's vision even as he adopted technologies promoted by agricultural institutions.

Although progressive farmers like the Hardimans purchased modern conveniences more easily than those on "inefficient" farms like the forty-acre farm of the Tomters, other farm people successfully purchased modern goods and raised their standards of living with an alternative vision of agriculture's future. In contrast to the image of the isolated nuclear farm family that dominated the agricultural institutions' vision of modern farming, many farm people often had to unite to gain access to modern conveniences. Changes in technology and living standards were not inevitably linked to a declining farm population or an increasing isolation of farm families. The oral history of Rangar and Margaret Segerstrom exemplifies how technological change could benefit entire rural communities and help preserve a community system of small family farms.[27]

Both Rangar and Margaret had roots in small family farms and close ethnic communities, and both had to work for wages as youths to assist their families and support themselves. Rangar and Margaret were both grandchildren of Scandinavian immigrants. Rangar's parents operated a forty-acre farm near River Falls, Wisconsin, and Margaret's parents had an eighty-acre farm near Mondovi, Wisconsin. Margaret, born in 1903, the oldest of seven children, worked as a hired girl near her family's home from the age of fifteen until her marriage. Rangar, born in 1896, was one of nine children. After his graduation from eighth grade in 1911, he attended River Falls Normal School instead of high school. In 1916, he graduated from the agriculture department, where he was introduced to modern agricultural techniques. Although he had planned to teach, Rangar felt teaching paid too poorly, and he went to Minneapolis to work as a shipping clerk. In 1918 he joined the navy. When he returned to Wisconsin in 1920, he managed farms in the Mondovi area and met Margaret; they married in 1921.

Although the Segerstroms wanted to modernize their farm, the context for these advances was different from that envisioned by the agricultural institutions. A former student of the Agricultural College of the River Falls Normal School, Rangar was interested in the new techniques of agriculture. However, he had little contact with county agents or the extension service until the 1930s, when they administered certain New Deal programs. Instead the Segerstroms joined the Farmers' Union, which shaped their views of modern farming. The Segerstroms described the group's goals as the improvement of the income of farmers and the raising of rural living standards — not unlike the stated goals of agricultural professionals. However, for the Segerstroms these goals included the entire community of farmers, not just "efficient" ones. The Segerstroms participated in cooperatives and practiced other survival strategies common to small family farms, even as they entered the consumer culture. They "learned to plan things and learned to get along with what we had without going into any debt." Mutuality, not separate spheres or gender hierarchy, characterized their marriage, and their work was gender-integrated. The Segerstroms valued saving, sharing, and community as they modernized their farm and their standard of living.

The Segerstroms married in the 1920s and started renting a farm in 1922. Kin systems were crucial to their ability to stay on the land. The farm they rented was for sale in the 1920s, and Rangar's sister and brother-in-law, who worked for the railroad in St. Paul, purchased it for fourteen thousand dollars. The Segerstroms rented from them on half shares for about eight years. Such assistance was crucial in 1922, as agriculture began its post–World War I decline. According to Rangar, hay, which was worth twenty dollars per ton during the war, dropped afterward to seven or eight dollars. Margaret described the hard times as a "good thing" because in these years they learned to save. The Segerstroms' farm was of moderate size (one hundred twenty acres). They practiced a four-year crop rotation that included twenty to twenty-five acres of timothy clover or oats; corn; hay; and pasture. Their dairy herd consisted of twenty milking cows and fifteen young cows. They also raised about a hundred hogs a year and kept 120 to 200 laying hens. Apples, plums, berries, and grapes provided additional income. The farm supplied food for the family and feed for all the livestock. Machinery included a plow, a drag, and a used drill and used grain binder (both purchased in 1924).

The house was not modern. The Segerstroms carried water from the springhouse, heated with a wood stove, and used kerosene lamps. Nevertheless, they made some improvements in the 1920s. In 1924, when farm prices had begun to level off after the precipitous postwar decline, they purchased a Model T for $360, with payments of $28 a month. Their choice of improvements indicates their position as tenants; while machinery and automobiles could be moved from farm to farm, housing improvements could not.[28] As it did for the Ericksons, the mention of a credit purchase marks the car as a departure from their usual pattern of consumption, but also shows that credit provided access to new goods. This credit purchase still occurred in the context of many cash-saving strategies.

The 1930s reinforced saving strategies as the Great Depression created an even harsher climate for farm stability. With the 1929 crash, the Segerstroms lost their checking account, which had contained seventy-five dollars, and farm prices continued to decline. In this context, kin and community, saving strategies and gender-integrated patterns of mutuality continued to be important. Political activism also increased. The Segerstroms had always participated in cooperatives; they now joined the Farmers' Union, which was an important element of the Democratic New Deal coalition that supported the alternative agricultural agencies such as the FSA. New Deal farm policies also altered the context of farm stability, and the Segerstroms' activism helped make these programs a success. As the Segerstroms said, they joined the Farmers' Union hoping to get more money for their products and a "better standard of living," but they also joined because they "knew [you] couldn't get somewhere alone."

The Segerstroms became farm owners in the 1930s; their kin and the New Deal programs helped make this possible. The Segerstroms' relatives, who owned the farm, wanted to sell. Rangar and Margaret purchased the farm in 1932 for sixty-five hundred dollars with the assistance of the Federal Land Bank. This was the first instance in the Segerstroms' oral history of government programs helping keep them on the land. Government programs also enabled the Segerstroms to improve their living standard. They benefited from the WPA, getting money for the use of their teams, better roads from the works project, and lime to improve their fields; the Soil Conservation Service (SCS); the AAA; and the REA.

Ownership enabled the Segerstroms to manage their farm and home. They cautiously added improvements, and their strategies meshed with community and family traditions. In the field, the Segerstroms practiced newer methods, but emphasized those that conserved the land and made the farm self-sufficient rather than those that were more capital intensive. Because of his training, Rangar was one of the first in his area to plant alfalfa, in 1928, and he practiced crop rotation. This supplied feed for livestock and was a cash crop; it also preserved the land. He usually bought secondhand machinery, and his choices of technology complemented the use of community labor. The neighborhood ring cooperatively threshed, filled silos, and shredded corn. The Segerstroms did not purchase a tractor for field work until 1945, when they bought a $360 International Harvester, and they continued to use horses until 1951. The tractor plowed and prepared the ground; the horses followed, planting corn or seeding grain. When asked why he did this, Rangar explained that there were few good mechanical planters then, and drawing them was difficult because a second person had to lift the planter at the end of each row. It was easier to use horses. In the fields, in other words, the Segerstroms used new techniques but implemented them in practical ways that complemented their cautious management strategies and the use of family and community labor to cut expenses.

In the barn, advances followed similar patterns. Many of these changes depended on the introduction of electricity through the REA and as a result of the prosperity of World War II. Advances in the barn not only increased the farm's income, but also reduced the labor of farm women. Rangar stated proudly that his herd of purebred Guernsey cows averaged four hundred pounds of butterfat each per year, and that "five or six of us around Mondovi had pretty good herds." Margaret explained the details of the dairy work. In the barn, a cement tank held the cream while water, pumped by a windmill or gas engine, kept it cool. Margaret separated the cream, at first by hand and later by operating the gas engine, and hauled the cream to Mondovi once or twice a week. By 1940, electricity powered the separator, and a milk hauler took the milk to the cooperative creamery to be separated. Rangar, however, preferred separating at home because they then had the skim to use for feed. The Segerstroms added milking machines and water to the barn in about 1940, a concrete silo in 1942, and a milkhouse in 1947.

Illustrating a gender-integrated sense of mutuality, the Segerstroms improved their home as they improved their farm, even when improvements were not connected to the production of income. The first substantial home improvements came after they purchased the farm in 1932. They removed a "rickety" porch and remodeled and enlarged the house. They also switched from wood to coal heat, though the date of this change is not clear from the interview. The Segerstroms had water in the house before it was added to the barn in 1940. The windmill filled a tank upstairs with water, which then ran down to the kitchen where it could be heated. Most home improvements came simultaneously with farm improvements. When electricity came to the region in 1938, the Segerstroms already had the house and barn wired for lighting and had purchased a radio and refrigerator; they did not get milking machines until 1940. Home and barn use of electricity still had to be balanced because there was not enough "juice" to do "much extra," such as use irons or stoves, in the house when someone used the milking machines in the barn. The Segerstroms added a new porch and basement in 1947 and central heating in 1961. They practiced a cautious plan of expansion that complemented community patterns of work exchange, reinforced patterns of mutuality within the family, and exemplified traditional strategies of making do and saving.

The role of community activism in altering farm consumption patterns is best illustrated by the arrival of electricity. Electricity did not come as a gift from the government or the agricultural institutions. The Segerstroms and the Farmers' Union were actively involved in bringing electricity to the Mondovi area. Although at the national level the AFBF and the Grange also supported the REA, Margaret described it as the "Farmers' Union's baby" and took pride in it as a cooperative achievement. Locally, Rangar and Margaret went from house to house to get the support of the three farmers per mile necessary for the REA to extend electricity throughout the area. These visits took place after supper, when it was easiest to find the family in the house. Rangar commented that one "pert' near had to get them in with the women" because, as Margaret added, "women could see" that electricity would make a difference. The arguments they used to convince their neighbors of the value of electricity were not the same as those used by agricultural professionals, but emphasized local values and patterns of saving. They argued that electric light was superior to kerosene, not only in quality but also in terms of safety. They asserted that it would be inexpensive, $3.50 per month for forty kilowatts, and that people had to pay cash for kerosene anyway. Since people did not have many appliances, they would "hardly use any juice" and could keep costs down. They also pointed out that the Northern States Power Company would have charged a thousand dollars just to "hook up" a farm even if it was close to the highway, and the REA was a cooperative effort and would provide the same service for nothing. When they succeeded and the electricity was "turned on," it was "a wonderful feeling." The Farmers' Union held a pancake supper to celebrate. The advance was not just for a single fam-

ily's standard of living, but an achievement for the rural community acting cooperatively.

The Segerstroms were not among the progressive, "efficient" farmers
who practiced capital-intensive farming and had a new, consumer-oriented standard of living in the 1910s and 1920s. They adapted the new
techniques promoted by the agricultural agencies, but at a slow pace, saving and making do, using family and community labor rather than spending cash and keeping their neighborhood ties. They also were not among
the "inefficient" farmers who could not keep their farms through the economic crisis of the 1920s and 1930s. Unlike poorer farmers, they had
enough resources to benefit from the programs of the New Deal, such as
REA, the AAA, and the SCS, and did not use the emergency relief programs that kept many poorer farmers alive, if not permanently on their
farms. Nevertheless, they did not believe that their own improving standard of living could come only through farm consolidation and the loss of
farms in rural communities. The Segerstroms and the Farmers' Union
local worked to stop farm foreclosures throughout their region. However,
by the 1940s and 1950s, the Segerstroms had entered a more cash-oriented
world of modern agribusiness, beginning to rely more on labor saving
devices than on community and family labor, and had begun to move
toward consumer purchasing rather than home production.

The vision of farming maintained by the Segerstroms and other farm
people may have included the products and techniques of the new agriculture, but it did not necessarily share its social ideology. They hoped to
improve their working lives, but thought this would happen only through
community action, not by following the ideal of an isolated nuclear family practicing capital-intensive agriculture and status-oriented consumption. They tied improvements for the family to improvements for the community. Although agricultural professionals believed benefits for the few
came only with the exclusion of many inefficient farm people, the Segerstroms believed that benefits came only from thinking about "all of the
people in place of a few of the people."

As government agencies sought to modernize rural life by encouraging
isolated farm families who bought new products for farm and home, farm
people entered the age of modernity by blending old and new practices.
Farm people often could not become consumers without continuing family strategies of making do and home production, or organizing their communities to share expenses. Professionals assumed that modern consumption and production required farm consolidation and a declining farm
population, but farm people adopted new products that blended with the
system of family farm agriculture. Many farm people wanted to improve
agriculture and raise their standards of living, but the loss of farm homes

and neighborhoods was not part of their view of a better agriculture. The dominant policies of agricultural institutions assumed there was no alternative, and failed to address the social questions the answers to which might have produced a modern agriculture that still maintained communities of small family farms.

CHAPTER 8

The "Farmer" and the "Farmer's Wife"

Gender Ideology and Changing Concepts of Work

If government policies were to succeed in altering family farm agriculture's production and consumption patterns, they first needed to redefine the gender relations and the work cultures of farm men and women. Professionals prescribed that modern farmers purchase tractors and buy fuel, rather than using horses who ate homegrown feed. They argued that the farmer's wife should buy an electric washer and purchase electricity, rather than using her own physical labor. Farmers should become businessmen, and farmers' wives should become homemakers. In this schema, farm men and women were both managers, but the farm and home were separate business activities.[1] This ideology separated male work from family and community, and judged its worth by new, professional business standards of efficiency. It separated women's household labor from the productive work of the farm enterprise and judged it by class standards of refinement and consumption. Class status, defined through capital-intensive agriculture and increased consumption, was inseparable from this modern vision of rural gender relations. Consequently, this ideology clashed with the labor-intensive work traditions of small farms that organized the relations of women and men through their interconnected labor as part of a family enterprise.

Although the dominant ideology of agricultural institutions assumed the subordination of women's work to male business concerns, female professionals challenged this subordination. Asserting the importance of women's labor, they, like urban female reformers, used women's separate sphere as a strategy for achieving more equality for farm women and greater respect for themselves as professionals. This challenge to male dominance resonated with many farm women, who recognized the potential for abuse in the customary and legal control of resources given to farm men. However, the strategies women on small farms used to gain greater access to resources did not grow from an ideology of separate spheres, but from a vision of their work as an integral part of the family farm economy. Although the debate about men's labor assumed men's status as the heads of families, the debate about women's labor more clearly articulated the ties between gender and class, between the patriarchal family structure and the changes of capitalist agriculture.

The promotion of a new set of gender relations for agriculture served a number of interlocking purposes. The new gender ideology reflected the interests of male professionals and business leaders and defined masculinity and femininity in ways that reinforced both class and gender hierarchies. First, the application of the ideology of separate spheres to the farm reaffirmed professional definitions of male prerogative, separated the world of masculine profession from feminine home and family, and reinforced the professional gender segregation that was occurring within agricultural institutions. Reformers hoped to lift farm men and women to a new middle-class status. This status not only separated male and female spheres, but also removed physical labor from farm work to make it a middle-class rather than a working-class job. In this ideology, farmers became businessmen who managed farms with brains and technology rather than working their farms with brawn. Farm women became professional homemakers relieved of the "drudgery" of farm labor by new home technology. The middle-class model viewed agriculture and business as separate from community, family, and home, and professionals became the arbiters who would teach farm people how to change their work, behavior, and attitudes.

Politically, many who promoted this gender ideology hoped to stave off challenges to both class and male dominance by creating middle-class farm families whose men were tied to capitalist business interests and whose women accepted domesticity, the priority of family, and their own subordinate role to farm men. As noted in chapter 5, the Farm Bureaus countered alternative grass-roots political and cooperative movements. By defining manhood in a way that made farmers businessmen, they sought to prevent farmers from identifying with workers and break political ties to labor. Male professionals defined womanhood to separate farm women from an identification with the woman's movement and make them the bulwark of a politically and socially conservative patriarchal family. A 1920 article in the *Farmer's Wife* stated this philosophy: "As American farmers are saving the business life of the nation in these days of stress, American farm women, in like manner, are saving the ideals of the home." Farm women, like farm men, the article continued, had a conservative role. While city women were giving up "jobs as homemakers," "shirking responsibility" and following the "jazz amusements" of the city, farm women "continue[d] to live" in the way in which "normal" wives and mothers should. In 1928, C. J. Galpin explained that the city was the home of unmarried women and men and small or childless families. To him, the farm would preserve "the American type family," the "child-bearing type." Some people in agricultural institutions feared not only radical class unrest and the growing immigrant population of the 1910s, but also the new directions in careers and the limitations in family size chosen by native-born white women. Just as the Red Scare of the 1920s assumed a link between the threats of labor and the woman's movement, agricultural professionals defined manhood and womanhood in ways that simultaneously countered class- and gender-based challenges to the political status quo.[2]

Finally, the ideology of gender relations promoted economic change. Changes in gender relations did not merely follow the industrialization of agricultural production; they were crucial to creating it. By measuring manhood in terms of capital-intensive farm practices and womanhood in terms of cultural uplift defined by new standards of consumption, professionals assured that only those who practiced capital-intensive agriculture could meet these standards. Inefficient farmers were in important ways less than men, failures who were outside respectable manhood. For women the class dichotomy opposed the domestically efficient and cultured woman who had leisure because of technology to the drudge. Ideology bound this drudge image to negative class images of men. The drudge was overworked because she had married an oafish, and probably inefficient, man who did not respect his wife. A man's respect for a woman, measured by her leisure, helped denote manhood and womanhood. Thus, the removal of women from production marked both the respectable woman and the professional farmer.

However, the removal of farm women from the drudgery of farm labor merely reshaped male control of decision making in the farm enterprise. Women's labor may have been eased by new technology, but men still decided whether farm resources should be invested to ease it. This is illustrated by an advertisement for a cream separator. First the advertisement makes a pitch to the farm man, promoting the economic and production value of the new technology: "Mr. Farmer. Kindly glance back again over the previous pages to read the headlines only. You will find there a number of highly important features possessed by no other separator in existence except the new Sharples. Each feature means either more cream, better cream, or less trouble." The appeal to the farm woman acknowledged her labor, but did not mention production or income:

Madam Wife: We hope that the reading of the foregoing pages has particularly brought out the points which interest you. The suction-feed is a *convenient* separator. It is certainly the easiest to clean and keep clean. The supply tank is but knee-high. The easy turning and the freedom to turn as fast or as slow as you please are certainly very important.

The advertisement recognized women's work on the farm and that women might have some input into farm decisions, but saw them primarily as subordinate workers, not as equal decision makers in this part of the farm enterprise. Men gained respectability by making good decisions based on efficient business practices; women gained respectability by gaining leisure from farm labor.[3]

Agricultural institutions promoted definitions of manhood and womanhood and gender relations that were rooted in class and gender hierarchies. Even challenges by women to male dominance within these professions reflected similar class hierarchies and definitions of womanhood. As programs based on the hierarchical definitions of gender relations moved into the countryside, they encountered different gender relations, ones that reflected a positive valuation of labor; the integration of women and men, family and business within the farm enterprise; and communal, not hierarchical, definitions of worth. Although gender hierarchy and a sexual division of labor existed within rural traditions of manhood and womanhood, farm men saw their work in relationship to the community and family, and farm women used an ideology that championed human worth based in labor and gender interdependence to challenge both class and gender hierarchies in ways women professionals could not. Altering work and consumption patterns not only reshaped the farm's relation to the market, but also the rules by which men and women negotiated resource sharing and decision making.

To change production required changing rural work cultures. Since work in family farm agriculture was characterized by a gender division of labor, modifying work practices dictated a transformation of the definitions of manhood and womanhood associated with that work. It also dictated that community sources of knowledge be replaced with the advice offered by professional experts, and family-centered decision making with judgments based on efficiency and status. Because agricultural professionals believed farm men to be the primary implementers of agricultural innovation, they needed to teach farm men new criteria for judging a good farmer. Professionals rarely challenged the manliness of traditional farmers. After all, the "manly" virtues of physical labor, independence, and self-sufficiency embodied in the image of the farmer had deep roots in America's cultural heritage. The question was not whether old-fashioned farmers were masculine, but whether they were modern and progressive. Class, as much as gender, framed the redefinition of the farmer's image. What the ideal farmer lost in working-class values of physical strength and independence, he gained in middle-class values of training, intelligence, and professionalism. This professional, managerial status came from the acceptance of the methods of capital-intensive agriculture.

The modern farmer was a businessman, a manager of the farm. The traditional skills of working the land differed from the ability to introduce the latest in modern technology and science and to understand markets and keep business accounts. The first step to becoming a farm manager was education, and experts staffing the colleges of agriculture, extension services, and high school agricultural departments taught farmers their professions. As C. J. Galpin pointed out in a 1918 publication, education was crucial for surviving in the new age of agriculture: "The fear of the hoe farmer has been that if he educated his boy he will run the risk of losing the boy from the farm to the city. The fear of the machine farmer may very well be that if he failed to educate his boy he will run the risk that the boy will not comprehend the modern science and art of agriculture." Tying the future of agriculture to education, science, and technology, experts and promoters ridiculed traditional methods and local sources of knowledge as "backward." As one advertisement for the *Country Gentleman* stated:

Are You a Stick in the Mud?

One who doesn't believe in such "pesky" contraptions as tractors? Who won't rotate crops or feed stock? Who bars all conveniences from his home? Who says, "What was good enough for grandfather is good enough for me?" If you are, I won't bother you. For I'm selling *The Country Gentleman*, the weekly journal of the hustling, up-to-date, progressive farmer.

Promoters of change used negative stereotypes to portray men who resisted new technology as stupid, unreasonable bumpkins.[4] Only education and modern methods could redeem them and elevate them to the status of progressive farmers.

Machinery, technology, and scientific methods changed farming from manual labor to intellectual labor, giving it a more middle-class status. According to a 1931 speech by rural sociologist Carl C. Taylor, who succeeded Galpin as head of the Division of Farm Population and Rural Life in 1937, machines and science freed farmers from the "mental paralysis which results from continuous fatigue." "Furthermore, the very processes of scientific and machine farming are direct stimuli to thinking. . . . the more complex farm machines give him new problems altogether. He does not, like the common factory worker, merely feed the machine." Scientific farming removed farmers from the ranks of labor and made them business managers. The modern farmer did not just work with nature to grow a crop, but through science and technology, controlled and managed the soil. He was a professional whose work demanded managerial and scientific skills, not those of "farming the land."[5]

As farmers became managers, business criteria dictated their choices. Modernization depended on the use of credit to expand and capitalize farm operations. Agricultural institutions and farm journals encouraged cordial relationships between farmers and bankers, and attacked farmers' resistance to debt and expansion. An advertisement in the *Country Gentleman* in the 1920s attacked the farmer's fear of debt as backward and unreasonable:

Out of Debt, But—

Henry Shepard had paid off his mortgage and was out of debt but his farm income was a mere pittance.

Henry's banker, the ad continued, suggested that Henry put in tile drains and add a silo. These improvements would pay for themselves through increased income. Henry was afraid to go into debt again, but "luckily, the banker was a man of vision and he lent him cash to make improvements—and so to make money." Promoters linked debt and improvements to increased income.[6] This vision ignored the instability of farm incomes and the reality that unpaid farm debts led to farm foreclosures, a problem that had become particularly acute with the overexpansion during World War I and the economic contraction of the early 1920s.

Professionals used the dichotomy of the "modern" and the "backward" farmer to redefine the concept of the agricultural ladder. By pairing this dichotomy with the notion of the survival of the fittest, they justified the displacement of small farmers and tenants. The rungs of the agricultural ladder consisted of laborers, tenants, and owners. The earlier image of the agricultural ladder invoked ideals of opportunity, with a farmer moving through each of these stages, up the rungs, to become a farm owner. Actual studies of tenancy in the late 1910s, the 1920s, and the 1930s showed that this "natural" progression did not mesh with reality. The proportion of tenants was too high, and tenants and farm laborers were older, not mere youths beginning their way up the ladder. To rationalize these trends, experts described tenants as inefficient businesspeople who did not make proper business decisions and refused to invest in new agricultural methods. More-efficient farmers moved to the top of the ladder and, as owners of smaller farms went out of business, the better farmers took on more land and became even more efficient farmers. Although some professionals in the 1930s questioned this ideology, most saw the class stratification of rural America, the increased size of farms, and the declining number of farmers as the inevitable and positive result of modern farmers' success and the weeding out of backward farmers.[7]

As agricultural institutions and farm business interests created a new middle-class image of farmers, the image of the farmer as worker persisted. Despite new technology, the work of farmers still was largely physical, not white collar. Drawings of men's ready-made clothing in the Sears catalog clearly distinguished between farmers and professionals. Men drawn in suits were slim, elegant, and sophisticated, suggesting a life of leisure and little toil. Men in overalls were muscular and often pictured with the tools of their trade. Professionals also maintained their status as experts, above practicing farmers—even progressive ones. Photographs from the 1920s and 1930s portray county agents and other agricultural experts interacting with farmers from a position of superior class, knowledge, and power. The agent is in white shirt and tie, the farmer in overalls. The agent always appears to lecture, "advising" the farmer in a clear pose of superior knowledge and control. Even when the farmer is speaking, the agent listens not as one who is learning, but as one who is judging. Even if farmers were professional managers, they were still in a class below the experts.[8]

The portrayal of farmers as sponges eager to soak up the wisdom of county agents does not accurately reflect the relationship of farmers and experts. Farm men may have adopted practices that professionals and advertisers promoted; however, they selected methods and gave them meaning from a perspective based in very different definitions of "good" farming and manhood. Farm men, like farm women, saw their work as part of family and community labor systems that made farming more than a business. The term *farmer* prioritized male labor on the farm and assumed both the male definition of that work (women were not seen as "farmers") and men's positions as heads of farm households. The meanings of "farmer" show the primacy of work, especially working the land, to rural definitions of manhood, but also its fundamental tie to a less articulated family economy. The community of farm men set the standards of masculine labor, and farm men learned valued work skills from practical experience and past generations. Farm men constructed the meaning of their work from shared communal values that did not privilege the opinions of wealthier farmers or professional experts, thus contradicting the class distinctions inherent in the concept of the progressive farmer.

Local definitions of good farming were not backward or out of touch with current agricultural trends. Some farmers eagerly sought information about the latest scientific methods from agricultural institutions and farm magazines; others had at least some contact with these sources of farm knowledge. Wisconsin farmers listed University of Wisconsin short courses, county agricultural schools, county agents, Farmers' Institutes, extension bulletins, 4-H Clubs, *Hoard's Dairyman*, the *Farmer's Wife*, the *Prairie Farmer*, the *Farm Journal*, the Soil Conservation Service in the 1930s, and farm organizations and associations as sources of knowledge. Farmers selected and tested this knowledge using criteria based on their community values and economic class.

As county agents began their field work, farm men challenged their assumptions and goals. These conflicts appear in the letters of Ernest Luther, one of the first county agents in Wisconsin (he began work in Oneida County in 1912). He was clearly tied to business interests, such as International Harvester, but kept these connections hidden from area farmers in order to encourage their participation and trust. However, the farmers' demands quickly placed him at odds with local agricultural businesses. Farmers demanded that Luther test their cream in order to challenge the local cream factory's grading procedures and prices. Despite the advice of his University of Wisconsin supervisor, Luther conducted these tests because he felt he could not promote dairying if farmers "just got cheated." Local farmers criticized him for spending too much time at one of the larger farms in the region, which suggests the agent's ties to more prosperous farms and the other farmers' insistence that agents serve the entire community. As Luther met with local farmers, he was impressed (and perhaps surprised) by the "good questions" farmers asked. He gained sympathy for the poorer farmers on "that jack pine land," but still played a superior role, hoping to "help out some of the poor fellows," and encouraged progressive farming as the answer despite the farmers' poverty; if they "only had a little money they would surely buy some [purebred] bulls." Despite these positive encounters he continued to suspect the character and responsibility of the poorer farmers: "But Professor, a good many are not too poor to spend good hard-earned money for drink." Despite the agents' attitudes, farmers clearly defined their own needs and were both open to and critical of the activities and practices promoted by county agents.[9]

Knowledge and work skills were often exchanged among men in the community. For example, when Jack Levin's father, a Jewish immigrant from Poland, moved out of Milwaukee to farm, his "old country" farming experiences were of little help. Through neighborly assistance, Levin learned the farm practices that worked in his new environment. Community exchange also played a role in the dissemination of information produced by agricultural institutions. Levin read farm magazines and extension service bulletins. When he read about cabbage worms, he wrote to the USDA for information on spraying poison. His cabbage plants were the only ones in his neighborhood to survive. When his neighbors asked him how he did it, he shared both his knowledge and his plants, providing seed for another crop. Levin learned farming in traditional and modern ways, and shared innovations with his neighbors.[10]

Farmers often preferred to gain knowledge from a local farmer who experimented than from outside experts. Practical experience, not just scientific knowledge, signaled a good farmer. Farmers trusted this knowledge because its source had participated in social and work exchanges and farmed under similar conditions. Arthur Wileden, a rural sociologist at the University of Wisconsin, recalled that neighbors scoffed at his parents for following the practices their children learned while attending the university. However, the Wiledens' neighbors copied their poultry practices. Wileden, like his parents' neighbors, noted the limitations of extension service and university demonstration farms. Although he thought them good for experiments and research, he felt they were too far removed from the typical reality of farms to be workable models. He felt farmers in his childhood neighborhood benefited more from the experiences of neighbors than from demonstrations of scientific farming.

Although communal exchange sometimes encouraged farmers to try new practices, the farmers' criteria for the adoption of innovations were rooted in class experiences distinct from those that shaped the business criteria of experts. Wisconsin farmer Norval Ellefson, who always looked to agricultural institutions as sources of new farming techniques, nevertheless understood the hesitancy of many of his neighbors. Whereas experts defined this hesitance as backwardness, Ellefson placed it in the context of farmers' unreliable incomes. Only a few of his neighbors were open critics of "book learning." Most hesitated to follow new techniques because their resources were limited, and they "couldn't afford to make many mistakes." Innovations had to be "proven out." One of his roles was to be the local farmer who could be trusted to test the success or failure of new methods. Farmers judged farming techniques not by progressive criteria, but by the economic realities of farming small family farms and their own community standards of effectiveness.[11]

Farmers often adopted innovations for reasons that contradicted the aims of capital-intensive farming. Wisconsin farmers undertook soil-conservation measures, using alfalfa, lime, or strip cropping. As one farmer said, these methods were important to "make the best of what you have." They could work on small family farms and did not require large acreage or expansion.[12] Wisconsin farmer Howard Brusveen acquired his work skills from past generations, his neighbors, and minimal contact with agricultural institutions. When asked how he got his farm knowledge, he replied that he "grew up with it" and learned in the "school of hard knocks." He read some farm papers, but he felt there was "a lot of hogwash in there, as far as that goes." Although he expressed distrust of agricultural institutions, he had participated in the 4-H Club program as a child, and this led his family to switch to purebred calves. He began using hybrid seed after a neighbor won a bushel of it and had success with it. In the 1930s, he followed some of the recommendations of the Soil Conservation Service, but these alterations blended with his traditional practice of crop rotation. Brusveen made innovations cautiously and selected those advances that fit his small farm and community traditions of farming.

When Brusveen discussed the state of agriculture in the 1970s, he believed that there was a lack of efficient farmers. Although "efficiency" was a term often used by the agricultural institutions, Brusveen defined it differently. "Good operators" used all of what the land could produce, but only in a way that preserved the land. Efficiency did not equal expansion and new technology, but smaller acreage both used and conserved. He believed that there was a "dangerously low level of skilled agriculture," and skill meant practical experience, not formal education or scientific knowledge. Brusveen noted, "If you don't have any down to earth experience with agriculture today you are going to hit the rocks in a hurry. It's a big business operation and if you're gonna borrow a half million dollars and pay fifteen percent interest . . . [without skills you could] be in a lot of trouble real quick." He acknowledged the vast changes in agriculture that made farming "big business," but believed that the skills of the past needed to be revived to make agriculture "efficient" for small family farms where farming was practiced as "a way of life."[13] Even in the very different agricultural economy of the 1970s, Brusveen inherently connected the success of agriculture to small farms and the success of the owners of those farms to community survival strategies and male work traditions.

Working-class definitions of good farming challenged hierarchical, middle-class definitions of progressive farming. Agricultural experts saw farm consolidation as inevitable and dismissed farmers who had difficulties as inefficient; farmers at the bottom rungs of the ladder saw other causes for their difficulties. Farmers who wrote to the FSA during the 1930s described drought conditions and poor prices as primary causes of farmers' problems. These problems were beyond the control of the farmers, not caused by poor management. Some analyzed their problems as part of the changing structure of agriculture and the pressures it created for farm consolidation. One Iowa farmer wrote that he wanted to farm, "but can't because there are three or four men who are trying to farm most of the counties in which I live. The most of the land is owned by loan companies mostly

Insurance, and they rent thousands and thousands of acres to one man which is not justice at all." Most of these farmers did not want to run huge farming operations; they wanted only small farms. An Illinois man wrote that he wanted land in the Ozarks because "I *don't* want a farm in Illinois as it takes to [sic] much money and is to [sic] big a bite for a poor man to undertake." Many knew that they were not alone and based their demands on their shared predicament with other farmers. A Nebraska man wrote, "now [it is] to the point what is to becum [sic] of men like me of which thair [sic] is thousands." Their demands were based on familial reasons, not commercial ones. These farmers wanted only small tracts of land to support themselves and provide food for their families. Their letters rejected farm consolidation and business efficiency as unjust. Modern agriculture violated their belief in an agriculture based on communities of small family farms.

These owners of small farms, tenants, and displaced farmers and farm laborers justified their demands by referring to their work skills, which formed the basis of their manhood and their right to farm the land. They requested, and sometimes demanded, assistance because they were good farmers. Most of the men began their requests by mentioning their farming skills. The phrases "I am a good farmer," "I have farmed all my life," and "I was born and raised on a farm" were their credentials. They asserted that the problems they encountered were not their fault, and that they did not want a gift, but merely a loan to give them a chance for a new beginning. They were hard workers, and this quality, they felt, ensured that the loans would be repaid and that they deserved a chance to return to farming, to rent or to buy a farm. These men were workers, not businesspeople, and farming was their "life work," a tradition based on inherited knowledge and well-practiced skills. They were not inefficient, but hard-pressed by economic crisis and the changing structure of agriculture. [14]

The technological innovation that most clearly symbolized the modern farmer was the tractor. By the 1930s, tractors could be used instead of horses in most field operations. The tractor symbolized the transition from farmer as worker to farmer as manager. The replacement of animal with machine power made the restructuring of agricultural production possible and removed hard physical labor from the job description of the farmer. It contributed to the industrialization of agriculture by decreasing the farm's labor needs and encouraging farm consolidation. The tractor became a symbol of farm prosperity and modernity; horse farming, a symbol of backwardness and poverty. [15] The transition redefined male work culture.

Many farmers shared the values of professionals and saw tractors as part of agricultural progress and a sign of status. Owning a tractor often suggested improved economic status and success as a progressive farmer. Elmer G. Powers, an Iowa farmer, noted his purchase of a used Farmall tractor in 1937 by saying that nearly all his neighbors had cultivating tractors, and he had "waited a long time for a more modern tractor." In this case, tractor farming was not only modern, but also the community standard for measuring a successful farmer. Many farmers used tractors to expand their operations. These farmers accepted definitions of masculine work that paired new technology with large-scale farming.

Farm expansion was not the only reason for a farmer to purchase a tractor, however; tractor technology also eased physical labor. Although this seems inconsistent with the value placed on hard work, male farm culture valued both physical strength and mechanical skills. Farmers did not romanticize the demanding toil of their work. Farm men often remembered the hard labor of horse farming they had experienced when young, and wanted to avoid it. John Faul, a North Dakota farmer, worked from "dark to dark," walking behind plows with water up to his knees. Howard Brusveen worked at a walking plow in 1930, at the age of twelve or thirteen, when he was so small that the handles were in front of his eyes. Even after new technology enabled him to ride rather than walk, he still described it as hard, uncomfortable work; it would "just about shake the liver out of you." Tractors eased this heavy labor, and the desire for some ease did not conflict with the farmers' view of masculinity.

Brusveen, who disliked the "hogwash" of agricultural publications, nevertheless embraced the tractor as a benefit even for small farmers because it saved cash. He purchased a tractor in 1942 because it would save on expenses for horses and feed. He had hogs, chickens, and cattle, and in dry years, particularly those of the 1930s, he found it hard to grow enough feed for them all on his small farm. The tractor was "not eating anything when it wasn't working," and the feed that would have gone to horses now went to stock animals. In 1946, he was the first in his neighborhood to buy a tractor with rubber tires. Brusveen's investment showed caution and no great desire to be modern; he continued to use that tractor until 1977. Brusveen's tractor fit his strategy of farm management, which emphasized cash-saving strategies, not expansion or modernity.[16]

Farmers who did not purchase or delayed purchasing tractors judged their worth as farmers by their ability to balance investment with saving; to produce what the farm needed on the farm; to use labor more than spending cash; and to rely on networks of exchange to enhance farm resources. Since farmers had little control over commodity prices, owners of small farms, in particular, developed strategies to control the cost of inputs. Tractor farming did not fit with these strategies. Tractors required the purchase of new kinds of machinery, and increased cash operating expenses that farmers previously could have met with resources supplied by the farm, family, or community. With tractors, farmers had to pay for fuel and repairs; feed for horses could be raised on the farm. The primary advantage of tractors, the savings in labor and labor costs, did not lead to direct cuts in expenses for owners of small farms, who relied on unpaid family or neighborhood labor, and the increased production did not necessarily lead to higher incomes to cover these increased costs. While horse farming often encouraged local exchanges of labor and feed, the money farmers spent on tractors went out of the local community. In contrast, horse farming increased self-sufficiency within the farm neighborhood and decreased market dependence. Farmers who expressed a preference for horse farming or bought tractors at a very late date often mentioned these objections to tractors.[17]

Other farmers defended their choice of horse farming as a work culture that connected them to past male work traditions and to family heritage. Two North Dakota farmers recalled growing up with their own teams, which no one else worked. They argued with siblings over whose team was best and worked with the same team for years. Each of these farmers was among the last in his neighborhood to purchase a tractor. Many farmers enjoyed working with horses. John Seltvedt, a North Dakota farmer, recalled that horse farming was hard work, but he always "agreed with" horses. Each horse had a personality, and horses "know who you are." They were partners, knowing the routines of work and leisure. Seltvedt's father had a team of horses for twenty-four years; Seltvedt worked his own team for sixteen years. He took excellent care of his horses, and "they took good care of me." Tractors could not evoke such feelings.[18]

As farmers made the transition from horses to tractors, many integrated the machine with male work traditions and community exchanges. North Dakotan John Vaage did not get a tractor until 1939, when he rented more land. The land was heavy sod, and he thought his horses were too slow. He and his sons used horses and tractors in the same fields, a practice that also appears in photographs in the USDA collections. Getting accustomed to tractors was not difficult for Vaage because he had worked with them for neighbors. Often a farmer would rent or borrow a tractor from a neighbor before buying one himself.[19]

Ultimately, however, tractors, combined with policies that promoted the consolidation of agricultural production and distribution, divided the community of farmers and undermined the exchanges that created male interdependence. Initially tractors most negatively affected those at the lower end of the economic spectrum. Many farm laborers and owners of small farms who relied on cash from hiring out their labor found that mechanization hurt their employment opportunities and made it more difficult to keep their farms. Studies in Illinois, Nebraska, and Kansas indicate that New Deal programs, particularly those of the AAA, enabled some landowners to buy tractors, farm more land, and use less help, which hurt other laborers, farmers, and farmers' sons in their own communities. Eventually, those who purchased tractors could also feel negative affects. Many farmers who purchased tractors, particularly in the 1920s, found that poor prices and drought kept them from paying their debts for machinery and endangered their ability to keep their farms in the 1930s.[20] In the long run, tractors decreased the physical labor of farming, but did not necessarily increase farmers' leisure or alter their sense of themselves as workers. John Vaage commented that the tractor made it possible to work longer hours than with horses, since tractors did not need to rest. For Vaage, the labor was easier, but he worked more hours in order to increase his income.

Modern farming transformed the work on small farms by decreasing its communal content and redefining survival strategies to decrease saving and increase production and income. This altered male work culture even as farm men retained their respect for hard work and their identity as farmers. Rangar Segerstrom described these changes by comparing his labor in the 1930s to his son's in the 1970s. Rangar used four horses to do all the work on his 120 acres. Everyone stopped for dinner at noon and supper at six, and even the "horses knew exactly what time it is." Twenty-two cows were milked by hand, which took two or three family members less than an hour, leaving plenty of time in the evening to attend meetings or visit neighbors. His son had 120 cows, so milking took more time. Because he needed cash income, his son also worked a second job as an International Harvester salesperson. Because he could not finish field work during the day, he did it at night with lighted machinery. Such long hours of labor happened only at harvest time during the "old days." Segerstrom concluded by blaming costly machinery for the change: "that's why they have to keep on so early and so late." He would "rather farm like when I did than the way they're farming now." The promise of modern agriculture, that its efficiency would lead to better income for professional farm businessmen, was fulfilled only for some, and the number of those few has continued to dwindle.[21]

The modern farmer's wife established the middle-class status of the farm family. Although farmers' physical work was appropriate to an image of masculinity but did not fit their new middle-class status, the physical work of farm women not only clashed with middle-class status, but also made them "unwomanly." Such labor signified the inferiority of rural life. Professionals and the farm press portrayed farm women who worked in the field, and sometimes those who worked with livestock, as drudges.

The middle-class farmer's wife, like her urban counterpart, worked only in the home, providing for her family. The new ideology even subsumed acceptable labor, such as poultry and gardening, under the heading of her new role as consumer. In these images, when women sold any surplus, they used their "pin money" to improve the home and provide cultural advantages for themselves and their children. This ideology trivialized women's work as producers and savers and ignored its real economic contributions, encouraging women to define themselves by their ability to improve the quality of life through consumption.[22]

Although this view of women's work dominated the ideology and structure of agricultural institutions, women in the fields of home economics and rural sociology conducted much of the research on and extension projects for women. Marginalized within their institutions, many of these professional women wanted to improve the status of women both in their professions and on the farms. As agricultural institutions redefined the structure and content of male farm work, female agricultural professionals attempted to define women's place in this modernized agriculture, sometimes accepting and sometimes questioning its tenets. Many professional women challenged the gender hierarchies inherent in these institutions and in the power relations of farm families. However, in most cases, these professionals accepted the class hierarchies found in professional agricultural ideology and policy. They rarely questioned the inequities of income distribution among farm families or the ways in which policies meant to aid farmers excluded poorer farm people. When professionals confronted farm women whose lives did not reflect their ideals, they did not condemn these women, but they also did not question that the new capital-intensive agriculture would change their lives in positive ways.

Ideas for improving the lives of farm women developed in relation to agricultural politics and the women's movement. Beginning in the early twentieth century, the *Farmer's Wife*, a monthly magazine published by the Webb Publishing Company of St. Paul, Minnesota, reverberated with the debate over women's place in modern agriculture.[23] In the 1920s and 1930s, the magazine had a circulation of more than a million and was particularly popular in the Midwest and Great Lakes regions. In 1939, the *Farm Journal* purchased the *Farmer's Wife* to get its lucrative advertising business in baby foods, cosmetics, and home appliances. Between 1939 and 1944, the two were combined under one cover but kept separate identities. Gradually, the women's section became smaller and, by August 1945, the magazine was again titled simply the *Farm Journal*. Reduced to a small women's section, "The Farmer's Wife" retained that title only in the table of contents.

In its earliest years, the *Farmer's Wife* actively supported the woman's movement and the country life movement. Reports on the suffrage movement, women's clubs, and the diverse organizations of farm women, including the International Farm Women's Congress, show that rural women were active participants in the woman's movement and rural reform. In these early years, the magazine had a populist style. For example, "The Home Club" contained readers' letters, which asked for advice from other readers. Rather than being addressed to an editor or staff writer, the letters began "Dear Sisters." The questions and replies could be practical, giving home remedies or advice on how to remake clothes, or deal with important issues such as problems within marriages, ways to define appropriate work roles, and questions of women's rights, including suffrage and the right to control income. The other departments reflected farm women's work, including sections on dairy, poultry and garden, health, beauty and fashion, fancywork, and a "Young Folks" page.

With a change in editorship by 1915, the journal became more closely associated with the professionalizing field of home economics and the programs of agricultural institutions. Reports from women's clubs now came from those affiliated with agricultural extension. "The Home Club" became "Our Home Circle," a column that provided advice from an expert. Increasingly, it focused narrowly on issues of homemaking, cultural improvement, and entertaining. The sections on child raising and domestic concerns increased, while poultry and dairy advice received less space. By 1917, "Use Your State College" replaced "Our Home Circle." By the 1920s, as advertising revenues became increasingly important, suggestions on home remedies and making do gave way to articles on the latest fashions and consumer goods.

The editorial policies of the magazine became more conservative on farm policy, labor policy, and women's issues, but maintained a pro-woman agenda. Editorials decried labor unions and closely paralleled the positions of the AFBF rather than organizations such as the NPL or the Farmers' Union. The magazine supported the General Federation of Women's Clubs, which was more conservative than other women's organizations, and encouraged rural women's clubs to affiliate. Paralleling the position of other "social feminists," editorials favored protective labor legislation rather than the Equal Rights Amendment. However, the magazine continued to report on the activities of the National Women's Party and the International League for Peace and Freedom, even during World War I and the 1920s, when these groups were controversial. Within a relatively conservative framework, the magazine continued to advocate improvement in the status of farm women. Although the editorials and fiction reflected the dominant ideology of agricultural institutions, the writers used language that increased rather than devalued the importance of women and their work.[24]

As female agricultural professionals considered the status of farm women in modern agriculture, they saw them losing class status in comparison to urban, middle-class women and losing gender status in relation to farm men. Although technology eased the work of urban women and farm men, farm women continued to toil in primitive conditions. These comparisons led to an image of farm women as overworked drudges. Middle-class urban women had access to laborsaving devices and other services, such as bakeries and laundries, much earlier. Investment in farm machinery often preceded similar laborsaving technologies in the home. These professionals hoped to lessen the physical toil of farm women by restricting their work to reflect middle-class standards of domesticity and by equalizing work demands between men and women on the farm. As in the nineteenth-century woman's movement, professionals reified separate spheres and domesticity and used the female sphere to challenge male dominance. They contested important inequities in rural gender relations, but did so from within the confines of middle-class definitions of womanhood and modern agriculture.

Professionals developed three strategies for improving the status of the modern farmer's wife. The first restructured the relationship between women's labor and that of the entire farm enterprise. Professionals attacked what might be called the "double burden" of a farm woman's labor: her work in the field and her work in the home. Redefining the farm woman from field worker to domestic laborer raised her social status. In the strategy's more prescriptive forms of the 1920s, writers glorified women's domestic role. However, in its more practical forms, professionals used this restructuring of women's work to attack what they viewed as inequitable divisions of labor on the farm and to decrease women's physical labor compared to that of men. Getting immediately to the heart of the inequities regarding work flexibility, Nellie Kedzie Jones wanted to separate women's work from that of men because women too often helped in the field while men rarely helped in the house. In some ways this view reinforced women's domestic role and native-born, middle-class ideals of womanhood. For example, Jones refused to teach girls in agricultural colleges to milk because it was "not a woman's work." However, she also challenged the priority of male work by demanding that men help with the laundry; "I wish it could be burnt into the consciousness of every man and every woman that washing under average farm conditions is a man's work." On the basis of the physical strength needed for the task, observed Jones, riding a mowing machine was much easier than doing the laundry.

Here Jones critiqued the technological changes and gender hierarchies that made male work less physical and made women's physical toil more "manly" than "men's work." Inherent within this was a critique of the male dominance of the new capital-intensive farming. However, Jones did not push the logic of this statement to promote a change in the gender division of labor. Instead, she proposed a separation of field and home work, with extra help and technology provided to farm women for home tasks.[25] In this way, she accepted class-based definitions of womanhood, while challenging the gender hierarchies that made women's work more easily exploited and less valuable in both agricultural institutions and family structures.

In similar ways, women professionals attacked the potential abuse of women's tendency toward self-sacrifice, which was imbedded in rural traditions of making do and home production. In doing so, however, they, like their institutions, also redefined women's labor in terms of consumption and technology, assuming levels of cash income that many farm people did not have. Professionals discouraged farm women from doing without or using their labor to produce on the farm what could be purchased at a cheaper price. As one expert advised:

The question should not be can I possibly get along without that?—but, can I bring myself to a higher degree of efficiency, to a state of more robust vigor, of more intense and joyous activity, by having the conserving appliances, by cooking more sustaining meals, by inducing them to wear shoes with thicker soles and coats of rubber or to stop work sooner? Can I get a little more efficiency out of myself and of my family and out of the workers in barn and kitchen by adopting these new-fangled ideas or devices?

Professionals attempted to change the way women viewed their relationship to labor and consumption. Nellie Kedzie Jones recommended that farm women give their time cash value and purchase soap and clothing rather than make them because "the latest and the best is none too good for the hardworked woman." Such advice encouraged farm women to enter the market economy by giving monetary value to their labor and by purchasing what could be made on the farm. It did not give them new ways to turn their time into cash.[26]

Although professionals attempted to lessen the work of farm women, they did not devalue the labor women did. They insisted that women's work in the home entitled farm women to their fair share of farm income. They decried the tendency of farm men to put resources into the farm first and challenged the patriarchal control of farm management and resources. For example, in "This New Freedom Stuff," a short story published in 1921 in the *Farmer's Wife*, the female protagonist proclaimed that women were equal contributors to the farm and that farm profits should be "divided between the house and the barn, so that where there was a convenience added in one place, there would be in the other." She organized a farm women's club and convinced her fiancé's mother to join. This outraged her fiancé. When she suggested that his mother had "sacrificed more than you realize," he replied to her challenge to male family control: "Mother doesn't care for those things. . . . She is essentially a home woman. She cares for her *family's* happiness, not her own. This 'new freedom' stuff is bolshevism, Madge." It took a near auto accident and Madge's driving and first-aid skill, which she had learned at the club, to convince him of the need to accept changes in women's roles. Here the modern woman, like the modern farmer, categorized traditional values as backward. However, the critique of male dominance is not aimed at an inefficient, oafish farmer, but at an efficient, modern one. Female professionals pointed out the abuses of male authority possible in the middle-class progressive farmer and challenged male dominance within modern agriculture itself.

But professional women balanced these demands for greater economic control of farm resources with an acceptance of women's essentially domestic and supportive position in the farm enterprise. For example, Nellie Kedzie Jones asserted that farm women's contributions to the farm, though separate, made them equal partners. She recommended that women have their own or joint accounts and that they force men to do business with them as if they were men. A woman was to be the "private secretary" and "co-equal," to keep financial records, and to know the "business side" of the farm. But the wife should advise and help manage, not veto decisions: "Be slow to criticize. Be sympathetic. Remember that the one who is doing the actual work knows and feels the difficulties as an onlooker never can." The separation of work roles gave men, the "actual" physical laborers, final control of the management of land, cash crops, and income, reinforcing their position of power as husbands. Although she advised farm women not to be "too timid" to take from the "family purse" what the home really needed, the family purse and the farm enterprise were still ultimately controlled by men.[27]

By arguing for women's separate sphere, agricultural professionals maintained a middle-class view of women's appropriate work roles and reaffirmed male control of the business side of farming. However, by defending the importance of women's sphere, they challenged many practices of male dominance within both agricultural institutions and farm families. Ultimately, their solutions to farm women's problems reaffirmed the vision of capital-intensive, consumer-oriented agriculture promoted by agricultural institutions, and shared their assumption of a prosperous farm constituency, even as they challenged its gender hierarchies.

In the second model for improving the status of farm women, professionals demanded access for farm women to the role of farm manager. Much less dominant in the literature, this argument also accepted the ideology of the new agriculture, but took its vision of the modern farmer and made it acceptable for women. The professionals had to defend women's ability to do the job and make the job more appropriate for women. This approach challenged male control of production and altered the sexual division of labor. So long as farming involved physical work that made it a working-class job, professionals hoped to remove women from production because it was unwomanly, but as farming became a respectable profession, some female experts challenged its exclusion of women.

Professionals used the ideas of scientific farming, which emphasized management rather than physical labor, to promote women in agriculture. Although it did not involve physical labor, managing was also a "manly" pursuit and did not easily fit with ideas of respectable womanhood. For example, in 1911, the *Farmer's Wife* reported that at a state Homemakers' Club meeting, eight Missouri women "hesitatingly admitted that they were farmers," not farmer's wives, and formed their own organization. Their conception of farm work emphasized supervisory and business skills rather than physical labor, and the magazine compared their efforts to those of other women who were pioneers in male-dominated vocations. When the Missouri women's club gave an agricultural scholarship in 1915 to a girl to "study practical farming," it stated: "It is desired that women be encouraged in the profession of agriculture, as well as in the profession of medicine and law."

While challenging women's exclusion from agriculture as a profession, professionals also carefully defended the pathbreakers' respectability and womanhood. The officers in the Missouri club were housekeepers and "even plead guilty to the vanities of modish costume and millinery." Three of the eight had children, and two had husbands in other businesses. It is unclear if the rest were widows or shared in the farm business with their husbands. The article defended the two single women who did not have "domestic ties" by noting that they actively participated in other clubs, fulfilling their "women's role" as their "brother's keeper" in society. In order to challenge exclusively male definitions of work, professional women had to prove farm women's respectability and womanhood through their familial and social ties.

Issues of respectability also required that these women's farms were affluent and modern. Farm women were professional when they operated mechanized farms, not when they did manual labor in the fields. However, even tractor farming did not necessitate a professional role for farm women. During World War I, agricultural institutions encouraged women to do field work because of the shortage of male laborers. Male professionals placed women in the role of subordinate workers, not professional farmers. A 1918 USDA article argued that women made superior tractor drivers because driving took "skill and close attention and ability to follow directions." A woman will assume she knows nothing and will follow instructions, it continued, while a hired man will assume he knows everything and will "monkey with the machinery" and be careless.

Although the USDA devalued women's skills and stopped promoting women's field work after the war, the *Farmer's Wife* continued to encourage this trend. The magazine held a more positive view of women's skills. It emphasized that the work did not harm women, and did not turn them into drudges. One fourteen-year-old North Dakota girl, the "child champion tractor operator," was described this way: "She does not look overworked either—indeed, she had every appearance of thoroughly enjoying her place at the wheel as mistress of the iron horse." This girl was in control of her work. She was the "mistress" of the machine, not a subordinate worker following directions. However, mechanized farming still determined her position in the field. The tractor made field work less difficult and opened it up as appropriate work for women and girls.[28]

The third method of improving women's status defended the importance of all women's labor on the farm. It appeared less frequently in the literature and occurred most often in connection with discussions of the experiences of real farm women. When farm women encountered the ideas of women professionals, they often questioned the assumptions that farms would be mechanized and that farm women could abandon field work and give up home production to become consumers. Although professionals acknowledged the differing realities of farm women's lives, they rarely, at least in their published work, questioned their own class-based assumptions or challenged the economic vision of agriculture promoted by their institutions.

Only rarely did professionals publish challenges to class-based assumptions about women's work. Writing to the *Farmer's Wife* in 1922, one author argued that thanks to the farm press, "the country woman has been shown that physical effort is a disgrace and a mark of stupidity and that her work out of doors is deplorable." She defended the physical labor of farm women and confronted the class content of this view of women's physical abilities. She questioned the logic that made it fashionable for rich girls to sweat playing tennis, swimming, or riding, but made it "reprehensible for a woman to perspire over necessary and productive labor." However, professionals rarely glorified women's physical labor in "men's work" as this author did.[29]

Professionals did laud the skills of actual farm women and their economic contributions as both income producers and income savers when that labor was appropriate "women's work."[30] The *Farmer's Wife*, even as it strengthened its domestic emphasis after 1915, continued to run articles on how farm women could increase their cash income by expanding some operations, such as poultry or fruit. In addition, they recognized the economic value of making do even if they did not approve of the self-sacrifice involved in it. A 1921 editorial, "Dignifying the Work of Farm Women," pointed out that women were "economic agents." It argued that authorities denied women's economic role because their activities, such as sewing and baking, took place in the home and were perceived as "having *saved* money instead of having *earned* it." The editorial sharply criticized the classification by the United States Bureau of the Census of farm wives as "women with no occupation." Professional women defended the value of farm women's "feminine" work, particularly against male-dominated practices that devalued it.[31]

Nevertheless, the professional literature implied that farm women used their income production to purchase home conveniences and cultural items, rather than to make essential contributions to farm survival. Some farm women criticized this assumption of farm affluence. One farm woman responded to the many articles about farm women easily purchasing conveniences through marketing women's products.

It is useless to say "make butter, raise gooseberries, chickens and so forth." All the women I know do that and their produce is always exchanged at the local grocery for provisions for the family and the man would be so injured in his feelings if it were disposed of otherwise that he would not be pleasant to live with. Do you really suppose the women do without labor-saving conveniences, pleasures and so forth because they are so stupid that they don't want them? It is because they haven't the money to buy them.

Although this suggests the possibility of conflict with men over resource allocation, a potential common ground for women professionals and farm women, it also makes clear that both farm men and farm women expected women's income to provide essentials for the farm family. The author criticizes professional women for blaming farm women's ignorance for their inability to purchase labor-saving devices. Professionals and the farm press failed to acknowledge the economic reality that women's income and production were used for essentials.

Professional women rarely examined the political issues of farm incomes or recognized that farm women might not be able to ease their work because of the general economic conditions of agriculture. The report of the First International Farm Women's Congress in 1911 illustrates the controversial nature of a class-based challenge to professional assumptions, even in the prosperous and less conservative Progressive Era. After a series of reports by university home economics extension leaders on farm women's need for conveniences, a farm woman from Colorado stirred "lively debate," saying: "As long as such conditions [low prices for farm products] exist, the farmer cannot make it any easier for his wife, and she has no right to expect any easier lot." The author of the article recognized the differences within the Congress: "The preceding theories of what women ought to do, of course had their place, but the actual facts of what they can do with the tools and contributions at hand—that is almost another problem." These women tied the improvement of farm women's lot not just to the end of male dominance on the farm, as professionals usually did, but to the improvement of economic conditions for small farmers. This point was too seldom recognized.[32]

Professional women understood women's subordination within the farm family and attempted to find ways to improve women's status within it, but developed strategies that worked best for farm women on more prosperous, mechanized farms. They had fewer solutions for women whose farms produced little cash to divide equally or required the economic contributions of women's field work and income-producing and income-saving activities. When examining the work of real farm women who could not meet domestic, middle-class ideals of female labor, professionals acknowledged the importance of this work and celebrated the strength of farm women. Although more local studies are needed, evidence also suggests that individual women agents, particularly those working in poorer areas, attempted to bend USDA or extension service policies to meet the needs of these women.[33] But, whether because of the limitations of working within these institutions or because of shared assumptions, no alternative voice of professional women arose to contest the policies that substituted technology for farm and home labor and separated men's and women's work. Professionals could commend the many activities that farm women actually performed as temporary necessities, but did not accept them as appropriate for long-range agricultural social or economic policy.

In contrast to the professional women, many farm women viewed their work as integral to the farm rather than separate from it and believed in the dignity of all their labor on the farm. Essentially, the farmer's wife was a farmer, a necessary worker in the farm operation. Farm women had strong local sources for their definitions of womanhood and their work culture. Women valued their abilities to make do and save, to produce goods for household use and local markets, to care for their families, and to perform work on the farm wherever it was necessary. Women's work was integral to the family and the farm, and women appreciated their own importance as workers in the farm enterprise.

Farm women knew the dominant middle-class ideals of womanhood, but many asserted the validity of their differences from this ideal. Farm women and professional women debated these issues in a 1923 report, "The Advantages of Farm Life," by Emily Hoag, associate economist at the USDA Division of Farm Population and Rural Life. Hoag conducted interviews and analyzed letters responding to an article in *Farm and Home* entitled "The Woman God Forgot" and a contest in the *Farmer's Wife* entitled "Would You Like Your Daughter to Marry a Farmer?" The respondents were slightly more educated and lived on slightly more prosperous farms than the nation's average, and most came from the upper Midwest. Even these farm women, prosperous readers of journals that promoted modern gender relations on the farm, found that the modern definitions of a farmer's wife did not match their reality.

First, these women took pride in their physical labor. Of the 1,506 letter writers, 899 specifically mentioned that they resented the implications of drudgery that appeared in the article. Instead, they felt "themselves proud workers worthy of respect and admiration." Like their male counterparts, they believed in physical labor. As a New York farm woman wrote, "The world's work must be done and I am no shirk." They, like their husbands, viewed themselves as workers of the land. "What does it matter," an Illinois woman wrote, "if we farmers do get some of God's clean soil on us in our labor, once in a while." This work did not undermine their womanhood; it proved it. A Minnesota woman wrote: "On the farm, I have always put my shoulder to the wheel and have helped whenever my help was needed in milking and feeding calves and hogs and have always felt I was a woman and fulfilling my mission in life." Farm women did not see themselves as unproductive consumers, but as proud producers and workers. They challenged the image that "worker" and "woman" were incompatible.

Farm women regarded their work in the field as evidence of their integral part in the farm operation. They did not resent it as a sign of drudgery or a violation of separate spheres; they were partners in a joint venture. Drawing lines between men's and women's work took second place to completing the work of the farm. A woman from the prairie agreed that modern farm life had progressed because she did not do outside work like her grandmother. However, she understood the situation "when our husbands are helping our neighbors with their harvest and hay, and we know they won't be home until late. Who wouldn't help out in a case of that kind?" This farm woman was glad she did not have to work so hard as her grandmother had, but was willing to help with "men's work" and took pride in her ability to do so. Here modernity blended with traditions that valued flexibility in task assignments.

Other farm women challenged the belief that a lack of modern conveniences signified drudgery and inequality. To these women, field work and making do were not inherently signs of subordination. Here a different challenge to gender hierarchies emerges: one that understood the economic restrictions of many farm families. A woman from the Corn Belt wrote:

True . . . there are many women who do not have the comforts of life, yet there are many men who do not have the necessary implements to farm with. To my mind, it is no worse for the average farm woman, if strong, to carry water, if not too far from the house, than it is for her husband to carry water for his horses, hogs, and cows, morning, noon and night. In my case being a renter on the same farm for six years, I have to do both. It is no worse for me to keep my house swept with a common broom than for my son who is now eighteen to keep the manure hauled from the barns with just a common wagon and pitchfork.

This woman opposed farm men's tendency to abuse and overwork farm women by adding the limitations "if she is strong," and "if not too far from the house." However, she also proclaimed the basic equality of the work and strengths of farm women and men. She challenged the class biases of the professional literature that assumed the technological transformation of all men's labor and separated a woman's gender deprivation from that of the class status of her family. Farm women could be abused by inequality and mistreatment, but hard physical labor and the absence of labor-saving devices did not necessarily mean that farm women were drudges or victims of patriarchal family structures alone.[34] Many farm women took pride in making do, and joined an awareness of the inequities within farm families to the inequities within agriculture itself.

Farm women, like farm men, selected and adapted new technology in ways that complemented their work culture. In some cases farm women's desires for devices that saved labor paralleled the suggestions made by professional women. However, the farm women were less likely to alter their "free" time from productive work to consumption. Farm women valued most the labor that made the greatest economic contribution to the farm, whether it involved making do or home production. They often put the farm first, a practice professional women criticized. Farm women's activities as producers and savers contributed to farm survival, children's opportunities, and farm expansion. Their work in the field also remained important on many farms, and changes in field technology rearranged their work, an analysis that rarely appeared in the professional literature because field and home were viewed as separate, not interdependent. In any case, farm women continued to value their economic contributions to the farm rather than embracing new roles as consumers.

When farm budgets allowed, farm women chose new technologies that eased the physical labor of household tasks. Farm women valued daily chores less than home production. They welcomed changes that lessened the labor of household tasks because they did not challenge the definition of themselves as workers for the farm. For example, a 1926 Illinois study of farm homes found that all of the homes with electricity used it for lighting. Electric lights not only provided better light, but also eliminated the care and cleaning of kerosene lamps, tasks that farm women often disliked. Farm women also welcomed water pumped into or near the house because it eliminated the chore of carrying water long distances. These advances lightened daily chores that farm women rarely romanticized.[35]

Farm women accepted changes that eased physical labor and resisted changes that led to an increase in their domestic chores. Much lore surrounded the arduous nature of the weekly wash, and farm women were proud of their ability to perform the task, but they rarely described it as satisfying work. Belt-powered washers and electric washing machines eased this physical labor, and the Illinois study found that the third most common home use of electricity was for electric washers. However, farm women often rejected the increased standards of cleanliness and increased labor that accompanied washing machines. One farm women scolded her city-raised daughter-in-law for putting clean clothes on the children every day, because she already had a big washload and thought her daughter-in-law's standard wasteful. When new technologies increased women's domestic work, farm women often rebelled. For example, the cream separator may have eased dairy work, but the intricate parts of the machine were difficult to clean. As a character in Willa Cather's *One of Ours* pointed out: "I could see the advantages of a separator if we milked half-a-dozen cows. It's a very ingenious machine. But it's a great deal more work to scald it and fit it together than it was to take care of the milk in the old way." Farm women often complained about the inconvenience of this "labor saver."

Although professionals believed laborsaving devices would increase farm women's leisure, farm women often used the "free" time to increase other kinds of farm work. The Illinois study of electric use found that although some tasks were shortened, the number of tasks increased. From the evidence in farm women's diaries, new types of washers, for example, seem not to have altered work routines significantly. The need for cash to pay for farm and home improvements or to balance uneven incomes kept most farm women working to save or produce money through their activities.[36] Women continued to make do even as their ability to purchase new goods increased.

Consequently, farm women were less likely to decrease the labor that made direct economic contributions to the farm enterprise or to replace their roles as savers and producers with the roles of purchasers. They employed "farm first" practices even in the domestic sphere. Many continued to perform productive tasks that were a source of pride. Although few farm women of economic means continued to use washboards, preserving and canning remained a farm woman's task even after canned goods and produce became more readily available in stores. Even home economists did not merely promote consumption, but taught the skill of shopping wisely for canned foods and new technological methods of home preserving. Farm women's vivid and detailed descriptions of food preservation and canning attest to the importance of these work traditions. Washing was a monumental task that farm women endured, but canning and food preservation was work that farm women enjoyed and valued for the skill it required, its economic contribution to the farm, its importance for family use, and its role in social life. Not until after World War II did farm women give up these productive activities and purchase rather than produce most of their families' food.[37]

Helping out in the field was also a crucial part of farm cash-saving strategies and a part of farm women's view of womanhood. Although new field technology altered the content of women's work, it did not alter the structure of their relationship to field work as part of the family labor system. Such technology did tend to intensify gender divisions of labor in farm families, particularly on more capital-intensive, specialized farms. But as smaller, general farms were mechanized, farm women still worked in the field in the busiest seasons and in tending to the more labor-intensive crops. Although men generally controlled new field technology, farm women did not necessarily leave the fields. If their work was needed, women still filled the vacuum.

Even on farms that practiced a stricter sexual division of labor, machinery did not exclude women from field work. For example, the family of Iowan Elmer Powers segregated men's and women's work, but when Powers and his son were busy, his wife or his daughter often assisted. In the 1920s, his wife plowed while he did other tasks. By the 1930s, his daughter Lillian assisted, even after the family purchased a used Farmall tractor. Lillian disked down stalks while her brother got a load of feed. She also worked when new machinery broke down or when the family could not afford hired help. When the corn binder broke, Lillian drove the team while her father husked. When the corn picker broke and help was difficult to find, Lillian took a "corn-husking vacation" from school. Machinery made women's and children's labor in the field less necessary, but did not eliminate it entirely.

On farms where women and children played a more active role in the field, new technology often expanded women's productive tasks or compensated for labor deficiencies. The family of Anna Pratt Erickson used technology to complement changes in the composition of the family labor force and flexibly redefined men's and women's work throughout the period. The Ericksons paired technological change with the movement of children on and off the farm. When Anna was married, her husband did the field work that involved machinery. When she was not married and her children were young, she hired out much of the field work to male neighbors with modern technology. To make the best use of family labor, the Erickson farm diversified and developed labor-intensive "women's" crops, such as potatoes, garden truck, and fruits. As her children got older, Erickson rented machinery, and she or her older children, all daughters, ran it. As her son, the youngest child, got older, he was more often the one to operate farm machinery, but not exclusively so. Mechanization of field labor coincided with the older daughters' switch to off-farm employment. Although field labor in many of the crops that required the use of machinery was defined as male labor, women always worked in the fields, sometimes from necessity, sometimes by their own choice.[38] As they did in home production, farm women maintained their work culture and often continued their active role in the farm enterprise, adapting new technology to the traditional structures of their work.

Farm women, like farm men, maintained their work culture, but changes in the economy and new technology, over time, altered farm women's labor. Like farm men, women used labor-saving devices to increase their economic contributions to the farm enterprise. In the 1920s and 1930s, the more widespread availability of consumer goods coincided with an unstable farm economy. By promoting farm and home practices that increased the need for cash income, agricultural policies ignored the need of farm people, both men and women, to use work to compensate for low incomes. A woman's work identity centered on her ability to save, make do, and produce family necessities on the farm. In the 1930s, women's cash-saving work often spelled the difference between survival and failure on small farms. This labor, generally respected by farm men and women alike, helped women negotiate claims to mutuality within the farm family. Their work was integral to family farm survival.

After World War II, these realms of women's economic contribution to the farm economy became less profitable. Consolidation in the poultry industry captured the markets of farm women's primary source of income, and the increased availability of mass-produced food made food as cheap to buy as to produce. As changes in agricultural production and marketing brought women's work more completely into the market economy, farm women lost their base for economic contribution to the farm enterprise. Women had to find new ways to earn income, and began to seek off-farm work. Though farm women continued their role as supportive farm laborers, they became more like their urban counterparts, contributing wages and unpaid household labor to the family economy. Although their work was still crucial for farm survival, it no longer seemed so integral to the farm economy itself. Women now negotiated for mutuality and respect within the family from a position more removed from agriculture, based on urban wage work or housework, which was the least valued form of women's labor.[39]

Changes in production and consumption altered gender-defined work cultures on family farms. Promoters assumed that new technology and increased consumption benefited both men and women. Although professional men assumed that modern farms preserved a separation of spheres and that the male business enterprise took precedence, professional women challenged the male domination of the farm family, promoted the importance of household labor, and challenged the unremitting physical toil that exploited farm women. But professional women did not see the potential patriarchy in separate spheres or the potential mutuality in a shared work enterprise. They assumed that prosperity and technology meant respect for farm women and that women's labor in the barn or field meant patriarchal dominance. Technology, however, did not automatically create patriarchal or mutual gender relations, and farm women pointed this out in their rejection of the drudge image.

Although technology did not make gender relations patriarchal or mutual, it did alter the work cultures of men and women. Women and men both welcomed relief from the hard physical labor of farm work. Sometimes they held to older work cultures, especially when their work contained skills valued by their society. For both farm men and women, new technology brought their work more fully into a cash economy. Both now bought what could have been produced by their labor on the farm. This, in particular, hurt women and men on poorer and smaller farms, who did not earn enough cash income from commodities to support the increased cash expenses. They worked longer hours and sacrificed more to keep their farms.

Despite these similarities, the move into the cash and consumer economy reshaped the work culture of women more than that of men. Women's ability to make do and to produce goods on the farm was one of the most valued parts of their work culture. Ultimately, a man could still be a farmer while driving a tractor because he still grew produce to sell in markets. Women, who purchased food rather than growing it, became wives more than farm wives. Although most farm people, particularly those on smaller farms, continued to see themselves as productive workers in family enterprises, the rules and options of the new economy changed the nature of work for both men and women. Men still earned cash income for the farm as they had in the past, but farm women could no longer earn cash while working on the farm, and their cash-saving and home production strategies no longer fit the farm's needs in an economy that increasingly demanded cash. Women lost a crucial lever for building mutuality in family relations. Though women's work eased, it lost much of its value as productive agricultural labor.

How You Gonna Keep 'Em Down on the Farm?

Mass Culture, Depression, and the Decisions of Farm Youths

Era Bell Thompson, an African American, grew up on a farm in North Dakota and was a high school student in Mandan, North Dakota, in the 1920s. In her autobiography, she reflected on an incident at a rodeo on the outskirts of town. Era Bell was assisting her father at a food stand when a Native American friend approached with her mother. The daughter purchased food and talked while her mother stood silent and smiled. Thompson's friend explained, "My mother don't speak American." Thompson reflected on the experiences of these two generations:

Old Country, I thought. Only it wasn't Old Country: it was this country. Nearly all my friends were second generation; their parents spoke the mother tongue, wore the native clothes, had the ways of the fatherland, even the Indians. In a sense I was second generation, too, only Pop had no other language, but in the ways of the world he was far ahead of me. My Latin and geometry didn't make any more sense to my father than they did to my friends' fathers. They didn't make too much sense to me.[1]

This experience of difference from their parents linked the youths coming of age in the rural Midwest in the 1920s and 1930s. Thompson, the daughter of a native-born African American, felt the generational divide much as the children of European immigrants did. Access to education transformed this generation's experience. High school attendance created more ties to towns, middle-class cultural expectations, and a youth peer-culture that no longer corresponded to the smaller rural neighborhoods experienced by older rural Americans. Even those youths who did not attend high school expected to travel longer distances in automobiles and believed that mass culture and commercial recreation were a part of life, not unique experiences.

At the time, professionals argued that automobiles, movies, and radios made a positive contribution in ending rural isolation, but also were negative in that they introduced urban mores and living standards, ultimately making farm youths dissatisfied and eager to abandon rural life. Historians have painted the 1920s as a time when rural youths fled the countryside looking for the advantages of consumer culture and modern forms of recreation. Most studies assume that movies, radios, automobiles, and jazz dance were urban by their very nature and were incompatible with rural cultural traditions. However, mass culture, commercial recreation, and more extensive education were also reshaping the experiences of urban youths of both the middle and working classes in this period. Rural youths, like their urban counterparts, became part of a new youth culture tied to changing patterns of consumption and recreation. Although these new patterns were in conflict with some aspects of rural culture, farm youths' acceptance of these new forms of behavior did not mean they had abandoned their ties to kin and the rural community.[2] However, economic realities in the 1920s and 1930s made it more difficult for them, particularly farm girls, to become independent adults and remain on family farms and in rural society. The availability of new forms of recreation and consumption may have exacerbated farm youths' dissatisfaction with farm incomes, but it was the absence of economic opportunities, as much as the bright lights of the city, that pushed farm youths cityward.

New forms of commercial recreation are most often associated with the urban environment because they require concentrations of people to make them mass entertainments. This does not make them urban by nature, but it does mean that access to the new forms of commercial recreation and consumer culture was structured differently for rural youths than for their urban counterparts. Differences in the spatial organization of rural life altered the ways in which farm youths encountered new forms of recreation. Urban youths escaped the restrictions of parental and community authority when inexpensive public transportation increased their independent mobility. In rural America, the automobile altered the social geography of recreation and increased youths' access to activities such as high school sporting events and movies. However, families most often controlled automobiles, and rural youths' mobility, more than that of their urban counterparts, had to be negotiated within the family.

Before the automobile, rural people's daily travel was limited geographically, and rural neighborhoods linked people in the open country, rather than linking farm and town people. The diary of Anna Pratt Erickson illustrates the nature of community formation in the open country both before and after the automobile. Before 1921, Erickson did not own a car; however, she was far from isolated. She often walked to neighbors' houses for visits or errands. Neighbors shared rides in horse-drawn buggies, or (later) cars, whenever they planned to go to town or church and often for pleasure rides or Sunday visiting. When trips to more distant towns were necessary, neighbors with cars often provided transportation; if not, Erickson and her family took the train.

Although farm people were rarely isolated, the automobile nevertheless enabled farm people to travel greater distances in shorter periods of time, giving them more choices about where they would go to create a social life. Rural residents whose neighborhoods had always expanded to meet social and economic needs now had more flexibility to adjust to changed conditions. Automobiles introduced new options, including commercial forms of recreation and social networks beyond the open-country neighborhood.

Farm people clearly valued the greater mobility cars offered. In the early years of the twentieth century, ownership of an automobile was a sign of prosperity. In one Iowa family history, the author recalled that the car was quite a status symbol. People would drive to town on Saturday nights to sit in their cars, listen to band concerts, and make their "car-less" neighbors jealous. More farm people bought cars as they became more affordable. The price of the Model T declined in the 1920s. Despite lower farm incomes, it took a smaller percentage of a farmer's crop to purchase a car in 1929 than it had in 1913. Between 1900 and 1940, automobiles changed from luxuries to necessities in rural areas. Although automobiles may have increased farm people's choices, as time progressed, many institutions such as churches, schools, and health care facilities that had once existed in local communities became available only in larger, more distant towns and cities.[3] By 1930, more than 80 percent of farm families in each state of the Midwest except Missouri owned automobiles.

Farm people did not necessarily use the automobile to become more urban or to abandon their local communities.[4] They often used the automobile to enhance the social ties that shaped their lives, rather than to alter them. In Erickson's case, the automobile clearly reinforced local ties. Erickson's access to an automobile came with her courtship and marriage to her second husband, Joe Mauritz, between about 1921 and 1926. The automobile facilitated visits to neighbors and trips to town, but the basic social networks remained the same. For example, Anna and Joe increased their trips to town on Saturday nights, but often they made these trips with friends from their rural neighborhood. They continued to visit neighbors on Sunday, but often went for rides to more distant towns or through the countryside, which provided a mobile setting for socializing. Anna still walked to her local club meetings, to church, and to school when Joe or one of her older daughters could not drive her. Neighbors still shared rides, but now Joe and Anna offered rides as well as taking them.

After her divorce, Erickson finally purchased her first car, a $525 Ford, in 1929. The event merited considerable space in the diary:

May 5 — then at 7 o'clock Clyde Southwick brot up our new ford. . . . May 6 — Fay [Erickson's daughter] ran the car to town and Morris [Erickson's son] run it home washed pails cans and strainers then I drove all afternoon Clyde teaching me. . . . then Loddie [future husband of Erickson's daughter Dot] helped us to empty out the machinery and showed us how to run the car in the shed.

Erickson marked the event in the following weeks with visits to neighbors. The family went to church and the children attended local church youth groups more consistently. For Erickson and others, the automobile became a new tool for building rural neighborhoods in traditional ways.[5]

Over time, however, patterns of social interaction and the geographic base of community subtly began to change. Hospitals reshaped rural birth rituals, and the automobile increased the accessibility of recreational opportunities in town and altered patterns of courtship. The births and courtships described in Erickson's diary illustrate both the integration of old and new forms and the general trend toward enlarging the local base of community recreation and friendship networks, particularly for youths accustomed to automobile travel and tied to towns through education or work.

Anna Erickson had always given birth in her home, with a physician attending, and female kin and neighbors assisting with work and sharing the birth rituals. As late as 1924, Anna gave birth at home. Her daughter Orma helped with the work, and other neighborhood women attended Anna before and after the birth, and at the baby's death a few days later. Ten years later, Erickson's daughter Dot had her first child; by then the birth rituals had changed significantly. By this date, the Ericksons had developed more connections to the regional center, Wausau. Dot had lived and worked there in 1928 and 1929 before marrying and returning to the rural neighborhood, Fay was a nurse in the hospital there, and Anna had been in the hospital for an operation in 1929. Dot went to a doctor in Wausau and gave birth at the hospital. The location separated those doing work for Dot from her and the baby. Anna and Lois (Anna's youngest daughter) worked for Dot at her home, and Dora Zubke, a neighbor, washed some quilts. Despite this change in the work rituals of birthing, the visiting rituals remained because automobiles enabled neighbors to go to Wausau. Neighborhood women visited Dot at the hospital and after her return home with the baby. When Dot had her second child, in 1938,

Fay came for two weeks to care for the older child and do the home chores, much as Anna had attended her sister-in-law when she gave birth in 1903. Although the hospital significantly altered the location and content of birth rituals, better transportation made sharing the event possible, if not in the same intimate ways.[6]

The automobile also altered the rituals of courtship. The first courtship recorded in the diary was that of Anna and her first husband, Conrad Erickson, in 1903 and 1904. It began when Anna arrived in Wisconsin to assist her brother and sister-in-law at the birth of their first child. She met Conrad through Sunday school and Christian Endeavor, the church youth group. The courtship began with Conrad taking Anna home after prayer meetings: "Conrad took me home sit up till 15 to 12." Visiting in the late evening was the most frequent of their pastimes, but they also went for rides ("Conrad and I went out three hours buggy riding"); visited neighbors and kin; and, infrequently, attended the opera house or dances. Only once did they go to Wausau, where "together we took the town in had lunch together then I started for home" [back to Illinois by train]. Trips to town were rare treats, not the primary occasions for courtship.

Erickson's courtship with her second husband, Joe, which lasted from 1920 to 1922, took place under very different circumstances. First, Anna was a widow with five children. She and Joe did not meet at youth groups, but through shared work in the neighborhood. Second, Anna was a member of the Presbyterian church, while Joe was Catholic; therefore, the church could not be the center of a social circle. Their courtship began with visits. They also took rides, but now the transportation was an automobile: "Joe Moritz [sic] came after dinner took us down Wertzburg way for a car ride." Joe also gave the family rides to church and became a part of family and neighborhood visiting patterns. In these ways, courtship followed the traditional social forms.

Conrad and Anna rarely went to town for entertainment, but Joe and Anna frequently did so. Trips to town served as an important weekend alternative to visiting, which shows the impact of the automobile even on the older generation. While the importance of visiting to courtship is exemplified by Joe's having visited twelve evenings during the busy month of August, Anna and Joe also went to town three evenings that same month. Their activities in town varied. Many events, such as plays or literary programs, some of which involved Anna's older daughters, were held at the high school. Other events in town that they attended included shows at the opera house, political speeches, town fairs, dances, traveling medicine shows, and a "home talent play" (community theater). Informal networks and visiting remained important, but events in town, particularly at the high school, replaced church activities as a primary source of recreation.

For Erickson's daughters, changing patterns of travel, education, and work made the town a much more important location for social life. The social life of young adults was focused on visiting, school entertainment, church youth groups, and dances at the opera house. High school events were of particular importance; this represents a significant change. The children spent leisure time in town and made friends in town. Nevertheless, many of their dates or escorts to school events or dances were boys whose names appear in the diaries as part of neighborhood social and work networks. The younger generation continued to integrate the two patterns of social life, visiting kin and neighbors as well as going to town events.

The courtship of Dot Erickson and Loddie Loskett during 1928 and 1929 is an example of how the younger generation maintained traditions while stretching them to include other social events. They traveled much greater distances, partly because Dot worked in Wausau; they attended dances and fairs, and simply went to town more frequently than Anna did during her first courtship. Nevertheless, visiting, local institutions, and neighborhood and kin ties were still vital to their social lives. Loddie started appearing regularly in the diary in 1928. It is not clear from the entries how Dot and Loddie met. Loddie's family was not in the Ericksons' immediate neighborhood, but came from the general area. Dot would come home from Wausau on weekends, and Loddie would visit her at the Erickson home, usually on Sundays. He also provided transportation, usually driving her back to Wausau on Sundays, and sometimes taking the whole family to visit her. By 1929, Loddie participated fully in the family's visiting networks. He visited the Ericksons even when Dot was not home, went with Dot to see neighbors and friends, and attended Sunday school and church with the Ericksons. Although much of their social life was probably unrecorded by Anna, it is clear that they maintained the values of the rural community even though they traveled to towns more frequently.[7]

Although automobiles gradually reshaped the geography of rural social networks and made town-centered activities more available, the economic realities of agriculture limited access to commercial recreation and consumer goods. The family system of labor in midwestern agriculture, like its spatial organization, made farm youths' encounters with mass culture different from those of their urban counterparts. Participation in mass culture required cash, and average rural cash incomes roughly equalled working-class urban incomes.[8] However, in contrast to their working-class urban peers, who earned individual cash incomes as wage workers, most rural youths were part of a family economy that did not include wages. Consequently, access to cash for recreation often came from the family purse and had to be negotiated in competition with other family needs.

In this context, commercial recreation could put a strain on the already tight budgets of farm families. Few such families spent much of their income on recreation. Most standard-of-living studies found that farm families spent between 8 percent and 12 percent of their incomes on "advancement" goods, which, in addition to recreation, included education (such as high school or college tuition), reading material, charitable and religious donations (including support for local churches), and organization dues. These statistics are probably even higher than average because sampling techniques were often biased to include more well-to-do farm families. When the studies broke down advancement spending, expenditures on recreation were very small. A 1927 Minnesota study found that only 8 percent of advancement expenditures, or about nine dollars a year, went to theaters and movies, and a third of the families spent nothing on these commercial entertainments.

Because recreation depended on disposable income, these expenditures varied by class. For example, a 1928 Iowa study found that half the families spent only one dollar of every hundred on advancement and the other half spent fifteen dollars or more of every hundred. Families who spent less than 1 percent of income on advancement lived on farms of 155 or fewer acres, and owners spent 8 percent for advancement while tenants and hired men spent less than 5 percent. These expenditures varied according to the prosperity or poverty of a region and the economic status of a given farm family. In addition, when economic times were hard recreation expenses were the first to be cut. Farm families in three Wisconsin counties spent between 3 percent ($12) and 6 percent ($29) of their yearly expenditures on recreation in 1929, but only 2 percent ($6) and 5 percent ($16) in 1933.[9]

New leisure and consumer standards challenged the strategies of making do that were developed in response to these economic realities. Many older farm people considered spending money on recreation wasteful. This conflicted with younger farm people's desire to be modern. Farm novels of the 1920s often depicted this cultural clash. The grandfather in Homer Croy's 1924 novel RFD #3 represented the view of the older generation. He saw "today's" youth as "harum-scarum children. . . . All they thought about was riding around in cars, staying out till all hours of the night and frittering away their money." The farm youth, Claude, in Willa Cather's One of Ours (1922) offers the young person's viewpoint. He knew that if he "ate out" when he was in town, he would be accused by his family of "putting on airs." "In the Wheeler family a new thrasher or a new automobile was ordered without a question, but it was considered extravagance to go to a hotel for dinner."[10]

Generational change is also apparent in rural attitudes toward play. Although many adult farm people did accept new forms of mass culture and commercial recreation, that recreation also challenged traditional modes of socializing. First, many older farm people did not dichotomize leisure and work time, and did not share the modern definitions of "play" that commercial recreation required. Agricultural professionals who hoped to promote recreation as necessary for a higher standard of living complained that farm people needed to be taught to play, and that they "will play only under a work camouflage."[11] Second, most rural recreation involved entire families. As they did in urban areas, new forms of commercial recreation often brought youths together in subcultures outside the realm of parental authority. Adults found traditional, supervised settings for youth recreation more appropriate than town-centered activities that were organized by commercial ventures and were not controlled by community mores. A 1936 Illinois survey found that parents approved of church activities, visiting, parties, and fairs as recreation for young people. They found town-centered activities, such as street carnivals, dances, and "street loafing," objectionable. Youths, on the other hand, accepted the idea of leisure time and wanted these new forms of recreation.[12]

While economic realities and cultural values affected all farm youths' access to recreation, the gendered structure of the family economy restricted farm daughters more than farm sons. In family farm agriculture, men controlled land ownership and men's labor was more associated with the cash-earning parts of the agricultural economy. Consequently, sons had access to wage work and independent cash incomes in rural areas, while daughters' access to independent wages often depended on education and employment outside the farm economy. In a 1937 Missouri study of white high school youths (ages 14–19), roughly equal numbers of boys and girls planned to attend college and work in the city. But more boys than girls planned to stay on farms (about 25% of boys and only 1% of girls), and more girls than boys planned to work in towns. When listing occupational preferences, boys could list farming, but girls had to find other occupations, such as teaching or nursing, that might keep them in the rural community. Farm girls' access to farm work came as daughters or wives. The former most probably translated into "no plans" or "other plans." If they were single women choosing to earn money independently, girls had to move off the farm.[13]

Daughters' independence and recreational choices were also limited by gender definitions of appropriate behavior. The activities of boys suggested both more mobility and a greater acceptance of physical activity than was the case for girls. Studies of the activities of young people (ages 14–24), particularly two Missouri studies done in 1927 and 1937, reveal that this applied to activities that were more traditional as well as those that were modern. Even though some home-centered and some mobile activities were shared by the sexes, boys enjoyed outdoor activities, such as hunting, trapping, and fishing, while girls spent leisure time in more home-centered activities, such as fancywork, sewing, and reading books and plays. In addition, girls seem to have been restricted from some activities that required learning physical skills. Girls mentioned hiking and running as activities, but desired to learn how to swim and ice skate. Boys, however, mentioned both swimming and ice skating as favorite activities.

Gender restrictions on physical activity persisted as modern pastimes were introduced. Some evidence suggests that participation became more gender-defined over time. For example, Missouri farm girls and boys equally enjoyed organized sports in the 1920s. In the 1927 study, a roughly equal proportion of boys and girls played baseball (boys, 58%; girls, 61%) and basketball (boys, 52%; girls, 48%). However, the 1937 study suggests that opportunities for boys expanded, while girls' opportunities were redefined to highlight sexual differences. By 1937, boys participated in large numbers in baseball (56%), basketball (53%), softball (66%) and volleyball (46%). Girls participated only in volleyball (52%) and softball (57%).[14]

Farm daughters also were more dependent on their families for access to community or town activities. Farm girls (and women) had less independent access to automobiles than did boys (and men). In the Missouri study, 72 percent of farm boys drove cars, but only 35 percent of farm girls did. In listing activities that they wanted to learn, 37 percent of farm girls wanted to learn how to drive, while only 6 percent of farm boys felt they needed or wanted to learn to drive. While most of the girls could travel to town with relatives or neighbors, they clearly had less independent mobility than their brothers to attend activities in towns or visit distant neighbors.[15]

Historically, farm women have organized events that integrated women and men, as well as participating in same-sex activities. Similar gender differences appeared in the kinds of recreational opportunities youths desired. Girls wanted to participate in more community-oriented activities (leading singing groups, giving readings, acting in plays) and organizations (4-H Clubs, Girl Scouts). When youths expressed how they believed their communities needed to change, girls wanted more "social" opportunities, boys more "recreational" opportunities. Such desires reflect boys' greater mobility and access to travel, and girls' restricted mobility and need to travel with family, neighbors, or other peers. In this way, girls continued recreational patterns of creating gender-integrated community leisure even as they participated in more modern recreation.[16]

A closer examination of three new forms of recreation—going to movies and dances and listening to the radio—illustrates how modern activities blended with and subtly altered traditional recreation and social ties, how youths more readily accepted and enjoyed the new leisure and commercial forms of recreation than adults did, and how gender and class structured the ways in which adults and youth encountered the changes of modern culture. Listening to the radio, because it was a recreation that took place in the home, blended most easily with rural traditions of work and socializing. Movies became a much more prominent part of a new youth peer culture; however, they, too, blended with some patterns of neighborhood socializing. Both introduced new patterns of consumption and behavior. The commercialization of dancing was the most controversial of the three because it challenged parental authority and community norms and was closely associated with youthful rebellion. The increased cost of these activities clearly limited access for poorer youths and farm daughters, but gender restrictions on mobility and behavior sometimes contradicted gender definitions of what should be appropriate recreation for women.

Radios were not a town-centered recreational activity, but provided entertainment in the home, and thus fit in with rural patterns of work and sociability. Radio was a form of mass culture that was clearly a family entertainment rather than a form of recreation specific to a certain age group. Families often listened together, and because using the radio did not take youths away from family or community supervision, less generational controversy surrounded it. In addition, radios blended well with rural social and work routines. Listening to the radio often was a community event; neighbors would visit and listen to the radio, talking about the programs and sharing the new experience. After a hard day at work, listening to the evening programming was a new form of relaxation. One Wisconsin farm woman recalled that her daughter "would rip into her chores and she'd come in and flop down on the floor and listen to 'Amanda of Honeymoon Hills.'"[17]

Because the radio was a family entertainment rather than an individual one, access to the radio was based more on class than on gender. The number of farm families that owned radios, small at first, increased dramatically over time. In 1925, radio ownership in the western Midwest ranged from a low of 4 percent of farm homes in Wisconsin to a high of 12 percent in Illinois. By 1940, the range was from 59 percent in Missouri to 85 percent in Iowa and North Dakota. Nevertheless, farm youths still trailed their rural nonfarm counterparts in access to radios.

Both farm boys and farm girls could listen to a family-purchased radio. Changes in technology over the period increased the access of farm daughters to the radio. In the early days of radio, radios often had to be built. The mechanical nature of radios made them a recreational choice of boys more than of girls. In the early Missouri study, 34 percent of boys "ran" the radio, while only 18 percent of girls did so. As this activity changed from running the radio to listening to the radio, girls' participation increased. Fifty-eight percent of farm girls listened to the radio, compared to 60 percent of farm boys. Radio clearly became an important form of recreation during the period from 1900 to 1940, and its use became less gender-defined.[18]

The content of radio programming sometimes supported rural cultural values and sometimes challenged them. On the one hand, radio programming often served rural interests. In their oral histories, farm people recalled listening to practical and rural-oriented shows, such as market and weather reports, agricultural programs, and cooking programs. Many farm people appreciated the Sunday sermons, especially when bad weather kept them from attending church. Others listened to local news and entertainment. North Dakota diarist Pauline Olson recalled listening to her own daughter singing "over the radio" from Minot, about ninety miles away.[19]

On the other hand, the radio connected rural people more directly to the larger national culture and to new patterns of consumption and leisure. For some traditional farmers, this new culture could be controversial. Two North Dakota farmers remembered a Norwegian neighbor who would not listen to sermons in English because "that isn't God's word." Progressive farmers could also reject innovation. Howard M. Jones, a minister, author, and part-time farmer, and the husband of pioneering home economist Nellie Kedzie Jones, purchased a radio in 1938 over his wife's objections. He won out because "she knows I hate jazz as hard as she does — also the vulgar advertising . . . but she knows I won't have it bawling all the time." Radio programs sometimes clashed with ethnic traditions, and it also conflicted at times with progressive farm values that perceived radio as crass and inappropriate for middle-class propriety.

Most farm people recalled the radio and the new cultural ties it created in more positive ways. For many, the radio was an amazing machine that brought the world closer and reported other wonders of the new age. One farm woman recalled, "My husband was so delighted with this new gadget that he sat up till midnight almost every night trying to bring in distant stations." The radio increased the immediacy of world and national events. Pauline Olson noted in her diary that she listened to the presidential inauguration of 1933, the New York Yankees' victory in the 1936 World Series, and reports about the 1937 floods along the Mississippi and Ohio Rivers. Entertainment programming encouraged acceptance of mass culture and consumption. Gerald and Fay Goodwin, Iowa farmers, remembered listening to "National Barn Dance," "Amos and Andy," and "Fibber McGee and Molly." After hearing music on the radio, Fay Goodwin would purchase recordings at the furniture store or drugstore in nearby Correctionville, Iowa. In the 1930s, probably because of the influence of radio sports, Missouri farm boys rated boxing as one of the leisure activities they most wanted to learn.[20] Radio introduced farm people to new forms of mass culture, leisure, and consumer goods, but it did not destroy their rural way of living.

In contrast to radios, movies were a town-centered activity, belonged more to a separate youth peer culture, and required access to transportation and individual spending money. Both of these had to be negotiated within the family. Movie attendance by farm youths could potentially challenge definitions of how family money should be spent and could require parents to accept youths' independent mobility. Transportation and cost meant that farm youths had much less access to movies than their counterparts in town did. In the 1927 and 1937 Missouri studies, about 90 percent of the village youths attended movies, while only about 75 percent of farm youths did.

Class also influenced farm youths' access to movies. Farm youths who did attend movies usually came from more prosperous farm families and were part of high school youth subcultures. Although the average family attended movies between five and ten times a year, farm families who were more active in organizations such as the Farm Bureaus and 4-H Clubs, who had better incomes, or who had children in high school attended movies slightly less than once a month. As farm budgets tightened during the Great Depression, the only farm families whose movie attendance did not decline substantially were the more prosperous families with children in high school.[21]

Because farm daughters had less access to wage work and less independent access to automobiles, one would expect them to have attended movies less than farm boys did. However, going to the movies was often part of family visiting as well as peer-group recreation. In the Missouri studies, farm girls' attendance at the movies lagged slightly behind boys' in 1927, but had surpassed it by 1937. Farm people combined going to the movies with weekly shopping trips, visits to older children and siblings who worked in town, and Saturday night socializing, whether with families, within groups of friends, or on dates. One Iowa farmer recalled that when he was young, "when we went into town, we just walked round and round the few blocks, talking and joking." He and his friends would attend a ten-cent silent movie, get "a hamburger and pop" afterward, and go home. The new commercial form of recreation was only a new way of spending time with those who were part of neighborhood and kinship networks.[22]

Although attendance at movies often fit into existing visiting patterns, the movies introduced new images of leisure and consumption. Experts saw movies as a form of leisure that should be available to farm people, but worried that movies would create urban tastes and that rural youths would become dissatisfied with rural living and leave their farms for the advantages of city life.[23] But the cultural transformation of the 1920s cannot be explained simply in terms of the dichotomy between urban and rural cultures. Movie images influenced rural culture in ways that paralleled their effect on traditional urban middle-class and working-class cultures. Economically, however, farm youths' experience was more like that of working-class youths; the movies introduced rural youths to new consumer attitudes and presented a way of living that was financially beyond their means. The economic, social, and cultural hegemony of "urban" life and its conflicts with rural values were similar to the conflicts between middle-class and working-class cultures within cities.

Movies also introduced new definitions of appropriate behavior for girls and boys. As historians of the movies have argued, movies encouraged athletics as a realm of success for boys, while sexual attractiveness was crucial for female success. Girls were particularly influenced by the models of female success appearing in the movies. While boys responded to the appeal of athletic heroes, girls sought the glamour of the female musical and dramatic stars. In the 1937 Missouri study, 31 percent of farm girls wanted to learn to tap dance, 23 percent wanted to learn to act, and 41 percent had already appeared in plays. The movies also influenced boys, though the activities in which girls were interested were considered less gender-appropriate for boys. Boys wanted to learn only three activities that were typically associated with girls' leisure time. Acting (15 percent of boys) and tap dancing (20 percent) were two of these activities. (Canning food was the third.) The skills associated with being in the movies (dancing and acting) were thought more appropriate for farm girls; boys adopted the recreational models of athletics.[24]

In contrast to radio and movies, dancing took both traditional and commercial forms. Traditional dances were an important part of the building of neighborhoods and family socializing. These dances took place in homes or in barns. Sometimes they were part of special events, such as weddings or end-of-the-harvest celebrations, but often they simply provided a break from routine and a chance to get together. In some communities dances were held as often as once a week. Local musicians provided music, and the dances included schottisches, polkas, waltzes, square dances, and two-steps. Farm people learned these dances through oral folk traditions. Iowa farmer Brownie McVey was a caller for dances in his neighborhood. He remembered learning this skill by simply "being there." The old terms were "hand me down from one generation to the next," and children learned the dances by being "dragged" out when the group was short a couple.[25]

In some cases modern practices were blended with traditions; a sense of community purpose and neighborhood control was maintained, but young people were allowed to share in mass culture. Isabel Baumann remembered hearing contemporary music and doing the Charleston at Wisconsin barn dances in the 1920s. Farm organizations, churches, and dance clubs also sponsored dances. In Shelby, Iowa, a group of young people would "pool their money and rent the hall [the local 'old opera house' and] bring in one of eight or nine small orchestras from the surrounding towns." Gradually, however, dances at dance halls in town or in the open country replaced barn and home dances as weekly social events; farm people reserved home dances for special occasions.[26]

But dancing, whether traditional or commercial, was controversial. Dancing in any form was opposed by many religious groups, and the practice thus could divide rural communities. A 1931 North Dakota study of rural community clubs found that controversies about dancing hurt such clubs in areas that had a variety of opinions on dancing. One Northwest Iowa farm couple remembered that dancing in their community was a part of most socials and Saturday night entertainments until Dutch settlers, whose church opposed it, moved into the area.[27]

The rise in the number of commercial dance halls created even more controversy. By the 1930s, dances increasingly took place in commercial halls. In a study of North Dakota service centers done between 1926 and 1936, the only institution whose numbers increased in the open country while decreasing in towns and cities was the dance hall. Dance halls were controversial for several reasons. First, they provided entertainment with national mass-media style. Dance halls presented jazz-influenced styles of music and dance that many people saw as indecent and sexually suggestive. A 1921 study of a Wisconsin town noted: "There are now two dance halls in town, one rather jazzy, and the other threatening to put permanent seats in and stop the dance because it is not what she wants to be in any way responsible for. She runs the movie." Commercial dance halls and "jazzy" music offered a threat to decency that movies did not.

The new dance halls also created controversy because many served liquor. Brownie McVey recalled a dance hall six miles from Havelock, Iowa, that could not obtain a permit to sell beer in 1934. The owners moved in four houses, built another, incorporated as a town, and gave themselves a permit. Even when the use of alcohol was not opposed by parents, commercial dance halls created an unchaperoned setting that operated outside community controls. Some youths who were forbidden to attend dance halls could get parental permission to attend local neighborhood home and barn dances, even when they served local "hootch."[28]

Part of the controversy about dancing was caused by its being an age-specific activity that was often associated with courtship. Most studies indicate that only 30 percent to 40 percent of farm people went to dances, but about 50 percent of farm youths participated in dances for leisure. Unchaperoned settings and sexually suggestive jazz dances created a challenge to parental authority. Dance halls increased the numbers and diversity of people that young people could meet from outside the neighborhood at a time when they were beginning to define their own lives, rebel against parental control, or look for marriage partners. Willa Cather's *My Antonia* describes the ethnic, class, and town/country differences that collided at town dances; North Dakotan Clara Jacobs met and danced with Indian men at dances in the 1930s; and Percy Hardiman recalled giving rides to eighteen or twenty black men who performed in bands at various high schools in his rural Wisconsin neighborhood. For many farm youths, going to a dance hall was a form of rebellion against local rules and parental restrictions. In some rural communities, however, continuity, rather than conflict, held sway. Iowa farmer Edna Rohwer described her father's generation spending recreation time at "Five Mile House," which was a saloon and dance floor, while her own generation went to a dance hall in Westside.[29]

Given the controversial sexual nature of the new dances, the unsupervised and heterosocial commercial dance hall environment, and the restrictions placed on rural daughters' mobility, dancing should have been a questionable activity for farm girls. However, dancing was culturally defined as a feminine activity. Although oral histories do suggest that girls were restricted from commercial dance halls more than boys were, girls were also more likely to dance than boys, though whether this was at commercial or community dances is unclear in the studies. In the 1927 Missouri study, 29 percent of girls and 19 percent of boys went to dances. Dancing was one of the recreational activities to which girls had more access than boys did, and one that boys wanted to learn, though this changed somewhat over time. While the percentages of girls wanting to learn to dance remained relatively stable, the number of boys wanting to learn to dance declined. Dancing was a physical and musical activity appropriate for girls, but boys preferred sports and saw their gender-appropriate musical activity as playing musical instruments rather than dancing.[30]

These three commercial forms of recreation, to differing degrees, both blended with and challenged traditions of rural communities. It was possible for farm youths to remain in agriculture and still participate in modern youth culture. It was, however, more difficult for farm daughters and for poorer farm youths to participate in commercial recreation than it would have been for their working-class, urban peers. These youths also had the fewest economic options for staying in agriculture and remaining in their rural communities even if they were satisfied with the social life. Although some rural youths disliked the pace of farm life or the work of farming, or resented the lack of access to recreational opportunities, the assumption that dissatisfaction with rural social life propelled youths cityward underemphasizes the economic realities.

In the studies that investigated young people's reasons for leaving rural communities, open hostility to farm life was rare. When asked directly if their farm communities were good places to live, an overwhelming majority of farm youths in most studies responded that they were. However, when youths were asked to choose between farm and town living, their discontent began to emerge. The economic content of this discontent becomes clear when the gender differences in the responses are considered. Girls were less satisfied with rural life than boys were. For example, in the 1927 Missouri study, only 33 percent of girls responded that they preferred to live on a farm, compared to 42 percent of boys. While the levels of recreational and social discontent for boys and girls were relatively equal, economic satisfaction clearly differed. Girls were more tied to the unpaid family economy than boys were. In the 1927 Missouri study, more boys earned and saved money than girls (58% and 45% compared to 20% and 24%). Earning and saving money were among the highest-placed items on the list of activities in which girls wanted to participate if they had the opportunity (40% and 48%). Economic discontent also affected poorer farm boys, with the percentages of both girls and boys wanting to earn money corresponding almost exactly to the percentages who said they wanted to live in a city (41% of girls, 27% of boys). When studies shifted from high school students to older youths who had migrated out of the rural community, they found that the economic situation was even more important. Forty-eight percent left for economic reasons, and 68 percent wanted to return if they could earn a living in their home community.[31]

As youths made the transition to adult work, their social ties to farm communities often remained strong. Automobiles aided the transition for rural children who moved to regional towns or cities for economic opportunities. Frequent trips home eased city life for those who were accustomed to the security of close family and neighborhood social ties. Siblings who lived in towns or cities also provided social, educational, and recreational opportunities for youths who remained on the farm. In the process farm people's social connections to area towns increased.

The economic choices of Wisconsin diarist Anna Erickson's five children illustrate the gendered nature of economic options and the relationships between youths' moves to adulthood and the rural social community. All five of the Erickson children attended high school. Erickson's four daughters continued their professional training and worked away from the farm community. They initially moved a small distance away to gain access to education or economic opportunity, and carefully maintained close connections to the home farm. Erickson's son, who was the youngest child, worked on the home farm and did not receive education beyond high school, but eventually took over the farm as an adult in the 1940s. The Ericksons' choices reflect broader patterns for farm youths. Girls received more education than boys did and worked away from home; boys found work in the farm community as farm laborers or operators.

Erickson's oldest daughter, Orma, was the first to leave the farm community. Eventually, she lived the farthest away and became most distant from the family. Orma boarded in town to attend high school, and graduated at the age of sixteen in 1921. After her graduation, Orma went to River Falls, Wisconsin, to attend summer training at a normal school. Although River Falls was not close to the home farm (it was about 150 miles away), kin remained important because Conrad Erickson's family lived in the River Falls area. In September, she took the teacher's examination and then secured a job in a school six miles from the home farm. During her stay there she frequently visited on weekends. The next year she returned to River Falls to continue school, and graduated in 1924.

After graduation, Orma probably held a job in Eagle River, Wisconsin (about ninety miles from Athens), until August 1926. Despite the distance, Orma visited home on holidays; for extended visits in the summer, when she was not teaching; on special occasions; and when the family needed her. For example, Orma returned in August 1924, when her mother was pregnant. Both she and her sister Dorothy (usually called Dot or, later, Dick in the diary) returned for the entire summer in 1926 to help Anna at the time of her divorce from Joe. In August 1926, Orma moved to Minneapolis and maintained kinship ties primarily through correspondence and gift exchanges. At some point Orma married Reuel Stratsma and moved to Wyoming. The couple made only one visit to Wisconsin in the 1930s.

Erickson's daughter Dot followed a similar early pattern, but her choices kept her closer to her family in Athens. Her first move from home, like Orma's, was to board in town while attending high school between 1921 and her graduation in 1925. Like Orma, she attended normal school in River Falls, but Anna did not record her graduation. Between 1925 and 1927, Dot either attended winter sessions or taught winter sessions near River Falls. As studies of women's employment indicate, working on the home farm without pay and doing domestic work were almost the only jobs for women in rural areas. During summer and fall, Dot worked at home on the farm and did housework for wages in town or for neighbors. While at River Falls, her visits home were infrequent, but when she worked in the area she visited home almost every weekend. At some point in 1926 or 1927, Dot was teaching rather than attending school. On 31 March 1928, Anna recorded that Dot resigned her position at the school and "came home for good."

Although Dot returned to the region, she did not stay on the farm. She worked at home and for neighbors from March until September, but then took a job in Wausau as a domestic. Before this, the Ericksons had only traveled to Wausau on business, but at this point, Wausau became an important part of the Erickson visiting network. Because the family had no car between 1926 and 1929, Dot relied on the bus, neighbors, and boyfriends to provide transportation home. After the family purchased a car, the trips to Wausau increased for Anna and, even more, for her other children. More often, however, Dot visited home, usually riding with her constant boyfriend and future husband, Loddie Loskett.

In December 1929, Dot moved to Chicago, the location of Loddie's business. Her visits home were less frequent, but her stays were extended. In both 1931 and 1932, she stayed on the farm and worked throughout the summer, which suggested that she had returned to teaching. During these stays, Dot and Loddie were instrumental in increasing and maintaining kinship ties with the family. Dot and Loddie frequently used their or Anna's car to visit or pick up the younger two daughters, who lived in Wausau in the 1930s. In October 1933, Dot and Loddie were married, and by 1934 they had returned to live in Athens, just as they were starting a family of their own. Because of her marriage, Dot was able to settle permanently in the farming community. Although Loddie's job still took him to Chicago frequently, Dot and Loddie settled into the Ericksons' social neighborhood.

The career choices of Fay and Lois resemble the decisions of their sisters, but their experiences differed because of the patterns established by the first two children. None of the three younger children boarded during high school; they first moved from home after graduation. Both Fay and Lois went to Wausau. This choice was much easier than the move to River Falls had been for the older girls, because the family had visited kin in and were familiar with Wausau. Fay went to the hospital in Wausau in 1929 to become a nurse, and Lois went to a normal school in Wausau in 1930 for teacher training. Fay did not visit home as much as either Dot or Lois had, probably because nursing offered less-flexible weekend hours than teaching did. Lois and Fay relied on bus transportation or ride sharing—particularly Lois, who knew many other students from Athens at the normal school.

Lois began teaching school in the fall of 1931, and she chose schools near the home farm. Each summer she returned to the farm to assist Anna, much as Dot had done before. This pattern continued until 1939, when

Lois traveled to Arizona. Lois returned to settle in Wausau in the 1940s. Fay remained in Wausau except for a three-month stay in Milwaukee in 1932. In the late 1930s, she moved to Chicago. Her trips from Chicago by train were less frequent than Dot's had been earlier, but she always visited for about two weeks each spring or summer and sometimes for holidays and special occasions. As Orma did, she maintained kinship ties by mail and gift exchanges as well as these yearly visits.[32]

Morris's experiences reveal both the advantages and the difficulties for young men expected to take on the responsibilities of the home farm. In some ways, Morris had more freedom than his sisters did. During high school, Morris, like his sisters, attended high school events, church youth group meetings, and dances. However, he had more independent mobility, traveling more frequently than his sisters had to other towns with friends. Although his sisters left home for school or jobs after finishing high school, Morris, the only son and the youngest child, was expected to work on the farm. He did not have to adjust to new communities or to a different work life; however, he did not have the opportunity to become an adult away from family supervision.

As Morris became an adult, tensions between Anna and him increased. Although issues of independence, work expectations, and opportunities created these tensions, Anna expressed her disapproval and Morris his rebellion through conflicts about appropriate recreation, leisure, and mobility. After his graduation in 1935, Morris began to be away from home more often in the evening. He took an agricultural short course at the high school and stayed in town to play basketball. By 1938, he still went to church and community events, but also went to movies and simply, as Anna put it, "went out." She recorded his trips with increasing disapproval. Anna wrote that Morris was "supposed to be in Athens . . . got in after 1." Later he went to Eau Claire "against my wish." "Morris beat it out after dinner with Joe Hare went to Wertzberg for all afternoon and played ball." By July 1939, Morris left "for the West" and stayed until September. Eventually, Morris returned to the farm, married, and took over its operation. Anna lived with Morris for a number of years, but she later moved in with Dot and eventually moved into a house of her own in town. Morris had farming opportunities that the daughters did not have; however, they had opportunities for education and travel that he gained only by rebelling against parental authority.[33]

While their experiences are not extraordinary, the Erickson children had advantages that many farm youths did not have. They all attended high school, the daughters all attended college or received professional training, and the son inherited ownership of a farm. Studies of youth activities and mobility done in the 1930s put these experiences into a broader context of social change. During the Great Depression, both staying in the open country and leaving were difficult for farm youths. Those who stayed were more likely to be young men than young women. In general, educational attainment and migration patterns flip-flopped, showing the impact of the Great Depression on the poorest farm youths. Iowa farm youths with less than an eighth-grade education, the most likely to leave in the 1920s, became the most likely to stay during the Depression. These youths could not compete for unskilled urban jobs and had few family resources to assist migration. Young people with some high school education but no diploma had been most likely to stay in rural areas before the Depression, but during the Depression, they migrated in greater numbers. These youths may have been in a more competitive position for urban employment.

Employment patterns in rural areas during the Great Depression remained tied to the family labor system, and youths who remained in rural areas were likely to work for little or no pay. Farm girls more than farm boys still remained firmly within an unpaid family labor force with severely limited opportunities for wage earning. The 1937 Missouri study found that most farm daughters earned less than seventy-five dollars a year, and two-thirds of them earned no independent income. These patterns were true for youths in high school and on relief. In the Missouri study, 24 percent of the boys worked outside the home for wages, compared to only 14 percent of the girls. Many families, however, compensated for this by giving daughters a share of the family income. Sixty percent of the boys and 85 percent of the girls recorded receiving spending money from their parents. Compared to their town counterparts, the study found that farm boys had more economic opportunities than town boys did, while farm girls had fewer economic opportunities than town girls did. However, all farm youths during the 1930s remained largely underemployed or within the family labor system. In the Missouri study, 87 percent of high school farm youths earned nothing or less than seventy-five dollars a year.[34]

Gender shaped the wage-earning opportunities of farm youths who stayed in rural areas and those who migrated. Of those youths who worked for wages off the farm in the Missouri study, most boys worked as farm laborers (26%), common laborers (17%), or clerks (10%). Boys who left their farm homes found employment in seasonal farm work, common labor, or relief programs such as the WPA or the CCC. Relief jobs were more readily available for boys than girls. In North Dakota, for example, 8 percent of young men aged fifteen to twenty-nine were employed by relief programs, compared to less than 2 percent of young women in the same age group. These jobs kept boys in rural areas but took them away from their local communities.

High school girls in the Missouri study found work while living on their home farms as domestics (15%) or clerks (10%). Although girls had fewer opportunities to get relief work, these jobs kept them in their local communities. Relief work employed most of the female high school students, with almost 50 percent earning wages at school through the National Youth Administration. (Only 15% of the boys were employed through the NYA.) Girls who left the home farm by marrying generally married farm laborers or unskilled workers. Girls who did not marry had more economic opportunities in towns than in rural areas. Many became domestics; others worked in cafés or factories. Those with more education could become teachers, nurses, clerks, or clerical workers. However, family resource allocation during the Great Depression tended to help boys' job opportunities while hindering those of girls. North Dakota and Wisconsin studies indicated that the Great Depression hurt farm girls' chances to attend high school. While the percentages of boys attending high school remained stable (though it was still lower than that for girls), percentages of girls attending high school declined, which hurt their employment options.

Studies of migration show that youths who left their farming communities did not move great distances. They were not seeking to escape from "backward" rural communities or the limitations of rural social lives. Many of those leaving remained in the open country or near their parents' farms. In a 1936 South Dakota study, six of ten boys who left home farms remained in the open country, and six of ten farmers' daughters who left home married farmers, and thus stayed on farms. More than 80 percent of North Dakota youths who migrated stayed in counties that adjoined the county in which the parental farm was located. Most of those who left the open country moved to towns and villages, not cities. If they moved to cities, these, too, were in adjoining areas. For example, rural youths from northwest Missouri migrated to Kansas City, St. Joseph, and Omaha. The only areas to have significant numbers of youths moving great distances were those of the Great Plains, where some youths moved to the Pacific Coast. Young women were more likely to leave the open country for towns and cities; young men were more likely to go greater distances when they left the home community.

These patterns changed as World War II began. A South Dakota study charted the changes that occurred between 1935 and 1941. About 75 percent of the youths in the study were children of farm owners, tenants, or laborers. Thirty-six percent of the men who migrated became farm operators; twice as many became tenants as became owners. Forty percent of the young women who migrated married farm operators (again, twice as many became tenants as became owners). During the Great Depression, farm youths generally remained near their family farms and stayed in agriculture, perhaps using or contributing to family resources. This pattern changed dramatically with World War II. In 1935, 50 percent of South Dakota migrants went into agriculture; in 1941, only 4 percent did so. With the changing job opportunities created by wartime, migration shifted not only out of agriculture, but also out of the state.

As the Great Depression ended, rural youths and their families had faced long-term economic problems. When the young people considered their futures, farming seemed to offer few opportunities. The Great Depression often had increased the work of farm youths as families tried to make ends meet and, because of smaller incomes, lessened their opportunities to participate in the types of recreational events that had become available in the 1920s. The decline in farm resources often led to a smaller share for farm youths, intensifying clashes within the patriarchal family structure. Hard times made farm life less attractive, particularly as urban jobs expanded during and following World War II. Jean Long, whose children grew up in the 1930s, described the choices her four children had made. Three of them wanted to leave agriculture. They felt that "life [was] too hard on the farm." Her two younger girls had no love of farming and had perhaps had little time to participate in school or town events. They felt that rural life was too limiting. Her son left the farm because he wanted to make a good living and wanted more independence, rather than working so closely with his father. The decline of family resources and economic opportunities for young people during the Great Depression also made it more difficult for youths who wanted to farm to get land. For Long's oldest daughter, who wanted to farm, the road was difficult. She and her husband worked at a tavern in a nearby town to earn cash in order to rent and later purchase their own farm. For the generations who grew up in these less prosperous years, who had more contact with towns and cities, who more readily accepted new standards of living and new farm and home technology, and who had more access to education, agriculture rarely provided the income to acquire these advantages.[35]

Farm youths in the 1920s and 1930s, like their urban counterparts, became a part of subcultures of youths that accepted commercial recreation as an element of modern life. Although the geographic and economic structures of the city potentially offered more access to commercial recreation, more independent mobility, and more economic independence, this did not necessarily mean that rural youths valued recreation or independence more than the emotional ties and economic and social security of farm communities. Farm youths experimented with new forms of behavior and leisure while continuing to participate in traditional forms of neighborhood sociability. Commercial recreation became more available to farm youths during the 1920s and 1930s, but it was difficult for them to become economically independent adults and remain on farms. This was particularly true for farm daughters, who were most restricted by the unpaid family system of labor, and for poorer farm youths, who were limited by inadequate farm incomes. The massive movement of youths out of rural communities came only after more than a decade of unemployment and underemployment in an agricultural depression, and accompanied the simultaneous rural contraction and urban expansion of economic opportunities during and following World War II. Economic limitations, as much as cultural attractions, framed farm youths' choice to move from country to city.

Conclusion

At the dawn of the age of modern agribusiness, rural America had suffered the ravages of a long-term depression. Josephine Johnson's 1935 novel *Now in November* dramatizes the devastation, illustrating both the importance of community and family survival strategies and their limits. Three fictional northeastern Missouri farm families represent different classes of farmers and the differing ways the Great Depression exhausted their resources. At the center of the story is the Harldeman family. After the father lost his job in a lumber factory, the family returned to a farm that had belonged to relatives. The land was rocky, but productive. This seeming security could not, however, hide the large mortgage. "Here was the land and the spring air full of snow melting, and yet the beginning of fear already—this mortgage, and Father consumed himself with sour irritation and the future dread." Although the drought hurt their crops, they used their cattle, dairy, orchard, and chickens to stay solvent. When the tax assessor came, he thought them "pretty well off," with a good house, cows, horses, sheep, chickens, plows, and a tractor. The father responded by pointing out that, in fact, they were "pretty well out," with empty barns and silos and not enough income to repay debts or pay taxes.

An encounter with a wandering beggar brings out the emotional impact of living on the edge. The Harldemans had food to eat, but there was still a "bitterness in sowing and reaping . . . when all that it meant was the privilege of doing this over again and nothing to show but a little mark on paper." Above all, they feared losing even this security. A man came to the Harldeman farm looking for work and asking for food for his family.

He assumed that the Harldemans were prosperous because "farmers have got food anyway." Mr. Harldeman replied to him, "A farmer's as pinched as any man. We don't raise stuff for the fun of giving," and ordered the man to get out. Harldeman disliked the man's "presumptuous attitude," but underneath was the fear:

I think it was that he didn't want to see him there, standing shabby with his jaundiced skin and his nose all slimy, looking like he was sick from his soul clear out and reminding Father of what might have happened to him if there hadn't been land to save us, and reminding him, too, of what might happen still.

Marget, the daughter who is the book's narrator, tried to catch the man to give him a few potatoes and carrots, but the image of the man, whom they pitied, and the "fear of what he had stood for" continued to haunt her.

The second family in the novel, the Rathmans, owned land that was flat and sheltered. Old Rathman had a "good market" for his grapes and wine. The family had no debt and "whatever grew on the land belonged to them." To Marget "they seemed so solid and so safe, and needed so little." Nevertheless, even their "prosperity" did not allow them to escape hard times. Drought hurt their strawberries and vegetables. The oldest sons left the farm. The youngest son worked in the city, and he and his wife spent beyond their means and did not work on the farm. The Rathmans had little available cash and had to have their telephone removed. The most devastating blow came when Old Rathman fell and broke his hip, leaving the family shorthanded at harvest time. At this point even Marget lost her envy: "the farm looked going-apart too, sending to seed." Family problems, disease, or injury could change even the security of ownership to poverty and distress.

The third family, the Ramseys, were black tenants who had to pay cash rent to a landlord. This family continuously lived on the edge. Christian Ramsey had rented the land for ten years and had been able to save only fifty dollars, which he had to spend on a new team. Early in the novel, Ramsey asked his neighbors for a loan to pay his rent. Rathman, though an owner, could not help: "I got land and vegetables, but no money!—Maybe I should have given him Kohlrappys to pay his rent." Racism compounded the Ramseys' poverty. Before making them a loan, a second neighbor advised Ramsey not to pay his wealthy landlord: "Let 'm try to shove you off and see what'll happen." Christian Ramsey replied, "you ain't a nigger. You don't have a wife and seven children. A nigger can't wait and see what'll happen. He *knows*."

While these three families illustrate different levels of rural poverty, Johnson also points to the similarity of their experiences. One incident in particular connects all the families. When the Harldemans' horse was ill,

Marget's father told her to ask the Ramseys for the use of their mule and told her to offer harvest labor in return. When she told the Ramseys that she had come to ask for help, "they looked surprised, and all of a sudden it occurred to me that we seemed to them as the Rathmans did to us. Safe. Comfortable. Giving appearance of richness, with our dairy and corn and chickens, our steers and team and orchard—although each thing was barely paying to keep itself." The Ramseys, the Harldemans, and the Rathmans shared the hardship of the Great Depression, and any prosperity was only relative and illusory.

The incident also suggests the limits of rural helpfulness as the need for cash grew and community resources dwindled. Ramsey readily agreed to let the Harldemans use his mule, but he refused the offer of work in exchange because he "don' think we'll be here to cut the corn." They again did not have the cash for rent, and none of their neighbors had a cash reserve to make a loan. When drought destroyed their crop, they were unable even to pay shares. Racism added to their problems. When a white neighbor tried to intercede on their behalf with the landlord, the landlord's attitude was that "niggers make poor tenants . . . a white man would have managed." The neighbor showed a solidarity of feeling with the Ramseys and asked if he thought "being niggers kept rain off the land." Unlike the unknown unemployed man who asked for help from the Harldemans, the Ramseys were a part of the rural neighborhood and the fear of poverty was now paired with anger and "the shame of being unable to help, of standing by, bound and helpless and seeing life make its assault on others." The neighbors assisted one another with food, exchanged work, and helped out in emergencies, but the problems that beset them, particularly for the poorest and most marginal, could not be solved by the traditions of neighborhood sharing.[1]

Johnson's novel distills the rural experiences of the Great Depression into the lives of three families, but these experiences must be multiplied to approach an understanding of its true magnitude. Stories like these are repeated in the letters farm people wrote to the federal government in the 1930s. The National Archives collection of letters in the records of the Rural Rehabilitation Division of the Farm Security Administration between 1935 and 1942 contains 113 boxes, each primarily filled with one-page letters from farm people throughout the country. These people were unable to pay their farm operating expenses or family living expenses, to pay rents or mortgages. They were about to lose farms or hoping to return to farms already lost. The 113 archive boxes contain only those people whose last names began with "A," "B," or "C." The original boxed collection was 389 feet in length. The magnitude of the collection and the poignancy of the letters it contains are a concrete and personal reminder of the devastation of the Great Depression for farm people and rural communities.

The Great Depression increased farm people's reliance on neighborhood sharing and women's labor in home production and making do, but ultimately depleted resources and the effectiveness of these survival strategies. In 1939, a Minnesota family with nine children had been living in a tar-paper shack and working forty acres of land for seven years. Neighbors helped them build a new home and also took up a collection that raised forty dollars for used furniture. But the family needed more assistance. The farmer had not received enough money from the sale of potatoes and vegetables to cover living expenses, much less the feed loan he was being pressed to pay. Although neighbors shared—and this was often a key to the persistence of farm neighborhoods—it was often not enough to counter rural poverty and low farm prices.[2]

The loss of income due to poor prices and drought put added burdens on women's ability to make do and produce goods to meet the needs of the family on the farm. Making do increasingly meant doing without. To keep from losing the land or to continue to pay rent, farm women had to manage family budgets with few resources. One Nebraska farm woman wrote for government assistance because her family's government loans had not been approved. Their banker disapproved of their efforts to use government sources of financial credit and had started foreclosure proceedings. They had used their money for feed and to pay debts, and her ability to make do was at an end.

We have nothing in the house to wear or to do with no curtains or rugs I have cut my shades and hemed [sic] them so much there isn't a yd. of goods left in them. My tub leaks it is past repair My dish pan is full of holes I have to do my washings on the board. I have only 2 everyday dresses with sleeves all wore out and 1 good 15 cent per yd print dress for Sunday no coat no hat no sheets or gowns in the house.

Other families were even worse off. Many stopped attending church or sending children to school because they lacked clothing or shoes. In some letters and oral histories, farm people would describe their poor conditions, but then they would say they were not "so bad off" because they at least kept food on the table, something that many in drought-stricken areas could not do.

Government assistance often enabled farm people to keep making do. Oral histories from Mountrail County, in western North Dakota, which had been hit particularly hard, show both the necessity of making do and the importance of New Deal relief programs in making that possible. Oscar and Ida Craft felt "helpless" in the 1930s. When asked if they were ever discouraged, Oscar replied, "Oh, God, don't tell me." Many mornings he would sit at the breakfast table and think "what's the use. One day just as hot as the other, and dry as the other." Ida helped keep the family going by churning and selling butter and trading eggs for groceries. She also planted a garden and "raised a little bit when it wasn't a blowin'." When the land would not even provide thistles for cattle feed and the market would not even offer a price to cover the costs of shipping them, they butchered their cattle and canned the beef. But "welfare" (government relief) often represented the margin of survival. The Crafts went to nearby Stanley to get surplus food and clothing. Ida had used flour sacks for underwear and sheets, but most of their clothes had "nothing more to patch." Oscar also worked on roads for the WPA and recalled that it was the "happiest time" because "nobody there [was] any better than I was. We was all alike at that time. . . . By God, you can talk to each other." Oscar remained close to some of these WPA friends even at the time of the interview in 1976. In a period when there was a crisis every year and the dust continued to blow, government assistance was essential for physical survival, but knowing people who shared rural poverty was necessary for emotional survival.[3]

Farm people often sensed that the Great Depression was destroying their farm neighborhoods. They did not suffer alone; they shared the experience with their friends and neighbors and more distant farm families. One Missouri farmer listed the name of each of his neighbors who suffered as he did: "Dear Mr. President Roosevelt there is 12 people. right here. that have their teams and all farming and have not got any place to go to. . . . here, are the names here in 2 miles square and it is all over the whole country that way." This letter combined the personal impact of the Great Depression on a specific neighborhood with the larger problem of small farmers throughout the country.[4]

Such connections often led farm people to take political action. The same people from western North Dakota who discussed their hardships and felt a sense of community suffering also proclaimed faith in the Farmers' Union or the NPL. The 1930s brought growth to these farm organizations and led to the creation of new groups, such as the Farm Holiday Association, which addressed the problems of the Great Depression with direct-action tactics, such as organizing milk strikes or physically halting farm foreclosures. The membership of these organizations often encompassed those farm people who needed government assistance. A 1934 study of Burke County, in western North Dakota, described the rural population of that hard-hit area as 40 percent "communist." These "communists" were members of or sympathizers with the United Farmers' League, a Communist-led farm organization, and they demanded relief as a right. The Farmers' Union and the Farm Holiday Association were also well organized in the county, and several politicians affiliated with the NPL held meetings in the area telling the people to demand relief. Farm people joined a myriad of groups to insist that government alter its agricultural and relief policies to help preserve their communities.

These groups built from the shared experiences of farm people but channeled their efforts beyond local strategies of survival into larger political and protest activities. Jean Long, a Farmers' Union leader in Wisconsin, recalled that her work as state rural recreation leader for the WPA led to increased growth for the Farmers' Union. By bringing farm people together for entertainment and recreation, she created the social places for them to discuss and share their problems and eventually to organize.[5] While many used community and family survival strategies, relied on government assistance, or both, other farm people took another step and joined farm organizations that attempted to address the causes of rural poverty.

Although government responded to this great need and to increased pressure from these political groups with experimental programs and relief measures, the overall direction and ideology of agricultural policy did not adjust to the crisis. Fundamentally, agricultural institutions continued policies that promoted increased production in their research and development programs, while trying to hinder the effects of these new methods by developing production controls on acreage and providing price supports. These policies moved in conflicting directions, and there was little analysis of the impact the policies would have on rural America. The institutions were so attached to definitions of progress that assumed the inevitability and benefits of increased production, larger farms, more costly farming methods, and a declining farm population that even the crisis of the Great Depression did not lead to a serious reevaluation of the direction of change.

The professionals most concerned with farm people displaced by these policies had little power; they were marginalized through a process of professionalization that used gender hierarchies to dismiss these concerns and questions. Because much farm labor was unpaid, provided either by women and youths within families or exchanged between neighbors, policymakers could easily dismiss this work and these workers and exclude them from agriculture's future. While agricultural policy seemed to evidence sympathy for the family farm, it privileged a certain type of family farm that introduced new capitalist-oriented production and a consumption-oriented family unit that had little in common with the existing system of families operating small farms. The methods of production and way of life of families on small farms were largely antithetical to the production and consumption goals of agricultural policies.

The fundamental changes in agricultural production that followed World War II originated in the institutional, ideological, and economic changes that took place during the first forty years of the twentieth century. As agricultural production was reorganized by government policy, the power of increasingly centralized agricultural corporations, and technological innovations, farm people migrated from rural America, and the survival strategies of community exchange and home production went with them. The transformation was not complete; hard work and making do, adapting and protesting persist as legacies of rural America's past. For some, these strategies continue to support survival and the preservation of family farms. Nevertheless, although rural communities and patterns of assistance in hard times persist, they are no longer integrated with daily patterns of work and exchange. Families share resources, family members contribute extensive labor to the family enterprise, and farm women still negotiate within patriarchal family structures, but the methods of contributing to the farm and the resources available for negotiation have changed dramatically.

An understanding of the gender relations and social structures of agricultural policy and rural communities is crucial for an understanding of the problems of contemporary agriculture. Farm women still continue their community-building labor and still integrate the social concerns of their families and their neighborhoods with the economic concerns of farming and agriculture.[6] However, as farm communities became more dispersed, as farm populations became smaller, and as farm production and living became more entwined with an international economy, it became more difficult to find security through the building of networks of mutuality. Crossing the barriers that separate neighborhoods, regions, and nations, and breaking down the barriers that separate the economic from the social, have become crucial in the attempt to address the problems created by fifty years of agribusiness development. From the past, before agriculture became "modern," come the visions that farm people had of integrating work and living, ways farm women sought to connect the needs of families, communities, and farms, and practices by which rural people together built flexible and adaptive human connections—visions that perhaps can provide clues about how to create another "new agriculture," one that can meet the needs of communities and the land more than simply the needs of production.

Notes

Introduction

1. Lyrics from Harriet R. Reeves, *Song and Dance Activities for Elementary Children* (West Nyack, N.Y.: Parker Publishing, 1985), 155–56.

2. Sarah Elbert explores the patriarchal meanings of this phrase in "The Farmer Takes a Wife: Women in America's Farming Families," in *Women, Households, and the Economy*, ed. Lourdes Beneria and Catharine Stimpson (New Brunswick, N.J.: Rutgers University Press, 1987), 173–97.

3. The critique of considering the family as a singular unit rather than as a dynamic relational unit was elaborated by Rayna Rapp, Ellen Ross, and Renate Bridenthal, "Examining Family History," *Feminist Studies* 5 (Spring 1979): 174–200.

4. In most of the rural Midwest, unpaid labor within family units was the norm, not simply an aberration applying only to female household labor. This is not to deny the importance of wage labor in the rural economy; there was a class of farm laborers who did not have ties to family farms, and a class of farmers who relied more on hired than on family labor. But on most small family farms in the Midwest, most wage work was an adjunct to unpaid family labor or exchanged community labor. Farmers often hired help to supplement family labor, and farm laborers often performed wage labor to supplement the family income or to get the money to establish their own operations.

5. For a full listing of these works and others mentioned in the text, see the bibliographical note.

6. Max J. Pfeffer, "Social Origins of Three Systems of Farm Production in the United States," *Rural Sociology* 48 (1983): 540–62; S. A. Mann and J. M. Dickinson, "Obstacles to the Development of a Capitalist Agriculture," *Journal of Peasant Studies* 5 (1978): 466–81.

7. Theodore Saloutos and John D. Hicks, *Agricultural Discontent in the Middle West, 1900–1939* (Madison: University of Wisconsin Press, 1951), 3–8; United States Bureau of the Census, *United States Census of Agriculture, 1945*, vol. 2, *General Reports: Statistics by Subject*, 292–93.

8. William Cronon, *Nature's Metropolis: Chicago and the Great West* (New York: W. W. Norton, 1991); Pfeffer, "Social Origins," 554–60; Susan Mann and James Dickinson, "State and Agriculture in Two Eras of American Capitalism," in *The Rural Sociology of Advanced Societies*, ed. Frederick Buttell and Howard Newby (Montclair, N.J.: Allanheld, Osmun, 1980), 283–325; Joan Jensen, *With These Hands: Women Working on the Land* (Old Westbury, N.Y.: Feminist Press, 1981), 100–104; Harriet Friedmann, "World Market, State, and Family Farm: Social Bases of Household Production in the Era of Wage Labor," *Comparative Studies in Society and History* 20 (1978): 583–85. A new direction in the study of the frontier and of women on the frontier would be provided by a more careful analysis of the gendered nature of expansion policies and the connections of the family labor system to the development of the growing economic system of national markets.

9. Charles Byron Kuhlmann, *The Development of the Flour-Milling Industry in the United States with Special Reference to the Industry in Minneapolis* (Boston: Houghton Mifflin, 1929), 130, 141–47.

10. Eric E. Lampard, *The Rise of the Dairy Industry in Wisconsin: A Study in Agricultural Change, 1820–1920* (Madison: State Historical Society of Wisconsin, 1963), 193.

11. The following information is drawn from an analysis of the United States Census of Agriculture for the years 1925, 1930, 1940, and 1950. United States Bureau of the Census, *United States Census of Agriculture, 1925*, part 1, *Northern States*, 6–9; *Fifteenth Census of the United States, 1930, Agriculture*, vol. 2, part 1, *Northern States*, 22–23, 30–31, and vol. 4, *General Reports*, 40, 107–8; *Sixteenth Census of the United States, 1940, Agriculture*, vol. 3, *General Reports: Statistics by Subject*, 37–38, 81, 96–97; *Seventeenth Census of the United States, 1950, Agriculture*, vol. 2, *General Reports*, 29–31.

12. For example, a national study done between 1924 and 1928 found that farm population increased in years when farm income was high and decreased in those when it was low. *Yearbook of Agriculture, 1930* (Washington, D.C.: USDA, 1931), 412–15.

13. Average farm size in the prairies increased from 142 acres in 1920 to 144 acres in 1930; in the plains it increased from 368.2 acres to 390.7 acres.

14. The farm population and the number of farms decreased, while farm size increased; however, tenancy rates did not begin their decline until economic recovery occurred during and following the war.

15. Data on net farm returns can be found in *Yearbook of Agriculture, 1925* (Washington, D.C.: Government Printing Office, 1926), 1342–43; *Yearbook of Agriculture, 1926* (Washington, D.C.: USDA, 1927), 1228–29; *Yearbook of Agriculture, 1927* (Washington, D.C.: USDA, 1928), 1133–34; *Yearbook of Agriculture, 1930*, 972–73; and *Yearbook of Agriculture, 1932* (Washington, D.C.: USDA,

1933), 894–95. For estimates of urban incomes in the 1920s, see Frank Stricker, "Affluence for Whom? Another Look at Prosperity and the Working Classes in the 1920s," *Labor History* 24 (Winter 1983): 5–33. Data on prices and incomes and increases in bankruptcies can be found in *Yearbook of Agriculture, 1910* (Washington, D.C.: USDA, 1911), 501, 512; *Yearbook of Agriculture, 1930,* 574–85, 972–73, 993–97; *Yearbook of Agriculture, 1932,* 894–95; *Yearbook of Agriculture, 1934* (Washington, D.C.: USDA, 1935), 700–701; and *Yearbook of Agriculture, 1935* (Washington, D.C.: USDA, 1936), 675–76, 680–85, 692.

CHAPTER 1   The Farm Family

1. Emily F. Hoag, "The Advantages of Farm Life: A Study of Correspondence and Interviews with 8,000 Farm Women," 1923, 51, USDA Bureau of Agricultural Economics (BAE), Division of Farm Population and Rural Life (hereafter cited as DFP&RL), Record Group 83, National Archives, Manuscripts, box 2. Similar views were expressed by farm girls; see Martha Foote Crow, *The American Country Girl* (1915; New York: Arno Press, 1974), 26–29.

2. Nancy Grey Osterud has effectively argued the inadequacies of "separate spheres" analysis for farm women in nineteenth-century New York; see *Bonds of Community: The Lives of Farm Women in Nineteenth-Century New York* (Ithaca: Cornell University Press, 1991). For a critique of the application of reproductive/ productive classifications for analyzing the work of farm women, see Carolyn E. Sachs, "The Participation of Women and Girls in Market and Non-Market Activities on Pennsylvania Farms," in *Women and Farming: Changing Roles, Changing Structures,* ed. Wava G. Haney and Jane B. Knowles (Boulder: Westview Press, 1988), 123–34.

3. Most studies of inheritance patterns in rural America indicate that male children received land while female children received movable goods or education. See, for example, Osterud, *Bonds of Community*; Kathleen Neils Conzen, "Peasant Pioneers: Generational Succession among German Farmers in Frontier Minnesota," in *The Countryside in the Age of Capitalist Transformation: Essays in the Social History of Rural America,* ed. Steven Hahn and Jonathan Prude (Chapel Hill: University of North Carolina Press, 1985), 259–92; Mark Friedberger, "The Farm Family and the Inheritance Process: Evidence from the Corn Belt, 1870–1950," *Agricultural History* 57 (Jan. 1983): 1–13; and Sonya Salamon and Ann Mackey Keim, "Land Ownership and Women's Power in a Midwestern Farming Community," *Journal of Marriage and the Family* 41 (Feb. 1979): 109–19. Some anecdotal evidence indicates that daughters inherited land when there were no sons in a family (as long as the daughters had married). With declining family size this pattern may become more frequent.

4. In the survey, home demonstration agents asked farm women in selected localities in representative counties to complete records of their working conditions. Florence E. Ward, "The Farm Woman's Problems," *USDA Department Circular* no. 148 (Nov. 1920): 3–11. The survey did not ask who performed this work, if the women did not. Many of these tasks may have been performed by children

under the supervision of women. Other good descriptions of the variety of women's work on farms include Nellie Kedzie Jones, "Is the Wife a Partner in the Domestic Firm?" originally published in the *Country Gentleman*, 7 June 1913, Nellie Kedzie Jones Papers, 1881–1950, Wis MSS RT, State Historical Society of Wisconsin; Clara L. Chambers, tapes 26 and 27, UC 1086A, Rural Women's Oral History Project (hereafter cited as RWOHP), State Historical Society of Wisconsin; Agnes Lee Oral History, tape 1, side 1, tape 689A, State Historical Society of Wisconsin; Margaret and Rangar Segerstrom, tape 2, side 1, tape 581A, Wisconsin Agriculturalists Oral History Project (hereafter cited as WAOHP), State Historical Society of Wisconsin; Ida Gullickson, TR17–0984 A&B, North Dakota Oral History Project (hereafter cited as NDOHP), North Dakota State Historical Society; Ethel Fosberg, TR8–0977 A&B, NDOHP; Myrna Bogh, tr. 11–16, OH4–23, Iowa Century Farms Oral History Project (hereafter cited as ICFOHP), Iowa State Historical Society; Elizabeth Ellis Hoyt, "Value of Family Living on Iowa Farms," *Iowa Agricultural Experiment Station Bulletin* no. 281 (June 1931): 232; Memo from H. C. Taylor to Secretary of Agriculture Henry Wallace, "Percent of Amount of Farm Work by Women and Children from Weekly Records, 1914–1920," 2 Mar. 1923, DFP&RL, General Correspondence, 1919–36, Office of the Secretary of Agriculture, Memoranda, 1922–28, box 12; Oscar Juve and Ilene Bailey, "The Labor and Leisure Year of the Farmer and His Wife," 1921, DFP&RL, Manuscripts, box 5; and George Von Tungeln, E. L. Kirkpatrick, C. R. Hoffer, and J. F. Thaden, "A Study of the Social Aspects of Rural Life and Farm Tenantry, Cedar County, Iowa," 80–90, DFP&RL, Manuscripts, box 8 (also published as *Iowa Agricultural Experiment Station Bulletin* no. 217 [Aug. 1923]). Other good descriptions can be found in the regular column "How Some Women Succeed: True Stories about Real Farm Women," appearing in the *Farmer's Wife* between May and December 1924. Photographs also show similar divisions of labor; see the collections of the USDA Federal Extension Service, Record Group 33-SC, Still Pictures Branch, National Archives (hereafter cited as NASPB), and Midwest and Northwest Region Files, Farm Security Administration—Office of War Information Photographs (hereafter cited as FSA Photographs), Photographs and Prints Division, Library of Congress.

5. Ward, "Farm Woman's Problems"; Segerstrom, tape 2, sides 1 and 2, WAOHP; FSA Photographs; DFP&RL, Marketing and Rural Life, 1902–38, Record Group 83-ML, NASPB; and Farms and Farming Files, Photographs, Iowa State Historical Society.

6. These generalizations about children and farm work are based on diaries, oral histories, and reminiscences. All the diaries are rich sources for this material. Some of the more descriptive oral histories are Clara Scott, tapes 28 and 29, RWOHP; Segerstrom, tape 1, side 1, WAOHP; Jean Long, tape 4, sides 1 and 2, tape 589A, WAOHP; Isabel Baumann, tape 1, sides 1 and 2, tape 809A, WAOHP; Arthur F. Wileden, tape 2, side 2, tape 3, side 1, tape 553A, WAOHP; Howard Brusveen, tape 1, side 1, tape 3, side 2, tape 894A, WAOHP; Percy S. Hardiman, tape 574A, WAOHP; Norval Ellefson, tape 1, side 1, tape 551A, WAOHP; Jack D. Levin Oral History, tape 1, side 1, tape 555A, State Historical Society of Wisconsin; Gul-

lickson, NDOHP; Alfred O. Berg, TR20–0986 A&B, NDOHP; Anna Dannewitz, MN3–0649 A&B, NDOHP; Jake and Clara Jacobs, MN12–0657 A&B, NDOHP; and Isaac and Dora Leopke, WE8–1061 A&B, NDOHP. Other good sources include "How Some Women Succeed," in *Farmer's Wife*; Hamlin Garland, *Son of the Middle Border* (1914; New York: MacMillan, 1923), 31–36, 48–52, 77–78, 85–87, 116–20, 125–40, 147–55; and Era Bell Thompson, *American Daughter* (Chicago: University of Chicago Press, 1946), 36–60, 98–102. Photographs reveal similar task assignments; see Work Files in the Midwest and Northern Plains States, FSA Photographs.

7. See E. L. Kirkpatrick, Rosalind Tough, and M. L. Cowles, "How Farm Families Meet the Emergency," *Wisconsin Agricultural Experiment Station Research Bulletin* no. 126 (Jan. 1935): 19–20; "Rural Industries Supplement Income on Farms, New Survey Shows," 30 Mar. 1934, DFP&RL, General Correspondence, Press Releases, box 17; letter of Ruth M. Jacobs, 12 Apr. 1976, Iowa Century Farms Records (hereafter cited as ICFR), Special Collections, MS96, Iowa State University; Scott, RWOHP; Segerstrom, tape 1, side 1, WAOHP; Baumann, tape 1, side 1, WAOHP; "How Some Women Succeed (Mary Theiss)," *Farmer's Wife* 27 (Dec. 1924): 222; Dannewitz, NDOHP; and Kate Olson, TR16–0983 A&B, NDOHP.

8. W. B. Siebert Papers, 1903–37, Orin G. Libby Manuscript Collection, Chester Fritz Library, no. 211, University of North Dakota, 1935–37.

9. There is some contradiction between the oral history sources and the diaries of grain farmers. Women in oral histories largely talk about their community work (cooking for the large threshing crews) during the threshing rituals rather than any labor they might have done during the harvest before threshing. Diary sources suggest that women did work on binders and in the fields preparing the grain for threshing.

10. Anne Isabel Francis Burke Papers, 1907–42, Orin G. Libby Manuscript Collection, Chester Fritz Library, no. 616, University of North Dakota.

11. E. G. Powers Diaries, 1920–42, Manuscripts, MS63, Iowa State Historical Society, entries for 1926–37. In a sample of about thirty oral histories in which all these factors were described, women on farms of fewer than 80 acres were most active in the barnyard and fields, while those with more than 240 acres were least active. Those farms between 80 and 240 acres show a diversity of arrangements, based on the needs of the farm and the preferences negotiated among family members. See Mary Neth, "Gender and the Family Labor System: Defining Work in the Rural Midwest," *Journal of Social History* 27 (Mar. 1994): 563–77.

12. "A Type of Foxfire History: Butler County, Iowa," Iowa Local History Collection (hereafter cited as ILHC), Special Collections, MS-80, M-2, Iowa State University. Martha Foote Crow, in a study of farm girls, called the oldest daughter, who was expected to perform all field and home tasks, the "crack-filler": *American Country Girl*, 102.

13. Juve and Bailey, "Labor and Leisure Year."

14. Frank Krueger Papers, 1881–1948, Microfilm 505, P84–1986, State Historical Society of Wisconsin, 1900–1901 and 1919–20. See also Juve and Bailey,

"Labor and Leisure Year." The changing expenses of farm families through the life cycle and how farm families met changing needs are described in E. L. Kirkpatrick, Rosalind Tough, and May L. Cowles, "The Life Cycle of the Farm Family," *Wisconsin Agricultural Experiment Station Research Bulletin* no. 121 (Sept. 1934). Another good description of how women's work changed is found in Chambers, tape 26, side 2, parts 1 and 2, RWOHP.

15. For a more in-depth analysis of ethnicity and the other factors shaping the gender division of labor, see Neth, "Gender and the Family Labor System."

16. Gerald and Fay Goodwin, OH4–29, ICFOHP; Bogh, ICFOHP.

17. Much of my discussion of the valuation of women's and men's work on the farm parallels that of Nancy Grey Osterud in *Bonds of Community*. My study has benefited from the sophistication of her analysis.

18. Good descriptions of daily chores can be found in Baumann, tape 1, side 2, tape 3, sides 1 and 2, WAOHP, and Garland, *Son of the Middle Border*, 116–20, 124–32. Garland also records how farmers accustomed to raising wheat found the change to livestock confining and dull: see 361–62. For a comparison of daily and seasonal work routines on different types of farms, see Juve and Bailey, "Labor and Leisure Year."

19. Descriptions of work organization are found in Nellie Kedzie Jones, "The New Home on the Old Farm," 28–33, a compilation of articles published in the *Country Gentleman* between 1912 and 1916, collected in the Nellie Kedzie Jones Papers, and "How Some Women Succeed (Louise Blankenship)," *Farmer's Wife* 27 (Sept. 1924): 102–3.

20. Siebert Papers and Powers Diaries.

21. Jones, "New Home on the Old Farm," 30–31, 46–47; Jones, "Is the Wife a Partner"; Leopke, NDOHP.

22. Descriptions of seasonal work routines are found in Jones, "New Home on the Old Farm," 34–37; Garland, *Son of the Middle Border*, 77–78, 86–87, 116–20, 125–28, 147–55; and the Agnes Lee interview, State Historical Society of Wisconsin. The photographs of the FSA also illustrate seasonal, periodic, and daily work routines very effectively: Farm Work Folders, FSA Photographs.

23. Lucille Hucke, OH4–63, ICFOHP; Walter and Emma Henderson, OH4–82, ICFOHP.

24. Anna Phillips, OH4–46, ICFOHP.

25. Dannewitz, NDOHP. Other examples of these traditions can be found in Christ Larson, MN1–0646 A&B, NDOHP; Oscar and Ida Craft, MN11–0656, NDOHP; Mr. and Mrs. Howard Stansbury, TR11–0979B, NDOHP; Hazel James, WE4–1057 A&B, NDOHP; Amy Bilsland, OH4–62, ICFOHP; and E. L. Kirkpatrick, P. E. McNall, and May L. Cowles, "Farm Family Living in Wisconsin," *Wisconsin Agricultural Experiment Station Research Bulletin* no. 114 (Jan. 1933): 10–11. In Kirkpatrick, Tough, and Cowles, "How Farm Families Meet the Emergency," the more prosperous Wisconsin counties of Green and Portage illustrate how families reintroduced these techniques in bad times, while Sawyer County, in the cutover region, illustrates how poorer families constantly used these techniques for survival and had little room to expand them during hard times. For a

discussion of the importance of these work patterns to family traditions, see Seena Kohl, "The Making of a Community: The Role of Women in an Agricultural Setting," in *Kin and Communities: Families in America*, ed. Allan J. Lichtman and Joan R. Challinor (Washington, D.C.: Smithsonian Institution Press, 1979), 175–86.

26. Good examples of these values playing a role in farm management decisions can be found in Segerstrom, WAOHP; Brusveen, WAOHP; and Harold Tomter, tape 715A, WAOHP. See also John W. Bennett, Seena Kohl, and Geraldine Binion, *Of Time and the Enterprise: North American Family Farm Management in a Context of Resource Marginality* (Minneapolis: University of Minnesota Press, 1982), chaps. 12–17.

27. Perry Anderson, WE16–1069, NDOHP.

28. See Hoyt, "Value of Family Living," 19–21, 201–7; Kirkpatrick, McNall, and Cowles, "Farm Family Living in Wisconsin," 7–11; "Meeting Agriculture's Old and New Problems with the Aid of Science," *Wisconsin Agricultural Experiment Station Annual Report Bulletin* no. 421 (Feb. 1932): 18–20; and Kirkpatrick, Tough, and Cowles, "How Farm Families Meet the Emergency," 4–7. See also George Von Tungeln, J. F. Thaden, and E. L. Kirkpatrick, "Cost of Living on Iowa Farms," *Iowa Agricultural Experiment Station Bulletin* no. 237 (Nov. 1928); Kirkpatrick, Tough, and Cowles, "Life Cycle of the Farm Family"; "Annual Family Living in Selected Farm Homes of North Dakota," Aug. 1928, DFP&RL, Manuscripts. Oral histories with good descriptions of women's work in food furnishing include Olson, NDOHP; Chambers, RWOHP; Tomter, tape 1, sides 1 and 2, WAOHP; Jacobs, NDOHP; Dannewitz, NDOHP; Anderson, NDOHP; James, NDOHP; Stansbury, NDOHP; O. M. "Mike" Smith and Theodore Olstad, TR1–0970 A&B, NDOHP; Gullickson, NDOHP; Fosberg, NDOHP; Bilsland, ICFOHP; and Cora Doty and Anna Smith, MN14–0659 A&B, NDOHP.

29. Krueger Family Papers, 1852–1965, Microfilm 748, State Historical Society of Wisconsin, June 1910. Income for 1919, for example, included $2,534 for milk, $315.15 for wheat, $615.82 for swine, $354.29 for poultry and eggs, and $225.14 for honey. Hardiman, tape 1, side 1, WAOHP; Ted R. Rask, interviewed by Marcie Hogan, North Dakota Depression Interviews (hereafter cited as NDDI), Special Collections, no. 274, University of North Dakota. See also Hoyt, "Value of Family Living," 204–6; Kirkpatrick, Tough, and Cowles, "How Farm Families Meet the Emergency," 19; "How Some Women Succeed (Mrs. Albert Lindbaugh)," *Farmer's Wife* 27 (Oct. 1924): 126; Cecilie Nelson, MN15–0660A NDOHP; Segerstrom, tape 2, side 1, tape 6, side 2, WAOHP; Smith and Olstad, NDOHP; Doty and Smith, NDOHP; Eunice K. Long, WE2–1055 A&B, NDOHP; Jacobs, NDOHP; Craft, NDOHP; Bilsland, tr. 5–6, ICFOHP; Lynn Kaspari, interviewed by Olyn Lack, NDDI; Mrs. Christ Mitzel, interviewed by Clinton Loble, NDDI; Fred Donahue, interviewed by Margaret Ruff, NDDI; Chambers, RWOHP; Tomter, tape 1, sides 1 and 2, WAOHP; "How Some Women Succeed (Mary Theiss)"; and "Let Us Counsel Together [Letter from Mrs. E.L.D.]," *Farmer's Wife* 17 (Feb. 1915): 262.

30. *Farmer's Wife* 16 (Feb. 1914) and 22 (Aug. 1919): 64. For examples of sewing and making over in one diary, see Anna Pratt Erickson Diaries, 1898–1959,

Microfilm 738, State Historical Society of Wisconsin, 2 Aug. 1906, 14 Sept., 15 Oct. 1910, 2 Mar. 1911, 12–13 Aug. 1932, 16 Jan. 1933, 26 Feb., 6 July 1934, 29 Apr. 1935, 4 Nov. 1937. See also Crow, *American Country Girl,* 186–87; "Planning the Costume," *Iowa Agricultural Extension Home Economics Bulletin* no. 9 (July 1916); Hoyt, "Value of Family Living," 207–13; Kirkpatrick, Tough, and Cowles, "How Farm Families Meet the Emergency," 13; poem on making do in the "dirty thirties," Gardar Homemakers Club, Pembina County, North Dakota Homemakers Club Histories, Collection SC924, North Dakota State University (hereafter cited as NDSU); Craft, NDOHP; Olson, NDOHP; Dannewitz, NDOHP; Anderson, NDOHP; Doty and Smith, NDOHP; Mrs. Christ Mitzel interview, NDDI; Maude Stephenson Moore, "Memories of the Early Days," Iowa Century Farms Manuscript Collection (hereafter cited as ICFMC), Special Collections, MS96, box 2, folder 46, Iowa State University; and Jean Westin, *Making Do: How Women Survived the '30s* (Chicago: Follett, 1976). An interesting analysis of feed companies trying to appeal to women by printing patterned feedsacks in the 1950s is found in LuAnn Jones, "From Feed Bags to Fashion: Southern Farm Women and Material Culture" (Paper presented at the Southern Association of Women Historians Conference, Chapel Hill, N.C., June 1991).

31. Erickson Diaries; Baumann, WAOHP; and Isabel H. Baumann Papers, 1924–76, MS 591, State Historical Society of Wisconsin. Nancy Grey Osterud has found similar class/gender systems in her study of the Nanticoke Valley in the twentieth century; see "The Gender Division of Labor, Class, and Ethnicity on New York State Farms during the Early Twentieth Century" (Paper presented at the Social Science History Association Meeting, Minneapolis, Oct. 1990). While Baumann and Erickson exemplify class distinctions in patterns of mutuality, one novel, written in 1912, examines class distinctions in women's subordination in farm families. In it, the protagonist's mother is physically abused by her husband and is controlled by his actions. Her life is filled with hard labor as well as abuse. The protagonist marries a college-educated man, hoping to escape the abuse of her uneducated family, only to find that he also controls her actions, though with methods other than physical abuse. Although she is not in the difficult position her mother was in, she is still not in an equal marriage. The novel's protagonist only gains control of her life when she inherits land and has her own economic base of support. See Dell H. Munger, *The Wind before the Dawn* (Garden City, N.J.: Doubleday, Page, 1912).

32. Craft, NDOHP.

33. Nelson, NDOHP. Attitudes toward the plight of women in authoritarian marriages were exemplified in a series of letters in the *Farmer's Wife.* The first letter described how one woman's husband never gave her money for clothes and never let her visit her mother, who was ill. The woman also had six children between the ages of three and fourteen. This letter brought a series of responses from other readers, offering advice of various sorts. One reader suggested she needed "courage tablets" and should stand up to her husband; if "he slaps you, you slap him back and have the last word." Another reader thought this too harsh; "I think love will conquer before harsh words." Another reader described her own situa-

tion, which was similar, and hoped women would get the ballot so that husbands could not make "slaves of their wives." Another woman suggested that she "take [her] troubles to God." Others suggested she have more "grit" and refuse to work until she got more income; that she only do work in the house, milk the cows, and care for the chickens; that she not submit tamely, but also not go into battle or fight; that she buy labor-saving utensils and be a little more selfish so her family would learn to be more unselfish. Finally a woman wrote that she was "riled" not at the writer, but at the "blame some of the sisters seemed to put on her and excuse the man." Only one letter suggested that she leave her husband; this woman had done this herself. See *Farmer's Wife* 15 (Dec. 1912) through 16 (Nov. 1913).

CHAPTER 2   Building a Rural Neighborhood

1. Jones, "New Home on the Old Farm," 66–68.
2. I use *neighboring,* a term that appears in oral histories from the region, to refer to the practice of building neighborhoods.
3. This argument was first made by Osterud, *Bonds of Community.*
4. The other factors Kolb identified as significant in 1941 were length of residence, tenure status, nationality, and age of head of household. See J. H. Kolb, "Trends of Country Neighborhoods: A Restudy of Rural Primary Groups, 1921–1931," *Wisconsin Agricultural Experiment Station Research Bulletin* no. 120 (Nov. 1933): 18–19, and John H. Kolb and Douglas G. Marshall, "Neighborhood-Community Relationships in Rural Society," *Wisconsin Agricultural Experiment Station Research Bulletin* no. 154 (Nov. 1944): 5–6. A 1920 study that disagreed with the Kolb findings and emphasized the importance of informal neighboring patterns and work exchange was E. L. Morgan and Owen Howells, "Rural Primary Groups of Boone County, Missouri," DFP&RL, Record Group 83, Manuscripts, box 7.
5. These distinctions, to a certain extent, were made by rural sociologists, though their tendency was to define both in terms of geographic locale. See Lowry Nelson, *Rural Sociology: Its Origin and Growth in the United States* (Minneapolis: University of Minnesota Press, 1969), 35–44.
6. Erickson Diaries.
7. Howard R. Klueter and James J. Lorence, *Woodlot and Ballot Box: Marathon County in the Twentieth Century* (Wausau: Marathon County Historical Society, 1977), 40–46, 53, 140–45, 151–53; P. H. Pactzold, "Map of Marathon County, State of Wisconsin," 1912, State Historical Society of Wisconsin; *Plat Book of Marathon County, Wisconsin* (Rockford, Ill.: W. W. Hixson, 1920), State Historical Society of Wisconsin; *Atlas and Farmers' Directory of Marathon County, Wisconsin* (St. Paul: Webb Publishing, 1930), State Historical Society of Wisconsin; and *Plat Book of Marathon County, Wisconsin* (Milwaukee: County Plat Book Publisher, 1947), State Historical Society of Wisconsin.
8. Klueter and Lorence, *Woodlot and Ballot Box,* 142–44, and John P. Johansen, "Immigrant Settlements and Social Organizations in South Dakota," *South Dakota Agricultural Experiment Station Bulletin* no. 313 (June 1937): 44–51. See

also J. H. Kolb, "Rural Primary Groups: A Study of Agricultural Neighborhoods," *Wisconsin Agricultural Experiment Station Research Bulletin* no. 51 (Dec. 1921): 22–27; Kolb, "Trends of Country Neighborhoods," 23–26; and Kolb and Marshall, "Neighborhood-Community Relationships," 6.

9. Sources besides Erickson's diary used to recreate her neighborhood include the plat maps cited in note 7; *Guide to Church Vital Statistics Records in Wisconsin* (Madison: Wisconsin Historical Records Survey, 1942); *Inventory of the County Archives of Wisconsin: Marathon County* (Madison: Wisconsin Historical Records Survey Project, 1940); *Marathon County, Wisconsin, Cemetery Inscriptions: An Every-Name Index* (Wausau: Marathon County Genealogical Society, 1986); the *Athens Record*; and Athens Directories, State Historical Society of Wisconsin. Rural sociologists of the time listed ethnic and religious homogeneity, strong neighborhood institutions, kinship ties, and secure tenure status as primary sources of stability in rural neighborhoods. In contrast to Erickson's neighborhood, Orange Township in Blackhawk County, Iowa, illustrates how these factors combined to make a stable, prosperous farm community. See George Von Tungeln, "A Rural Social Survey of Orange Township, Blackhawk County, Iowa," *Iowa Agricultural Experiment Station Bulletin* no. 184 (Dec. 1918): 402–3, 405–6, 412, 423–26.

10. Studies done in South Dakota, Missouri, and Illinois all showed the importance of visiting; see Walter L. Slocum, "The Influence of Tenure Status upon Rural Life in Eastern South Dakota," *South Dakota Agricultural Experiment Station Circular* no. 39 (May 1942): 4, 13; Henry J. Burt, "Contacts in a Rural Community," *Missouri Agricultural Experiment Station Research Bulletin* no. 125 (Aug. 1929): 4–5, 72–74; and D. E. Lindstrom, "Forces Affecting Participation of Farm People in Rural Organization," *Illinois Agricultural Experiment Station Bulletin* no. 423 (May 1936): 79–80, 92–93.

11. Kolb and Marshall, "Neighborhood-Community Relationships," 25. On the social aspects of the creamery, see Floyd Lucia, tape 2, side 1, tape 552A, WAOHP, and Segerstrom, tape 2, side 1, WAOHP.

12. Nellie Kedzie Jones, "Company Coming," in "New Home on the Old Farm," 53–55; Erickson Diaries, 28 Dec. 1917–19 Feb. 1918. This pattern of recording visitors was true for neighbors as well as relatives. It can also be found in Frank Krueger Papers, 11 July–12 Aug. 1901, and Burke Papers, Jan. 1928.

13. Throughout the text, I will refer to people with the names used by Erickson in the diary. Often, Erickson identified her female neighbors as "Mrs." rather than giving a first name. This emphasizes women's concern with familial connections. Some close female friends of a similar age and daughters of friends were referred to by their first and last names. Erickson usually used both first and last names for male neighbors. In general, when Erickson referred to someone by a first name only, that person was a member of her family.

14. Erickson Diaries, 8–15 Jan., 7–14 Sept. 1928.

15. Mr. and Mrs. L. V. Kunkel, WE11–1064, NDOHP; Jacobs, NDOHP. See also letter from C. R. Hoffer to C. J. Galpin, 19 July 1921, DFP&RL, Study Pro-

jects, 1919–22, Minnesota File, box 8, and Kolb and Marshall, "Neighborhood-Community Relationships," 15.

16. See Von Tungeln, "Orange Township," 439–48, and George Von Tungeln, "A Rural Social Survey of Lone Tree Township, Clay County, Iowa," *Iowa Agricultural Experiment Station Bulletin* no. 193 (Mar. 1920): 246–47. Sunday visiting appears in nearly all the diaries and oral histories I have examined. The patterns of Sunday visiting can be found in any part of Erickson's diary, but the letter writing was more frequent in the later years when her daughters lived farther away. Erickson also visited less frequently in the year when she was solely responsible for the farm and her children were young; however, she visited more frequently after her divorce from Joe than she did while married to him.

17. Examples of interactions with Margaret Copple in the Erickson Diaries: 13 Nov. 1923; 14 Feb., 16 Mar., 1 Apr., 25, 27 May, 18 June, 17 Oct. 1924; 16 Jan., 28 Feb., 15 Mar., 15 June 1925; 24 Mar., 8 May, 1, 3 July 1927; 30 Aug., 9 Dec. 1928; 22 June, 30 Aug., 10 Sept. 1929; 31 Aug. 1930; 12 Jan., 9 Aug. 1931; 28 Feb., 8 July 1932; 27 Apr., 9 June 1933; 10 Aug., 10 Nov. 1937.

18. Morgan and Howells, "Rural Primary Groups of Boone County," 51–53; J. O. Rankin, "Nebraska Farm Tenancy: Some Community Phases," *Nebraska Agricultural Experiment Station Bulletin* no. 196 (Oct. 1923): 25–26; Kolb and Marshall, "Neighborhood-Community Relationships," 25; Slocum, "Influence of Tenure Status," 10–11.

19. Most diaries reveal that work was primarily done by extended kin, particularly when they were settled on nearby farms. Neighborhood exchanges were most common when extra labor was needed, particularly at threshing and harvest time. When their children were too small to work, the diarists generally exchanged work with nearby relatives. Only one diarist had a hired man in addition to family help consistently through the busy season from planting to harvest. See Powers Diaries.

20. Other examples of butchering exchanges found in diaries: Frank Krueger Papers, 9 Nov. 1900; Burke Papers, Sept. 1919, Nov. 1926 and 1927, Dec. 1931; Siebert Papers, 1 June 1936, 2 Dec. 1937. Those in oral histories include Berg, NDOHP; Jacobs, NDOHP; Brusveen, tape 4, side 1, WAOHP; Hardiman, tape 4, side 1, WAOHP; and Tomter, tape 2, side 1, WAOHP.

21. Erickson Diaries, 27–30 Nov. 1906; 5 Feb., 12–13 Nov. 1908; 23 Dec.–4 Jan. 1917; 10–16 Jan., 5 Dec. 1918; 22 Dec. 1919; 18 Jan., 17 Dec. 1922; 15 Dec. 1923; 4 Feb., 7 Nov. 1924; 14 Nov. 1925; 22, 28 Nov. 1926; 9–20 Jan., 2–6 Dec. 1927; 18 Dec. 1928; 14 Mar. 1929; 7–8 Mar. 1930; 22–27 Dec. 1931; 4–19 Jan. 1934.

22. Threshing is universally mentioned in diaries and oral histories. Other examples of wood-chopping exchanges are found in Segerstrom, tape 2, side 1, WAOHP; Ellefson, tape 3, sides 1 and 2, WAOHP; and Burke Diaries, 1931. In Iowa and Wisconsin, exchanges of labor in corn husking or silo filling were sometimes more important than those in threshing. For husking, see Bertha Gabelmann Diaries, 1912–66, D45, box 1, Iowa State Historical Society, 7 Sept.–11 Nov. 1912; Powers Diaries, Oct. and Nov. 1932 and 1937 (by 1937 Powers sometimes used a corn picker); and Bogh, tr. 17, ICFOHP. For silo filling, see Henderson, tr.

12–14, ICFOHP; Baumann, tape 3, side 2, WAOHP; Segerstrom, tape 6, side 2, WAOHP; and Frank Krueger Papers, 12 Sept.–1 Oct. 1919. Other forms of work exchange could include canning and plucking turkeys for Thanksgiving or Christmas markets; see Siebert Papers, Aug., 16 Nov., and 11–19 Dec. 1937.

23. Wood cutting: Erickson Diaries, 12 Oct.–Nov. 1935; 4, 11 Nov., 7 Dec. 1937. Threshing and silo filling: Erickson Diaries, 3–8 Sept. 1924; 3–31 Aug. 1934; 8 Aug.–5 Oct. 1935; 2 Aug.–10 Oct. 1936; 1 Aug.–30 Sept. 1937.

24. Erickson Diaries, 23 Dec. 1919–4 June 1920. During this period, new buildings were frequently public buildings, such as community halls, schools, and churches, rather than barns. One example can be found in Mary Alma Barrett Still Papers, 1910–14, MS63, North Dakota Institute for Regional Studies, NDSU. In 1910 the Still men helped build a local school. Other examples of labor donated for community buildings are found in DFP&RL, Marketing and Rural Life, 1908–38, Neg. 6519, Record Group 83-ML, box 13, NASPB.

25. Erickson Diaries, 11 Oct. 1934. Berry sales: 26 June 1919, 25 June 1932; garden produce sales: 11 Oct. 1921; potatoes: 1 Oct. 1923, 29 Oct. 1926, 1 Aug. 1929, 30 Sept. 1930.

26. Erickson Diaries. Selling potatoes: 16 Mar. 1926, 15 Mar. 1928, 11 Jan., 28 May 1929, 30 Sept. 1930; cow breeding: 25 Dec. 1918, 7, 15, 27 Jan. 1919, 27 May 1929, 30 Jan. 1935; arranging and settling: 11 Nov. 1912, 13 Mar. 1918, 21 May 1927, 18 Sept. 1932, 30 Jan, 22 Apr. 1935, 2 Apr. 1938.

27. Erickson Diaries, 26 Sept. 1926, 10 Oct. 1928. Berries and poultry: 13 Sept. 1928, 5 Sept. 1929, 4 Feb. 1932; Zettlers: May, June 1936; Agnes Hanson: 31 Mar., 17, 22 Apr., 22–23 May 1927. Gifts exchanged between Kulas and Erickson: 31 Mar. 1918, 20 Mar., 10 Oct. 1919, 24 Mar., 25 Nov. 1921, 1 Sept. 1924, 24 Aug. 1926, 1 Apr. 1927, 21 June 1931, 24 Sept. 1932, 25 Dec. 1935. See also Hoag, "Advantages of Farm Life," 106.

28. Erickson Diaries. Eggs: 30 Mar., 19 Dec. 1918, 20 Mar. 1919, 24 Mar. 1921; rides given: 11 Dec. 1929, 14 Jan. 1931, 13 Feb., 14 Dec. 1934; rides received: 6 Dec. 1922, 1 Sept. 1925, 7 Apr., 7 Sept. 1927. See also Jacobs, NDOHP, and Smith and Olstad, NDOHP.

29. Brusveen, tape 4, side 1, WAOHP. He describes his neighborhood as tightly knit, with work exchanges lasting into the 1950s. Another close neighborhood is described in Gullickson, NDOHP. Nancy Grey Osterud argues that men's work relations were described more often in monetary terms and women's more often in terms of direct personal relationships. See Osterud, *Bonds of Community*. In general, my research supports these conclusions for farm people in the Midwest in the twentieth century; however, it also suggests that men, although tied more closely to a cash and wage economy, also perceived their work and exchanges in terms of personal ties to neighbors as friends or kin. In part these distinctions may be related to the types of sources used. Osterud found account books and men's diaries as evidence for the dominance of the cash economy in their lives. The men's diaries that I found from the Midwest did not include account records but closely paralleled women's diaries in their form and their descriptions of neighborhood exchange. The source that most clearly revealed men's placement of exchange in

social contexts was oral histories. Perhaps nineteenth-century written records (diaries, account books) reflect a literary culture that encouraged men to see their work in connection to the cash economy, while parallel oral traditions continued to link men to a community vision of their economic exchanges.

30. Burke Papers, 20 Oct. 1908, 26 Feb. 1910, 16 Dec. 1919, 27 July 1927. Iowa diarist Bertha Gabelmann, whose diary stretched from 1912 to 1966, also recorded community and personal events in a brief, direct style, but suggested intimacy by adding markings at either side of the entry: a drawing of wedding bells for marriages, crosses to mark a death. Gabelmann Diaries, 13 July 1918, 16 July 1934. Elizabeth Hampsten discusses the use of language by women diarists in the Midwest. She argues that women diarists used repetition and patterning in style and content to "assert a pattern [of events] and to blur distinctions between recurring and unique events." See Elizabeth Hampsten, *Read This Only to Yourself: The Private Writings of Midwestern Women, 1889–1910* (Bloomington: Indiana University Press, 1982), 20–21, 55–73. I found this true for rural women but also for the farm men whose diaries I read. The one exception is Elmer Powers's published diary, which more closely fits the different style Hampsten attributes to educated women. However, his unpublished diaries reveal more of Powers's personal and family life than did the diary he wrote to submit for publication in *Wallace's Farmer*. Portions of the latter diary were published as *Years of Struggle: The Farm Diary of Elmer G. Powers, 1931–1936*, ed. H. Roger Grant and L. Edward Purcell (Ames: Iowa State University Press, 1976).

31. Pauline Olson Diaries, 1926–69, MSS A-140, North Dakota Historical Society, 24 Jan. 1931; 7, 31 Aug. 1934.

32. Olson Diaries, 18 Aug. 1932.

33. Olson Diaries, 6 Oct. 1932, 2 July, 29 Mar. 1933. Other examples: 16 Apr., 6 May 1935.

34. Segerstrom, tape 2, side 1, WAOHP; Craft, side A, NDOHP.

35. Erickson Diaries, 15 Feb., 3 June–7 July, 5 Aug.–2 Sept. 1905; 23 May–23 Aug. 1908; 24 Mar.–10 May 1911; 13 July–11 Aug., 24 Mar. 1912; 2 Nov.–19 Dec. 1913; 22 Mar. 1914; 1 Jan.–12 Mar. 1917. That men were more distant from the childbirth experience can also be seen in Powers Diaries, 16 and 20–29 Aug. 1922. Powers's primary role at this time was to take his wife to help his sister-in-law and to help his brother make funeral arrangements after the death of the baby. Compare this to the death of Anna's sixth child, in which women played the primary roles: Erickson Diaries, 4 Aug.–6 Sept. 1924. Other births: 24–28 Aug. 1903, 31 Aug.–10 Nov. 1934, 25 Mar. 1935, 2 Nov. 1937, 2 Sept.–2 Oct. 1938.

36. It may have been common for men to perform nursing duties for other men. There may have been cultural taboos against women being exposed to the bodies of men who were not relatives. I did not find any discussion of this in my sources.

37. Erickson Diaries, 18–31 Dec. 1917, 1 Jan.–18 Mar., 13 July 1918. Erickson also received aid during her separation and divorce; see the months of July and August 1925, July through December 1926, February 1927, and September and October 1929. See also Nellie Kedzie Jones's advice to farm women on being good

neighbors during illness and death: "When Death Comes to the Farm Home," *Country Gentleman*, 15 Nov. 1913, and "True Neighborliness When Sickness Comes," *Country Gentleman*, 11 Oct. 1913, Nellie Kedzie Jones Papers. Erickson's diary confirms that neighbors assisted those who had a death in the family. She both received and gave assistance. Examples in other diaries: Olson Diaries, 13–22 Mar. 1934; Powers Diaries, 30 Oct.–11 Nov. 1933; Siebert Papers, 12–20 Nov. 1935; Gabelmann Diaries, 26 Feb.–10 Mar. 1927; Still Papers, 26 Apr.–7 May 1912, 21 Jan.–2 Mar. 1914. Some families relied more on relatives than on neighbors. Generally these were families with adult children who still lived in the neighborhood. This was somewhat true for Erickson, who relied more on her daughters for daily work when death and illness occurred, but depended on neighbors for visiting and emotional support (and occasional work).

38. Erickson Diaries, 7 Aug. 1921, 3 Mar. 1927, 24 Nov. 1930, 12 Sept. 1931, 11 June, 22–24 Oct. 1933, 25 Nov. 1937, 22 May, 20 Aug. 1938.

39. Erickson's gift exchanges occurred in most years at Christmastime (Dec. 23–31) and around birthdays in mid-April. After her mother and sister died (in 1923) gift exchange declined, but it increased as her daughters left home after 1926.

40. Goodwin, tr. 4–5, ICFOHP. Other examples of chivarees are given in the ICFOHP; see Bilsland, tr. 7–8, and Henderson, tr. 28–29. A chivaree is also mentioned in Still Papers, 16 June 1913.

41. Erickson Diaries, 14–15 Mar. 1922, 14 June 1938, 18 June 1939.

42. Institutions and informal community life sometimes meshed. In Orange Township, Iowa, by 1916, there was one consolidated school and one church, and social interactions focused primarily on these two institutions. In other areas, one or the other institution might dominate. In Lone Tree Township, Iowa, there was no church in the open country, and village churches were poorly attended. But when school consolidation was proposed, country neighborhoods voted to consolidate grades seven through twelve, but to keep their one-room neighborhood schools for grades one through six. See Von Tungeln, "Orange Township," 411–16, 423–26, and "Lone Tree Township," 231–33, 263–69.

43. Although women were often excluded from official leadership roles in churches and schools, they still created their own auxiliary groups and used such informal activities as fund-raising and social gatherings to expand their power in the institutions. Church and school activities also provided opportunities for farm youths to form age-group networks. For example, much of Anna's courtship with Conrad took place at church-related activities, and church groups such as Christian Endeavor and the Epworth League served as places where her children could meet friends.

44. Anna's church attendance reflects the diversity of her neighborhood and how friendship ties sometimes countered religious divisions. Anna had been raised in the German Methodist Episcopal church, but joined the Presbyterian church when she married. Although her second husband was Catholic, she and the children remained in the Presbyterian church. Many of Erickson's closest friends belonged to different churches. Sometimes socializing carried over into church attendance, and the Ericksons would attend other churches with friends or simply

for convenience, going to a night service when they had missed a morning one, or sometimes going on a weeknight or even twice on Sunday. They attended the Lutheran church's English service, the German Methodist Episcopal church, the Catholic church, and what Anna called the "Evangelist Church." They occasionally attended special camp meetings or revivals. There were also periods when Erickson rarely attended any church (when her children were very young and after Conrad's death), but still maintained an active social life within her informal neighborhood. While the Ericksons' school more closely mirrored the informal rural neighborhood than the churches did, it was still primarily a socializing place for children, not for the entire neighborhood. However, Erickson's involvement with the school suggests how women's child-rearing responsibilities grew into community support for rural institutions. Erickson made regular yearly visits to the school and frequently invited teachers to dinner or to other neighborhood events. She followed the education of her children closely, noting in her diary when they took eighth-grade exams and when they graduated.

45. The church picnic was usually held in June, though sometimes in July, and the Christmas program was held on Christmas Eve. Erickson attended these events consistently throughout the years covered by her diary. The school picnic usually took place in May (though sometimes in late April or early June), and the Christmas program took place in late December. The picnic and Christmas program were also occasions to visit her own daughters when they were teaching in nearby schools. Besides school- and church-sponsored annual events, there were other annual community celebrations that the Ericksons attended somewhat regularly. The one they most often attended was the Athens fair, which took place in late August or September. Erickson frequently entered produce in competition. Other such events included the Harvest Home picnic in Illinois (Aug. or Sept. 1901–2); the Community Club picnic (Aug. in the 1920s and 1930s) and July 4th celebrations (1914, 1916, 1918, 1924, 1931, 1934). These types of events had more importance in some communities than in others. Old Settlers' picnics were particularly popular in ethnic communities; see Olson Diaries, 11 July 1935, 9 July 1936, and Siebert Papers, 19 July 1936, 18 July 1937. Orange Township, Iowa, had a harvest picnic, a picnic on the last day of school, and 4th of July celebrations. Most of the diaries also record some 4th of July celebrations (Frank Krueger Papers, Gabelmann Diaries, Powers Diaries, Burke Papers, Siebert Papers, Still Papers, and Olson Diaries). See also Doty and Smith, NDOHP, and Hardiman, tape 4, side 1, WAOHP. School or church Christmas programs are also described in Fosberg, NDOHP; Baumann, tape 1, side 2, WAOHP; Tomter, tape 2, side 1, WAOHP; Still Papers, Dec. 1912; Siebert Papers, 19, 23 Dec. 1937; and Olson Diaries, 24 Dec. 1931. A good description of a school program is given in Alida Goodman, 18 Dec. 1980, tr. 3–4, Country School Legacy Oral History Project (hereafter cited as CSLOHP), Orin G. Libby Manuscript Collection, Chester Fritz Library, Collection 740, Interview 9, University of North Dakota.

46. Similar events occurred in 1928 when Erickson's daughter Orma and her husband Reuel visited from Wyoming (July 24–Aug. 8). The whole family went berry picking at the Kulases' farm, made jam to send to Auntie Fulmer, visited the

neighbors, helped with the family work (fixing dinner, doing the wash), and went to Wausau for a family portrait ("first time we all were together in six years"). Once again, work traditions, neighborhood visiting, and gifts were used to integrate Anna's grandchildren into the family traditions that Anna and her daughters had experienced as children. These family traditions connected the children to the lives of the previous generations.

47. Examples of visits include Earl, 14–21 Jan. 1906, 19–28 May 1923; Charley, 14 May 1904, 12–15 July, 6 Oct. 1906, 29–31 July 1922; to Illinois, 13 June–17 July 1912, 26 Nov.–2 Dec. 1917, 24 Feb.–3 Mar. 1923, 11–12 Aug. 1928; Orma, 24 July–8 Aug. 1928; June, 21–23 Aug. 1925, 12–17 Aug. 1927, 5–7 July 1933, 28 Dec. 1933–1 Jan. 1934; and Mother Erickson, 6–13 May 1904, 8–18 Oct. 1910, 24 May–3 June 1915, 11–14 Aug. 1921, 5–7 Aug. 1928.

CHAPTER 3 Communities Divided

1. Von Tungeln, "Orange Township," 448–50.

2. Class distinctions have generally been defined by the urban, industrial experience, with loss of land rights seen as the initial stage of urban proletarianization. Thus, class status in the countryside is usually defined in terms of farm ownership versus tenancy or wage labor. However, just as historians have recognized the emergence of a new urban middle class under industrial capitalism, they must reconsider class in rural America; they need to move beyond dichotomies of who controls the means of production (land ownership vs. tenancy or wage labor) and combine this with other measurements, such as standards of living (income levels), capitalization, and degrees of participation in the market. The impact of changes in capitalist economic organization on work and class status in rural America is only beginning to be understood; most of the current studies focus on the early development of a market economy in the eighteenth and early nineteenth centuries or on the era of modern agribusiness after 1945.

3. The states in which the value of land and buildings of owners exceeded that of tenants were Missouri, North Dakota, and Nebraska. Data from United States Bureau of the Census, *United States Census of Agriculture, 1925* — Summary, Part I: The Northern States, 6–9, 20–22.

4. Examples of economic studies include John F. Timmons, "Landlord-Tenant Relationships in Renting Missouri Farms," *Missouri Agricultural Experiment Station Bulletin* no. 409 (Aug. 1939); L. F. Garey, George H. Lambrecht, and Frank Miller, "Farm Tenancy in Clay County, Nebraska," *Nebraska Agricultural Experiment Station Bulletin* no. 337 (Jan. 1942); and H. P. Hanson, "Farm Tenancy in South Dakota," *South Dakota Agricultural Experiment Station Circular* no. 25 (Apr. 1939). Standard-of-living studies include Rankin, "Nebraska Farm Tenancy"; J. F. Thaden, "Standard of Living on Iowa Farms," *Iowa Agricultural Experiment Station Bulletin* no. 238 (rev. Nov. 1928); J. O. Rankin and Eleanor Herman, "A Summary of Living in Nebraska Farm Homes," *Nebraska Agricultural Experiment Station Bulletin* no. 267 (Jan. 1932); Margaret Reid, "Some Factors Affecting Improvement in Iowa Farm Family Housing," *Iowa Agricultural*

Experiment Station Bulletin no. 349 (June 1936); and Rainer Schickele, "Farm Tenure in Iowa: Facts on the Farm Tenure Situation," *Iowa Agricultural Experiment Station Bulletin* no. 356 (Feb. 1937).

5. Tenants left twice as frequently as owners did, and managers three or four times as frequently. Most neighborhoods, however, still had a solid core of farm families. A third of Nebraska farms remained with the same farmer in the same tenure status, and 60% of those who left (both owners and tenants) stayed within the same general community. Rankin, "Nebraska Farm Tenancy," 3, 14–22, 25–30.

6. Slocum, "Influence of Tenure Status," 5–6, 12–14.

7. Jones, "New Home on the Old Farm," 57–64, and "Going into Partnership with the Woman in the Tenant House," *Country Gentleman*, 12 Sept. 1914, in the Nellie Kedzie Jones Papers; Howard Murray Jones to his sister, Ada, 13 Oct. 1911, 13 Aug. 1912, Sept. 1914, 3 Dec. 1916, Howard Murray Jones Papers, 1890–1940, Wis MSS RN, State Historical Society of Wisconsin. Their favorite hired man was Reuben, a neighbor's son who shared the Joneses' values. Eventually he went to the University of Wisconsin and studied scientific agriculture.

8. Hardiman, tape 5, side 1, WAOHP.

9. Powers Diaries, 15 Aug. 1927, 5 Nov. 1927, 9 Apr. 1937.

10. George W. Hill and Ronald A. Smith, "Man in the 'Cut-over': A Study of Family-Farm Resources in Northern Wisconsin," *Wisconsin Agricultural Experiment Station Research Bulletin* no. 139 (Apr. 1941): 44, 31–58, 60–61. The relief/non-relief distinction dominated all community divisions. There are few studies of economically marginal farm people in the Midwest before the 1930s, when their increasing numbers made them harder for policymakers and academics to ignore.

11. Andrew Vekkund, TR14–0981 B, NDOHP. Some of the time periods given may not be exact; the interviewee was eighty-nine. In the interview in 1976, Vekkund said "now, I'm settin' perty," with 154 acres worth nine hundred dollars an acre.

12. From the agricultural data for this period, it is difficult to determine how many farm-owning families hired wage laborers. During the years between 1923 and 1933, the farm-owning families whose income data was used for the agricultural census spent, on average, about 12% of their receipts on hired labor in the East North Central and West North Central regions. Given the existing wage rates for hired labor in the two regions, this would have paid for one worker for about seven to eight months, if the cash spent did not account for in-kind boarding, or about five to six months if it did. Data drawn from two tables, "Distribution of Gross Income from Agricultural Production" and "Farm Wage Rates: Averages and Index Numbers," in the *Yearbook of Agriculture* for the years 1923–33.

13. He felt his wages were adequate and that one could save money if one behaved oneself, did not buy everything one wanted, and did not get drunk. John Seltvedt, TR9–0978 A&B, NDOHP; Von Tungeln, Kirkpatrick, Hoffer, and Thaden, "Cedar County," 111, 103–11. See also Olson, NDOHP.

14. Segerstrom, tape 2, side 1, WAOHP.

15. Erickson Diaries, 19 Aug. 1918, 22 Apr., 30 May, 16 Nov. 1919, 31 Mar. 1921, 17 July 1922, 16 Feb. 1930, and obituaries 1952. After moving from Athens,

Gore lived in Minnesota until 1932, when he moved to Missouri. The Gore farm was taken over by Bill Bernea. There was little conflict recorded between neighbors in the Erickson Diaries. Most of the conflicts occurred with the family of Erickson's second husband. For example, Erickson complained about her neighboring brother-in-law, who waited until 21 May to work on a fence "to pay for the hay he *cut* on my land *last July*." This was the only such complaint I found in the diary. Erickson Diaries, 21 May 1923.

16. Tomter, tape 1, side 1, WAOHP.

17. Charles Lively to C. J. Galpin, 30 Nov. 1920, DFP&RL, Study Projects, 1919–22, Minnesota File, box 8; K. H. McGill, Lawrence Vaplon, N. E. Woodard, Robert Crichton, and Katherine Wilson, "A Survey of Rural Problem Areas: Hodgeman County, Kansas," 1 Aug. 1934, 7–8, 99–100, DFP&RL, Federal Emergency Relief Administration (hereafter cited as FERA) Rural Problem Reports (hereafter cited as RPR), box 5; Fosberg, NDOHP; and Tomter, tape 1, side 2, WAOHP. See also Jacobs, NDOHP; Johansen, "Immigrant Settlements and Social Organizations," 1–63; and E. A. Willson, "Social Organizations and Agencies in North Dakota," *North Dakota Agricultural Experiment Station Bulletin* no. 221 (Aug. 1928): 13–15.

18. Neal Weber, "Russian-German Settlements in McHenry County, North Dakota," 1927, Orin G. Libby Manuscript Collection, Chester Fritz Library, MS497, University of North Dakota; Long, NDOHP.

19. Kolb, "Rural Primary Groups," 34; Gabelmann Diaries, 9, 16 June, 7 July 1918. The services continued to alternate between German and English at least through the 1920s; see 27 Jan. 1927; Henderson, tr. 8–10, ICFOHP; and Jacobs, side A, NDOHP. See also Howard Murray Jones Papers, 24 Oct. 1917, 30 June 1918.

20. Goodman, tr. 1–2, 8–9, CSLOHP. See also Winifred Guthrie Erdman, tr. 8–11, Interview 30, CSLOHP. Many of the second-generation immigrants retained fond memories of teachers who first introduced them to English. Erich Lenz, a fourteen-year-old German-Russian immigrant to South Dakota in 1921, had a Norwegian schoolteacher. At the time of the interview in 1979, the two were still in touch; they had visited and exchanged gifts even though Lenz lived in Wisconsin and the teacher in Oregon. Erich Lenz Oral History, tape 3, side 1, tape 774A, State Historical Society of Wisconsin.

21. Carl C. Taylor and E. W. Lehmann, "Ashland Community Survey: An Economic, Social, and Sanitary Survey in Howard County, Missouri," *Missouri Agricultural Experiment Station Bulletin* no. 173 (July 1920): 3–4, 7–8, and Carl C. Taylor to C. J. Galpin, 28 Feb., 30 Apr., 12 May, 28 Oct., 16 Dec. 1920, DFP&RL, Study Projects, 1919–22, Missouri File, box 9. Taylor had difficulty getting the results of his Missouri studies published. Both the USDA and the Missouri Agricultural Experiment Station refused to publish them because of pressure from the local community. C. C. Zimmerman included some of the results in his book *The Changing Community*, and Fred Yoder did so in his dissertation at the University of Wisconsin. Taylor finally published the results fifteen years later in a mimeograph, *Rich Land, Poor Man*. See Nelson, *Rural Sociology*, 177–84.

22. Taylor to Galpin, 28 Feb. 1920, DFP&RL; Morgan and Howells, "Rural Primary Groups of Boone County." For a briefer description of a similar black farm neighborhood in Kansas, see McGill et al., "Hodgeman County," 6–8, 100–101.

23. The organization of Native American communities was very different from the European-American patterns of family farm agriculture that are the basis of this study. For an interesting examination of how government policies attempted to impose European-American family farm agricultural practices and gender roles on Native Americans, see Delores Janiewski, "Making Women into Farmers' Wives: The Native American Experience in the Inland Northwest," in Haney and Knowles, *Women and Farming,* 35–54.

24. Nelson, NDOHP; Jacobs, NDOHP.

25. Henderson, tr. 1, 5–8, 18–21, ICFOHP; Larson, NDOHP; Jacobs, NDOHP. See also Doty and Smith, NDOHP.

26. Joe Cvancara, MN10–0655 B, NDOHP; Charlie Juma, MN24–0669 A&B, NDOHP. A Jewish settlement in Arpin, Wisconsin, encountered similar problems. Eighteen Jewish families settled Arpin in 1904 or 1905. Max Leopold cooperated with neighboring non-Jewish farmers and was active in local politics and the cooperative feed warehouse. The settlement prospered until after World War I, when agricultural prices declined. However, Leopold believed the primary reason for the decline was the fear that children would marry outside the Jewish faith. Max Leopold Oral History, tape 1, sides 1 and 2, tape 567A, State Historical Society of Wisconsin. See also Jack D. Levin Oral History, tape 1, sides 1 and 2, for the problems of a single Jewish family moving to a farm. The Levins returned to the city primarily because there was no community for a Jewish school or synagogue and no "Jewish relationships." In addition, the Charles Shepard Papers, 1848–1959, Microfilm 78, State Historical Society of Wisconsin, briefly describe similar problems encountered by a black settlement in Grant County, Wisconsin. The community, founded in 1848, at its largest had a hundred settlers, but by 1958 had only one black resident. The crisis period came after World War I, when the black church closed and youths moved to cities to find appropriate marriage partners.

27. Baumann, tape 1, side 1, tape 2, side 2, tape 3, side 1, WAOHP. The only part of her conversion that "rankled" Baumann was having to be rebaptized. A change in the ceremony's words to "in case you have not been baptized you are now baptized" satisfied her. It is unclear whether such conversions were unusual in her experience. At one point in the interview, she said they were uncommon, but later she stated that there were lots of mixed marriages and conversions at the time.

28. Thompson, *American Daughter,* 27, 33–35, 44–46, 55, 59, 75, 93, 98. Thompson's father was also active in local politics and the NPL.

29. Ibid., 21–22, 75–77.

30. Ibid., 10–11, 17–18, 59–67, 83–84, 116–18, 105–6, 107–10. Dissatisfaction on the new farm also arose because of the death of Thompson's mother, which created a "cold soberness that drew them [the boys] farther and farther away from Father, and I lived between two camps; the one guarded by self-pity and silence,

the other by bitter restlessness" (108). The mother's death also reveals how well the Thompsons were integrated into the neighborhood. They received aid and assistance from kin, the distant black community, and the local neighbors (89–92).
    31. Ibid., 72–73.

CHAPTER 4 Defining the Rural Problem

    1. Support for the USDA's development largely came from business-oriented farmers and agricultural industries. Although the scientists and professionals based in the land-grant college system supported the expansion of the USDA, they were more likely to see the USDA as a threat to their autonomy, and they attempted to limit its authority.
    2. The Grange was most directly involved with education and the land-grant colleges. In general, the Farmers' Alliance emphasized a different sort of education than that offered in the land-grant colleges. It stressed economic and cooperative principles. In the twentieth century, the Farmers' Union followed a similar pattern of alternative political and economic education for its members.
    3. The county agent system of agricultural extension was first developed in the South and was funded by the General Education Board created by John D. Rockefeller. In the Midwest, the USDA promoted efforts to extend the county agent system, but most often early financing came from business interests. The Midwest was the second most active region before 1914, with 151 agents in twelve states. In general, however, the land-grant colleges in the Midwest preferred to work through institutes and short courses. They became more actively involved in county agent work to counter the growing influence of the USDA. The creation of the Federal Extension Service did cause conflict over control and jurisdiction between the USDA and the land-grant colleges.
    4. The 1912 correspondence of Wisconsin county agent Ernest Luther illustrates these issues. Some of his early demonstrations were coordinated with an agent from International Harvester, who offered him a job when he "got done here." Luther described his talks and demonstrations as well attended, and he clearly worked with a diverse group of farm people. He performed milk tests for farmers to challenge those of a local cream factory, even though his supervisor advised him to stay out of the controversy. He also got into political trouble by spending too much time at one farm and attempting to make it a "demonstration plot." Later he received praise (and supplies) from a fertilizer company. Ernest L. Luther Papers, Wis MSS WH, State Historical Society of Wisconsin.
    5. The Country Life Commission was composed primarily of academics from the land-grant colleges and journalists from the farm press, with one representative from the Farmers' Union, who was added when southern agricultural journalists demanded another representative from the South. The country life movement was in some ways a strategy on the part of the land-grant colleges to assure their control of extension programs and funds. This would counter any growth of the USDA in this field and also keep control from state departments of agriculture.

State departments of agriculture often were responsive to pressure groups, including farmers' organizations.

6. Garrard Harris, *The Treasure of the Land: How Alice Won Her Way* (New York: Harper and Brothers, 1917), 64–67. See also *Third Wisconsin Country Life Conference* (Madison: University of Wisconsin College of Agriculture, 1913), 33–37.

7. "Credo of the Agricultural Labor Branch," 1–2, Interchurch World Movement Staff Seminar, 5 Jan. 1920, DFP&RL, General Correspondence, 1919–36, box 13. See also H. Paul Douglass, "Migratory Labor in the Wheat Harvest," 15–16, 40–44, 59, and supp. 4–5, Interchurch World Movement Rural Surveys, 1919, DFP&RL, General Correspondence, 1919–36, box 13. The report also encouraged the use of increased mechanization and diversification to lessen the need for seasonal workers. Other sources that show fears of a "class consciousness" among farmers and a desire to create a middle-class farm group to counter it are C. J. Galpin, "A Proposed Alliance of City and Farm," *Kiwanis Magazine*, 22 Jan. 1926; DFP&RL, General Correspondence, 1919–36, box 4; and confidential memo from the Secretary of Agriculture to Mr. Thompson, n.d., DFP&RL, General Correspondence, 1919–36, Office of the Secretary of Agriculture, Memoranda File, box 12, July 1928–June 1934. The concern about a farm "class consciousness" also appeared in a field report to Galpin from western Minnesota in 1920. The farmers of that region were "conscious of their economic position but not class conscious to the point of action." Lively to Galpin, 10 Dec. 1920, DFP&RL, Study Projects, 1919–22, Minnesota File, box 8.

8. A 1916 study of the 6,600 teachers in rural Wisconsin found that only 24% had normal-school training, compared to 52% of teachers in state-graded schools. Eugene Merritt and K. L. Hatch, "Some Economic Factors which Influence Rural Education in Wisconsin," *Wisconsin Agricultural Experiment Station Research Bulletin* no. 40 (Oct. 1916): 25–26. Samples of the discussion of the need to improve rural ministers can be found in *Second Wisconsin Country Life Conference* (Madison: University of Wisconsin College of Agriculture, 1912), 25–38.

9. Marie Mynster Fiedler, *In Retrospect: Teaching in North Dakota* (n.p.: North Dakota Teachers Association, 1976), 21. See also Leila C. Ewan, tr. 30–33, 30, North Dakota Country School Legacy Oral History Project (hereafter cited as NDCSLOHP), Orin G. Libby Manuscript Collection, Chester Fritz Library, Collection 740, Interview 30, University of North Dakota.

10. *First Wisconsin Country Life Conference* (Madison: University of Wisconsin College of Agriculture, 1911), 11.

11. Ernest L. Luther to K. L. Hatch, 28 Feb., 4 Mar. 1912, Luther Papers. See also Emily Hoag to C. J. Galpin, 7 May 1921, DFP&RL, General Correspondence, 1919–36, box 12.

12. Gregory M. Hooks and William L. Flinn, "Toward a Sociology of Rural Sociology," *Rural Sociologist* 1 (May 1981): 130.

13. Nelson, *Rural Sociology*, 23–33, 123–25. Rural social scientists, in general, came from upper-middle-class rural homes and saw themselves as an elite guiding the progress of rural America; see Harry C. McDean, "Professionalism in the

Rural Social Sciences, 1896–1919," *Agricultural History* 58 (July 1984): 365–72.

14. Nelson, *Rural Sociology*, 34–47; Charles Josiah Galpin, *My Drift into Rural Sociology* (Baton Rouge: Louisiana State University Press, 1938), 1–37.

15. Nelson, *Rural Sociology*, 22–23, 123–30; Galpin, *My Drift into Rural Sociology*, 21–29; Wileden, tape 1, side 1, tape 2, side 2, tape 7, side 1, WAOHP.

16. Nelson, *Rural Sociology*, 34–46, 123–30; Galpin, *My Drift into Rural Sociology*, 34–40, 46.

17. Galpin, *My Drift into Rural Sociology*, 51–52, 35–45; Nelson, *Rural Sociology*, 177–82.

18. Galpin, *My Drift into Rural Sociology*, 30–32, 59–62; E. L. Kirkpatrick, "Rural Young People 15–25 Years of Age," Third Purnell Conference, 1933, DFP&RL, General Correspondence, 1919–36, box 17. The narrowing of rural sociology can also be seen in the career of John M. Gilette. Gilette's research supported the NPL from 1916 to 1921, but ended with the backlash of the 1920s, to be replaced by "objectivity." Privately he continued to support reform. See Kenneth J. Dawes, "John M. Gilette: A Case Study in Rural Social Reform" (Paper presented at the Second International Institute on Social Work in Rural Areas, 1984), in the John M. Gilette Papers, Orin G. Libby Manuscript Collection, Chester Fritz Library, Collection 48, University of North Dakota. See also Nelson, *Rural Sociology*, 107–61, and Wileden, tape 1, side 2, tape 2, side 2, tape 6, side 2, tape 7, side 1, tape 8, side 1, tape 9, side 1, part 2, tape 10, side 1, part 2, WAOHP.

19. Letters that illustrate these conflicts can be found in DFP&RL, General Correspondence, 1913–19. These include Mayme Sloan to Ernestine Noa, 8 Feb. 1914; T. N. Carver to Ernestine Noa, 10 Feb. 1914; Noa to C. W. Thompson, 6 Sept. 1914; and Thompson to Noa, 16 Sept. 1914. Letters in DFP&RL, General Correspondence, 1919–36, include C. J. Galpin to Emily Hoag, 14 July 1921, and Hoag to Galpin, 24 June 1921. See also Anne M. Evans File, 12 July 1916, DFP&RL, Field Reports; J. O. Rankin to C. J. Galpin, 6 Oct. 1921, and Galpin to Rankin, 11 Oct. 1921, DFP&RL, Study Projects, 1919–22, Nebraska File; and Galpin to George Von Tungeln, 9 Mar. 1922, DFP&RL, Study Projects, 1919–22, Cedar County, Iowa. Nellie Kedzie Jones said of her first job as a home economist at Kansas State University, "They were not looking for doctorates in those days [the 1880s]; they wanted biscuits." From the *K-Stater*, Oct. 1954, in the Nellie Kedzie Jones Papers.

20. C. J. Galpin to Anna Clark, 28 Jan. 1922, DFP&RL, General Correspondence, 1919–34, box 1; Memorandum from C. J. Galpin to Dr. Taylor, 8 Mar. 1921, DFP&RL, General Correspondence, 1919–37, box 8.

21. Anna Clark to C. J. Galpin, 28 Jan., 24 Feb. 1922, DFP&RL, General Correspondence, 1919–34, box 1.

22. Material used by the Subcommittee on Research, 39th Annual Convention, 1925, DFP&RL, General Correspondence, box 15; Galpin, *My Drift into Rural Sociology*, 42–45, 53–55. For an interesting discussion of the assumptions and ideology in these studies, see Henry C. McDean, "'Reform' Social Darwinists and Measuring Levels of Living on American Farms, 1920–1926," *Journal of Economic History* 43 (Mar. 1983): 79–85.

23. C. J. Galpin, "Recent Losses in Farm Population," 29 Nov. 1927, 6–7, DFP&RL, General Correspondence, 1919–36, box 5 (published in *Wallace's Farmer*, 5 Mar. 1928); "The Standard of Living of the Farm Population in the United States for the Period 1919–1927," 1–10, DFP&RL, General Correspondence, 1919–36, Articles, 1928–30, box 5. See also "Farm Population Reaches New Low Point," 14 Mar. 1929, 3, DFP&RL, General Correspondence, 1919–36, Articles, box 4, and "National Policy on the Conservation of the Farm Population and the Farm Home," from House of Representatives Document 195, "Report of the National Agricultural Conference, January 23–27, 1922," 67th Cong., 2d Sess., in DFP&RL, General Correspondence, 1919–36, box 4. This attitude was also apparent in the prosperous period; see *First Wisconsin Country Life Conference*, 33–35.

24. This process of defining a chronic problem as an "emergency" also plagued the development of food relief policies and the use of agricultural surpluses. See Janet Poppendieck, *Breadlines Knee-Deep in Wheat: Food Assistance in the Great Depression* (New Brunswick, N.J.: Rutgers University Press, 1986).

25. Rural Relief Studies, DFP&RL: Waubaunsee County, Kans., 18–20; Johnson County, Mo., 16; Hickory County, Mo., 22; Richardson County, Nebr., 12.

26. Agricultural economics was a male-dominated field, with women relegated to lower levels as statisticians or home economists. Nevertheless, agricultural economics was always more open to "feminized" fields than were the sciences. Although no historical studies exist of women in the BAE, some home economics projects were clearly tied to reform efforts in the 1930s. For example, studies of dietary needs done by the Bureau of Home Economics were used to support BAE policies intended to develop higher incomes for urban and rural workers.

27. RPR: Oneida County, Wisc., 67–68, 118–19, 124–25, and Aitkin County, Minn., 48. For examples of hostility to organized farmers' relief groups, see RPR: Beltrami, Minn., 8–9, 16–17, and Burke County, N.D., iii, 37–39, 80.

28. Wileden, tape 9, side 1, part 2, tape 10, side 1, part 2, WAOHP.

29. FSA Photographs; Office of the Secretary of Agriculture, Historical File (hereafter cited as Historical File), 1900–1959, Record Group 16–G, NASPB. Like the FSA, the BAE was more likely than other agricultural agencies to study a rural community as a whole rather than focusing on prosperous farm families. The BAE photographs, however, rarely focused on the pathos of rural poverty to the extent that the FSA photographs did.

CHAPTER 5 Reorganizing the Rural Community

1. C. J. Galpin and D. W. Sawtelle, "Rural Clubs in Wisconsin," *Wisconsin Agricultural Experiment Station Bulletin* no. 271 (Aug. 1916): 3–6; C. J. Galpin, "Rural Social Centers in Wisconsin," *Wisconsin Agricultural Experiment Station Bulletin* no. 234 (Jan. 1914): 3–8; C. J. Galpin, "The Social Anatomy of an Agricultural Community," *Wisconsin Agricultural Experiment Station Research Bulletin* no. 34 (May 1915): 19–26, 32–34. See also J. H. Kolb and Arthur Wileden, "Special Interest Groups in Rural Society," *Wisconsin Agricultural Experiment Station Research Bulletin* no. 84 (Dec. 1927): 4–7.

2. C. J. Galpin and J. A. James, "Rural Relations of High Schools," *Wisconsin Agricultural Experiment Station Bulletin* no. 288 (Mar. 1918): 16–20. See also C. R. Hoffer to C. J. Galpin, 8 Feb. 1922, DFP&RL, Study Projects, 1919–22, Minnesota File, box 8.

3. Ernest L. Luther to K. L. Hatch, 24 Feb. 1912, Luther Papers; Kolb, "Rural Primary Groups," 47–50, 76–77; J. H. Kolb, "Service Relations of Town and Country," *Wisconsin Agricultural Experiment Station Research Bulletin* no. 58 (Dec. 1923): 8–12, 35–36, 38–58, 70–78; Kolb, "Trends of Country Neighborhoods," 23; J. H. Kolb and R. A. Polson, "Trends in Town-Country Relations," *Wisconsin Agricultural Experiment Station Research Bulletin* no. 117 (Sept. 1933): 12–13, 15–21, 24–29; Morgan and Howells, "Rural Primary Groups of Boone County," 40–44, 59; "Study of Webster City, Iowa, as a Trade Center," 1–57, DFP&RL, Study Projects, 1919–22, Iowa File, box 7. Diaries also show the use of various trade centers. The best for listing kinds of purchases are the Gabelmann Diaries and the Still Papers. Most of the interviews in the WAOHP also describe marketing and trade center practices. Other trade center studies include H. Bruce Price and C. R. Hoffer, "Services of Rural Trade Centers in Distribution of Farm Supplies," *Minnesota Agricultural Experiment Station Bulletin* no. 249 (Oct. 1928); C. C. Zimmerman, "Farm Trade Centers in Minnesota," *Minnesota Agricultural Experiment Station Bulletin* no. 269 (Sept. 1930); C. E. Lively, "Growth and Decline of Farm Trade Centers in Minnesota, 1905–1930," *Minnesota Agricultural Experiment Station Bulletin* no. 287 (July 1932); Paul H. Landis, "South Dakota Town-Country Relations, 1901–1931," *South Dakota Agricultural Experiment Station Bulletin* no. 274 (Sept. 1932); and Paul H. Landis, "The Growth and Decline of South Dakota Trade Centers, 1901–1933," *South Dakota Agricultural Experiment Station Bulletin* no. 279 (Sept. 1933). The South Dakota and Minnesota studies are particularly good at linking the failure of small trade centers to local farm conditions, such as periods of drought in South Dakota between 1911 and 1916, the price crisis of the early 1920s, and the decline in the number of rural post offices; however, none of the studies tries to correlate the decline in trade centers to the value of land or consolidation of land ownership. Some problems exist in comparing these studies because of the different definitions of hamlet, village, and town. A chart of what items were bought in which type of trade center or store appears in "Meeting Agriculture's Old and New Problems," 22–23.

4. Zimmerman, "Farm Trade Centers in Minnesota," 34–37; Price and Hoffer, "Services of Rural Trade Centers," 37–45.

5. Donald G. Hay, "Social Organizations and Agencies in North Dakota: A Study of Trends, 1926–1936," *North Dakota Agricultural Experiment Station Bulletin* no. 288 (July 1937): 5–6, 13–20. On elementary schools, see Wayne E. Fuller, *The Old Country School: The Story of Rural Education in the Middle West* (Chicago: University of Chicago Press, 1982). Fuller emphasizes the nineteenth century and the Progressive Era, with only one chapter dealing with developments in the 1920s, but many consolidation battles continued into the 1940s and 1950s. For example, see Ellefson, tape 5, sides 1 and 2, WAOHP.

6. Galpin and James, "Rural Relations of High Schools," 24; Galpin, "Social Anatomy of an Agricultural Community," 23.

7. Von Tungeln, Kirkpatrick, Hoffer, and Thelen, "Cedar County," 54–57; J. H. Kolb, "Service Institutions for Town and Country," *Wisconsin Agricultural Experiment Station Research Bulletin* no. 66 (Dec. 1925): 6–7; Kolb, "Trends of Country Neighborhoods," 36–37, 55–56; Willson, "Social Organizations and Agencies," 23; Hay, "Social Organizations and Agencies," 15–17, 21; Galpin and James, "Rural Relations of High Schools," 11–12, 22–23; Kolb and Polson, "Trends in Town-Country Relations," 24–25; Kolb and Marshall, "Neighborhood-Community Relationships," 26–27; Landis, "Growth and Decline," 34; Morgan and Howells, "Rural Primary Groups of Boone County," 69–70.

8. "Study of Webster City," 58; Kolb, "Service Institutions for Town and Country," 6–7, 12–13; Galpin, "Social Anatomy of an Agricultural Community," 14–16, 23; Kolb, "Rural Primary Groups," 53; Kolb and Polson, "Trends in Town-Country Relations," 10–11; Willson, "Social Organizations and Agencies," 23; J. H. Kolb and J. A. James, "Wisconsin's Rural Youth: Education and Occupation," *Wisconsin Agricultural Experiment Station Bulletin* no. 437 (Nov. 1936): 3–4, 6–7. Wisconsin had the highest percentage of farm boys aged 14–20 out of school, but other states in the Midwest had more than 50% as well: Minnesota 59.6%, Iowa 54.3%, and Illinois 54.2%. Net farm incomes in Wisconsin fell from $2,406 in 1918 to $1,023 in 1924, while net city incomes increased from $2,204 to $3,224, and net village incomes increased from $1,896 to $1,937. Average tax payments for farmers went from $134 to $264, for city dwellers from $124 to $270, and for villagers from $72 to $143. See "Gleanings from Science," *Wisconsin Agricultural Experiment Station Annual Report Bulletin* no. 388 (Dec. 1926): 23–24. Oral histories reveal some of the sacrifices farm families made to send children to high school. Wileden, tape 1, side 1, WAOHP; Baumann, tape 1, sides 1 and 2, WAOHP; Tomter, tape 1, side 2, WAOHP. See also Fiedler, *In Retrospect,* 21–27.

9. Willson, "Rural Community Clubs in North Dakota: Factors Influencing Their Success or Failure," *North Dakota Agricultural Experiment Station Bulletin* no. 251 (Aug. 1931): 18–20; C. J. Galpin and Emily F. Hoag, "The Rural Community Fair," *Wisconsin Agricultural Experiment Station Bulletin* no. 307 (Nov. 1919): 3–9, 30–34. The traditional oyster supper, which often was held to celebrate the end of a working season, could be reshaped into a "potato bake" to encourage the potato industry. See DFP&RL, Marketing and Rural Life, 1902–38, Neg. 14621, Record Group 83-ML, box 15, NASPB. See also C. L. McNelly, *The County Agent Story: The Impact of Extension Work on Farming and Country Life in Minnesota* (Berryville, Ark.: Braswell Printing, 1960), 116–18; and J. H. Kolb and A. F. Wileden, "Rural Organization Handbook: Capable Leadership, Constructive Programs, Cooperative Membership, the Three 'Cs' of Success," *Wisconsin Agricultural Experiment Station Bulletin* no. 384 (1926). Farmers' clubs were praised for their inclusion of women by leaders of women's farm groups; see *Farmer's Wife* 15 (June 1912): 37–38.

10. On the early development of farmers' clubs, see McNelly, *County Agent Story,* 21–22, 57–58, 116–18; Galpin and Sawtelle, "Rural Clubs in Wisconsin,"

4–5, 9–10; and *Third Wisconsin Country Life Conference,* 100–107. The farmers' club movement was strongest in Wisconsin and Minnesota. Long-term studies of clubs are Willson, "Rural Community Clubs in North Dakota," 14–31, and D. E. Lindstrom, "Local Group Organization among Illinois Farm People," *Illinois Agricultural Experiment Station Bulletin* no. 392 (June 1933): 133–35, 141–49, 154–60, 165. Total numbers of clubs are hard to determine, but two North Dakota studies found 136 community clubs in the state in 1926, and also noted that farm people most often affiliated with a local rural organization or none at all. See E. A. Willson, H. C. Hoffsommer, and Alva H. Benton, "Rural Changes in Western North Dakota: Social and Economic Factors Involved in the Changes in Number of Farms and Movement of Settlers from Farms," *North Dakota Agricultural Experiment Station Bulletin* no. 214 (Jan. 1928): 86–88, and Hay, "Social Organizations and Agencies," 62–73.

11. Willson's study of North Dakota community clubs found that the objectives of two-thirds of the clubs were social, while only one-third included education and agricultural practices and 18% included promoting community welfare; "Rural Community Clubs in North Dakota," 28. The Illinois study found that social activities dominated the farmers' clubs and community clubs, and these made up more than one-third of all social clubs studied; Lindstrom, "Local Group Organization," 153, 163. See also Kolb and Wileden, "Special Interest Groups in Rural Society," 35–41, 61–71. Information on the Skillet Creek Farmers' Club can be found in William Toole Papers, Wis MSS IE, State Historical Society of Wisconsin; Galpin and Sawtelle, "Rural Clubs in Wisconsin," 9–12; *Third Wisconsin Country Life Conference,* 100–107; and Still Papers, 1, 22 June, 13 July 1912. Although socializing was their primary activity, many club members also undertook community service projects. For example, between 1919 and 1920, near Niagara, North Dakota, farmers built a park, including a kitchen, pavilion, baseball park, ice house, lavatories, cement walks, picnic tables, improved roads, and electric lighting for buildings. See Wayne C. Nason, "Rural Planning: Recreation Places, the Social Aspects," DFP&RL, Manuscripts, box 7 (published as "Rural Buildings for Business and Social Uses," *USDA Farmers' Bulletin* no. 1622 [Apr. 1930]).

12. The need to organize by special interest groups rather than by locality is discussed in Kolb and Wileden, "Special Interest Groups in Rural Society," 4, 7, 95–96; Kolb, "Trends of County Neighborhoods," 51–54; and Willson, "Rural Community Clubs in North Dakota," 8–9, 20. Comparisons of farmers' clubs with the Farm Bureaus and Homemakers' Clubs are found in McNelly, *County Agent Story,* 56–60, and Lindstrom, "Local Group Organization," 131, 141–53, 163. The Farm Bureau connections to extension services were actual policy in most states; see Gladys Baker, *The County Agent* (Chicago: University of Chicago Press, 1939). One exception was Wisconsin, where the extension service's refusal to be formally connected to the Farm Bureau led to conflict between the two organizations and the provision by the extension service of educational services to a greater variety of farm organizations, such as the Farmers' Union. See Wileden, WAOHP, and Long, WAOHP.

13. Saloutos and Hicks, *Agricultural Discontent in the Middle West,* 56–82,

113–26, 147, 219–21; Leonard and Iva Rensick, tr. 3, OH4–11, ICFOHP; Von Tungeln, "Orange Township," 407–8; and "Four Decades of Farmer Cooperation," Gilette Papers, box 6, folder 10.

14. On social aspects of local and larger cooperatives, see Willson, "Rural Community Clubs in North Dakota," 100; Kolb and Wileden, "Special Interest Groups in Rural Society," 13–14, 27–31, 62–63, 65–67; and Morgan and Howells, "Rural Primary Groups of Boone County," 45–46. On increasing affiliation and centralization of cooperatives, see Saloutos and Hicks, *Agricultural Discontent in the Middle West*, 63, 73–82, 130–46, 225–28, 231–46, 309–20; Galpin, "Social Anatomy of an Agricultural Community," 10–11; Kolb and Polson, "Trends in Town-Country Relations," 4, 8; Theodore Macklin, "Cooperation Applied to Marketing by Kansas Farmers," *Kansas Agricultural Experiment Station Bulletin* no. 224 (Oct. 1920): 16, 27, 34; H. Bruce Price, "Farmers' Co-operation in Minnesota, 1917–1922," *Minnesota Agricultural Experiment Station Bulletin* no. 202 (Jan. 1923): 5–13, 17–18; F. L. Thomsen and G. B. Thorne, "Cooperative Marketing for Missouri," *Missouri Agricultural Experiment Station Bulletin* no. 253 (July 1927): 6–15; and L. M. Brown and R. J. Penn, "Cooperatives in South Dakota," *South Dakota Agricultural Experiment Station Bulletin* no. 328 (Apr. 1939): 12–13.

15. Lowell K. Dyson, *Farmers' Organizations* (New York: Greenwood Press, 1986), 14–17.

16. Thomsen and Thorne, "Cooperative Marketing for Missouri," 28–35. USDA photographs promoted cooperation by picturing the business end of marketing as much as the farm end. They showed large rooms of clerical workers or managers working in a New York City office as representatives of centralized efficiency. See DFP&RL, Marketing and Rural Life, 1902–38, Negs. 14848, 14849D, 17115, Record Group 83-ML, boxes 2 and 3, NASPB.

17. Baker, *County Agent*, xiv–xv; McNelly, *County Agent Story*, 55–60; Lindstrom, "Local Group Organization," 141, 149, 153–59, 163–65.

18. Lindstrom, "Forces Affecting Participation of Farm People," 103–5, 115–17; Lindstrom, "Local Group Organization," 156–59; Kolb and Wileden, "Special Interest Groups in Rural Society," 13; Willson, "Social Organizations and Agencies," 58–60; Saloutos and Hicks, *Agricultural Discontent in the Middle West*, 89–96, 255–85; Baumann, tape 5, side 2, tape 6, sides 1 and 2, WAOHP; Baker, *County Agent*, xiv–xv, 99; McNelly, *County Agent Story*, 76–85. Over half of the Farm Bureau members were in six states, most of them in the older regions of the Midwest—Iowa, Illinois, Ohio, Michigan, Indiana, and Texas.

19. *Farmer's Wife* 13 (May 1912): 376; *Farmer's Wife* 23 (Nov. 1920): 183; Anne Evans speech to the General Federation of Women's Clubs, 17 May 1916, DFP&RL, General Correspondence, 1913–19; Anna Clark to C. J. Galpin, 2 Nov. 1920, 25 Jan. 1922, DFP&RL, General Correspondence, 1919–34, box 1; Memo from C. Thompson to C. Brand, "Summary of Work, 1916," DFP&RL, General Correspondence, 1913–19; and Willson, "Social Organizations and Agencies," 61–62. On the early history of women's organizations, see Von Tungeln, "Orange Township," 437–38; Velma Lloyd, tr. 14, OH4–69, ICFOHP; Baumann, tape 4, side

1, WAOHP; and *Extension Program Annual Report, Williams County, 1923*, North Dakota Cooperative Extension Service, North Dakota Institute for Regional Studies, NDSU.

20. Homemakers' Club Histories Project, Alfalfameda Homemakers Club, SC 942, NDSU; Anne M. Evans, "Memo and Report of Western Trip, including Illinois, Kansas, and Iowa," 10–30 June 1916, and "Significant Examples of Women's Rural Organizations," DFP&RL, Field Reports, box 4.

21. Evans, "Memo and Report of Western Trip," and Nason, "Rural Buildings," 17–18.

22. Erickson Diaries, 16 Sept. 1915, 8 Nov. 1922, 2 Dec. 1925, 3 Aug. 1927, 16 Apr. 1930. On poultry marketing: Anne M. Evans, "Value of Women's Organizations in Direct Marketing" (memorandum of trip to Pike County, Ill., 6–26 Aug. 1917), and Anne M. Evans, "State Reports to the Farm Women's National Conference," 23 Oct. 1917, DFP&RL, Field Reports, box 4. On cooperative laundries, see Home Culture Club Records, 1904–79, River Falls MSS CK, River Falls Area Research Center, State Historical Society of Wisconsin; River Falls Cooperative Creamery Company, Minutes and Financial Book, 1912–37, 16 Aug. 1913 and 30 Dec. 1914, River Falls Sc 3, River Falls Area Research Center, State Historical Society of Wisconsin; Galpin and Sawtelle, "Rural Clubs in Wisconsin," 36–41; *Third Wisconsin Country Life Conference*, 94–99; *Fourth Wisconsin Country Life Conference* (Madison: University of Wisconsin College of Agriculture, 1914), 9–14; Rural Planning Surveys, DFP&RL, Clipping File, box 18; and Nason, "Rural Buildings," 17–20. By 1918, the laundry had 1,113 patrons. In 1924, it had three delivery trucks and employed about eight people.

23. Erickson Diaries, which mention "club at Stremers, Miss Feeny was there," 25 Jan. 1927. The *Athens Record*, 3 Feb. 1927, reported that Miss Regina Feeney, the county demonstrator, talked on "clothing budgets," and Nellie Kedzie Jones explained the Farmers' Week held in Madison. Erickson's obituary in the *Athens Record*, 26 Nov. 1959, reported that she was a founding member of the Johnson Homemakers Club and served as its secretary for many years. The Home Demonstration Agent Reports for Marathon County indicate that Erickson's daughter Dot ("Mrs. Loddie Loskot") took a leadership role in the Franklin club (Edgar, Wisc.) as an adult. She was president in 1940–41. Erickson's daughter-in-law, Mrs. Morris Erickson, also participated in the Johnson Homemakers Club and in county and district meetings in the 1950s; see *Athens Record*, 19 Nov. 1959. See Home Demonstration Agent Reports, Marathon County, 1921, University of Wisconsin Home Economics Extension, Steenbock Library Archives, University of Wisconsin. In 1919, an agent reported that a "good social time" was the primary objective of the clubs, and that she wanted clubs to be autonomous and not dependent on her assistance. Nevertheless, reports still emphasize home programs and home improvements (the Federal Extension Service report forms required that this information be reported).

24. On the development, structure, and educational purpose of Homemakers' Clubs, see McNelly, *County Agent Story*, 51–54; Lindstrom, "Local Group Organization," 141, 153, 163–65; Grace E. DeLong, "A Brief History of Home Demon-

stration Work in North Dakota," NDSU; North Dakota Extension Agent Annual Reports, Williams County, 1922–23, North Dakota Cooperative Extension Service, NDSU. Descriptions of the types of programs designed by extension services are found in M. C. Burritt, *The County Agent and the Farm Bureau* (New York: Harcourt, Brace, 1922), 6; McNelly, *County Agent Story*, 88; Hay, "Social Organizations and Agencies," 23–25; "State Wide Activities of the College of Agriculture," *Nebraska Agricultural Experiment Station Circular* no. 19 (Jan. 1923). The county extension reports of NDSU provide lists of proposed programs and those that were actually chosen by local clubs. See North Dakota Extension Agent Annual Reports, Williams County, 1923–24, 1924–25, 1926. The section quoted is on p. 31 of the 1926–27 report. The local nature of women's clubs, the small numbers of members per club, and the consequent high participation rates are discussed in Lindstrom, "Local Group Organization," 149, 156–59; Kolb and Wileden, "Special Interest Groups in Rural Society," 71–73; Kolb, "Trends of Country Neighborhoods," 53–54; and Hay, "Social Organizations and Agencies," 22–24. On the conflict between rural and town women's clubs, see Williams County Assistant Extension Agent Annual Reports, 1929–30 and 1937–38, NDSU.

25. Saloutos and Hicks, *Agricultural Discontent in the Middle West*, 128–30, 219–20, 230–31, 280–85, 291–305; McNelly, *County Agent Story*, 28, 38–39, 58–60; Wileden, tape 7, side 1, tape 8, side 1, part 2, tape 9, side 1, part 1, WAOHP; Segerstrom, WAOHP; Ellefson, tape 4, side 2, WAOHP; Craft, NDOHP.

26. Saloutos and Hicks, *Agricultural Discontent in the Middle West*, 161–63; Smith and Olstad, NDOHP; Seltvedt, NDOHP; Long, NDOHP; Craft, NDOHP; Segerstrom, tape 2, side 2, WAOHP; Long, tape 2, side 1, WAOHP.

27. On IVA, see Craft, NDOHP, and Long, tape 5, side 1, WAOHP. On social aspects of meetings, see Hay, "Social Organizations and Agencies," 59, 60–61, and Long, tape 5, side 2, WAOHP. On women's activities, see Segerstrom, tape 3, side 2, tape 4, side 1, WAOHP, and Craft, NDOHP. See also Long, tape 2, sides 1 and 2, tape 4, side 1, tape 5, side 2, tape 6, side 1, tape 7, side 1, WAOHP; Tomter, tape 2, side 1, WAOHP; and Long, NDOHP. Many North Dakota Farmers' Unions were previously community clubs, which illustrates the flexibility of Progressive Era reforms as they were adopted by farm people. See Willson, "Rural Community Clubs in North Dakota," 14–15, and Willson, "Social Organizations and Agencies," 58–60.

28. On the democratic structure of the Farmers' Union, see Saloutos and Hicks, *Agricultural Discontent in the Middle West*, 219–25, 231, and Thomsen and Thorne, "Cooperative Marketing for Missouri," 78–79. On the appeal of groups like the NPL and the Farmers' Union to diverse groups of farm people, see Slocum, "Influence of Tenure Status," 13; Rankin, "Nebraska Farm Tenancy," 27–31; and Hay, "Social Organizations and Agencies," 59–61. Quotes on political ideology from Oscar Craft and Cora Doty; Craft, NDOHP, and Doty and Smith, NDOHP. See also Seltvedt, NDOHP; Smith and Olstad, NDOHP; and Long, NDOHP.

29. While these organizations had similar aims and in general worked cooperatively, there were regional variations. In Nebraska and Kansas, strong Farmers' Union states, there was little support for the NPL, and the Nebraska Farmers'

Union was politically conservative. Sometimes these alternative organizations also would work cooperatively at the local level with the Farm Bureaus, particularly in livestock areas. For example, in 1924, the Nebraska, Kansas, and Missouri Farmers' Unions, the Missouri Farmers' Association, and the Missouri Farm Bureau cooperated in livestock shipping exchanges in Omaha, Nebraska; St. Joseph, Missouri; and Sioux City, Iowa. However, they competed in St. Louis and Kansas City. Saloutos and Hicks, *Agricultural Discontent in the Middle West*, 225–29, 231–40, 301–5, 317–18; Morgan and Howells, "Rural Primary Groups of Boone County," 45–46; Thomsen and Thorne, "Cooperative Marketing for Missouri," 64–65.

30. Segerstrom, tape 1, side 2, part 1, tape 2, side 2, tape 3, side 1, tape 5, side 1, WAOHP; Long, tape 2, side 1, tape 5, sides 1 and 2, WAOHP; Tomter, tape 2, side 1, WAOHP; Ellefson, tape 2, side 1, tape 4, side 1, WAOHP; Craft, NDOHP; Doty and Smith, NDOHP; Seltvedt, NDOHP; and Smith and Olstad, NDOHP.

31. Siebert Papers, 15 Feb., 13 Mar. 1936, 2 June 1937, and Tomter, tape 2, side 1, WAOHP. Other examples: Rich Valley Homemakers Club (Esmond, N.D.) Records, 1938–69, Mar. 1932, MS 58, NDSU; Olson Diaries, 7–8 Apr. 1936, 24 Jan. 1939. The Williams County Agent Annual Report, 1926–27, NDSU, records that the new agent hoped "to be friendly" with the new Farmers' Union. In Wisconsin, the extension service cooperated with the Farmers' Union. Like Homemakers' Clubs, 4-H Clubs may have been more responsive to local communities; they were organized by both male and female county agents, and the Smith-Lever Act, which created the Federal Extension Service, required that 25% of each state's funds be spent on club work. See Kathleen Hilton, "Growing Up Female: Girlhood Experience and Social Feminism, 1890–1929" (Ph.D. diss., Carnegie Mellon University, 1987), 187–93.

32. Willson, "Rural Community Clubs in North Dakota," 14, 18–19; Kolb, "Service Relations of Town and Country," 68–70; and Slocum, "Influence of Tenure Status," 13. A Missouri study in 1927 estimated that only half of the farmers in Missouri were involved in cooperative marketing. See Thomsen and Thorne, "Cooperative Marketing for Missouri," 25. See also Rankin, "Nebraska Farm Tenancy," 27–30.

33. The county agent was approved by a vote of 2,871 to 2,322, carrying only sixteen of the twenty-five townships in the open country. By contrast, the proposal won substantial support in towns, carrying eight of the nine towns in the county. Extension Program Annual Reports, Traill County, 1926, 1936, North Dakota Cooperative Extension Service, NDSU; Willson, "Rural Community Clubs in North Dakota," 26, 89, 96–97; Hay, "Social Organizations and Agencies," 59–61. In other counties in North Dakota, resistance to farm organizations reflected the views of German-Russian immigrants, who organized around local churches and disapproved of secular organizations.

34. E. L. Kirkpatrick, "Cedar County, Iowa, Study Report," 7–8, 12–14, DFP&RL, Study Projects, 1919–22, box 7; Von Tungeln, Kirkpatrick, Hoffer, and Thaden, "Cedar County," 110. See also W. Baumgartel to C. J. Galpin, 3 July 1920, DFP&RL, General Correspondence, 1919–34, box 1.

35. Brusveen, tape 1, side 2, tape 6, side 1, tape 7, side 1, part 2, WAOHP.

CHAPTER 6 Community Work and Technological Change

1. Willa Cather, *One of Ours* (New York: Knopf, 1922), 157; Anderson, NDOHP; George A. Pond and Louis B. Bassett, "Cost of Combine Harvesting in Minnesota," *Minnesota Agricultural Experiment Station Bulletin* no. 266 (May 1930): 24–25.

2. J. Sanford Rikoon, *Threshing in the Midwest, 1820–1940: A Study of Traditional Culture and Technological Change* (Bloomington: Indiana University Press, 1988). A parallel study of technological change in threshing on the Great Plains in this period is Thomas D. Isern, *Bull Threshers and Bindlestiffs: Harvesting and Threshing on the North American Plains* (Lawrence: University of Kansas Press, 1990).

3. Goodwin, tr. 20, ICFOHP; Brownie L. McVey, tr. side 1, p. 7, side 2, p. 1, tape OH4–6, ICFOHP. Photographic examples can be found in almost all agricultural collections. For some examples in literature, see Garland, *Son of the Middle Border*, 50–58, 147–56; Hamlin Garland, *Boy Life on the Prairie* (1899; New York: Unger, 1959), 148–61, 248–63; Homer Croy, *RFD #3* (New York: Harper and Brothers, 1924), 27–40; and Lorna Doone Beers, *Prairie Fires* (New York: Dutton, 1925), 90–105.

4. Erickson Diaries, 26 Aug. 1911, 3 Oct. 1918, 24–25 Sept. 1919, 11–31 Aug. 1922, 3–18 Sept. 1924; Olson Diaries, 2–22 Aug. 1932, 20–21 Aug. 1934, 22 July–3 Aug. 1936; Siebert Papers, 21 July–22 Aug. 1935; Burke Papers, 13–25 Sept. 1928, 21 Aug. 1929; Still Papers, 6 Aug.–16 Sept. 1914.

5. J. W. McManigal, *Farm Town: A Memoir of the 1930s* (Brattleboro, Vt.: Stephen Greene Press, 1974), 35–39. Other descriptions of corn harvests include Hucke, tr. 6–7, ICFOHP; Rensick, tr. 4–5, ICFOHP; Moore, "Memories of the Early Days"; Bert S. Gittens, "Morton to Stevens to Gittens," 26–28, ILHC, Special Collections, MS-80, M-26, Iowa State University; "Type of Foxfire History"; Oakley B. Collier, "The Story of Our Branch of the Collier Family," ICFMC; Gabelmann Diaries, 27 Sept.–11 Nov. 1912, 16 Oct. 1918, 19–23 Oct. 1937; and Powers Diaries, 25–31 Oct. 1932, 1–23 Nov. 1933, 4 Oct.–18 Nov. 1936.

6. Garland, *Son of the Middle Border*, 156, 160, and *Boy Life on the Prairie*, 162–67, 264–71. See also McVey, tr. side 2, p. 1, ICFOHP.

7. Olson Diaries, 14 Aug. 1935, 22 July 1936; Siebert Papers, 3–6 Aug. 1935; McManigal, *Farm Town*, 22–31.

8. McManigal, *Farm Town*, 22–23; McVey, tr. side 2, p. 1, ICFOHP; Thompson, *American Daughter*, 14–15; Goodwin, tr. 20–21, ICFOHP; Ethel Tiefeatheler, tr. 8, OH4–43, ICFOHP.

9. Erickson Diaries, 24 Sept. 1919; Still Papers, 21 Aug. 1914; Powers Diaries, 2 Aug. 1927; Croy, *RFD #3*, 27. See also Goodwin, tr. 20, ICFOHP.

10. Other improvements were also made to the thresher, such as the ability to blow the straw directly into the barn or to stack it with minimal human assistance.

11. Don D. Lescohier, "Conditions Affecting the Demand for Harvest Labor in the Wheat Belt," *USDA Bulletin* no. 1230 (Apr. 1924); Croy, *RFD #3*, 28; Fosberg, NDOHP; Jacobs, NDOHP; McManigal, *Farm Town*, 23–28; John Vaage, MN8–

653B and 654A, NDOHP; Larson, NDOHP; and Wileden, tape 3, side 1, WAOHP. The host's responsibility for stacking the straw might also have been a holdover from earlier traditions in which stacking the straw required skill, and individual farmers could be particular about how it was done, depending on how they intended to use it. I found few oral sources that described stacking the straw in this way. See also Vekkund, NDOHP, and Collier, "Collier Family."

12. Lescohier, "Conditions;" Don D. Lescohier, "Sources of Supply and Conditions of Employment of Harvest Labor in the Wheat Belt," *USDA Bulletin* no. 1211 (May 1924); Loepke, NDOHP; John Faul, WE27–1076, NDOHP.

13. Croy, *RFD #3*, 30–34; Jacobs, NDOHP. See also Powers Diaries, 31 July, 4 Aug. 1922, 18 July 1932, 29 July 1937.

14. Jones, "Cooking for a Crew," in "New Home on the Old Farm"; Erickson Diaries, 24 Aug. 1919; Gullickson, NDOHP; Henderson, tr. 18, ICFOHP.

15. Fosberg, NDOHP; Jacobs, NDOHP; James, NDOHP; Tiefeatheler, tr. 8–9, ICFOHP; Stansbury, NDOHP; Larson, NDOHP.

16. Tiefeatheler, tr. 8–9, ICFOHP; Henderson, tr. 18–19, ICFOHP; Fosberg, NDOHP; Collier, "Collier Family."

17. Baumann, tape 3, side 1, WAOHP; Jones, "Cooking for a Crew," 48; Henderson, tr. 18, ICFOHP; Fosberg, NDOHP. Other descriptions: Chambers, RWOHP; Brusveen, WAOHP; Julius and Hulda DeJong, OH4–52, ICFOHP; Bilsland, tr. 8–9, ICFOHP; James, NDOHP; Larson, NDOHP; Stansbury, NDOHP; Jones, "Cooking for a Crew," 43–49; Tiefeatheler, tr. 8–9, ICFOHP; Erickson Diaries, 26 Aug. 1911, 13 Aug. 1937. Two of the few who mention the clean-up chores are DeJong and Baumann.

18. Powers Diaries, 18–20 Aug. 1937; Hucke, tr. 6, ICFOHP; Bilsland, tr. 8, ICFOHP; DeJong, ICFOHP; Beers, *Prairie Fires*, 99–104.

19. Tomter, tape 2, side 1, WAOHP; Goodwin, tr. 20–21, ICFOHP; Jacobs, NDOHP; Faul, NDOHP. See also Croy, *RFD #3*, 30–31.

20. Goodwin, tr. 20–21, ICFOHP; Chambers, RWOHP; Jacobs, NDOHP.

21. Descriptions of children's work and play are found in many sources, including the following: Goodwin, tr. 20, ICFOHP; McManigal, *Farm Town*, 24–28; Fosberg, NDOHP; Fred Hawthorn and Robert Hawthorn, "Idlewild Farm: A Century of Progress" (Lake Mills, Iowa: Graphic Publishing, 1976), in ILHC, Special Collections, MS-80, Iowa State University; Powers Diaries, 7–21 July 1932; Long, tape 4, side 2, WAOHP; and Garland, *Son of the Middle Border*, 150–53. Some of these jobs were also done by older men, which shows the full life cycle of male threshing work. See, for example, Thompson, *American Daughter*, 15.

22. Garland, *Son of the Middle Border*, 147, 150–53; Thompson, *American Daughter*, 15; Olson Diaries, 27 Aug. 1938. See also Faul, NDOHP.

23. Moore, "Memories of the Early Days"; Baumann, tape 3, side 1, WAOHP. See also Croy, *RFD #3*, 38–39, and Hamlin Garland, "A Branch Road," in *Main Traveled Roads* (1891; New York: Signet Classics, 1962), 18–26. Rikoon also notes the importance of folklore surrounding courtship during the threshing. For men, this often took the form of practical jokes played on single men who might be interested in impressing a particular woman. Rikoon does not discuss women's tales of

courtship surrounding the harvest. Rikoon, *Threshing in the Midwest*, 130.

24. Lescohier, "Conditions;" Emil Rauchenstein and C. A. Bonnen, "Successful Threshing Ring Management," *Illinois Agricultural Experiment Station Bulletin* no. 267 (May 1925): 375–91; Peter O. Paulson, TR5–0974 A&B, NDOHP.

25. Jacobs, NDOHP. Another account of a tightly knit ethnic community and cooperative ownership is found in Brusveen, tape 1, side 2, tape 3, sides 1 and 2, tape 4, side 1, WAOHP. Farmers' Union leaders who recalled cooperative ownership are Long, WAOHP; Segerstrom, tape 2, side 2, WAOHP; and Ellefson, tape 2, side 2, WAOHP. An example of cooperative ownership in North Dakota is found in James, NDOHP. The Wisconsin interviews with Farm Bureau leaders were more likely to indicate custom threshing with cooperative work rather than cooperative ownership. This trend was less evident in North Dakota.

26. Vaage, NDOHP; Long, tape 4, side 2, WAOHP; Vekkund, NDOHP; Stansbury, NDOHP; Anderson, NDOHP; Bilsland, ICFOHP; Seltvedt, NDOHP; Hardiman, tape 4, side 2, WAOHP; DeJong, ICFOHP.

27. Goodwin, ICFOHP; Larson, NDOHP; James, NDOHP; Jacobs, NDOHP.

28. McVey, tr. side 2, pp. 2–3, ICFOHP. Some threshing rings were organized into very formal organizations, but this does not seem to have been common.

29. Siebert Papers, 21 July–20 Sept. 1937; Frank Krueger Papers, 17 Sept.–11 Oct. 1900. See also Gabelmann Diaries, 24 July–18 Sept. 1916, 12–15 July 1934.

30. Siebert Papers, 21 July–20 Sept. 1937; Frank Krueger Papers, 17 Sept.–11 Oct. 1900, 3 Aug.–25 Sept. 1919. Descriptions of labor exchange can also be found in Tiefeatheler, tr. 8, ICFOHP; Bilsland, tr. 8–9, ICFOHP; Fosberg, NDOHP; Hardiman, tape 4, side 2, WAOHP; Long, tape 4, side 2, WAOHP; Tomter, tape 2, side 1, WAOHP; Rauchenstein and Bonnen, "Successful Threshing Ring Management," 375–91; and Faul, NDOHP.

31. Beers, *Prairie Fires*, 90–92; Douglass, "Migratory Labor in the Wheat Harvest," 1, 59; R. C. Miller and Alva N. Benton, "Combine Harvesting in North Dakota," *North Dakota Agricultural Experiment Station Bulletin* no. 220 (June 1928): 6; Alva H. Benton and Harold E. Serelstad, "The Combined Harvester-Thresher in North Dakota," *North Dakota Agricultural Experiment Station Bulletin* no. 225 (May 1929): 47; Pond and Bassett, "Cost of Combine Harvesting in Minnesota," 24. One novel that gives a sympathetic portrayal of the seasonal laborer and his moves from agricultural to urban employment is G. D. Eaton, *Backfurrow* (New York: G. P. Putnam's Sons, 1925).

32. Douglass, "Migratory Labor in the Wheat Harvest," 2–4; Lescohier, "Sources of Supply," 22.

33. Lescohier, "Sources of Supply," 1, 3–5, 9–11; Douglass, "Migratory Labor in the Wheat Harvest," 8–10. See also William Baumgartel to C. J. Galpin, 12 June 1920 and 3 July 1920, DFP&RL, General Correspondence, 1919–34, box 1, and photographs for Lescohier, "Sources of Supply," and "Conditions," BAE, Division of Land Economics, 1911–47, Record Group 83-G, box 17, NASPB.

34. Jacobs, NDOHP; Paulson, NDOHP. See also Seltvedt, NDOHP; Vaage, NDOHP; Douglass, "Migratory Labor in the Wheat Harvest"; Lescohier, "Sources of Supply" and "Conditions"; and Thompson, *American Daughter*, 52–55. North

Dakota, in general, had more cooperative efforts with the IWW because of the NPL.

35. Paulson, NDOHP; Jacobs, NDOHP; Berg, NDOHP; Anderson, NDOHP. See also Larson, NDOHP. For descriptions of returning workers, networks, and "good workers," see Long, NDOHP; James, NDOHP; Larson, NDOHP; Stansbury, NDOHP; Still Papers, 10 July 1913; and Burke Papers, 10–23 July 1938. Douglass noted in "Migratory Labor in the Wheat Harvest" that most workers did not rely on newspapers or advertisements; "information [circulated] through untraceable channels from man to man." He also noted that these sources of information were very accurate, and jobs were often arranged through correspondence, relatives, and friends. Lescohier found this to be less common. About 11% of the farmers in North Dakota and Kansas in his study hired the same workers from year to year; however, the category also carries the notation "advance contract made with them." Arrangements may have been more informal than this suggests. Such arrangements may have been undercounted. Lescohier, "Conditions," 31.

36. Paulson, NDOHP; Fosberg, NDOHP.

37. Vaage, NDOHP; Jacobs, NDOHP; James, NDOHP; Larson, NDOHP. See also Burke Papers, 21–23 Oct. 1907, 4–21 Sept. 1908, 1–7 Sept. 1919, 30 Aug.–11 Sept. 1926, 18 Aug., Oct. 1927, 16–25 Aug. 1930, 1–7 Aug. 1932, and 8–26 Aug. 1935. The diary records the places where the threshing rig and cook car worked every season from 1907 to 1927, when the Burkes quit threshing and sold their machine. Even after the family stopped operating the rig, the older sons continued to go "away threshing" throughout the 1930s, earning money for high school and college.

38. Douglass, "Migratory Labor in the Wheat Harvest"; Lescohier, "Sources of Supply" and "Conditions," 21.

39. Erickson Diaries, 3 Oct. 1918, 18–21 Aug., 24 Sept. 1919, 23 Aug. 1920, 11–26 Aug. 1922, 3–18 Sept. 1924, 28 Aug.–3 Sept. 1926, 12–26 Aug. 1927, 11 Aug. 1932, 1–28 Aug. 1934, 3–28 Aug. 1935, 1–13 Aug. 1937.

40. Women were not encouraged to operate farm machinery or to be knowledgeable about it; this may also have shaped Erickson's decision. However, many farm women did operate farm machinery. Erickson worked in the fields and had looked for machinery with Joe, so the lack of encouragement probably had less influence on her. She could have had her son or neighbors provide technical knowledge, if she herself did not have it.

41. Powers Diaries, 4 July–8 Aug. 1922, 29 July–11 Aug. 1927, 5–30 July 1932, 29 July–24 Aug., 1 Oct. 1937.

42. This discussion is based on Lescohier, "Conditions." The farm sizes for this study were significantly different from farm size averages appearing in the 1920 census. Average farm sizes in the study compared to average state farm sizes were: Kansas, 537 to 275 acres; Nebraska, 271 to 339 acres; and North Dakota, 539 to 466 acres. Since smaller farms were more likely to use family and exchange labor, the study probably overrepresents the importance of hired workers in Kansas and North Dakota and underrepresents their importance in Nebraska. The average farm sizes for those farms that hired no labor and the percentages of farms

in the study that hired no labor were Kansas, 302 acres, 11%; Nebraska, 208 acres, 44%; and North Dakota, 320 acres, 29%.

43. Although Kansas farmers also boarded their workers, the study does not describe how the boarding work was organized in that state. Since the author mentions women exchanging work in Nebraska, the boarding work may have been done by individual women with hired help in Kansas. The significantly larger numbers of workers in Kansas could have added tremendously to the work of farm women if help was not hired or exchanged. Cook cars were used in large numbers only in North Dakota and South Dakota (14% of farms in South Dakota and 19% of farms in North Dakota). They were not found at all in Kansas or Nebraska, though there were a few in Oklahoma.

44. Lescohier, "Conditions," 16–17; Miller and Benton, "Combine Harvesting in North Dakota," 5–6; Mack M. Jones, "The Combine Harvester in Missouri," *Missouri Agricultural Experiment Station Bulletin* no. 286 (May 1930): 3–4; L. A. Reynoldson, R. S. Kifer, J. H. Martin, and W. R. Humphries, "The Combined Harvester-Thresher in the Great Plains," *USDA Technical Bulletin* no. 70 (Feb. 1928): 1–3. The following discussion of combines is drawn from these and other studies of combines, including L. A. Reynoldson, J. H. Martin, and W. R. Humphries, "Shall I Buy a Combine?" *USDA Farmers' Bulletin* no. 565 (Apr. 1928); Pond and Bassett, "Cost of Combine Harvesting in Minnesota," 1–30; Benton and Serelstad, "Combined Harvester-Thresher in North Dakota"; and Gabriel Lundy, K. H. Klages, and J. F. Goss, "The Use of the Combine in South Dakota," *South Dakota Agricultural Experiment Station Bulletin* no. 244 (Sept. 1929).

45. Powers Diaries, 13 July 1937; Paulson, NDOHP; Vaage, NDOHP; Ellefson, tape 2, side 2, WAOHP; Brusveen, tape 3, side 1, WAOHP; Faul, NDOHP. Combine farming also did not necessarily change the value placed on hard work and the use of labor to keep costs down. Gerald Goodwin (ICFOHP) purchased a smaller two-row combine (for picking corn) rather than the larger four-row combine to keep from going into debt. "Our theory is that where you got 200 acres of corn to harvest, the two row machine we got takes it up in good shape. It takes a few more hours in the field, but for the money, can spend the hours rather than go in debt. So many people spend the money for big new machines so they can hurry up and go to Florida."

46. Hardiman, tape 4, side 2, WAOHP; Chambers, RWOHP.

CHAPTER 7 Consumption and the Isolated Nuclear Farm
Family Ideal

1. The *Country Gentleman*, 1921, Ayer Advertising Agency Collection (hereafter cited as Ayer), Curtis Publishing Company, book 652, box 395, National Museum of American History, Smithsonian Institution (hereafter cited as NMAH).

2. *Farm Journal*, 1929, Ayer, book 487, box 275.

3. Edwin C. Powell, editor of *Farm and Home*, to C. J. Galpin, 18 Jan. 1921, and Galpin to Powell, 20 Jan. 1921, DFP&RL, General Correspondence, 1919–36, box 12. On the links of advertisers and the farm press to agricultural institutions,

see also C. J. Galpin to Mr. Russell, 19 Mar. 1927, DFP&RL, General Correspondence, Office of the Secretary of Agriculture, Memoranda, 1922–28, box 12, and the letters collected in the "Standard of Living, Miscellaneous" file, DFP&RL, Manuscripts, box 4. Examples of increased emphasis on consumer goods can be found in the *Farmer's Wife* in the 1920s and in the Ayer and Warshaw Collections at NMAH. See, for example, "American Agriculturalist: Why It Is the *Spokesman* of the *Substantial* Business Farmers of the Middle States," Warshaw Collection of Business Americana (hereafter cited as Warshaw), Collection 60, box 36, NMAH, and advertisements from the *Country Gentleman*, 1916–21, Ayer, Curtis Publishing Company, book 652. See also "Material Used for Subcommittee on Research," 16 Nov. 1925, DFP&RL, General Correspondence, box 15.

4. The *Country Gentleman,* 1921, Ayer, Curtis Publishing Company, book 652, box 395; E. L. Kirkpatrick, "Tentative Outline for Sourcebook on Rural Standards of Living," used at the 1930 Conference on American Country Life at the College of Agriculture of the University of Wisconsin (data from 1922–24), DFP&RL, Manuscripts, box 4; E. L. Kirkpatrick, "The Farmer's Standard of Living: A Socio-Economic Study of 2,886 Farm Families of Selected Localities in Eleven States," DFP&RL, Manuscripts, box 4. On the idea of advertising as "capitalist realism," see Michael Schudson, *Advertising, the Uneasy Persuasion: Its Dubious Impact on American Society* (New York: Basic Books, 1984), 209–33; Roland Marchand, *Advertising the American Dream: Making Way for Modernity, 1920–1940* (Berkeley and Los Angeles: University of California Press, 1985), xviii; and T. J. Jackson Lears, "From Salvation to Self-Realization: Advertising and the Therapeutic Roots of the Consumer Culture, 1880–1930," in *The Culture of Consumption: Critical Essays in American History, 1880–1980,* ed. T. J. Jackson Lears and Richard Fox (New York: Pantheon Books, 1983), 17–30.

5. C. L. McNelley termed this a shift from the old philosophy of "better farming" to the new "art of graceful living," in *County Agent Story,* 182. Kirkpatrick, "Tentative Outline for Sourcebook"; "Movements of Population from Farms to Cities, 1917–1926," DFP&RL, General Correspondence, Office of the Secretary of Agriculture, Memoranda, 1922–28; "Standard of Living of the Farm Population"; W. H. Baumgartel to C. J. Galpin, "Suggestions in re to North Dakota Farm Tenancy Bulletin," 1924, in "Farm Tenancy: An Analysis of Two North Dakota Tenant Communities," DFP&RL, Manuscripts, box 3. The linkage of economic and social visions can be found in most of the standard-of-living studies, in farm magazines, and in press releases of the DFP&RL. In addition to those cited above, these include Kirkpatrick, "Farmer's Standard of Living"; Tables, Miscellaneous, DFP&RL, General Correspondence, box 17; Webster County, Iowa, advertisements and reports, 1921, DFP&RL, Study Projects, Iowa File, box 7; J. O. Rankin, "Tenancy through New Eyes, 1919–1922," DFP&RL, Study Projects, Nebraska File, box 9; "Modern Conveniences in Nebraska Farm Homes," DFP&RL, Press Release, General Correspondence; "Living Conditions in Rural America," *Farmer's Wife* 23 (June 1920): 3; Von Tungeln, Kirkpatrick, Hoffer, and Thaden, "Cedar County"; Hay, "Social Organizations and Agencies"; John P. Johansen, "One Hundred New Homesteads in the Red River Valley, North Dakota: A Study of the

Resettlement and Rehabilitation of Farm Families," *North Dakota Agricultural Experiment Station Bulletin* no. 304 (June 1941); Willson, Hoffsommer, and Benton, "Rural Changes in Western North Dakota"; Von Tungeln, Thaden, and Kirkpatrick, "Cost of Living on Iowa Farms"; Thaden, "Standards of Living on Iowa Farms"; Hoyt, "Value of Family Living"; D. E. Lindstrom and W. M. Dawson, "Selectivity of 4-H Club Work: An Analysis of Factors Influencing Membership," *Illinois Agricultural Experiment Station Bulletin* no. 426 (Aug. 1936); Ward, "Farm Woman's Problems," 8–9; and "Annual Family Living."

6. Lantern Slides, 1904–41, Bureau of Plant Industry, Soils and Agricultural Engineering, Record Group 54-LS, boxes 9–12, NASPB. See also F. Cranefield, "The Improvement of Home Grounds," *Wisconsin Agricultural Experiment Station Bulletin* no. 105 (Dec. 1904). In many ways these model farm homes are direct descendants of the progressive farmer-designed homes of the late nineteenth century described by Sally McMurry, *Families and Farmhouses in Nineteenth-Century America* (New York: Oxford University Press, 1988). However, as McMurry notes, by the Progressive Era, progressive farm-home design was the domain of experts, not farm people themselves, and the choices of farm people were increasingly limited.

7. *Third Wisconsin Country Life Conference*, 26–33; "Gleanings from Science," 6–11. See also "Farm Homes," *Wisconsin Agricultural Experiment Station Bulletin* no. 353 (Jan. 1923); Jones, "New Home on the Old Farm," 3–26; and Wallace Manikowski, "Windmill Electric Lighting and Power," *North Dakota Agricultural Experiment Station Bulletin* no. 105 (Aug. 1913). On actual adoption of these technologies, see United States Bureau of the Census, *United States Census of Agriculture, 1945*, vol. 2, *General Reports: Statistics by Subject*, 317–19. The Midwest had more tractors, ranking at the top when compared to other regions, but for running water and electricity it ranked below the other northern regions of the country.

8. Ted R. Rask interview, NDDI; Community Studies (hereafter cited as Community Studies), Haskell County, Kans., Negs. 41867, 41887, 41888, 41898, 41968, and 41970, and Shelby County, Iowa, Negs. 4402–4, 44205–7, 44208, BAE, Division of Economic Information, Prints and Photographs, 1939–42, Record Group 83-G, NASPB; Lantern Slides, Bureau of Plant Industry, Soils and Agricultural Engineering, boxes 12–14, Record Group 54-LS, NASPB; Federal Extension Service, 1906–42, Negs. S2178, S11904C–S11944C, S17274C, S21579C, S22208C, S22842C, and S22870C, Record Group 33-SC, NASPB. Extension photographs focus more frequently on better homes. See also Willson, Hoffsommer, and Benton, "Rural Changes in Western North Dakota," 100–105.

9. Photographs showing community recreation include Historical File, 1900–1959, Neg. 53700L, Record Group 16-G, NASPB; and DFP&RL, Marketing and Rural Life, 1902–38, Negs. 6376, 6399, 6519, 6523, 6809, 7323, 14621, and 60309, Record Group 83-ML, NASPB. Family-oriented recreation examples are Historical File, Negs. 10,139 (REA), 8190, C7327, S3880, S-18197C, FCI-164, AAA-6539, 78,115 (SCS), and S2177C, and Federal Extension Service, Negs. S4318C, S5318C,

S22231C, S22822C, S22839C, S22870C, and S23782C, Record Group 33-SC, NASPB.

10. The images of nuclear families enjoying leisure and consumer goods parallels what Roland Marchand calls the "family circle" theme in advertising. See Marchand, *Advertising the American Dream,* 248–54.

11. Hoyt, "Value of Family Living," 196; Margaret G. Reid, "Status of Farm Housing in Iowa," *Iowa Agricultural Experiment Station Research Bulletin* no. 174 (Sept. 1934): 292; "Annual Family Living," 3; Kirkpatrick, Tough, and Cowles, "Life Cycle of the Farm Family," 8; and Kirkpatrick, McNall, and Cowles, "Farm Family Living in Wisconsin," 1–2, 10–11.

12. Doty and Smith, NDOHP; Stansbury, NDOHP; and K. H. McGill, "A Survey of Meade County, Kansas," 11 Aug. 1934, RPR, box 5. See also Hoag, "Advantages of Farm Life," 97–98; Fosberg, NDOHP; and Segerstrom, tape 1, side 1, WAOHP.

13. Because of Garland's "extravagance," the unusual way in which he earned his money, and his failure to associate with neighbors, the community saw him as "ungracious," and he was not particularly "well liked." See Hamlin Garland, *A Daughter of the Middle Border* (1921; New York: Grosset and Dunlap, 1926), 17, 71, 84, 101, 154–55, 186; Garland, *Son of the Middle Border,* 101; and Extension Agent Annual Reports, Williams County, 1924–25, NDSU. See also Crow, *American Country Girl,* 125–26, 139–42, 181; Craft, NDOHP; Hoag, "Advantages of Farm Life," 55–57; and Lorna Doone Beers, *A Humble Lear* (New York: Dutton, 1929), 346.

14. Croy, *RFD #3,* 52–53, 73–74, 101–7, 231. See also Cather, *One of Ours,* and "Neighbor Rosicky," in Willa Cather, *Obscure Destinies* (New York: Vintage Books, 1974).

15. Baumann, tape 1, side 2, tape 3, side 1, WAOHP; Long, tape 1, side 2, tape 4, sides 1 and 2, WAOHP.

16. Nellie Kedzie Jones, "The City Guest on the Farm," 28 Sept. 1912, Nellie Kedzie Jones Papers; Margaret Lynn, *A Stepdaughter of the Prairie* (New York: MacMillan, 1914), 63–79. This is a common theme in rural novels. See also Croy, *RFD #3,* 166–87; Garland, *Son of the Middle Border,* 189–97; and Hamlin Garland, *Rose of Dutcher's Coolly* (New York: Harper and Brothers, 1895), 82–90.

17. E. L. Kirkpatrick and Carl Kraenzel, RPR, box 14, Oneida County, Wisc., 28 July 1934, 127, and Paul Landis and Gordon Randlett, RPR, box 10, Burke County, N.D., Sept. 1934. See also Letters to the Editor, *Farmer's Wife* 16 (July 1911): 51, and *Farmer's Wife* 23 (Nov. 1920): 183; Extension County Agent Annual Report, Traill County, 1928, North Dakota Extension Service; and Wileden, tape 1, side 1, WAOHP.

18. The story of independent and rural telephone service has not yet been studied adequately by historians. The best analysis is Claude S. Fischer, "Technology's Retreat: The Decline of Rural Telephony in the United States, 1920–1940," *Social Science History* 11 (Fall 1987): 295–327. In 1934, only 3% of AT&T's phone service was rural. More than 29% of all independent connecting stations were rural. "The Bell system has left two-thirds of the rural telephone service to independent tele-

phone companies" (N. R. Danielian, *A.T.&T.: The Story of Industrial Conquest* [1939; New York: Arno Press, 1974], 21). See also John Brooks, *Telephone: The First Hundred Years* (New York: Harper and Row, 1975), 188–89, 196–97. By 1939, AT&T and the Bell System controlled 83% of all phones in service and 91% of all telephone plants (Brooks, *Telephone,* 205).

19. United States Bureau of the Census, *United States Census of Agriculture, 1945,* vol. 2, *General Reports: Statistics by Subject,* 317–19, 320–21, 328, 330. Electricity was much more prevalent in urban areas. In 1920, 50% of nonfarm homes had electricity; in 1930, 80% did. In 1930, only 10% of farm homes in the country had electricity, and it was not until 1946 that 50% of farm homes had electricity. In the late 1920s, 71% of urban homes had bathrooms, compared to 33% of rural homes. Susan Strasser also points out that running water was slower to become available than electricity because it was harder to make a profit from it than from electricity. See Susan Strasser, *Never Done: A History of American Housework* (New York: Pantheon Books, 1982), 67–103.

20. American Telephone and Telegraph, 1920–41, Ayer, Collection 59, NMAH, and Sears, Roebuck & Co. Catalogs, Reels 2 (Fall 1897), 7 (Fall 1905), 13 (Spring 1910), 18 (Spring 1915), 24 (Fall 1920), 28 (Fall 1925), 31 (Spring–Summer 1930), 35 (Spring–Fall 1935), and 39 (Spring 1940), Microfilm 692, NMAH Library.

21. Gabelmann Diaries, 25 Oct., 18 Nov. 1912, Jan.–Mar. 1916, 24 May, 14 Sept. 1918, 2–4 Feb. 1934, 3–24 Jan. 1939. Gabelmann recorded her purchases and used modern conveniences, such as cameras, but she also maintained ties to her German heritage, subscribing to the *Deutsche Hausfrau* ($1.25) and the *Deutsche Farmer* ($1.00) in 1918 (24 May) and writing sections of her diary in German. Shopping in unusual ways, in unknown cities, from traveling peddlers, and from mail-order houses were often recalled as happy events. One North Dakota farm woman recalled making out catalog orders for everything "from the skin out," including overshoes, mittens, dried fruit, and groceries. See Doty and Smith, NDOHP; Wileden, WAOHP; Dannewitz, NDOHP; Fosberg, NDOHP; and Thompson, *American Daughter,* 55–59, 64.

22. Olson Diaries, 25 Nov. 1937, 2 Nov. 1935, 22 Apr. 1936, 24–30 July 1937; Burke Papers, 12 Apr. 1907, 30 Mar. 1908, 2 Dec. 1919, 27 Oct. 1932, Jan.–Feb. 1933, 2 Nov. 1938, 3 July 1939. See also Powers Diaries, 24–25 Jan. 1922, 18 Jan., 3 Sept. 1932, 31 Apr. 1937, and Still Papers, Mar. 1912, 5 Oct., 7 Dec. 1914.

23. Erickson Diaries, 5 Nov. 1901, 2 Nov. 1913, 10 Feb. 1915, 8 Dec. 1919, 16 Oct. 1925, 20 May, 9 Aug. 1931, 1, 16, 29 Jan. 1933, 20–25 July 1934, 12 Jan., 14 Feb., 16 Oct. 1935, 27 Mar., 9, 19 Aug., 3 Dec. 1936, 31 May, 23 June, 6 July, 3 Dec. 1937, 7 Jan., 21 Mar., 9 Oct., 12 Apr., 3, 21 July, 22 Sept., 16 Nov., 3 Dec. 1938.

24. Hardiman, tape 1, sides 1 and 2, tape 2, sides 1 and 2, WAOHP; Tomter, tape 1, sides 1 and 2, tape 2, side 2, WAOHP.

25. The narrative structures of their stories also parallel the structures of the farm organizations of which they were members. Tomter was a member of the gender-integrated, community-based Farmers' Union; Hardiman a member of the gender-segregated, agricultural institution–sponsored Farm Bureau.

26. For a study of how Illinois farm people used electricity when it and equip-

ment were provided for free, see E. W. Lehmann and F. L. Kingsley, "Electric Power for the Farm," *Illinois Agricultural Experiment Station Bulletin* no. 332 (June 1929).

27. Segerstrom, WAOHP.

28. The differences between tenant and owner housing and how tenure status influenced consumption in Iowa are described in Reid, "Status of Farm Housing in Iowa," 351–82. Tenants generally purchased movable improvements, such as automobiles, machinery, radios, and washing machines, since they could not depend on a long-term residence in any one home. Other factors that affected quality of housing were land values, proximity to urban areas, incomes, and the age of the houses.

CHAPTER 8   The "Farmer" and the "Farmer's Wife"

1. See, for example, "Mr. and Mrs. American Farmer," *Farmer's Wife* 19 (July 1916): 27; "Reports of Committee Eleven: Farm Population and Farm Home," 3, DFP&RL, General Correspondence, 1919–36, Agricultural Conference Materials, Record Group 83, box 4; and Galpin and Sawtelle, "Rural Clubs in Wisconsin," 41.

2. Editorial, *Farmer's Wife* 22 (May 1920): 395, and "The Child-Rearing Family at Stake," DFP&RL, General Correspondence, 1919–36, Articles for Publication, 1921–June 1927, box 4. See also "Cities for Adults; Farms Are for Children Says Doctor Galpin," record of speech to Missouri State Teacher's Association, Nov. 1928, DFP&RL, General Correspondence, Press Releases, box 16. Much of this discussion parallels the conservative justifications for promoting suburbs and increased purchases of home appliances. See Delores Hayden, *The Grand Domestic Revolution: A History of Feminist Designs for American Homes, Neighborhoods, and Cities* (Cambridge: MIT Press, 1981), 22–28.

3. Sharples Separator advertisement, Warshaw, Collection 60, Drawer 77, NMAH.

4. Galpin and James, "Rural Relations of High Schools," 3–5; 1919 advertisement for the *Country Gentleman*, Ayer, 1916–19, book 652, NMAH.

5. C. C. Taylor speech at Farm and Home Program, University of Wisconsin, 6 Feb. 1931, DFP&RL, General Correspondence, 1919–36, box 7.

6. Advertisement for the *Country Gentleman*, 1920, Ayer, book 652. See also Harris, *Treasure of the Land*, 99, 108.

7. Although tenancy studies examine many causes of tenancy, this ideology is still apparent in their acceptance of overall trends. See, for example, Baumgartel to Galpin, "Suggestions," 1–11; George Von Tungeln and Harry L. Eills, "Rural Social Survey of Hudson, Orange, and Jesup Consolidated School District, Blackhawk and Buchanan Counties, Iowa," *Iowa Agricultural Experiment Station Bulletin* no. 224 (Nov. 1924): 208–15, 239; and Willson, Hoffsommer, and Benton, "Rural Changes in Western North Dakota," 5–7, 22–46. The "weeding out" of inefficient farmers led to better incomes for those remaining, and this justified the reorganization. By the 1930s, some tenancy studies questioned these assumptions,

looking at such issues as corporate ownership of land and its effect on increased tenancy. See, for example, Ray E. Wakeley, "Differential Mobility within the Rural Population in Eighteen Iowa Townships, 1928 to 1935," *Iowa Agricultural Experiment Station Research Bulletin* no. 249 (Dec. 1938): 297–303, and Schickele, "Farm Tenure in Iowa." The recognition of new problems, however, did not necessarily result in a change in ideology. Programs to assist tenants were often aimed at those who "deserved" assistance and could qualify as efficient, businesslike farmers. As the president of the AFBF said at a symposium on tenancy, government money should be given to landowners and they should be allowed to use it to "bring selected tenants up" and integrate them into the "credit system." See "Farm Tenure in Iowa, Part III: The National Symposium on Land Tenure Held in Des Moines, February 1937," *Iowa Agricultural Experiment Station Bulletin* no. 357 (Apr. 1937). See also W. G. Murray and H. W. Bitting, "Corporate-Owned Land in Iowa, 1937," *Iowa Agricultural Experiment Station Bulletin* no. 362 (Jan. 1937), and Johansen, "One Hundred New Homesteads," 11.

8. Sears, Roebuck & Co. Catalogs, Reels 18 (Spring 1915), 24 (Fall 1920), 28 (Fall 1925), 31 (Spring–Summer 1930), 35 (Spring–Fall 1935), Microfilm 692, NMAH Library. Photographs of county agents and farmers in USDA Federal Extension Service (hereafter cited as Extension Photographs), Negs. SC3008C, SC22191C, Record Group 33-SC, NASPB. Unlike male agents, home extension agents were photographed in less formal poses, often talking with the farm women rather than lecturing them. The poses in the photographs of home extension agents varied more than those in the photographs of male agents.

9. Ernest Luther to Prof. K. L. Hatch, 10, 17, 24 Feb., 10, 19 Mar., 12 June, 24 Dec. 1912; and Hatch to Luther, 19 Feb., 25 Mar. 1912, Luther Papers.

10. Jack D. Levin Oral History, tape 1, side 1 and 2, State Historical Society of Wisconsin. Novels also show a combination of traditional and modern ways of learning farm techniques. For example, Alexandra, the protagonist of Willa Cather's *O Pioneers!*, creates a prosperous farm by practicing new techniques, such as building a silo, but she also listens to the advice of "crazy Ivar," whose knowledge of the land comes from tradition and intuition. She blends progressive ideas on the farm with a sense of tradition and admiration for her heritage. Cather was critical of modern farming that ignored traditions because it was wasteful in its use of money and resources and made habits of consumption and the use of machinery. The generations that farmed in these ways did not have the spirit of the pioneer generation or its sense of tradition or feelings for the land. Another novel that blended progressive styles of farming with older values was Henry Oyen's *Big Flat*. In it the main character encourages his neighbors to try new farming techniques, including tractor power. But he also encourages cooperative purchase of this technology and leads a local battle against the area's exploitive big business. In the end, it is the action of the old-fashioned lumberjack-farmers that wins the battle against big business, not the scientific methods of the hero, even if they represent the future of the region's agriculture. See Willa Cather, *O Pioneers!* (1913; Boston: Houghton Mifflin, 1941), 22–28, 31–37, 42–45, 83–94; Cather, *One of Ours*,

101–3; and Henry Oyen, *Big Flat* (New York: George H. Doran, 1919), 60–66, 77–78, 90–117, 192–99, 245–94.

11. Wileden, tape 1, side 1, tape 5, side 1, WAOHP; Ellefson, tape 1, side 2, tape 2, sides 1 and 2, tape 3, side 1, WAOHP. Other farmers used the perspectives of their organizations as a guide for their choice of new methods. For example, the Segerstroms refused to read *Hoard's Dairyman* because they disagreed with its anti–Farmers' Union editorial policy. See Segerstrom, tape 2, side 2, WAOHP.

12. Ellefson, tape 2, side 2, tape 1, side 2, WAOHP. See also Segerstrom, tape 2, side 2, tape 3, side 2, WAOHP; Brusveen, tape 1, side 1, tape 6, side 1, WAOHP; Baumann, tape 4, side 1, WAOHP; Hardiman, tape 1, side 2, WAOHP; Wileden, tape 1, side 1, tape 5, side 1, WAOHP; Jack D. Levin Oral History, tape 1, side 2, State Historical Society of Wisconsin; Max Leopold Oral History, tape 1, side 1, State Historical Society of Wisconsin.

13. Brusveen, tape 1, sides 1 and 2, tape 2, side 2, tape 3, side 2, tape 6, side 1, tape 7, side 1, part 2, WAOHP.

14. Joe Baringer to Franklin Delano Roosevelt (FDR), 19 Dec. 1940; J. H. Ament to FSA, 16 Aug. 1941; Ed Alden to FDR, 28 Aug. 1939, USDA, Records of the Farm Home Administration, Rural Rehabilitation Division of the Farm Security Administration (hereafter cited as FSA Letters), 1935–42, Correspondence Relating to Complaints, Record Group 96, National Archives. See also O. A. Adams to FDR, 6 Feb. 1936; Thomas Abromovitz to FDR, 7 Dec. 1937; Mrs. O. J. Armstrong to FDR, Oct. 1937; Ralph Abernathy to FDR, 12 Nov. 1940; C. D. Arnold to Resettlement Administration, 15 Nov. 1936; Earl Arnold to FSA, 26 Jan. 1939; Ralph Adams to FSA, 15 Nov. 1937; and Tom Allen to FDR, 7 Jan. 1937, FSA Letters.

15. "New Science from Old Art," *Wisconsin Agricultural Experiment Station Annual Report Bulletin* no. 410 (Feb. 1930): 126; P. E. Johnston and J. E. Willis, "A Study of the Cost of Horse and Tractor Power on Illinois Farms," *Illinois Agricultural Experiment Station Bulletin* no. 395 (Dec. 1933); Johansen, "One Hundred New Homesteads," 21–27. See also Hawthorn and Hawthorn, "Idlewild Farm."

16. Powers Diaries, 9 July, 29 Aug. 1932, 31 May, 1 June 1937; Faul, NDOHP; and Brusveen, tape 1, sides 1 and 2, tape 3, sides 1 and 2, WAOHP. See also Anderson, NDOHP; Ellefson, tape 1, side 1, tape 2, side 2, WAOHP; and RPR, box 9, Dawes County, Neb., case interview, Hoaglund.

17. Even the research on agricultural institutions in the 1930s noted potential difficulties for small farmers; see note 15. See also Henderson, ICFOHP.

18. Berg, NDOHP; Stansbury, NDOHP; Seltvedt, NDOHP; Craft, NDOHP; Larson, NDOHP; Hucke, ICFOHP.

19. Vaage, NDOHP; Segerstrom, tape 2, side 2, WAOHP; Johansen, "One Hundred New Homesteads," 21–27; DFP&RL, Community Studies, Shelby County, Iowa, Neg. 44129, Record Group 83-GF, NASPB, and FSA Photographs, Neg. LCUSF34–60838-D.

20. Rural Relief Studies, DFP&RL: Woodford County, Ill., June 1935, 2–4, box 3; Richardson County, Neb., June 1935, 12, box 7; Jefferson County, Kans., May 1936, 8–9; Russell County, Kans., 37, 63, box 4; Powers Diaries, 4–8 Oct.

1937; RPR, box 9, Cheyenne County, Neb., case interview, Irwin Sanders family, 1–2; Hodgeman County, Kans., 87–88; case file, Anton Braumagel, 1939, FSA Letters; Arnold Adamson to Representative Karl Stefen, Apr. 1937, FSA Letters; FSA Photographs, Negs. LCUSF34-4320-E and LCUSF34-2896-D; Vaage, NDOHP.

21. Segerstrom, tape 5, side 1, WAOHP.

22. See Extension Photographs, S22893C, NASPB, and "Standard of Living, Miscellaneous" file, DFP&RL, Manuscripts, box 2. Negative images of women working in the fields are often associated with poorer classes of farmers and immigrants. See, for example, Crow, *American Country Girl*; Memo to Secretary Wallace from the Acting Chief of the Bureau of Agricultural Economics, 5 Oct. 1923, DFP&RL, General Correspondence, 1919–36, box 12; Willa Cather, *My Antonia* (1918; Boston: Houghton Mifflin, 1954), 123–32, 147–49; Garland, *Main Traveled Roads*, 104–15; Hamlin Garland, *Prairie Folks* (1892; New York: MacMillan, 1899), 83–117; and Eaton, *Backfurrow*, 208–18. Images of class were associated with the promotion of consumer goods. For example, a 1904 advertisement for a "ball bearing washer" showed one picture of a woman with muscled arms, poorly dressed, chained to a scrub board and tub. In contrast, the second showed a fragile-looking woman, dressed in ruffles and bonnet, seated by a tub cranking a spinner washer. *Northwestern Agriculturalist* 19 (Feb. 1904), in Warshaw, Drawer 77, Miscellaneous Periodicals, NMAH.

23. The *Farmer's Wife*, according to Mari Jo Buhle's *Women and American Socialism, 1870–1920*, was originally the title of the official newspaper of the National Women's Alliance in the 1890s. This organization promoted the "'natural unity' of temperance, suffrage, labor and agrarian radicalism." I have not found any direct connection between this newspaper and the magazine, except their location in Minnesota. Mari Jo Buhle, *Women and American Socialism, 1870–1920* (Urbana: University of Illinois Press, 1983), 87–89.

24. *Farmer's Wife: A Woman's Farm Journal* (St. Paul: Webb Publishing). Examples of these trends can be found in these issues: 16 (May 1911): 8–10; 16 (Aug. 1911): 78–83; 16 (Dec. 1911): 195–96, 207; 16 (Feb. 1914): letters; 18 (Jan. 1916): 189; 18 (Mar. 1916): 252; 19 (July 1916); 19 (Sept. 1916): 74; 20 (July 1917): 36–38; 22 (Feb. 1920): 255; 22 (Apr. 1920): 353; 22 (May 1920): 395; 23 (Nov. 1920): 183; 33 (June 1921): 467, 472; 33 (Oct. 1921): editorial; 33 (Feb. 1922): editorial; 25 (Oct. 1922): 133, 160; 26 (Nov. 1923): editorial. See Theodore Peterson, *Magazines in the Twentieth Century* (Urbana: University of Illinois Press, 1964), 168; Frank Luther Mott, *A History of American Magazines, 1885–1905* (Cambridge: Harvard University Press, 1957), 4:341; and copies of the *Farm Journal* and the *Farmer's Wife,* 1939 to 1945. The following discussion comes from an examination of the *Farmer's Wife,* the publications and reports of home economics professionals, and the records of extension service–affiliated Homemakers' Clubs.

25. Nellie Kedzie Jones, "Pioneering in Home Economics," *K-Stater* (Oct. 1954): 6–7; "New Home on the Old Farm," 11, 29, 31; "Things to Omit to Save Labor and Strength," 9 Nov. 1912, Nellie Kedzie Jones Papers. See also Kirkpatrick, Tough, and Cowles, "Life Cycle of the Farm Family," 14–15, and Edith

Brown Kirkwood, "Sylvia Comes Home," installments in *Farmer's Wife*, 20 (May 1917) to 20 (Aug. 1917).

26. Crow, *American Country Girl*, 125–26; Jones, "Things to Omit." The combination of efficiency and technology can be traced back to the beginnings of home economics, though the types of labor-saving devices changed substantially between the 1890s and the 1920s. See "The Kansas Agricultural College," *American University Magazine* 2 (Oct. 1895): 497–508, Nellie Kedzie Jones Papers. See also Crow, *American Country Girl*, 103–12, 124, 147–50, 157–66, 235–47, and Kirkwood, "Sylvia Comes Home." Nellie Kedzie Jones paired her promotion of technology with practical tips that all farm women could afford. She claimed that "we are to blame if our work is never done," and, for example, told farm women not to clean every room of the house each week, but to alternate them. She also had a more critical view of laborsaving devices than many of her peers did. She suggested that farm women evaluate devices carefully because some did not save labor; rather, they increased cleaning time, demanded large quantities to justify their use, or often had a "high pressure process" that demanded extreme "nervous energy" to operate. See Jones, "New Home on the Old Farm," 2–3, 32; "To the Woman Who Doesn't Care," 26 Oct. 1912; and "The Labor of Labor Savers," 27 June 1914.

27. Marjorie Sawyer, "This New Freedom Stuff: Friend Husband Had to Come to It and Say Fervently, 'God Bless the Club,'" *Farmer's Wife* 33 (July–Aug. 1921): 499, 516; Nellie Kedzie Jones, "How Timidity Handicaps the Homemaker," 12 Oct. 1912, and "Become Your Husband's Business Partner," 11 Jan. 1913. See also "Rural Social Development," *Third Wisconsin Country Life Conference*, 14–17, 25–26; and Trudy Midgett to C. J. Galpin, 8 Dec. 1921, DFP&RL, General Correspondence, 1919–34.

28. Frances Pearle Mitchell, "The Missouri Women's Farmers' Club," *Farmer's Wife* 16 (May 1911): 11; Ann M. Evans, "Field Report on Western Trip, 1915," DFP&RL, Field Reports, box 4; I. W. Dickerson, "Women Operate Farm Machinery," *Farmer's Wife* 21 (June 1918): 8; Florence L. Clark, "Power Farming for Women," *Farmer's Wife* 23 (Aug. 1920): 86. During both World War I and World War II, the USDA promoted women working in the fields; see photographs in Historical File, Negs. N-4028, AAA-8956, AAA-8910, Record Group 16-G, NASPB; and DFP&RL, Farm Management Investigations, 1896–1922, Neg. 13612, Record Group 83-F, NASPB. Other articles from the *Farmer's Wife* on demanding access to new technology and on women as independent farmers include "How Some Women Succeed (Mrs. Matthew Scott)," *Farmer's Wife* 16 (July 1911): 51; Bernice H. Irwin, "In the Dairy," *Farmer's Wife* 21 (Aug. 1918): 63; Alice Wilson, "We Three Women Kept the Farm," *Farmer's Wife* 25 (Oct. 1922): 444, 461–62; "How Some Women Succeed (Alice Peck and Anna Fisher)," *Farmer's Wife* 26 (Mar. 1924): 396–97; "How Some Women Succeed (Mrs. Charles Kruger)," *Farmer's Wife* 27 (Aug. 1924): 64–65; and Ruth E. Morrison, "Westward Ho! Farmerettes," *Farmer's Wife* 21 (Feb. 1919): 198–99. See also Nellie Kedzie Jones, "Shall the Spinster on the Farm Be Independent?" 15 Aug. 1914, Nellie Kedzie Jones Papers; Crow, *American Country Girl*, 109–20; and Adda F. Howie Papers, 1904–36, Wis

MSS QL, State Historical Society of Wisconsin. Howie's position in agriculture and agricultural colleges was defended as being within traditional women's roles; see, for example, Walt Mason, "She Bosses Wisconsin Farmers," and Larry F. Graber, "America's Outstanding Woman Farmer," Howie Papers. Novels also promoted women as agricultural operators and managers, but for many different reasons. In Dell Munger's *Wind before the Dawn*, the wife has an incompetent, abusive husband who goes deeply into debt, and Munger asserts women's need for more control in farm decisions to prevent such situations. In G. D. Eaton's *Backfurrow*, the wife takes over the farm after her husband's plans for expansion fail. In this case, the husband was suited for "higher pursuits" of an academic and intellectual nature, while the wife had a "greater attachment to the soil" and was "basically a peasant in mind and nature," and had a "primitive patience." His thoughts on marketing "were probably much more intelligent" than hers, but she was more "given to the problem." In Willa Cather's *O Pioneers!* Alexandra takes over the operation of the family farm because of her vision and management skills, while her brothers do the field work. In Mae Foster Jay, *The Orchard Fence* (Boston: W. A. Wilde, 1935), the farmer's daughter attends agricultural college and brings scientific, mechanized farming methods to the home farm, managing to make profits despite the serious agricultural depression. In both fictional and true stories of farm women as independent farmers, their status can be single, widowed, or married to a man who does not farm. If they are married to a farmer, they are partners rather than managers, even if they keep the financial records, because men control decisions about field management.

29. Mary Meek Atkinson, "My Ideas on the 'Tired Farm Woman,'" *Farmer's Wife* 25 (Oct. 1922).

30. For example, see "How Some Women Succeed," *Farmer's Wife* 26 (Mar. 1924): 396–97. The series continued throughout the year, and while women who fit all three models appeared, most of the women performed physical labor on the farms, produced income, and did domestic chores at some time in their lives and in the history of their farms.

31. "Dignifying the Work of Farm Women," *Farmer's Wife* 23 (Jan. 1921); *Farmer's Wife* 19 (Dec. 1917): 94; "Our Big Business: We Farm Women with Expert Help Can Control the Poultry Industry," *Farmer's Wife* 19 (Jan. 1917); Grace Viall Gray, "Mother and Daughter, Partners: Together They Earn Money without Leaving the Farm Home," *Farmer's Wife* 19 (June 1916): 3; "Why Farmers' Wives Should Keep Poultry," *Farmer's Wife* 15 (Feb. 1913): 272; Nellie Kedzie Jones, "Is the Wife a Partner." One of the earliest projects of women professionals in the DFP&RL was to coordinate rural and urban women's clubs to organize markets for poultry and eggs, and thus increase the income of farm women. They encountered both success and failure, some of the latter caused by misunderstandings between producers and consumers. See the field reports of Anne M. Evans on her efforts in Illinois and Missouri, 1917, DFP&RL, Field Reports, box 4. There are few records of these kinds of projects in the 1920s, and even in the 1910s supervisors sometimes criticized women workers for organizing too much rather than simply studying problems in an academic way. Home economics extension programs

and bulletins were dominated by domestic topics, such as sewing and cooking, but income-earning jobs, such as poultry raising and cheese making, also appeared. Programs concerning field work or agricultural problems in general were rare, though some did exist, particularly in the 1930s with the introduction of new policies and agencies. See the annual reports of county agents, Extension Program Annual Reports, Williams County, 1916–39, and Traill County, 1928–40, NDSU; Iowa State College of Agriculture, Agricultural Extension Department, *Home Economics Bulletins* nos. 1–115 (1915–28); and Iowa Master Farm Homemakers Guild, Special Collections, MS-60, box 3, Iowa State University.

32. Letter from Mrs. E.L.D., *Farmer's Wife* 17 (Feb. 1915): 262; "The First International Farm Women's Congress," *Farmer's Wife* 16 (Dec. 1911): 195–96. See also Miss Edna White, comment at Conference on Farm Life Studies, May 1919, DFP&RL, General Correspondence, box 15. A summary of negative responses to the question "Would you like your daughter to marry a farmer?" pointed most often to poor economic conditions and the inability to earn an income from farming. Reasons included debt, substandard homes, poor markets, high taxes, overproduction, the "sins of the commission man," financial uncertainty, problems of tenants, weather conditions, and women's own lack of money. Other complaints included poor churches and schools, the drudgery and monotony of rural life, poor health care, childbirth problems, and lack of doctors. The summarizer seemed not to accept these reasons. Women should work to change their communities, the summarizer said, and economic conditions "hit all farmers" and all businesses; therefore, poverty was the result of cruelty, laziness, and ignorance, and did not show that agriculture was any worse than other businesses. Hoag, "Advantages of Farm Life," and *Farmer's Wife* 25 (Oct. 1922): 133, 160.

33. Not all agents ignored the problems of poorer farm people. Annual reports submitted by the North Dakota home extension agent in Williams County showed flexibility; the agent introduced programs to help farm women, such as clothing exchanges, a "food on a limited budget" project, and lessons in how to make soap and polishes and repair furniture. The agent in Marathon County, Wisconsin, also promoted basic advances such as screens as well as electric appliances. Although the agent at first was frustrated with results that "were not too good," she also found that women want to improve their homes "when their income increases and they are able to carry their plans through." See Assistant Extension Agent Annual Reports, Williams County, 1929–39, NDSU, and Home Demonstration Agent Reports, Marathon County, 1921 and 1946, 22, University of Wisconsin College of Agriculture, Home Economics Extension, Steenbock Library Archives, University of Wisconsin. See also Joan M. Jensen, "Canning Comes to New Mexico: Women and the Agricultural Extension Service, 1914–1919," *New Mexico Historical Review* 57, no. 4 (1982): 361–86, and Kathleen C. Hilton, "And Now She's Plowing with the Mule: Race and Gender in U.S.D.A. Policy, 1907–1929," in *Southern Women: Hidden Histories*, ed. Betty Brandon, Elizabeth Turner, Virginia Bernhard, Elizabeth Fox-Genovese, and Theda Purdue (Columbia: University of Missouri Press, 1994).

34. For the "work side," see Hoag, "Advantages of Farm Life," 5, 8, 10–12,

15–17, 54–55, 37, 42–43; for the "social side," see 95 and the appendix containing a summary of data and the backgrounds of respondents.

35. Lehmann and Kingsley, "Electric Power for the Farm"; Baumann, tape 3, side 1, WAOHP; Segerstrom, tape 1, side 1, WAOHP; Long, tape 4, side 1, WAOHP; Anderson, NDOHP.

36. Lehmann and Kingsley, "Electric Power for the Farm," 400; Cather, *One of Ours*, 18; Long, tape 1, side 2, WAOHP; Burke, Oct. 1908, Nov.–Dec 1919, Jan. 1920. Jean Long believed that electricity did not lighten the workload but made it possible for women to finish their work more quickly, which freed them for Farmers' Union meetings in the evenings. Another description of the difficulties of washing separators is found in Scott, RWOHP, tapes 28 and 29. However, even new washing machines were not unanimously welcomed. North Dakotan Anna Dannewitz had a washing machine with a motor on it, but because there was no place for it in her home, she had to wash outside even in cold weather. Before that she had used a tumbler-type washer, but "for saving time," she did "pretty well washing on a board." For her, the new technology created as many inconveniences as it eliminated, and old technology was the labor saver. See Dannewitz, NDOHP; Olson, NDOHP; Fosberg, NDOHP; Long, tape 1, side 2, WAOHP; Baumann, tape 3, side 1, WAOHP; and Hoag, "Advantages of Farm Life," 36. In Anna Burke's diaries the switch from machine washing to hand washing was significant enough to be mentioned. Burke Papers, 27 Oct. 1932, Feb. 1933.

37. Dannewitz, NDOHP; Smith and Olstad, NDOHP; Gullickson, NDOHP; Doty and Smith, NDOHP; Erickson Diaries, 29 July 1919, 26 July 1921, 12 June 1929, 25 Aug. 1931, 25 July 1934, 14 Feb. 1935, 19 Aug. 1936. Washboards are prominent only in photographs of poorer homes, but canning is pictured in both poor and higher-income homes. Sometimes poorer families relied more on other ways of preserving, such as cellars, than did wealthier ones. Photographs of washing: FSA Photographs, Negs. LCUSF33–11274-M3, LCUSF33–11532-M2, LCUSF33–11533-M5, LCUSF34–3055-E, LCUSF34–3097-D, LCUSF34–4405-E; Extension Photographs, Negs. 33SC1241C, 33SC1267C; Iowa State Historical Society Collections, folders on Houses and Households-Domestic Chores, Cooper Collection (1910); Mary Howell and Lillie Coon (1910); and Gabelmann Diaries. Photographs of preserving, canning, or shopping for food: FSA Photographs, Negs. LCUSF33–11466-M6, LCUSF34–4354-D, LCUSF34–6221-D, LCUSF34–7522–2D, LCUSF34–29145-D, LCUSF34–31144-D, LCUSF34–31204-D, LCUSF34–61518-D, LCUSF34–61696-D; Extension Photographs, Neg. 33SC-22893C; Historical File, Neg. AAA8565.

38. Powers Diaries, 21, 29 Apr., Sept.–Oct. 1922, 21 Sept. 1927, 4 July, 31 Oct. 1932, 1 Jan., 19 Apr., 19–20 July, 27 Sept. 1937, and Erickson Diaries, 26 June–July 1919, July–Aug. 1928, July–Aug. 1929, May–Oct. 1930, June–Oct. 1932, May–Oct. 1933, May–Oct. 1934, May–Oct. 1935. Other examples of women doing field work with new technology or using milking machines for dairy work include Long, tape 1, side 2, tape 4, sides 1 and 2, WAOHP; Chambers, tape 26, side 2, parts 1 and 2, RWOHP; Scott, tape 28, sides 1 and 2, RWOHP; Craft, NDOHP; Bogh, tr. 8–9, ICFOHP; and Gabelmann Diaries, July–Aug., 27 Sept., 7, 31 Oct.,

4–11 Nov. 1912, 11 July 1913, 12–26 July, 7–10 Sept. 1916, Aug.–Oct. 1933, July 1934, Oct. 1937. See also Nancy Hendrickson Photographs, Collection 25 B17, North Dakota State Historical Society. The importance of women's work to farm survival was particularly clear in the 1930s, and some studies noted women's increased work in the fields. See RPR, Grant County, N.D., v–vi, and Rural Relief Reports, Hutchinson, S.D., 14–15, DFP&RL.

39. Some men and women left farms to find additional work, leaving the other family members with more tasks to perform around the farm. The role of off-farm work in earlier periods deserves more attention. Off-farm work was important for farm survival during the frontier period and the Great Depression; in particular regions, such as the cutover areas of Wisconsin and Minnesota; and for poorer farmers. Children's off-farm work also played an important part in the family farm labor system. However, it seems that off-farm work for married farm women was rare before World War II.

CHAPTER 9   How You Gonna Keep 'Em Down on the Farm?

1. Thompson, *American Daughter* (1946; reprint, St. Paul: Minnesota Historical Society Press, 1986), 147–48.

2. Descriptions of recreation can be found in Burke Papers, Jan.–Dec. 1918; Siebert Papers, 16 May–4 July 1937; Notes on photographs 44215–44219, Shelby County, Iowa, Division of Economic Information, Prints and Photographs, 1939–42, Community Studies, box 33, Record Group 83-G, NASPB; Kolb and Marshall, "Neighborhood-Community Relationships," 15, 22–28; Hoyt, "Value of Family Living," 230–32; Randall C. Hill, E. L. Morgan, Mabel V. Campbell, and O. R. Johnson, "Social, Economic, and Homemaking Factors in Farm Living," *Missouri Agricultural Experiment Station Research Bulletin* no. 148 (July 1930): 13–16; E. L. Morgan and Henry J. Burt, "Community Relations of Rural Young People," *Missouri Agricultural Experiment Station Research Bulletin* no. 110 (Oct. 1927): 16–26; Rankin, "Nebraska Farm Tenancy," 32–40; J. O. Rankin, "The Use of Time in Farm Homes," *Nebraska Agricultural Experiment Station Bulletin* no. 230 (Dec. 1928): 8–11, 39; Donald Hay, James Greenlaw, and Lawrence Boyle, "Problems of Rural Youth in Selected Areas of North Dakota," *North Dakota Agricultural Experiment Station Bulletin* no. 293 (June 1940): 59–61; E. L. Kirkpatrick, J. H. Kolb, Creagh Inge, and A. F. Wileden, "Rural Organizations and the Farm Family," *Wisconsin Agricultural Experiment Station Research Bulletin* no. 96 (Nov. 1929): 24–25; Kolb and Polson, "Trends in Town-Country Relations," 24–26; Hoag, "Advantages of Farm Life," tables 4 and 10; Ruth Millicent Wood, "The Psychological Basis of a Nationwide Program for Rural Outdoor Recreation" (Master's thesis, Boston University, 1925), Thesis and Letter File, DFP&RL, Manuscripts, box 6; and "Attitudes and Problems of Farm Youth," 14–19, DFP&RL, Manuscripts, box 1. Good descriptions of rural recreation can also be found in the following interviews: Leonard and Carrie Stanford, tr. 14–15, OH4–48, ICFOHP; Tiefeatheler, tr. 14, ICFOHP; Rensick, tr. 6, ICFOHP; Goodwin, tr. 19–29, ICFOHP; McVey, tr. 14–15, ICFOHP; Bilsland, tr. 10–11, ICFOHP;

Bogh, tr. 11–17, ICFOHP; Tomter, tape 1, side 1, tape 2, side 1, WAOHP; Baumann, tape 1, side 1, tape 2, side 2, WAOHP; Hardiman, tape 4, side 1, WAOHP; Kunkel, NDOHP; Anderson, NDOHP; Faul, NDOHP; Vaage, NDOHP; Doty and Smith, NDOHP; Jacobs, NDOHP; and Dannewitz, NDOHP. See also Anson W. Buttles Diaries and Papers, 1856–1906, Wis MSS IR, State Historical Society of Wisconsin, 16–30 Nov. 1899; Still Papers, 5–30 Oct., 27 Nov. 1914; Gabelmann Diaries, 2 Sept.–8 Oct. 1918; Bertha Gabelmann photographs, Photograph Collection, Iowa State Historical Society; Powers Diaries, 9 Apr. 1922; Krueger family photographs, "Six Generations Here: A Family Remembers," exhibit, State Historical Society of Wisconsin Museum; and FSA Photographs, Midwest and Northwest Regions, Recreation and Social Life Files.

3. Moore, "Memories of the Early Days"; Michael L. Berger, *The Devil Wagon in God's Country: The Automobile and Social Change in Rural America, 1893–1929* (Hamden, Conn.: Archon Books, 1979), 44–45, 147–73, 205–13. See also Von Tungeln and Eills, "Rural Social Survey," 243–45. Other descriptions of first cars are found in Baumann, tape 2, side 1, WAOHP; Wileden, tape 3, side 1, WAOHP; Vekkund, NDOHP; Berg, NDOHP; Jacobs, NDOHP; and Faul, NDOHP. On the lack of economic and social status associated with the "farm car," the Model T, see Croy, *RFD #3*, 112.

4. Farm people were more likely to travel to area towns than to larger urban centers. See Baumann, tape 2, side 2, WAOHP, and Ellefson, tape 1, side 2, tape 3, side 1, WAOHP. Trips to regional cities are frequently described in novels. For example, see Garland, *Rose of Dutcher's Coolly*, 9, 154–73; Lynn, *Stepdaughter of the Prairie*, 63–79; and Croy, *RFD #3*, 53–54, 231–59. In a 1920s study of farm and village youth, more than 57% of farm boys and 60% of farm girls reported trips to towns or cities for business or pleasure fewer than 80 times per year; 33–35% recorded fewer than 40 visits; 23% of farm boys and 19% of farm girls reported more than 160 trips, and 45% of farm girls reported 120–59 trips. See "Attitudes and Problems of Farm Youth," 17.

5. Erickson Diaries, 14 Jan. 1905, 9–13 July 1913, 5, 23 Jan. 1915, 25, 29 Jan., 14 Apr. 1918, 10 May 1919, 15 Sept. 1921, 24 Jan., 24 Apr., 4, 28 May, 3 June, 29 Aug., 11–21 Oct. 1922, 11–13 Feb. 1927, 1 June 1928, 9 Jan., 5–20 May, 2–13 June 1929. Other diaries show the same patterns of visiting and social networks before and after the acquisition of automobiles. Family changes, such as death and marriage, seemed to lead to more alterations in visiting patterns than cars did. Car sharing is also described by Long, tape 4, side 2, WAOHP.

6. Erickson Diaries, 4–31 Aug. 1924, 28 Sept.–12 Nov. 1934, 2 Sept.–3 Oct. 1938. Erickson's delivery in 1924 was premature, so it is unclear if the home birth was by choice or necessity.

7. Erickson Diaries, 8 Sept. 1903–22 Mar. 1904, 1 June 1920–15 Mar. 1922, 29 Aug.–31 Dec. 1926, 13–27 Feb. 1927, 28 Nov. 1928–31 Dec. 1929, 27 Aug.–2 Sept. 1930, 29 May–1 June, 4 July–20 Sept. 1931, 8 Aug.–17 Sept. 1934.

8. Statistics on net farm returns can be found in the USDA *Yearbook of Agriculture* for the years 1925 (1342–43), 1926 (1228–29), 1927 (1133–34), 1930 (972–

73), and 1932 (894–95). For estimates of urban incomes in the 1920s, see Stricker, "Affluence for Whom?" 5–33.

9. Carl Zimmerman and John Black, "How Minnesota Farm Family Incomes Are Spent: A One Year's Study, 1924–1925," *Minnesota Agricultural Experiment Station Bulletin* no. 234 (June 1927): 26–27; Von Tungeln, Thaden, and Kirkpatrick, "Cost of Living on Iowa Farms," 29–30, 50; Thaden, "Standard of Living on Iowa Farms," 89, 122–26, 129, 131–34; Kirkpatrick, Tough, and Cowles, "How Farm Families Meet the Emergency," 15–30, 39. See also Hoyt, "Value of Family Living," 221–22; E. A. Willson, "Incomes and Cost of Living of Farm Families in North Dakota, 1923–1931," *North Dakota Agricultural Experiment Station Bulletin* no. 271 (June 1933): 18–25; Rankin, "Use of Time in Farm Homes," 8–11, 39–40; Kirkpatrick, "Farmers' Standard of Living," 46–52; Carl Zimmerman and John Black, "Factors Affecting Expenditures of Farm Family Incomes in Minnesota: Analysis of 1926 Survey," *Minnesota Agricultural Experiment Station Bulletin* no. 246 (July 1928): 1–29, and Kirkpatrick, Kolb, Inge, and Wileden, "Rural Organizations and the Farm Family," 20–25.

10. Croy, *RFD #3*, 119; Cather, *One of Ours*, 10. See also "The Neglected Crop or the Farmers' Spare Time," 16 Nov. 1927, USDA Radio Service Office of Information radio drama, DFP&RL, General Correspondence, Press Releases, box 17.

11. Rankin, "Nebraska Farm Tenancy," 41. See also Kolb, "Trends of Country Neighborhoods," 55–56; C. J. Galpin, "The Farmer's Recreation Problem," 22 Jan. 1926, 1–3, DFP&RL, General Correspondence, 1919–36, box 4; C. C. Taylor, speech to Farm and Home Program, University of Wisconsin, 6 Feb. 1931, 1–4, DFP&RL, General Correspondence, 1919–36, box 7; Wood, "Rural Outdoor Recreation"; Craig S. Thaws to Ruth Wood, 13 Jan. 1925, Thesis and Letter File, DFP&RL, Manuscripts, box 6; Kolb and Marshall, "Neighborhood-Community Relationships," 23, 26–27; and W. F. Kumlien, "What Farmers Think of Farming," *South Dakota Agricultural Experiment Station Bulletin* no. 223 (Apr. 1927): 14.

12. Lindstrom and Dawson, "Selectivity of 4-H Club Work," 260–63; Morgan and Burt, "Community Relations of Rural Young People," 15–16.

13. E. L. Morgan and Melvin W. Sneed, "The Activities of Rural Young People in Missouri," *University of Missouri Agricultural Experiment Station Research Bulletin* no. 269 (Nov. 1937): 14–24, 47–53.

14. Morgan and Burt, "Community Relations of Rural Young People," 22–36; Morgan and Sneed, "Activities of Rural Young People," 44–60.

15. Morgan and Sneed, "Activities of Rural Young People," 13, 44, 54, 58. See also Bruce L. Melvin and Elna Smith, *Rural Youth: Their Situation and Prospects, Works Progress Administration Research Monograph* 15 (1938; New York: De Capo Press, 1971), 78–79. Automobiles were in general considered a masculine form of technology, although women's access to them increased after World War I, even in rural areas. The Missouri study indicates that farm girls may have had even less access than their counterparts in rural towns (41% of whom drove cars and 31% of whom wanted to learn), while farm boys had slightly more access to cars than town boys did (68% of whom drove and 7% of whom wanted to learn). Older married women probably had even less access. For example, Anna Erickson

did not learn to drive a car when she was married to Joe, but her daughters did. She only learned when she was no longer married. Photographs of groups and families posed beside cars almost always show men or boys at the wheel. See, for example, Mary Jane Chapman Fawcett Photograph Collection, 1900–1920, PA 145, Iowa State Historical Society, and the subject binders of the photographic collection of the North Dakota Historical Society. See also Gittens, "Morton to Stevens to Gittens," 38–39. One of the Gittens family's favorite stories was about the author's mother, Beatrice, who wanted to drive. The father, Tom, decided to let her do it one day. She did well until entering the garage. Then she did not know how to put on the brakes; she only took her foot off the accelerator. Mineral sacks kept her from going through the garage. This became one of the father's favorite "funny" stories until he told it to a car salesman after Beatrice had said that if they ever bought a new car she was going to be taught to drive. The salesman did not laugh; he said "Tom, I don't think that's funny. When you bought that car, someone spent a lot of time teaching you to drive." The story was rarely mentioned again. Men usually bought and controlled cars, and women often had to insist on learning to drive and risked being ridiculed or teased if they were slow learners. However, male control of transportation was often recorded even in horse-and-buggy days, when men would use horses in the field or were responsible for harnessing. A 1912 novel by Dell H. Munger, which criticized the subordination of women in farm families, showed how male control of transportation and strictures about appropriate female behavior restricted the heroine's mobility. See *Wind before the Dawn*. In the Missouri study, 80% of farm boys drove horses, while only 69% of farm girls did so.

16. Morgan and Burt, "Community Relations of Rural Young People," 22–36; Morgan and Sneed, "Activities of Rural Young People," 44–60.

17. Chambers, tape 26, side 2, parts 1 and 2, RWOHP. Examples of visiting and radios are found in Powers Diaries, 18 Jan. 1932; Moore, "Memories of the Early Days"; Ted R. Rask interview, NDDI; Craig S. Thaws to Ruth Wood, 13 Jan. 1925; and McVey, tr. 14–15, ICFOHP.

18. United States Bureau of the Census, *United States Census of Agriculture, 1945*, vol. 2, *General Reports: Statistics by Subject*, 317–21, 328, 330; Morgan and Burt, "Community Relations of Rural Young People," 22–31; Morgan and Sneed, "Activities of Rural Young People," 44–60. See also Hay, "Social Organizations and Agencies," 7–8; Rankin, "Use of Time in Farm Homes," 22–25, 39–40; Hoyt, "Value of Family Living," 221, 230–31; Kumlien, "What Farmers Think of Farming," 12; "What's New in Farm Sciences," *Wisconsin Agricultural Experiment Station Annual Report Bulletin* no. 405 (Feb. 1929): 19–20; Kirkpatrick, Kolb, Inge, and Wileden, "Rural Organizations and the Farm Family," 21–25; Kolb and Polson, "Trends in Town-Country Relations," 27–28; Kirkpatrick, Tough, and Cowles, "How Farm Families Meet the Emergency," 15–17; Powers Diaries, 3 Feb., 18 Mar. 1932; and Siebert Papers, 3–25 Jan. 1936.

19. Olson Diaries, 18 Dec. 1932, 2 Nov. 1935. See also Burke Papers, 10 Nov. 1926; Erickson Diaries, 29 Jan. 1933, 16 Nov. 1938; Hill, Morgan, Campbell, and Johnson, "Social, Economic, and Homemaking Factors," 13–15; Kirkpatrick,

Kolb, Inge, and Wileden, "Rural Organizations and the Farm Family," 21–25; Custer County, S.D., 20, and Meade County, S.D., 22, Relief Studies, DFP&RL, box 8; and Powers Diaries, 30 Oct. 1932.

20. Smith and Olstad, NDOHP; Howard Murray Jones Papers, June 1938; Moore, "Memories of the Early Days"; Olson Diaries, 2, 11 Nov. 1935, 4 Mar. 1933, 6 Oct. 1936, 20 Jan. 1937; Goodwin, tr. 28, ICFOHP; Morgan and Sneed, "Activities of Rural Young People," 54–56. See also Siebert Papers, 17–30 Feb. 1936, 25 Jan. 1937; Brusveen, tape 5, side 2, tape 6, side 1, WAOHP; McVey, tr. 14–15, ICFOHP; Vekkund, NDOHP; Edna Rohwer, tr. 12, OH4–32, ICFOHP; Powers Diaries, 20 Jan. 1932; and Faul, NDOHP.

21. Morgan and Burt, "Community Relations of Rural Young People," 22–25; Morgan and Sneed, "Activities of Rural Young People," 44–46; "What's New in Farm Sciences," 19–20. The earliest date that movies appear in the diaries is 1908. Oral histories and diaries generally mention the first movies sometime between 1915 and 1925. The decline in attendance at movies in the 1930s is found in several studies of standards of living. See Kirkpatrick, Tough, and Cowles, "How Farm Families Meet the Emergency," 29–30, 39; Rankin, "Use of Time in Farm Homes," 8–11, 39; Rankin, "Nebraska Farm Tenancy," 32–40; Zimmerman and Black, "Minnesota Farm Family Incomes," 26–27; Hoyt, "Value of Family Living," 221; "Science Safeguards: Crops, Livestock, and Farm Income," *Wisconsin Agricultural Experiment Station Annual Report Bulletin* no. 430 (June 1935): 155–56; Kirkpatrick, Kolb, Inge, and Wileden, "Rural Organizations and the Farm Family," 24–26; and Kirkpatrick, Tough, and Cowles, "Life Cycle of the Farm Family," 26–28.

22. Morgan and Burt, "Community Relations of Rural Young People," 22–25; Morgan and Sneed, "Activities of Rural Young People," 44–46; "Type of Foxfire History." See also McManigal, *Farm Town,* 75; Chambers, tape 27, side 1, RWOHP; Tomter, tape 1, side 1, WAOHP; Burke Papers, 22 Apr. 1908, 14 Feb. 1911, 9 Apr. 1914, 6 Nov. 1915, 17 July, 23 Oct. 1926, 25 Sept. 1933, 18 Feb. 1934; Powers Diaries, 11 Sept. 1927, 16 Feb. 1932, Driving Record 1922–23; Erickson Diaries, 21–28 May 1924, 8 Aug. 1926, 25 Apr. 1937, 4–16 Mar. 1938; and Siebert Papers, 8–9 May 1937.

23. Woods, "Rural Outdoor Recreation," 29–30; Morgan and Burt, "Community Relations of Rural Young People," 22–31. The acceptance of commercial forms of recreation as a measure of the quality of rural life is implicit in the studies of standards of living, and the belief that the absence of recreation led to the rural-to-urban migration of the 1920s is often explicit, particularly in the studies of rural youth and rural population. The ambivalence toward commercial recreation and its acceptance as a measure of the quality of life also exists in studies of urban living standards.

24. Morgan and Sneed, "Activities of Rural Young People," 54–56.

25. Vaage, NDOHP; Smith and Olstad, NDOHP; Goodwin, tr. 19, ICFOHP; McVey, tr. 10–11, ICFOHP. Other descriptions of traditional house and barn dances can be found in Rensick, tr. 9–10, ICFOHP; Larson, NDOHP; Doty and Smith, NDOHP; Jacobs, NDOHP; Fred Donahue interview, NDDI; Baumann,

tape 2, side 2, WAOHP; and Eleanor Gates, *Biography of a Prairie Girl* (New York: Century, 1902), 118–23.

26. Baumann, tape 2, side 2, WAOHP; Community Studies, Shelby County, Iowa, photo caption 44223, NASPB. See also McVey, tr. 10–14, ICFOHP; Cvancara, NDOHP; Hardiman, tape 4, side 1, tape 13, side 2, WAOHP; Cather, *My Antonia,* 194–205, 221–30; Garland, *Son of the Middle Border,* 169–70; Craig S. Thaws to Ruth Wood, 13 Jan. 1925; and Kirkpatrick, Tough, and Cowles, "Life Cycle of the Farm Family," 26–27. Diaries also present a mix of town and home dances. See Still Papers, Jan. 1911; Burke Papers, 12–18 Jan. 1912; Siebert Papers, 1–20 May, 14–15 Sept. 1937; Erickson Diaries, 29 Apr. 1921, 20 Nov. 1925, 11 July, 29 Aug., 8, 29 Sept., 5 Nov. 1926, 23 Feb., 29 May, 5 June, 17 July, 22 Aug. 1927, 9–11 Dec. 1928, 26 May 1929, 7 Aug. 1932, 31 Dec. 1934, 11 June 1935. The trend in Erickson's diary was for town dances to replace home dances, although the location of many dances was not recorded. See also FSA Photographs, Midwest Region, Recreation, Music, and Social Life Files, Negs. LCUSF34–26876-D, LCUSF34–294671-D, LCUSF34–64586-D, and LCUSF34–64589.

27. Rensick, tr. 6, ICFOHP; Willson, "Rural Community Clubs in North Dakota," 46–54.

28. Hay, "Social Organizations and Agencies," 75; Kolb and Marshall, "Neighborhood-Community Relationships," 26–27; McVey, tr. 14, ICFOHP. See also E. G. Sanderson to C. J. Galpin, 2 Apr. 1921, DFP&RL, General Correspondence, box 17; Bilsland, tr. 10, ICFOHP; Smith and Olstad, NDOHP; Emma Brossart Jangleward, NDDI; Goodwin, tr. 19–20, ICFOHP; Hardiman, tape 13, side 2, WAOHP; Jacobs, NDOHP; Rohwer, tr. 11–16, ICFOHP; Faul, NDOHP; Anderson, NDOHP; and Wood, "Rural Outdoor Recreation," Letter File.

29. Cather, *My Antonia*, 194–230; Jacobs, NDOHP; Hardiman, tape 13, side 2, WAOHP; Rohwer, tr. 11–16, ICFOHP. However, interethnic contact was not limited to town or commercial dance halls. Christ Larson (NDOHP) remembered that all neighborhood groups, including Germans, Finns, Swedes, Norwegians, and Danes, attended Saturday night barn dances near Coulee, North Dakota. Other information on dance is drawn from "What's New in Farm Sciences," 19–20; "Science Safeguards," 155–56; Kirkpatrick, Kolb, Inge, and Wileden, "Rural Organizations and the Farm Family," 24–25; Hay, Greenlaw, and Boyle, "Problems of Rural Youth," 59–60; Morgan and Burt, "Community Relations of Rural Young People," 22–36; Morgan and Sneed, "Activities of Rural Young People," 44–60; and Willson, "Rural Community Clubs in North Dakota," 46–54.

30. Morgan and Burt, "Community Relations of Rural Young People," 22–36; Morgan and Sneed, "Activities of Rural Young People," 44–60.

31. Morgan and Burt, "Community Relations of Rural Young People," 4, 16, 22–36, 50–62; Morgan and Sneed, "Activities of Rural Young People," 14–24, 47–53; Hay, Greenlaw, and Boyle, "Problems of Rural Youth," 24–37. See also "Attitudes and Problems of Farm Youth," 14, 19, 29, 59, 62.

32. Erickson Diaries, 1921–39. Other diaries that show the use of the automobile for maintaining kin ties are found in the Frank Krueger Papers, Burke Papers, and Siebert Papers.

33. Erickson Diaries, 1931–39. For specific examples cited, see 30 Mar., 11 Nov. 1938, 14 Apr., 18 July, 3 Sept. 1939, and 29 Dec. 1940.

34. Morgan and Sneed, "Activities of Rural Young People," 14–24. The following analysis is drawn from Wakeley, "Differential Mobility"; Morgan and Sneed, "Activities of Rural Young People"; Hay, Greenlaw, and Boyle, "Problems of Rural Youth"; W. F. Kumlien, Robert McNamara, and Zetta Bankert, "Rural Population Mobility in South Dakota," *South Dakota Agricultural Experiment Station Bulletin* no. 359 (Apr. 1942); Kolb and James, "Wisconsin's Rural Youth"; and Rural Relief Studies, 1935–36, DFP&RL. These studies generally include a section about youth. See, for example, Jefferson, Saline, and Waubaunsee Counties, Kansas; Jackson, Harding, Custer, Hand, Grant, and Meade Counties, South Dakota; Hall County, Nebraska; and Franklin, Holt, Douglas, Pemiscott, Ray, Hickory, Johnson, Adair, and Newton Counties, Missouri.

35. Long, tape 5, side 1, WAOHP.

Conclusion

1. Josephine Johnson, *Now in November* (New York: Simon and Schuster, 1935), 4–5, 76–81, 96–102, 120–22, 156–59, 163–72, 218–23, 227–31.

2. Mrs. William Bankard to Eleanor Roosevelt, 21 Mar. 1939, FSA Letters. See also Mr. and Mrs. F. L. Albertson to FDR, 29 Oct. 1935, FSA Letters.

3. Mrs. Fred Adams to Mr. R. G. Tugwell, 17 Apr. 1936, FSA Letters; Craft, NDOHP. Other interesting descriptions of the Great Depression in Mountrail County are found in Jacobs, NDOHP; Larson, NDOHP; and Doty and Smith, NDOHP. See also Faul, NDOHP, and Kirkpatrick, Tough, and Cowles, "How Farm Families Meet the Emergency."

4. Walter Banks to FDR, n.d., FSA Letters. See also Mrs. Winifred Amsden to Secretary of Agriculture, 7 Sept. 1938, FSA Letters, and Mrs. Lou Allsup to FDR, 23 Mar. 1936, FSA Letters.

5. Craft, NDOHP; Doty and Smith, NDOHP; RPR, box 10, Burke County, N.D.; Long, tape 5, side 2, tape 6, side 1, WAOHP. Sometimes the most poverty-stricken did not participate in these organizations, though that depended on the region or state. One example of protest by those at the bottom of the agricultural ladder was when Missouri sharecroppers, evicted from their land, lived along U.S. Highway 61 to draw attention to their problems. See FSA Photographs; Louis Cantor, *A Prologue to the Protest Movement: The Missouri Sharecropper Roadside Demonstration of 1939* (Durham, N.C.: Duke University Press, 1969); Fannie Cook, *Boot-Heel Doctor* (New York: Dodd, Mead, 1941); and John Allen to Congress, 9 Jan. 1939, FSA Letters. Many farmers remained largely apolitical in orientation and tried to survive by using local resources and government programs; see Larson, NDOHP.

6. Contemporary farm women's roles in political activism and the strengths in both their approach to leadership and their integration of social and economic issues are discussed in Lorna Clancy Miller and Mary Neth, "Farm Women in the Political Arena," in Haney and Knowles, *Women and Farming*, 357–80.

Bibliographical Note

Since I began this project, there has been a boom in rural social history and the history of farm women. While this book is clearly a part of the scholarship that tells the long-range story of the development of capitalism in rural America, it is also indebted to the work of many other scholars, applying theoretical perspectives from rural sociology, incorporating gender analysis from many fields of feminist scholarship, exploring issues raised by scholars of the urban working class and mass culture, and building on studies of agricultrual science and technology, agricultural institutions and economics, and agrarian political movements.

Much of the social history of rural America has focused on the growth of capitalism in the eighteenth and nineteenth century or after World War II. Examples of work on the earlier period can be found in Steven Hahn and Jonathan Prude, eds., *The Countryside in the Age of Capitalist Transformation: Essays in the Social History of Rural America* (Chapel Hill: University of North Carolina Press, 1985), and a full discussion of this literature and its debates can be found in Alan Kulikoff, "The Transition to Capitalism in Rural America," *William and Mary Quarterly* (Jan. 1989): 120–44. Also significant is William Cronon, *Nature's Metropolis: Chicago and the Great West* (New York: W. W. Norton, 1991). Little of this work carefully examines the relationship between capitalism and patriarchal family gender relations. One exception is Christopher Clark, *The Roots of Rural Capitalism: Western Massachusetts, 1780–1860* (Ithaca: Cornell University Press, 1990).

Literature on the history of post-1945 agriculture includes Pete Daniel, *Breaking the Land: The Enclosure of Cotton, Tobacco, and Rice Cultures, 1880–1984* (Urbana: University of Illinois Press, 1985); Jack Temple Kirby, *Rural Worlds Lost: The American South, 1920–1960* (Baton Rouge: Louisiana State University Press, 1987); John L. Shover, *First Majority—Last Minority: The Transforming of Rural*

Life in America (DeKalb: Northern Illinois University Press, 1976); Mark Fried-berger, *Farm Families and Change in Twentieth-Century America* (Lexington: University Press of Kentucky, 1988); and Peggy F. Barlett, *American Dreams, Rural Realities: Family Farms in Crisis* (Chapel Hill: University of North Carolina Press, 1993). Again, gender analysis is rarely central to these works, but other scholars, including Deborah Fink, *Open Country, Iowa: Rural Women, Tradition, and Change* (Albany: State University of New York Press, 1986), and Rachel Ann Rosenfeld, *Farm Women: Work, Farm, and Family in the United States* (Chapel Hill: University of North Carolina Press, 1985), have shown how women were cru-cial in the transition to modern agribusiness.

Sociologists also are studying the relationship between capitalist agriculture and different methods of organizing agricultural labor, including family farm agri-culture. These include Max J. Pfeffer, "Social Origins of Three Systems of Farm Production in the United States," *Rural Sociology* 48 (1983): 540–62; S. A. Mann and J. M. Dickinson, "Obstacles to the Development of a Capitalist Agriculture," *Journal of Peasant Studies* 5 (1978): 466–81; Susan Mann and James Dickinson, "State and Agriculture in Two Eras of American Capitalism," in *The Rural Soci-ology of Advanced Societies,* ed. Frederick Buttell and Howard Newby (Mont-clair, N.J.: Allanheld, Osmun, 1980), 283–325; Patrick H. Mooney, "Toward a Class Analysis of Midwestern Agriculture," *Rural Sociology* 48 (1983): 563–84; Harriet Friedmann, "Household Production and the National Economy: Con-cepts for the Analysis of Agrarian Formations," *Journal of Peasant Studies* 7 (1980): 158–84; and Harriet Friedmann, "World Market, State, and Family Farm: Social Bases of Household Production in the Era of Wage Labor," *Comparative Studies in Society and History* 20 (1978): 545–86.

Other historical, sociological, and anthropological studies do not address the transition to capitalism as a central question, but provide greater depth in their analysis of families and communities. My examination of the cultural meaning of economic exchange is indebted to Marcel Mauss, *The Gift: Forms and Functions of Exchange in Archaic Societies* (New York: W. W. Norton, 1967); John W. Ben-nett, Seena Kohl, and Geraldine Binion, *Of Time and the Enterprise: North Amer-ican Family Farm Managment in a Context of Resource Marginality* (Minne-apolis: Univeristy of Minnesota Press, 1982), 9–20; and Carol Stack's study of resource sharing among poor, urban blacks, *All our Kin: Survial Strategies in a Black Community* (New York: Harper and Row, 1974). One must also acknowl-edge the pioneering community study of Merle Curti, *The Making of an Ameri-can Community: A Case Study of Democracy in a Frontier County* (Stanford, Calif.: Stanford University Press, 1959). Other studies of frontier and settled agri-cultural communities include John Mack Faragher, *Sugar Creek: Life on the Illi-nois Prairie* (New Haven: Yale University Press, 1986); Jan L. Flora and John Stitz, "Persistence and Capitalization of Agriculture in the Great Plains during the Set-tlement Period: Wheat Production and Risk Avoidance," *Rural Sociology* 50 (1985): 341–60; Hal S. Barron, *Those Who Stayed Behind: Rural Society in Nine-teenth-Century New England* (Cambridge: Cambridge University Press, 1984); and Jane Marie Pederson, *Between Memory and Reality: Family and Community in Rural Wisconsin, 1870–1970* (Madison: University of Wisconsin Press, 1992). Inheritance patterns also are being studied by social historians and sociologists, including Kathleen Neils Conzen, "Peasant Pioneers: Generational Succession among German Farmers in Frontier Minnesota," in Hahn and Prude, *Countryside*, 259–92; Mark Friedberger, "The Farm Family and the Inheritance Process: Evidence from the Corn Belt, 1870–1950," *Agriculatural History* 57 (Jan. 1983): 1–13; and Sonya Salamon, *Prairie Patrimony: Family, Farming, and Community in the Midwest* (Chapel Hill: University of North Carolina Press, 1992).

The history of farm women and the study of gender in rural settings is reshaping our knowledge of the transition to capitalism and the nature of rural communities and families. The best theoretical integration of class and gender questions and their implications for an analysis of rural transformations is by Latin-American historian Florencia E. Mallon, "Patriarchy and the Transition to Capitalism: Central Peru, 1830–1950," *Feminist Studies* 13 (Summer 1987): 400–403. Comparative sociology also offers methods of viewing agricultural policy with a gendered analysis: see Cornelia Butler Flora, "Public Policy and Women in Agricultural Production: A Comparative and Historical Analysis," and Kathleen Cloud, "Farm Women and the Structural Transformation of Agriculture: A Cross-Cultural Perspective," in *Women and Farming: Changing Roles, Changing Structures*, ed. Wava G. Haney and Jane B. Knowles (Boulder: Westview Press, 1988), 281–99. The need to make "private" issues of gender and family central to understanding "public" issues, such as economic change, was first proposed by Michelle Zimbalist Rosaldo, "The Use and Abuse of Anthropology: Reflections on Feminism and Cross-Cultural Understanding," *Signs* 5 (Spring 1980): 174–200. Its value was proven in Mary Ryan's pathbreaking study *Cradle of the Middle Class: The Family in Oneida County, New York, 1790–1865* (Cambridge: Cambridge University Press, 1981).

Joan Jensen, in her numerous articles, collected in *Promise to the Land: Essays on Rural Women* (Albuquerque: University of New Mexico Press, 1991), *With These Hands: Women Working on the Land* (Old Westbury, N.Y.: Feminist Press, 1981), and *Loosening the Bonds: Mid-Atlantic Farm Women 1750–1850* (New Haven: Yale University Press, 1986), has pioneered the history of farm women. The work of Nancy Grey Osterud has sharpened the theoretical tools for cutting across the barriers of public and private, combining economic and gender analysis in creative ways in such works as *Bonds of Community: The Lives of Farm Women in Nineteenth-Century New York* (Ithaca: Cornell University Press, 1991); "The Valuation of Women's Work: Gender and the Market in a Dairy Farming Community during the Late Nineteenth Century," *Frontiers* 10 (1988): 18–24; "Land, Identity, and Agency in the Oral Autobiographies of Farm Women," in Haney and Knowles, *Women and Farming*, 73–87; and "Gender and the Transition to Capitalism in Rural America," *Agricultural History* 67 (Spring 1993): 15–29.

Other important work on the history of farm women include Sarah Elbert, "The Farmer Takes a Wife: Women in America's Farming Families," in *Women, Households, and the Economy*, ed. Lourdes Beneria and Catharine Stimpson (New Brunswick, N.J.: Rutgers University Press, 1987), 173–97, "Women and

Farming: Changing Roles, Changing Structures," in Haney and Knowles, *Women and Farming*, 245–64, and "Amber Waves of Gain: Women's Work in New York Farm Families," in, *"To Toil the Livelong Day": American Women at Work, 1780–1980*, Carol Groneman and Mary Beth Norton (Ithaca: Cornell University Press, 1987), 250–68; Carolyn E. Sachs, *The Invisible Farmers: Women in Agricultural Production* (Totowa, N.J.: Rowan and Allanheld, 1983), 24–33, and "The Participation of Women and Girls in Market and Non-Market Activities on Pennsylvania Farms," in Haney and Knowles, *Women and Farming*, 123–34; Cornelia Butler Flora and John Stitz, "Female Subsistence Production and Commercial Farm Survival among Settlement Kansas Wheat Farmers," *Human Organization* 47 (Spring 1988): 64–69; Stephanie McCurry, "Defense of Their World: Gender, Class, and the Yeomanry of the South Carolina Low Country, 1820–1869" (Ph.D. diss., State University of New York at Binghamton, 1988); Joan E. Cashin, *A Family Venture: Men and Women on the Southern Frontier* (New York: Oxford University Press, 1991); LuAnn Jones, "'Mama Learned Us to Work': Farm Women in the Twentieth-Century South" (Paper presented at the Southern Historical Association Meeting, Lexington, Ky., Nov. 1989); Mary Neth, "Gender and the Family Labor System: Defining Work in the Rural Midwest," *Journal of Social History* 27 (Mar. 1994): 563–77; Seena B. Kohl, "The Making of a Community: The Role of Women in an Agricultural Setting," in *Kin and Communities: Families in America*, ed. Allan J. Lichtman and Joan R. Challinor (Washington, D.C.: Smithsonian Institution Press, 1979), 175–86, and Kohl, *Working Together: Women and Family in Southwestern Saskatchewan* (Toronto: Holt, Rinehart, and Winston, 1976); Deborah Fink, *Agrarian Women: Wives and Mothers in Rural Nebraska, 1880–1940* (Chapel Hill: University of North Carolina Press, 1992); Delores Janiewski, "Making Women into Farmers' Wives: The Native American Experience in the Inland Northwest," in Haney and Knowles, *Women and Farming*, 35–54; and Sarah Deutsch, *No Separate Refuge: Culture, Class, and Gender on an Anglo-Hispanic Frontier in the American West, 1880–1940* (New York: Oxford University Press, 1987).

Expanding on the work of E. P. Thompson and Herbert Gutman, labor historians have examined the meaning of work, community, and mass culture for working-class and middle-class Americans. Examples are Susan Porter Benson, *Country Cultures: Saleswomen, Managers, and Customers in American Department Stores, 1890–1940* (Urbana: University of Illinois Press, 1986); Jacquelyn Dowd Hall, James Leloudis, Robert Korstad, Mary Murphy, LuAnn Jones, and Christopher Daly, *Like a Family: The Making of a Southern Cotton Mill World* (Chapel Hill: University of North Carolina Press, 1987); Roy Rosenzweig, *Eight Hours for What We Will: Workers and Leisure in an Industrial City, 1870–1920* (Cambridge: Cambridge University Press, 1983); and Lizabeth Cohen, *Making a New Deal: Industrial Workers in Chicago, 1919–1939* (Cambridge: Cambridge University Press, 1990).

There has been little examination of mass culture and consumption in rural America in the twentieth century, in part because much social analysis has defined "progress" as the transition from a traditional rural culture to a modern urban one. An example is James H. Shideler, "Flappers, Philosophers, and Farmers: Rural-Urban Tensions of the Twenties," *Agricultural History* 47 (Oct. 1973): 283–99. Theoretical work that avoids such dichotomies in cultural analysis includes Thomas Bender, *Community and Social Change in America* (New Brunswick, N.J.: Rutgers University Press, 1978); T. J. Jackson Lears, "The Concept of Cultural Hegemony: Problems and Possibilities," *American Historical Review* 90 (June 1985): 567–93; and Clifford Geertz, *The Interpretation of Cultures* (New York: Basic Books, 1973). Some recent works that move beyond the rural/urban dichotomy in their studies of rural culture include Sally McMurry, *Families and Farmhouses in Nineteenth-Century America* (New York: Oxford University Press, 1988), and LuAnn Jones, "From Feed Bags to Fashion: Southern Farm Women and Material Culture" (Paper presented at the Southern Association of Women Historians Conference, Chapel Hill, N.C., June 1991).

Studies that provide important background on the technologies, consumer goods, and mass culture that altered rural America are Gordon L. Weil, *Sears, Roebuck, USA: The Great American Catalog Store and How It Grew* (New York: Stein and Day, 1977); Reynold M. Wik, *Henry Ford and Grass-Roots America* (Ann Arbor: University of Michigan Press, 1972); Michael L. Berger, *The Devil Wagon in God's Country: The Automobile and Social Change in Rural America, 1893–1929* (Hamden, Conn.: Archon Books, 1979); Virginia Scharff, *Taking the Wheel: Women and the Coming of the Motor Age* (New York: Free Press, 1991); Claude S. Fischer, "Technology's Retreat: The Decline of Rural Telephony in the United States, 1920–1940," *Social Science History* 11 (Fall 1987): 295–327; Lary May, *Screening Out the Past: The Birth of Mass Culture and the Motion Picture Industry* (Chicago: University of Chicago Press, 1980); and Daniel Horowitz, *The Morality of Spending: Attitudes toward the Consumer Society in America, 1875–1940* (Baltimore: Johns Hopkins University Press, 1985).

The development of advertising in this period is discussed in Daniel Pope, *The Making of Modern Advertising* (New York: Basic Books, 1983); Michael Schudson, *Advertising, the Uneasy Persuasion: Its Dubious Impact on American Society* (New York: Basic Books, 1984); Roland Marchand, *Advertising the American Dream: Making Way for Modernity, 1920–1940* (Berkeley and Los Angeles: University of California Press, 1985); and T. J. Jackson Lears, "From Salvation to Self-Realization: Advertising and the Therapeutic Roots of the Consumer Culture, 1880–1930," in *The Culture of Consumption: Critical Essays in American History, 1880–1980,* ed. T. J. Jackson Lears and Richard Fox (New York: Pantheon Books, 1983), 17–30. These works do not include advertising to rural markets. One exception is Susan Smulyan, "'A Latchkey to Every Home': Early Radio Advertising to Women," *American Quarterly* (forthcoming).

On the development of different youth cultures and their ties to mass culture, commercial recreation, and consumerism, see John Modell, *Into One's Own: From Youth to Adulthood in the United States, 1920–1975* (Berkeley and Los Angeles: University of California Press, 1989); Paula S. Fass, *The Damned and the Beautiful: American Youth in the 1920s* (New York: Oxford University Press, 1977); Kathy Peiss, *Cheap Amusements: Working Women and Leisure in Turn-of-the-Century*

New York (Philadelphia: Temple University Press, 1986); Beth L. Bailey, *From Front Porch to Back Seat: Courtship in Twentieth-Century America* (Baltimore: Johns Hopkins University Press, 1988); and Cohen, *Making a New Deal.*

Visual images found in photographs and art provide a rich resource for scholars of rural America. My use of family photographs was influenced by an exhibit presented by the State Historical Society of Wisconsin entitled "Six Generations Here: A Family Remembers"; Julia Hirsch, *Family Photographs: Context, Meaning, and Effect* (New York: Oxford University Press, 1981); and Steven Zeitlin, Amy J. Kotkin, and Holly Cutting Baker, *A Celebration of American Family Folklore: Tales and Traditions from the Smithsonian Collection* (New York: Pantheon Books, 1982). On the FSA photographs, see F. Jack Hurley, *Portrait of a Decade: Roy Stryker and the Development of Documentary Photography in the Thirties* (Baton Rouge: Louisiana State University Press, 1972); Karin Becker Ohrn, *Dorothea Lange and the Documentary Tradition* (Baton Rouge: Louisiana State University Press, 1980); and Edward Steichen, ed., *The Bitter Years, 1935–1941: Rural America as Seen by the Photographers of the Farm Security Administration* (New York: Museum of Modern Art, 1962). For analyses of the photographs of different agricultural agencies, see Pete Daniel, Mary A. Foresta, Maren Stange, and Sally Stein, *Official Images: New Deal Photography* (Washington: Smithsonian Institution Press, 1987). An excellent analysis of the images of farm men and women in WPA art is Barbara Melosh, *Engendering Culture: Manhood and Womanhood in New Deal Public Art and Theater* (Washington: Smithsonian Institution Press, 1991). A theoretical study of the use of photographs is John Berger, *About Looking* (New York: Pantheon Books, 1980).

Studies of the literary image of farmers include Henry Nash Smith, "Western Farmer in Imaginative Literature, 1818–1894," *Mississippi Valley Historical Review* 36 (Dec. 1949): 179–90; R. Richard Wohl, "The 'Country Boy' Myth and Its Place in American Urban Culture: The Nineteenth-Century Contribution," *Perspectives in American History* 3 (1969): 77–156; and Roy W. Meyer, *The Middle Western Farm Novel in the Twentieth Century* (Lincoln: University of Nebraska Press, 1965).

The Midwest as a region does not have the developed literature that the South and West do. Recent works on the Midwest include James H. Madison, ed., *Heartland: Comparative Histories of the Midwestern States* (Bloomington: Indiana University Press, 1988); Andrew R. L. Cayton and Peter S. Onuf, *The Midwest and the Nation: Rethinking the History of an American Region* (Bloomington: Indiana University Press, 1990); and Kenneth Walker, *A History of the Middle West: From the Beginning to 1970* (n.p., 1972).

Some of the works on nineteenth- and twentieth-century farm organizations are Scott McNall, *The Road to Rebellion: Class Formation and Kansas Populism, 1865–1900* (Chicago: University of Chicago Press, 1988); Mary Jo Wagner, "'Helping Papa and Mamma Sing the People's Songs': Children in the Populist Party," in Haney and Knowles, *Women and Farming*, 319–35; Dennis Nordin, *Rich Harvest: A History of the Grange, 1857–1900* (Jackson: University of Mississippi Press, 1974); Donald Marti, *Women of the Grange: Mutuality and Sisterhood in Rural*

America, 1866–1920 (New York: Greenwood Press, 1991); Robert L. Morlan, *Polticial Prairie Fire: The Nonpartisan League, 1915–1922* (1955; St. Paul: Minnesota Historical Society Press, 1985); Karen Starr, "Fighting for a Future: Farm Women of the Nonpartisan League," *Minnesota History* 48 (Summer 1983): 116–37; Theodore Saloutos and John D. Hicks, *Agricultural Discontent in the Middle West, 1900–1939* (Madison: University of Wisconsin Press, 1951); Hal S. Barron, "Bringing Forth Strife: The Ironies of Dairy Organizations in the New York Milkshed, 1880–1930," and Nancy Grey Osterud, "Farm Crisis and Community Revitalization in the Nanticoke Valley of New York State in the Early Twentieth Century" (Papers delivered at the Association of Living History Farms and Agricultural Museums Annual Conference, Indianapolis, June 1989); M. C. Burritt, *The County Agent and the Farm Bureau* (New York: Harcourt, Brace, 1922); Melvin Dubofsky, *We Shall Be All: A History of the Industrial Workers of the World* (Chicago: Quadrangle Books, 1969); John L. Shover, *Cornbelt Rebellion: The Farmers' Holiday Association* (Urbana: University of Illinois Press, 1965); and Lowell K. Dyson, *Red Harvest: The Communist Party and American Farmers* (Lincoln; University of Nebraska Press, 1982).

Women's historians have begun to explore differences in the way women organize to promote social change. Important works include Mari Jo Buhle, *Women and American Socialism, 1870–1920* (Urbana: University of Illinois Press, 1983), and Elsa Barkely Brown, "Womanist Consciousness: Maggie Lena Walker and the Independent Order of Saint Luke," *Signs* 14 (Spring 1989): 610–33. A comparison of women's activism in the Farmers' Union and in Homemakers' Clubs is made in Mary Neth, "Building the Base: Farm Women, the Rural Community, and Farm Organizations in the Midwest, 1900–1940," in Haney and Knowles, *Women and Farming*, 339–55. For an analysis of farm women's political activism historically and in the present, see Lorna Clancy Miller and Mary Neth, "Farm Women in the Political Arena," in Haney and Knowles, *Women and Farming*, 357–80.

David B. Danbom, *The Resisted Revolution: Urban America and the Industrialization of Agriculture, 1900–1930* (Ames: Iowa State University Press, 1979), first suggested the conflict between progressive reformers and farm people. A study of rural reformers that focuses on institutions is William L. Bowers, *The Country Life Movement in Ameria, 1900–1920* (Port Washington, N.Y.: Kennikat Press, 1974). Studies of the development of agricultural institutions include Roy V. Scott, *The Reluctant Farmer: The Rise of Agricultural Extension to 1914* (Urbana: University of Illinois Press, 1970); Wayne D. Rasmussen and Gladys L. Baker, *The Department of Agriculture* (New York: Praeger Publishers, 1972); C. L. McNelly, *The County Agent Story: The Impact of Extension Work on Farming and Country Life in Minnesota* (Berryville, Ark.: Braswell Printing, 1960); and Gladys Baker, *The County Agent* (Chicago: University of Chicago Press, 1939).

Much of the literature on agricultural institutions is based in the history of science and is more concerned with the development of science than with the political, social, or economic conditions of agriculture or farmers. The best of this literature includes Charles Rosenberg, *No Other Gods: On Science and American Social Thought* (Baltimore: Johns Hopkins University Press, 1961); Margaret Rossiter, *The Emergence of Agricultural Science: Justis Liebig and the Americans, 1840–1880* (New Haven: Yale University Press, 1975); Alan I. Marcus, *Science and the Quest for Legitimacy: Farmers, Agricultural Colleges, and Experiment Stations, 1870–1890* (Ames: Iowa State University Press, 1985); Donald B. Marti, *To Improve the Soil and the Mind: Agricultural Societies, Journals, and Schools in the Northeastern States, 1791–1865* (Ann Arbor: University Microfilms, 1979); and David Danbom, "The Agricultural Experiment Station and Professionalization: Scientists' Goals for Agriculture," *Agricultural History* 60 (Spring 1986). A suggestive overview is David B. Danbom, "Publicly Sponsored Agricultural Research in the United States from an Historical Perspective," in *New Directions for Agriculture and Agricultural Research: Neglected Dimensions and Emerging Alternatives,* ed. Kenneth A. Dahlberg (Totowa, N.J.: Rowman and Allanheld, 1986), 107–31. Few existing works examine the ties between corporate agricultural interests and agricultural institutions. One exception is Deborah Fitzgerald, *The Business of Breeding: Hybrid Corn in Illinois, 1890–1940* (Ithaca: Cornell University Press, 1990). David Noble's *America by Design* (New York: Knopf, 1977) is suggestive of methods useful in approaching this topic.

Studies of the professionalization of the social sciences in agricultural institutions include Gregory Hooks and William L. Flinn, "The Country Life Commission and Early Rural Sociology," *Rural Sociologist* 1 (Mar. 1981): 95–100; Harry C. McDean, "Professionalism in the Rural Social Sciences, 1896–1919," *Agricultural History* 58 (July 1984): 365–72; Harry C. McDean, "Professionalism, Policy, and Farm Economists in the Early Bureau of Agricultural Economics," *Agricultural History* 57 (Jan. 1983): 64–82; Harry C. McDean, "'Reform' Social Darwinists and Measuring Levels of Living on American Farms, 1920–1926," *Journal of Economic History* 43 (Mar. 1983): 79–85; Joel P. Kunze, "The Purnell Act and Agricultural Economics," *Agricultural History* 62 (Spring 1988): 131–49; Gregory Hooks, "Critical Rural Sociology of Yesterday and Today," in *Studies in the Transformation of U.S. Agriculture,* ed. A. Eugene Havens, Gregory Hooks, Patrick H. Mooney, and Max J. Pfeffer (Boulder, Colo.: Westview Press, 1986), 1–25; and Lowry Nelson, *Rural Sociology: Its Origin and Growth in the United States* (Minneapolis: University of Minnesota Press, 1969).

On agricultural policies, professionals, and institutions in the 1930s, see Gregory Hooks, "A New Deal for Farmers and Social Scientists: The Politics of Rural Sociology in the Depression Era," *Rural Sociology* 48 (1983): 386–408; Sidney Baldwin, *Poverty and Politics: The Rise and Decline of the Farm Security Administration* (Chapel Hill: University of North Carolina Press, 1968); Theodore Saloutos, *The American Farmer and the New Deal* (Ames: Iowa State University Press, 1982); Richard S. Kirkendall, *Social Scientists and Farm Policies in the Age of Roosevelt* (Columbia: University of Missouri Press, 1966); and David E. Hamilton, *From New Day to New Deal: American Farm Policy from Hoover to Roosevelt, 1928–1933* (Chapel Hill: University of North Carolina Press, 1991).

Few studies of women in agricultural institutions, agricultural science or social sciences, or rural social work exist. Studies of women in extension services include Joan M. Jensen, "Canning Comes to New Mexico: Women and the Agricultural

Extension Service, 1914–1919," *New Mexico Historical Review* 57, no. 4 (1982): 361–86, and Kathleen C. Hilton, "And Now She's Plowing with the Mule: Race and Gender in U.S.D.A. Policy, 1907–1929," in *Southern Women: Hidden Histories*, ed. Betty Brandon, Elizabeth Turner, Virginia Bernhard, Elizabeth Fox-Genovese, and Theda Purdue (Columbia: University of Missouri Press, 1994). On the development of home economics, see Glenna Matthews, *Just a Housewife: The Rise and Fall of Domesticity in America* (New York: Oxford University Press, 1987). On women in agricultural science, see Margaret W. Rossiter, *Women Scientists in America: Struggles and Strategies to 1940* (Baltimore: Johns Hopkins University Press, 1982). A general study of women in higher education is Barbara Miller Solomon, *In the Company of Educated Women: A History of Women and Higher Education in America* (New Haven: Yale University Press, 1985). Studies of sociology, social work, and social welfare agencies, though not their rural branches, include Rosalind Rosenberg, *Beyond Separate Spheres: Intellectual Roots of Modern Feminism* (New Haven: Yale University Press, 1982); Clarke Chambers, *Seedtime of Reform: American Social Service and Social Action, 1918–1933* (Minneapolis: University of Minnesota Press, 1963); Linda Gordon, "Black and White Visions of Welfare Activism, 1890–1945," *Journal of American History* 78 (Sept. 1991): 559–90; Linda Gordon, ed., *Women, the State, and Welfare* (Madison: University of Wisconsin Press, 1990); and Susan Ware, *Beyond Suffrage: Women in the New Deal* (Cambridge, Mass.: Harvard University Press, 1981). Unfortunately, there are no studies of women in the Resettlement Administration, the FSA, or the USDA.

Rural education and religion also need more scholarly attention. The existing literature includes Wayne E. Fuller, *The Old Country School: The Story of Rural Education in the Middle West* (Chicago: University of Chicago Press, 1982); Wayne E. Fuller, "Making Better Farmers: The Study of Agriculture in Midwestern Country Schools, 1900–1923," *Agricultural History* 60 (Spring 1986): 154–68; Jeffrey W. Moss and Cynthia B. Lass, "A History of Farmers' Institutes," *Agricultural History* 62 (Spring 1988): 150–63; Gary E. Moore, "The Involvement of Experiment Stations in Secondary Agricultural Education, 1887–1917," *Agricultural History* 62 (Spring 1988): 164–75; and James H. Madison, "Reformers and the Rural Church, 1900–1950," *Journal of American History* 73 (Dec. 1986): 645–68.

Studies of agricultural technology and economics include Allan G. Bogue, *From Prairie to Corn Belt: Farming on the Illinois and Iowa Prairies in the Nineteenth Century* (Chicago: University of Chicago Press, 1963); James H. Shideler, *Farm Crisis, 1919–1923* (Berkeley and Los Angeles: University of California Press, 1957); and John T. Schlebecker, *Whereby We Thrive: A History of American Farming, 1607–1972* (Ames: Iowa State University Press, 1963). Studies examining the importance of technological change to farm women's labor include Joann Vanek, "Work, Leisure, and Family Roles in Farm Households in the United States, 1920–1955," *Journal of Family History* 5 (Winter 1980): 422–31; Corlann Gee Bush, "'He Isn't Half So Cranky as He Used to Be': Agricultural Mechanization, Comparable Worth, and the Changing Farm Family," in Groneman and Norton, *To Toil*, 213–32; and Katherine Jellison, *Entitled to Power: Farm Women and Technology, 1913–1963* (Chapel Hill: University of North Carolina Press, 1993).

Index

Page numbers in italics refer to illustrations.

Eagle River, Wis., 260
Eau Claire, Wis., 262
Ebert family, 62
education, agricultural, 101–2, 105, 126–
  28; and consumption, 189–91; farmer
  response to, 145, 205–6, 208, 220–23;
  and farm organizations, 127–28; local
  sources of knowledge, 220–24. *See also*
  professionalization
eggs: economic contribution, 31–32; and
  local exchange, 59–63, 136–37; as
  women's work, 19, 35
electricity, 35, 120, *162–63*, 190–91, 197–
  201, 205–6, 211, 239
Ellefson, Norval, 181, 222
English, 25, 83, 89
Equal Rights Amendment, 229
Erickson, Anna Pratt: and automobiles,
  245–49; birth of children, 64–66, 247;
  and community institutions, 68–69;
  and consumption, 203–4; courtship,
  248–49; death of husband, 62, 66;
  divorce, 34, 260; and extended kin, 69–
  70; and family authority relations, 33–
  35, 262; gift exchange, 67–70; marriages, 67–68; neighborhood described
  42–44; neighborhood maps, 46–49;
  and product exchange, 60–62; relations
  with neighboring tenants, 80; and
  threshing, 155, 171–73; and visiting, 44–
  54; in women's club, 136, 138; and work
  exchange, 55–59, 171–73; work in field,
  241
Erickson, Conrad, 33–34, 42, 53, 55, 62,
  65, 66, 248
Erickson, Dorothy (Dot), 42, 54, 55, 57,
  61, 65–66, 172, 204, 247–48, 260–61
Erickson, Fay, 42, 204, 247–48, 261–62
Erickson, Lois, 42, 65, 247, 261–62
Erickson, Morris, 42, 57, 65, 68–69,
  172–73, 204, 262
Erickson, Orma, 42, 65–66, 69, 172, 247,
  260
ethnicity: and agricultural policies, 189;
  and farm organizations, 144–45; and
  gender division of labor, 25; and marriage, 88–89, 92; mixed-ethnic neighborhoods, 88–93, 244; and neighborhood formation, 43, 82–85; relations

between ethnic groups, 75; and relief
  policies, 118–19
Evans, Anne, 136–37
exchanged work, 41, 54–59, 73–74, 76, 88,
  90. *See also* threshing
extension service, 105, *161*, 164, 172, 236;
  and consumption, 189–90, 192; creation of, 101–2; and farm organizations,
  127–28; farm people's attitudes toward,
  143–45, 222. *See also* education, agricultural; Farm Bureau; 4-H Clubs;
  Homemakers' Clubs; professionalization
fairs, agricultural, 101, 127–28
family labor system: and access to leisure,
  251; cash commodities, 29–30; children's labor in, 20–22, 24–25; daily
  chores, 26; defined, 18; home production, 29–32; and neighborhood formation, 41, 44–53; periodic work, 26–27;
  seasonal work, 27–29; and youth
  opportunity, 259, 263. *See also* gender
  division of labor
Fargo, N.Dak., 144
Farm Bloc, 132
Farm Bureau, 35, 75, 130, 144–45, 172,
  255; and agricultural businesses, 132–
  33, 140; and agricultural institutions,
  133, 140; and centralized marketing,
  133; and extension service, 101, 133–34;
  and gender, 133; membership of, 134–
  35; origins of, 132–33; social organization of, 133, 141. *See also* American
  Farm Bureau Federation
farm consolidation, 10, 99–100, 212,
  219–20, 223–24, 226–27
Farmer-Labor party, 105, 132, 143
Farmers' Alliance, 99–100, 131
farmers' clubs, 77, 127. *See also* community clubs
Farmers Home Administration, 119
Farmers' Institutes, 101
Farmers' Union (Farmers' Educational
  and Cooperative Union), 37, 81, 105,
  132, 145, *160*, *161*, 208–9, 211, 229,
  271–72; conflict with Farm Bureaus,
  139–41; formation of, 131; membership
  of, 134, 141–42; and New Deal, 118;
  organization of, 140–41; relations with

Library of Congress Cataloging-in-Publication Data

Neth, Mary.
    Preserving the family farm : women, community, and the founda-
tions of agribusiness in the Midwest, 1900–1940 / Mary Neth.
        p.   cm. — (Revisiting rural America)
    Based on the author's thesis (doctoral)—Virginia Polytechnical
Institute and State University.
    Includes bibliographical references and index.
    ISBN 0-8018-4898-9 (hc: alk. paper)
    1. Middle West—Rural conditions.   2. Rural families—Middle
West.   3. Farmers' wives—Middle West.   4. Agriculture and state—
Middle West.   I. Title.   II. Series.
HN79.A14N48   1995
307.72'0977—dc20

94-21695